Examine the Evidence®

Ralph O. Muncaster

HARVEST HOUSE PUBLISHERS

EUGENE, OREGON

EXAMINE THE EVIDENCE®
Copyright © 2004 by Ralph O. Muncaster

Portions of the material herein are drawn from the author's previous books *Are There Contradictions in the Bible?; Can Archaeology Prove the New Testament?; Can Archaeology Prove the Old Testament?; Dismantling Evolution; Evidence for Jesus; How Is Jesus Different from Other Religious Leaders?; A Skeptic's Search for God; What Is the Trinity?;* and *Why Does God Allow Suffering?*

EXAMINE THE EVIDENCE is a registered trademark of The Hawkins Children's LLC. Harvest House Publishers, Inc., is the exclusive licensee of the federally registered trademark EXAMINE THE EVIDENCE.

Published by Harvest House Publishers
Eugene, Oregon 97402
www.harvesthousepublishers.com

Library of Congress Cataloging-in-Publication Data
Muncaster, Ralph O.
Examine the evidence / Ralph O. Muncaster.
p. cm.
Includes bibliographical references and index.
ISBN 0-7369-1295-9
1. Apologetics. I. Title.
BT1103.M85 2004
239—dc22   2004012482

*In loving memory of my
grandfather and namesake,
Ralph Olsen—
his abundant love will forever
remain an inspiration.*

Acknowledgments

Much thanks to Michael Spicher, master in Christian Apologetics at Southern Evangelical Seminary, for his tireless and unselfish assistance in the technical editing of this project; and to Drs. Norman Geisler and Thomas Howe, professors at Southern Evangelical Seminary, for working with Mr. Spicher as advisors.

Thanks also to Kurt Goedelman of Personal Freedom Outreach* for his generous provision of the photos of Holy Land archaeological sites.

* Personal Freedom Outreach is "a non-profit, non-denominational group with three goals: to educate Christians about the dangers and heretical doctrines of religious cults, to use the Gospel of Jesus Christ to reach members of those cults and to warn Christians of unbiblical teachings within the church itself." Their Web site is at www.pfo.org. They may also be contacted at P.O. Box 26062, St. Louis, MO 63136; (314) 921-9800.

Contents

Preparation for Your Journey to Greater Faith

WARNING—a deadly plague will hit you!

The news cuts through the heart of the entire world. Newspapers, TV, media of all types announce an outbreak of a new virus that lives on dust particles in the upper atmosphere. The "Dybbuk" virus is blown around the world on a daily basis and sweeps down to earth periodically. Eventually it is destined to infect every man, woman, and child on the planet. Contracting the virus means the slowest, most excruciating death imaginable. Victims experience a scorching sore throat, making it almost impossible to eat. Gradually a searing, burning sensation seeps into blood vessels and moves throughout the body. Every part seems to be engulfed in an inferno—a fire that can't be quenched. Sores break out on the skin. Tiny worms that accompany the virus grow in the sores and multiply, spreading everywhere while gnawing at rotting flesh. Slowly, ever so slowly, the eternal fires close the body's capillaries—disabling one appendage at a time, until finally enough blood is not available to serve the brain. There is no cure...only prevention.

Yet the prevention is certain, and it simply requires a bit of time, research, and commitment to obtain. Several medical journals are available to everyone, each revealing possible antidotes—but only one works. The correct vaccine is not hard for an individual to identify—however, there are people trying to convince everybody that their favorite alternative is "right." It is up to each person to select one, *and only one,* antidote to use. In this imaginary world, each selection must be secret, so there are no "research studies" to guide in the process. If the right one is selected, the person will be spared. Otherwise, the terrible fate awaits them.

Your group of close friends consists of John, an aggressive salesman; Mary, a calm housewife; Richard, a young scuba diver; and Joan, a poverty-stricken street person. All are stunned by the news of the worldwide epidemic. In response, they all immediately go out and purchase several potentially life-saving medical journals.

Amazingly, even though no one knows when a gust of "infected wind" might sweep down from the troposphere—it could happen any day—only Joan starts researching the journals right away.

"I'll get to it next week," says Richard, who is planning a diving trip to the Cayman Islands.

Mary is apathetic. "I'm not too worried," she says. "I'm a good person who keeps active and stays pretty healthy, so I don't really expect anything bad to happen."

"We haven't had any deaths in our area yet," chuckles John as he ambles out the door with golf clubs thrown over his shoulder. "I'll get to it soon, but I've got an important client to impress."

Joan, struggling financially and emotionally, keeps mostly to herself, and after two weeks discovers the "right" antidote.

What would you do? Opt for a vacation? Be apathetic? Focus on your business or your golf game? Or start researching?

Time passes. One by one, your friends fall victim—devastated by the unstoppable plague. How horrible it is to see each of them "felled." Repeatedly, tears fill your eyes, and you wonder why they placed so much priority on other things or didn't care enough to investigate the curse that was certain to hit all of them.

The Dybbuk Plague Story Models a Christian Decision

Every man, woman, and child on Earth will eventually die. Like the Dybbuk plague, nobody can avoid it. And everyone will have an eternity of intense suffering unless he or she obtains the gift of salvation through Jesus Christ. Furthermore, everything we need to know to have a joyous life on earth and an eternal life in God's presence can be learned from one book—the Bible—providing we take the time to learn about and accept God's gift of Jesus Christ. Other books are available and promoted by other people. The key is discovering the "right antidote" for ultimate redemption with God.

However, as in the above example, even though all people know they will eventually die, very few ever take the time to objectively analyze the truth about eternity. Often people have other priorities like vacations or careers—or they are simply apathetic. Perhaps most often, people simply believe that all religions are basically the same and they don't take the time to discover the differences. This usually means accepting the religious beliefs of family or friends.

The Bible teaches that there is only one way (one antidote) to eternal life (John 14:6). Moreover, God has provided abundant evidence that this one way is true and certain. Evidence is everywhere—from historical records to scientific support to miraculous prophecies to archaeological discoveries. Only Christianity can provide such enormous support. This text examines that evidence.

Jesus—the wonderful Redeemer from God—called each of us who discovers this "miraculous gift" to tell others about it. Though the Dybbuk plague is an imaginary model of the situation that faces all of mankind, the consequences of religious choice before death are real. While everyone carries his or her own responsibility to seek out the true relationship with God, it is also incumbent upon all of us to tell others. How terrible it would be to know your friends and loved ones would suffer needlessly on Earth and in eternity...simply because they never received the right "antidote" to sin. You can tell them. You can teach others to tell their loved ones too. This book will help you.

This Book Will Prepare You to S.H.A.R.E.

Telling others about Jesus can, and should, be easy, natural, and fun—not a dreaded confrontation as is felt by some people. A program that involves a bit of preparation and that can utilize other, readily available tools, called S.H.A.R.E., shows how to share the great news about Jesus with others. (See pages 571–572.)

An Adventure of Discovery

Get ready for a fascinating journey, rich with insight into the Christian faith. Moses spent 40 days on the mountain to be instructed by God in the Ten Commandments. Jesus spent 40 days with his disciples teaching them after the resurrection. In the following book you will be taken through 40 lessons (chapters) of belief. At the conclusion, your faith in Christianity should be stronger than ever because you will gain much greater insight into the facts and evidence supporting Christianity. So buckle your seatbelt and get set to start!

—ɯ—   —ɯ—   —ɯ—

40 Lessons of Belief

The Bible is the blueprint for Christianity. But, many have asked, how accurate is it? Were the original words reliable or merely someone's fantasy? Were myths created and then written down many centuries later? Were words accurately transmitted from the original records, or were mistakes made? Did the church later change the Bible to suit its needs? Questions like this abound.

Others may ask what evidence supports the Bible. Is it consistent with other records of world history? Is there archaeological evidence to support its claims? Is the Bible consistent with scientific knowledge? The answers to these and other questions will lead to an exciting adventure of discovery into the wealth of evidence supporting Christianity.

Christianity Is a History-Based Religion

It is extremely significant that Christianity is a history-based religion. Of all the world religions, only Judaism (Christianity's Old Testament foundation) and Christianity are truly history-*based*. Only Christianity relies entirely on one set of historical events (the crucifixion and resurrection). Islam, while also having much history-based information, *does not have doctrine based on any claim or evidence of divinity* from its leader, Muhammad. And Eastern religions, like Buddhism, Hinduism, and the religion created by Confucius, while started by historical people, do not have doctrine or any claims of divine knowledge that depend on any specific historical event(s) of their lives.

> Christianity is the only truly history-based religion—meaning that its essential belief is based on two historical events. This allows it to be verified and tested, whereas other religions must be sustained solely on weaker philosophical beliefs.

Christianity depends completely on the death and resurrection of Jesus Christ. If these two prophesied events did not occur, then Christianity is moot and meaningless. When the Bible is broken down into its simplest form, the entire Old Testament essentially reviews mankind's break from God and the need for a sacrificial sin offering. The ultimate answer to reconciliation was then forecast, through prophecy, to be a forthcoming perfect sacrifice from God himself—Jesus Christ. Without this ultimate sacrifice, there would be no reconciliation with God. So, the historical fact of the crucifixion (the promised sacrifice) is absolutely essential.

While the crucifixion was the actual sacrifice necessary to redeem humanity, the resurrection is also vital to Christianity. This is because all the claims of Jesus to be the Messiah who would allow a restored relationship with God depend on his reality as a valid spokesperson—in this case God himself, in human form. The resurrection is the proof of this claim to be God. The proof is not only in the spectacular event of his overcoming death—something nobody else has done—but also in his accurate prophecy of this event. Fulfillment of prophecy is a critical test of something—in this case Jesus—being of God (see part 3).

Deciding to Follow the Proven Word of God

Since Christianity is history-based, it can be verified and tested. If it can be shown to be accurate, especially to a high degree of "divine" certainty (if we can demonstrate it to be divinely inspired), then it would be wise to adhere to its direction and reject belief and doctrine that contradict it. These are actions that should seem obvious to an objective person because many issues—most importantly, all of eternity—lie in the balance. Even so, many people knowing this either refuse to investigate Christianity—or simply refuse to accept it based on the knowledge they have.

Why would someone reject Christianity if it is truly verifiable as being from God? Some of the most common reasons are

- they don't really understand how to obtain a relationship with God (that is, the gospel message)

- they don't understand the consequences of not having an eternal relationship with God (John 3:36)

- they are immersed in a family-based, community-based, or culture-based religion and are unwilling to investigate others

- they are apathetic

- they are afraid of investigating religion (this is like being afraid to go to the doctor for fear that something will be found to be wrong)

This book is designed to be a personal program to help you discover the evidence supporting Christianity leading to: 1) stronger faith, 2) increased love for God, and 3) preparation to tell others of Jesus.

Yet if Christianity is true, if it is the only way to have a relationship with God for all of eternity (as the Bible indicates), then it would be a horrible tragedy for someone to not at least have an opportunity to understand the good news of the gospel, the support behind it, and the consequences of not following it. Certainly this is an essential reason for Jesus' ultimate command to go out and "make disciples" of everyone.

The Importance of Building Rational Faith

Some people think that only *having faith* in God, even the God of the Bible, is all that is important. They would say, sometimes rather proudly, that there is no need for them to have facts to support their faith. However, if we assume the Bible is clearly God's inspired Word, then we must understand that God's command is *not* that we "blindly" accept ideas about God. The risk in doing this should be obvious. It could lead to acceptance of various cult ideas that lead to either premature "death" on Earth (consider Jim Jones, David Koresh, or Marshall Applewhite of Heaven's Gate)—or eternal death by following a false religion.

Such "blind faith" can easily result from following family and friends in selecting religious beliefs instead of making an honest, objective investigation of the truth. Since Christianity is history-based, it is easily tested. However attractive someone's religious beliefs might be, it doesn't matter at all if the beliefs aren't true. And sincerity, no matter how heartfelt, is not a good gauge of truth. Regardless of how someone is lured away from the truth, the Bible indicates that the consequences are devastating. This entire book deals with verifying evidence for God, Jesus, and the Bible.

In regard to the people who are susceptible to *blind faith,* they often open their Bible and point to Hebrews 11:6:

A Verse to Memorize

Without faith it is impossible to please God, because anyone who comes to him must believe that he exists and that he rewards those who earnestly seek him (Hebrews 11:6).

The tendency is to read the first part of this verse and stop: "Without faith it is impossible to please God..." This would seem to justify simply accepting what the Bible says (or what people think the Bible says) without question. However, the remainder of the verse provides other critical information about faith. It indicates "anyone who comes to him [God] must *believe* that he exists." As a human being, belief is based on a thought process developed from investigation, testing (sometimes subconsciously), rational thought, and experiences. Therefore, the implication is that the faith, which Webster's dictionary defines as "unquestioning belief," is based on a "sense" that something is true. *The basis for that unquestioning sense, however, is all important.* As human beings we have the opportunity to rationally consider our beliefs, which normally come from a *more rational* test or experience. And since Christianity is *history*-based, it *provides opportunity for rational testing.*

The last part of Hebrews 11:6 is also critical to understanding how faith pleases God. It says that God "rewards those who earnestly seek him." Again, we see that God does not simply want "blind faith" but instead desires that people earnestly seek him, which would certainly imply that a human use all the gifts God has provided—especially the mind—to know God.

In summary, Hebrews 11:6 essentially says we should seek God with everything we are (spirit, strength, and mind) and that we will be rewarded. Presumably, a key reward will be rational, strong belief. Such strong belief then leads to solid, unbreakable faith.

The Apostles Needed Rational Faith

Consider the early apostles. They had all the direct teaching of Jesus, yet when he was crucified they fell away. Their faith was shattered. Why? Because it wasn't yet supported by a rational belief that Jesus was who he said he was—God in human form. Upon the resurrection, this all changed. Then the disciples had proof. They had a rational reason to believe. They could have simply believed upon faith before the resurrection, yet they didn't...and they knew Jesus directly. They had even seen his many miracles. Jesus knew how the disciples would act before he died. If Jesus anticipated that the disciples who knew him personally would need rational evidence supporting his claim to be God, why wouldn't he likewise expect us to want (sometimes need) evidence as well?

Rational Belief and Faith to *Know* God

The Bible commands us to test everything to know that it is from God.

A Verse to Memorize

Test everything. Hold on to the good (1 Thessalonians 5:21).

Developing rational belief helps us

1. **know** God (we are rewarded when we seek God—Hebrews 11:6)
2. **love** God (we love God with our mind—Mark 12:30)
3. **share** God (we can be prepared to give a reason for our hope through Jesus Christ—1 Peter 3:15)

This verse does *not* say test everything except the Bible. It says to test *everything*, including the very words of the Bible and those who claim to speak for it. Certainly the reason to test everything is to know that teaching and information we base our life and eternity on is actually from God, and not from some false prophet. The Bible also provides the ultimate test—100-percent perfect prophecy (see part 3):

_____A Verse to Memorize_____

I am God, and there is no other;
I am God, and there is none like me.
I make known the end from the beginning,
from ancient times, what is still to come.

—Isaiah 46:9-10

This verse proclaims God as unique—"there is no other"; "there is none like me." Furthermore, it indicates *how* God is unique—"He makes known the end from the beginning." There are many other places in the Bible where prophecy is indicated and used as a test of something truly being from God. For this reason, considerable attention is given to the historical prophetic evidence of God, Jesus, and the Bible in this book.

As noted above, developing a rational belief in God is important at the outset of establishing a relationship with him to know that it is the "right" God that we are "getting to know." Following the wrong god can be disastrous. So many influences can lead someone to a wrong belief: family, friends, a community, an inspirational leader, habits, or apathy. Selecting the right authority to guide the knowledge of a relationship with God is critical. It would make sense that the authority would be other than human since human beings can make mistakes and have misplaced motives. Humans can change. Something that transcends humanity, such as the written words of a holy book like the Bible, would be a more permanent, more dependable authority. This book will demonstrate why the Bible is trustworthy as that authority.

Rational Faith and Belief to *Love* God

Jesus taught that the greatest commandment of all is to love God with all our heart, soul, strength, and mind:

A Verse to Memorize

Love the Lord your God with all your heart and with all your soul and with all your mind and with all your strength (Mark 12:30).

This verse indicates that we are to love God with our *whole being*. To simplify understanding, Mark defined the ways we should love God. *Heart* indicates the core (including emotion) love God desires, perhaps likened to the human emotional love we feel for others. *Soul* indicates a spiritual love that transcends humanity. It's an innate love that exists within our being—the sense that there is a God we can and should be connected with. *Strength* indicates the love God expects through our actions. Whether it's someone actively serving others demonstrating God's love, or someone on a deathbed serving as an inspiration through faith and courage, God wants us to love him with whatever strength he's providing.

Finally, the above verse clearly shows that loving God with all our being, also involves loving him with our *mind*. He does not put it in second place to emotional, spiritual, or service-oriented love. It is integrated fully. And why shouldn't it be? God provided human beings with something unique among all creatures—a mind. Since we are created in God's image, we know that this even reflects (to some very small degree) the mind of God. We are called to love him with our mind. That kind of love implies a rationally based understanding of who God really is, and an awe-inspiring love because of it.

Rational Faith and Belief to *Share* God

Jesus' last words to the disciples were to go out and share the gospel:

A Verse to Memorize

Go and make disciples of all nations, baptizing them in the name of the Father and of the Son and of the Holy Spirit (Matthew 28:19-20).

This is a vital command for everyone who has a relationship with God through Jesus Christ. The reason is that the only way to be redeemed into a proper relationship with God for all of eternity is through Jesus—by believing in his sacrifice on the cross and his resurrection and making a decision to accept him as both Lord and Savior.

A Verse to Memorize

I am the way and the truth and the life. No one comes to the Father except through me (John 14:6-7).

It is vitally important for people to know of and accept God's gift of redemption through Jesus Christ. What could be more clear than the statement that only those believing in Jesus will have eternal life? (In the full sense

Whoever believes in the Son has eternal life, but whoever rejects the Son will not see life, for God's wrath remains on him (John 3:36).

of the original language, "believing" means complete trust in Jesus.) Moreover, it is equally clear that those rejecting him (or not accepting him) will not see life and will have to endure God's wrath. What a choice—eternal life or God's wrath! This leads to the second greatest commandment Jesus taught:

A Verse to Memorize

The second is this: "Love your neighbor as yourself." There is no commandment greater than these (Mark 12:31).

Knowing the dire need to accept Jesus as Lord and Savior, how can one truly love one's neighbor as oneself without sharing the gospel—and obeying Jesus' command to "make disciples of all men"?

—∿— —∿— —∿—

Two Ways to Use This Book

This book will help in all of the above: 1) knowing God, 2) loving God, and 3) sharing God. Although it is intended to be read in sequential order, it is designed so that any segment can be read as a stand-alone section. Further, it is designed to be read at one of two levels:

1. *Strictly enjoyment*—Some will want to read *Examine the Evidence* strictly for enjoyment in their own journey of faith. Let your curiosity take you on an

adventure of biblical discovery. Look at the table of contents and go to areas of interest. Page through the text, stopping wherever your interest is drawn to. Or if you have a specific question, attempt to find the answer using the reference and indexing options available.

> Do we really love another person who doesn't know Jesus if we don't share the gospel with him or her?

2. *Serious study*—Others will want to take a more serious approach and study the material for teaching others or for evangelism. First, it would be wise to assess your knowledge of the historical foundation for the Bible and Christianity. If you feel it is somewhat weak, the special "Seven Independent Studies" (part 6) are designed in outline form as a guide to help you gain a clear understanding of the history of the Bible and church, and how it fits with the history of the world. If your knowledge of the Bible and Christianity is already strong, you may want to begin with the part 1 text immediately. For serious study, the text is designed to be covered sequentially.

Features for Easy Learning

The following features will help organize your thinking and learning in either case:

- *Extensive cross-referencing:* Useful references are placed throughout the text.

- *Important information:* Information that is important for learning is placed in sidebars next to the text.

- *Memorize this:* Important information or scripture that should be memorized is highlighted by special shading.

- *Fascinating facts:* Information that is of particular interest is boxed.

- *Test yourself:* At the end of each chapter is a quiz that can assist you in evaluating your knowledge of the content of what you've read.

- *Evangelism recommendation:* Helpful guidelines for use of Examine the Evidence series evangelism booklets are included with a special marking at the end of each chapter in the "Group Study" homework suggestions.*

 ✝ Example of Evangelism Recommendation

- *Group study:* A group-study program is offered at the end of each chapter. This provides guidelines for 40 sessions that can be selected for Bible study classes, for workshops, or for small groups.

- *Special group-study tools:* Appendix A provides guidelines for using this book for group study.

So regardless of the reasons for your interest in this book, simply sit down, relax, and start going through it. Think about your own questions. Or think about people who might benefit from the insights you will learn. You may sense direction for a particular educational need. If so, take a moment to outline a personal study plan covering the areas of specific interest to you.

> *Always be prepared to give an answer to everyone who asks you to give the reason for the hope that you have. But do this with gentleness and respect.*
> —1 Peter 3:15

---

* See also the S.H.A.R.E. program for evangelism in appendix A.

Most importantly, be prepared to enjoy your journey into the evidence for the Christian faith. Know with full assurance that by the time you have completed this book you will have at your fingertips the information necessary to do what the apostle Peter exhorted us to do.

Part 1

Evidence of God's Existence in Creation

The delicate beauty of a butterfly. The thundering power of the surf. The scent of a rose. The majesty of the Alps. The harmony of the rain forest. The spectacle of the heavens. The wonder of a newborn baby. All of these things speak to the glory of God. All of these things are evidence of his existence. All of these things are "clearly seen" and indicate his divine power and nature, making any doubt of God's existence "without excuse." Perhaps the strongest evidence for the existence of God is the evidence of his creation of life— which also includes the evidence that evolution of life by random chance is unreasonable; and some would say, impossible.

Observational
Evidence of Creation

As the Bible describes in Romans 1:20, God's "eternal power" and "divine nature" can be clearly seen from what he has created, so that mankind is "without excuse" (in not recognizing God). When one carefully considers life itself, it is quite simple to recognize if something is created or not.

Though most of this section deals with *hard evidence* (see pages 33-34 for definition of hard and soft evidence), there is some *soft evidence* we should still consider. This evidence is based on straightforward logic. For example, a missionary once said he had explained the concept of evolution—that man had descended from apes—to a group of natives living in the Amazon. He was immediately greeted by roars of laughter. They couldn't understand how anyone would believe such a thing.

Today we have DNA technology, other findings from molecular biology, and much other evidence that indicates the natives' laughter was well-founded. But let's take a closer look at the logic displayed by the natives. We should not dismiss the simple process of observation that made them laugh.

Random or Created?

The example of the Amazon natives illustrates something that has been apparent throughout human history. Human beings, having a mind, can readily recognize whether something is purposely created or occurred by random chance. Something created, designed, or built has a form that defies randomness. It appears to have a purpose. Think of Stonehenge. In essence it's simply a collection of rocks. But the careful shaping of the rocks, their placement, their consistency in size, and their pattern leads us to recognize that the rocks did not accumulate by accident. They were shaped and placed intentionally, though we can only speculate as to how and why.

Likewise, imagine you're taking a walk in the desert. You might step over hundreds of stones, here and there kicking one away. Suddenly one "stone" catches your eye. It has obviously been purposefully shaped. After a moment, you recognize its form as an arrowhead. There is no doubt in your mind that it is something that was created. It has a form. It apparently has a purpose. And it is normal and intuitive to reach that conclusion.

As a further example, consider the "Monkey Face" rock formation on Smith Rock, at Smith Rock State Park in Oregon.

Courtesy of Oregon State Parks and Recreation Department.
Contact: www.oregonstateparks.org or 1-800-551-6949.

When you look at it, the rock does resemble a monkey. But was it purposely created? No. It's obvious to any observer. You could call the rock "gorilla rock," or "dinosaur-head rock," or many other things. Does it glorify monkeys? Or was it just randomly formed and happens to look like a monkey's head? (Today many rock climbers love to climb Smith Rock, but it wasn't created for that purpose.)

Now, consider another rock, one that we all recognize, Mount Rushmore.

This "rock" was obviously created. In fact, it's a rock that's been turned into a monument. It took purposeful energy and design to create it. And it has a clear purpose—that of honoring four great presidents.

The above example demonstrates how natural it is to see the difference between created things and randomly developed things—even with simple rock formations.

The Systems Inside Living Things

Dealing with a design in rocks is simplistic compared to the complexities of life. Let's take our comparison a step further. Imagine that you've landed on another planet. You encounter a robot-like creature with multiple parts. Perhaps it has headlight-like "eyes." Maybe it has numerous steel-lever "arms." And you notice that it rolls around on a complex set of wheels that can be raised and lowered to fit the terrain. You would intuitively know that the robot had been created. In fact, you would recognize that human beings have been able to create such things.

Yet, for instance, the same types of motors that would be used in such a robot are found *by the trillions in the human body*. They have the same basic parts—but they're 200,000 times smaller than a pinhead. (See page 96 for more information about these "ATP motors.") Every cell in our body has hundreds of these motors. And in terms of efficiency, at the center of the motor is a wheel that turns at about 100 revolutions per second.[1] Today's molecular biology has made it even easier for us to understand we have been created by some incredibly intelligent designer, now that we can investigate the amazing biological machinery we can't even see.

All this is nothing new. Even in ancient times people would notice the intricate details of a flower—all the minute, complex components. Or they would observe a centipede—so small, yet so complex. Looking at more complex creatures, they would ask, how did all the body parts seem to "know" how to form themselves together? How did they "know" where to go? How did they "know" how to diagnose and repair themselves? How did they "know" how to grow? How did these creatures "know" how to reproduce? The questions go on and on. Even on the "macroscale" of complete plants and animals, their complexity and design has been obvious for millennia.

Let's look at one more example gained from the recent major advances in molecular biology: the amazing harmony of the "factory system" of a human cell. Gerald Schroeder, who holds a PhD from MIT, describes it this way:

Other than sex and blood cells, every cell in your body is making approximately two thousand proteins every second. A protein is a combination of three hundred to over a thousand amino acids. An adult human body is made of approximately seventy-five trillion cells. Every second of every minute of every day, your body and every body is organizing on the order of 150 thousand, thousand, thousand, thousand, thousand, thousand, amino acids into carefully constructed chains of proteins. Every second; every minute; every day. The fabric from which we, and all life is built, is being continuously rewoven at a most astoundingly rapid rate.[2]

It defies logic to pretend that such complex systems— systems that work together in such a precise and harmonious way—came about randomly. It is plainly absurd.

Hard Evidence Versus Soft Evidence

Hard science is science that draws conclusions from mathematical equations or using data obtained from reliable, highly predictable experiments. Hard sciences include physics, astronomy, engineering, chemistry, and molecular biology. Soft sciences are the sciences that make a study of a subject using the best available observation and knowledge, although not having an abundance of available hard evidence with which to draw conclusions. Soft sciences include geology, paleontology, anthropology, and basic biology.

Hard-science experiments and calculations have led to the laws and formulas of physics, thermodynamics, chemistry, and engineering—all hard sciences, and all extremely predictable. These are the sciences that allow us to build bridges and buildings with confidence, knowing they are structurally sound. These are the sciences that allow us to land men on the moon or launch space probes that travel immense distances predictably. And these are the sciences that allow us to make refrigerators, microwave ovens, and medicines. Every day, we plan our lives in accordance with the hard sciences. Think about it. Every time we drive a car, go over an overpass, go up an elevator, drink treated water, or take medicine we are placing our very lives in the hands of what hard science has learned. Fortunately, hard science is *extremely* reliable. *Soft science is not.*

How Evolutionists Use Soft Science to Teach Evolution

Soft science has been used for years in teaching evolution in public schools. Some of the soft-science observations that are said to be evidence for evolution include common body-part studies (homology), common embryonic studies (embryology), and misuse of the study of *microevolution* to support *macroevolution*.

As we more thoroughly examine these and other claims below, again and again we'll see that such observations fail to provide solid evidence for the theory of evolution. The fossil record (soft science), so highly regarded by many, has failed. Logic and intuition have failed. And the hard-science world of physics has certainly failed evolutionists. Now the greatest frontiers in the study of origins—molecular biology, astrophysics, and probability analysis—are failing evolutionists as well.

Although some dedicated evolutionists are still searching for reasonable hard-science answers, the theory of evolution can no longer pretend to rely on hard science. Instead it relies on unsupported speculation or falls back on outdated soft-science ideas. Nonetheless, new evidence that makes evolution implausible is not taught in our schools yet. Rather, evolution continues to be vigorously taught in our educational system. We should ask ourselves this question: Why?

Evolution Is Assumed to Be True

Unfortunately, we live in a society where evolution is assumed to be fact. Research of literature written by evolutionists indicates that conclusions were drawn based on the *starting assumption* that evolution is fact. Various theories were then considered to see which one best fit the "fact" of evolution. In such cases, evolution itself was never questioned. It was never suggested that intelligent, supernatural design might actually be a more reasonable theory and have more evidence to support it. The assumption that evolution is fact has held sway for decades, and it will only change as scientists choose to promote the facts that are now abounding from hard science.

A Closed System of Thinking

In a textbook designed for sixth graders entitled *Earth Science* (published in 2001 and endorsed by the National Geographic Society) evidence of early indoctrination in evolution can be found. Peppered throughout the text was the *presupposition* of evolution:[3]

- "Plant life evolved on land."

- "By this time, animals began to move onto land with the plants."

- "Birds evolved from dinosaurs."

- "Fossil evidence shows that ancestors of the present-day whales and dolphins once lived on land."

The point is that children are indoctrinated that evolution is a *fact*. And now, well over a hundred years after

Darwin's landmark book, this indoctrination is established in many people's minds—in spite of new evidence. It is only because of these many years of presupposition that evolution remains in textbooks. It keeps perpetuating itself like this:

1. People want to know about the origin of life.

2. People go to those who are thought to be experts (evolutionists).

3. People are told the evolutionary theory, modified a bit since Darwin's time.

4. Nobody questions the "experts." Evolution becomes entrenched in the educational system.

> Evolution is presupposed as fact by most evolutionists. A closed system of thinking has caused the idea that evolution is "scientific" and that creation is "religion" to endure. Therefore evolution continues to be taught in schools.

An example of this is a cover story in *Time* magazine from October 1996. Robert Wright states in his article "Science and the Original Sin,"

> As a story of creation, the book of Genesis long, long ago crumbled under the weight of science, notably Darwin's theory of natural selection.[4]

Sadly, Robert Wright and the *Time* editors are simply uninformed about the facts.

The Facts Are Coming to Light

Now, even dedicated evolutionists recognize that neo-Darwinism is nothing more than a theory—despite their own pre-assumption that it is a fact. Such scientists repeatedly describe theoretical steps of evolution using words and phrases like "maybe," "possibly," "we think that," "if," and so on. In fact, not a single one of the critical transitional steps identified by evolutionists has any strong evidence—and this problem is admitted by the evolutionist architects themselves! This hardly sounds like a theory that has logically crushed theories of supernatural creation, such as intelligent design.

Today, evidence from modern hard science is enabling scientists like biochemist Dr. Michael Behe, astrophysicist Dr. Hugh Ross, and mathematician Dr. William Dembski to counter outdated thinking. We are seeing changes in how the evidence is viewed. In fact, the common presupposition of evolution as fact may soon be behind us.

One final point should be made as Christians learn how to use hard science to demonstrate the glory of God. It would be ludicrous to *deny* that astronomers can predict an eclipse, or that engineers can build a safe bridge, or that chemists can anticipate a chemical reaction. These are hard sciences that we have learned to trust. Most people want their children to learn about such sciences. These and similar sciences accurately put men on the moon and send space probes with pinpoint accuracy to Mars and Jupiter at exactly the predetermined time.

Later in this text, the same hard sciences will be used to demonstrate powerful support for the God of creation and for the accuracy of the Bible. Hard science will also be used in the discussion of *general revelation* (God through his creation) and *special revelation* (God through his Word—the Bible). Hard science provides our knowledge of the universe and God's general revelation, as well as the plethora of evidence showing consistency between science and the Bible. Christians should be careful not to criticize hard sciences because they have proven to be so trustworthy and predictable.

Readers are urged to keep this thought in mind in the discussion of general revelation (including knowledge of the universe—page 61) One shouldn't try to go both ways. In other words, we would lose credibility if we claim that advanced mathematics and laws of physics are reliable as long as we are looking at eclipses and sending space probes to Mars and Jupiter but then suddenly claim the equations and laws of physics fall apart when we are evaluating the boundaries (and age) of the universe—using precisely the same astronomical principles, mathematical models, and methods. Mathematics and laws of physics are constant.

As a general rule, embracing hard science and questioning soft science is both the right, and the most effective, way to present God, the Bible, and eventually Jesus to a nonbelieving world.

Observational Myths Used in Teaching Evolution

Myth #1: Homology

Homology is the myth that observed similarities between various creatures "proves" they had a common evolutionary ancestor. For example, humans, bats, and grasshoppers all have knees—an evolutionist using homology might claim, therefore, that they all had a common ancestor.

This argument falls apart, however, when compared to the argument for an Intelligent Designer (Creator). Obviously, a good designer applies a successful system to like mechanisms—like designing wheels on skateboards, bicycles, and cars.

Myth #2: Microevolution Equals Macroevolution

Evolution simply means "change" (in the sense of "unfolding"). "Naturalistic evolution" would then mean "change because of causes that occur in nature without the involvement of an intelligent agent." However, the most common definition of evolution—the definition used in our school system—implies much more. It implies *the change of one reproducing species into another reproducing species.* Darwin's book *On the Origin of Species* lays a reasonable foundation for the idea of natural selection (see page 40). But many biology textbooks take a major leap in the dark and also cite it as the foundation for the concept of inter-species evolution. Let's look at a more precise definition of the terms.

Microevolution. Evolution (change) does occur within individual species. Perhaps the safest way to identify a species is by *genotype* (its genetic makeup). Some might identify a genotype as a reproducing species.

Considerable variety exists within the genetic structure of any species. For example, a human being may be blue-eyed, brown-eyed, have dark or light skin, be short or tall, fat or skinny...the list goes on and on. All of these potential variations exist within the human DNA encoding for an individual. As modern science has discovered, the "mapping," or the makeup, of the human genome is 3.2 billion base pairs of DNA. This information allows an enormous amount of flexibility for humans and other creatures to adapt to their surroundings. This type of adaptation can be called *microevolution.* It has been observed, and it is accepted by virtually everyone.

Macroevolution. Neo-Darwinian evolutionary theory is based on the concept that one reproducing species can change into another. This process can be called *macro*evolution.

Today we can understand that leaps of improvement can happen within a species because it already has the capability within its existing DNA. But a species can be "improved" only "microevolutionarily"—in the sense of survival to meet circumstances. For another instance, bacteria that show statistically valid long-term variations in DNA structure (because their rapid procreation cycle allows for rapidly mutating populations—see page 130) still remain bacteria. *There is simply no evidence, even in this case, of a structural change in the DNA of bacteria that turns them into more complex organisms.* (The word "strain" is most appropriate to describe the changed varieties of bacteria.)

Natural selection. The tendency for favorable genes to predominate in a species in order to allow the survival of the fittest has been termed *natural selection.*

Darwin was right. Natural selection is obvious. But it only works within a certain genotype. There have been many studies that demonstrate that gene pools favorable under certain circumstances survive and proliferate to help an *existing* species. But doesn't it seem logical that an intelligent designer would design such adaptability into any creation? Only an inept designer would engineer a mechanism that would fail if a single environmental circumstance changed. Even human designs include compensating mechanisms—for instance, redundancy of systems in airplanes.

What about new breeds of dogs or new types of wheat? Don't these represent genetic changes that create new species? We have been able to tinker with existing DNA to

Microevolution is change within a species and is true.

Macroevolution is change from one species to another and has never been proven. Microevolution does not prove macroevolution.

Natural selection is the process in which a gene pool with a survival advantage will dominate a population. It is observed within microevolution, but not macroevolution.

actually improve some aspects of species through selective breeding. Some dogs seem more attractive as pets, wheat can become more abundant, and cows can produce more milk. But while human artificial breeding (or even accidental mutation) can sometimes "improve" an organism in one sense, inevitably it harms the organism in other ways.

Myth #3: Embryology Supports Evolution

Since Darwin recognized problems in substantiating his theory of evolution from the evidence of the fossil record and gradual changes, he hypothesized that evidence of embryonic similarities would support his claims. And indeed, the well-known drawings of embryos made by the German biologist Ernst Haeckel (1834–1919) seemed to show similarities between the embryos of various species. From the drawings, conclusions were made that supported Darwinian evolution.

Unfortunately, these drawings and conclusions were shown to be fraudulent. The fraud involved: 1) misrepresentation of the embryos prior to the drawings; 2) inconsistent selection of stage and age, and distorted drawing of the embryos; and 3) deception about which species were actually used. Haeckel was simply trying to support his own ideas.[5]

Myth #4: The Miller–Urey Experiments Created Life in the Laboratory

Virtually anyone exposed to the teaching of biology in the past five decades has been told that, in 1953, Stanley Miller, along with his mentor, Harold Urey, developed a scientific means of simulating the earth's early environment and, within it, was able to create the "building blocks of life." This is enormously misleading.

First, these "building blocks of life" consisted of only a few amino acids—very far from the complex proteins, nucleotides, and organized information necessary for life. It is similar to manufacturing a drop of black ink and claiming you have created the building block for an encyclopedia.

Second, Miller and Urey's simulation of the early-earth environment has been widely criticized. They artificially blocked out oxygen and "trapped" only the amino acids favorable to life. However, there is no way to explain how this could have happened on the early earth.

Third, it is almost never mentioned that the vast majority of components produced in these experiments were destructive "tar"—which would have *eliminated* any early life. The bottom line is, an impressive laboratory setup in biology textbooks has misled people into thinking that "science has created life." Nothing could be further from the truth.

 ## Test Yourself

1. Quote a Bible reference that indicates that "man is without excuse" when it comes to recognizing that God's presence, power, and divinity are apparent in nature.

2. What examples would you use to tell someone that the difference between design and random creation is obvious?

3. What is hard science? What is soft science?

4. What is homology? Embryology? Microevolution used to show macroevolution? Why do they not make sense as evidence for evolution?

5. What are the problems with the Miller–Urey experiments?

Chapter 1 Group Study

Homework Preparation (do prior to group)
Read: Romans 1:20; Isaiah 44:24; chapter 1 of this text; and pages 4–7, 21–22 in *Creation vs. Evolution.*✝ Familiarize yourself with appendix B. Also go to www.evidenceof god.com and familiarize yourself with tools regarding creation vs. evolution.

Opening Prayer
Discussion: The "watchmaker" example in *Creation vs. Evolution* (pages 21–22) seems exaggerated. Nobody would so foolishly consider the "evolution of a watch." Yet people readily believe in the evolution of a far more complex human. Discuss why.

Practical-Experience Game
Role-playing: The objective is for the "Christian" to present the "nonbeliever" with compelling evidence using simple observation alone, that God exists. The nonbeliever should use arguments employed in "normal" teaching of evolution.

Closing Prayer

Analyzing the
Fossil Record

Ancient, fossilized bones and ancient creatures such as dinosaurs *are* fascinating. It seems like these remains can bring us closer to the way the Earth really was long, long ago. But we must take great care in what we conclude from such soft evidence, keeping in mind that we are dealing with a soft science that is making speculative conclusions.

The fossil record is often evaluated starting from the assumption of evolution—which is a theory in crisis. It is relatively easy to show that the fossil record *contradicts* evolution.

Courtesy of www.creationism.org

45

The Crux of the Fossil Controversy

Many evolutionists claim that the fossil record confirms evolution. Others are embarrassed that it doesn't. Why is there this controversy?

Those who maintain that the fossil record confirms evolution all too often start from the assumption that evolution is a fact and then seek evidence to fulfill their belief. For example, they will search out similar-looking body structures and hope thereby to demonstrate that different species have a common ancestry. In reality this demonstrates nothing. An equally valid argument could be made that these species were created different and complete, maybe even at different points in time.

Think about it. Old human skulls are often used as examples of the evolution of man. This is very weak proof. Look at different skull shapes in existence around the world today. Millions of years from now, someone could unearth Asian, European, and African skulls and make that same mistake, hypothesizing that one was the ancestor to the other.

The assumption of evolution doesn't fit the model for good science. Instead, a reasonable hypothesis should be drawn first, carefully defining the parameters for its proof. For example, suppose it was hypothesized that fish evolved into frogs (an idea many evolutionists hold). Test criteria could then be established to see if the hypothesis could be fulfilled. For example, transitionary life-forms would be sought that had fins with stubs, and others in which those stubs actually started to become legs. We would be looking for fossil evidence showing that the fish body started to take on the form of a frog. We might look for indications that gills were starting to turn into lungs. These kinds of scientific tests would help provide objective evidence of a change from fish to frogs.

The reason why so many biologists—whether they believe in evolution or not—don't think that the fossil record provides evidence for evolution is because all the organisms that make up the fossil record are fully formed and fully functional. We don't find lizards with small pieces of feathers starting to form on their scales. Fossilized life-forms either have feathers or they don't. We don't find organisms with only retina casings. They either have eyeballs or they don't. We don't find any with stubs for legs. They either have legs or they don't.

What Sort of Change Does the Fossil Record Show?

The fossil record actually shows that ancient specimens have forms virtually identical to life-forms in existence today. Below are some examples:

- "The oldest fossils of land-dwelling animals are millipedes, dating to more than 425 million years ago. Incredibly, the archaic forms are nearly indistinguishable from certain groups living today."[1]

- "The Florissant Fossil Beds in Colorado are internationally renowned for the variety and quantity (over 60,000 specimens) of fossils discovered. These fossils date to about 35 million years ago, roughly the halfway mark between the age of the dinosaurs and the first humans. The finds include over 1100 different species of insects. According to the National Park Service's Geologic Resources Division, 'the fossils indicate that insects 35 million years ago were much like those today.' "[2]

- "A fossil dealer found fossilized jellyfish encased in about 12 vertical feet of rock, which, scientists say, represents a span of time of up to 1 million years. According to a Reuters article, 'The fossilized jellyfish appear similar in size and characteristics to their modern brethren.' "[3]

If the fossil record confirms anything, it confirms the reality of little change. Plants and animals that existed millions of years ago are much like plants and animals today.

Is the Fossil Record Complete?

Charles Darwin wrote in *On the Origin of Species* that

natural selection can act only by the preservation and accumulation of infinitesimally small inherited modifications, each profitable to the preserved being.[4]

He went on to ask,

Why, if species have descended from other species by insensibly fine graduations, do we not everywhere see innumerable transitional forms? Why is not all nature in confusion [he is talking about today's plants and animals] instead of the species being as we see them, well defined?[5]

Finally, he wondered,

But, as by this theory innumerable transitional forms must have existed, why do we not find them embedded in countless numbers in the crust of the earth?[6]

At Darwin's time, we had unearthed relatively few fossils compared to the countless millions we have to analyze today. But the validity of his point hasn't changed. If the fossil record actually demonstrated evolution, we would have found "innumerable" transitional species showing infinitesimally small variations.

Today, researchers have concluded that the fossil record is virtually complete in what it has to reveal. For instance,

> A study in the Feb. 26, 1999, issue of *Science* combines data analysis of hundreds of early ancient mammal fossils with a mathematical model of evolutionary branching patterns to determine the completeness of the fossil record prior to 65 million years ago. The researchers concluded that the fossil preservation rate is high—high enough that the probability that modern mammals existed more than 65 million years ago without leaving fossils is just .2 percent (two-tenths of one percent). Study author Christine Janis, professor of ecology and evolutionary biology at Brown University, proclaimed, "The fossil record for that period is good enough for us to say that those species would most likely have been preserved if they had been there."[7]

The Numbers Just Don't Add Up

Today, tens of millions of fossils have been unearthed and categorized. We have defined 250,000 distinct fossilized species. If true transitional forms existed, we should have at least the same number of transitional species—perhaps far more, given that many small changes would have taken place over time.

Even if we consider *punctuated equilibrium,* which theorizes sudden, abrupt evolutionary change and is a suggested alternative to the gradual neo-Darwinian model (see page 54), an abundance of true transitional fossils should still be present. And in line with neo-Darwinian theory, we would also expect the gaps between developing, diverging species to be small.

The numbers just aren't there, though.

First, there are *no true transitional species* in the fossil record at all. (Only fully formed fossils with similar appearances are thought by some biologists to be transitions.)

Second, *the rapid appearance of many separate, fully formed species*—in the Cambrian explosion (see below)—contradicts the gradualism proposed by neo-Darwinists. (It also confounds the molecular biologists who have to confront the questions of *irreducible complexity* and mutation through vast DNA change—see chapters 7 and 8.)

In the intelligent-design paradigm, however, we would expect fully formed, fully functional creatures to suddenly appear. And naturally, there would be differences—gaps—between the various species. This is exactly what the fossil record indicates.

The Cambrian Explosion

During a very short period of time—thought to be from 525 to 550 million years ago—an incredible "explosion" of fully formed creatures appeared. Among them were more than 100 species of soft-bodied animals, an enormous number of small shelled organisms, and many others, such as the Burgess Shale arthropods. Scientists have named this period after Cambria, Wales, where large fossil beds were studied in the 1800s.

-------------------- Key Concept --------------------

The Cambrian explosion, which scientists estimate occurred 525-550 million years ago, reveals the presence of over 100 new species at once. This agrees with the Bible and is a problem for evolutionists.

Paleontologists Speak Out

With so many fossils now available to view, and no real missing links having been found, evolutionists who are not committed to "making the evidence fit the theory" are speaking out. Some try to downplay the importance of the lack of transitional species. British zoologist Mark Ridley declares,

> The gradual change of fossil species has never been part of the evidence for evolution. In the chapters on the fossil record in *On the Origin of Species*, Darwin showed that the record was useless for testing between evolution and special creation because it has great gaps in it. The same argument still applies....In any case, no real evolutionist, whether gradualist or punctuationist, uses the fossil record as evidence in favor of the theory of evolution as opposed to special creation.[8]

Interestingly, Ridley seems to echo what Darwin had lamented—the "gaps," or lack of fossils to be analyzed. As we've seen, this is no longer the case today, as pointed out by T.N. George as far back as 1960:

> There is no need to apologize any longer for the poverty of the fossil record. In some ways it has become almost unmanageably rich. And discovery is outpacing integration.[9]

Acknowledging the Gaps

Noted molecular biologist Michael Denton, who holds both an MD and PhD, examined the gap problem in his well-known book *Evolution: A Theory in Crisis*. The back cover of the book summarizes his views:

> Not only has paleontology failed to come up with
> the fossil "missing links" which Darwin anticipated,
> but hypothetical reconstructions of major evolu-
> tionary developments—such as that linking birds to
> reptiles—are beginning to look more like fantasies
> than serious conjectures.[10]

Even though some evolutionists attempt to use the fossil
record to construct an apparent progression of plants and
animals, the gaps cause this progression to fall apart, as evolutionary paleontologist George Gaylord Simpson observes:

> This [the gap in the proposed progression of horses]
> is true of all thirty-two orders of mammals....The
> earliest and most primitive known members of every
> order already have the basic ordinal characters, and
> in no case is an approximately continuous sequence
> from one order to another known. In most cases the
> break is so sharp and the gap so large that the origin
> of the order is speculative and much disputed.[11]

Simpson later notes,

> This regular absence of transitional forms is not con-
> fined to mammals, but is an almost universal phe-
> nomenon, as has long been noted by paleontologists.
> It is true of almost all orders of all classes of animals,
> both vertebrate and invertebrate. A fortiori [even
> more strongly], it is also true of the classes, and of
> the major animal phyla, and it is apparently also true
> of analogous categories of plants.[12]

It is not hard at all to find paleontologists who acknowledge that the many gaps in the fossil record essentially dis-
mantle it as evidence for evolution. Here is a sampling of
what has been said:

Given that evolution, according to Darwin, was in a continual state of motion...it followed logically that the fossil record should be rife with examples of transitional forms leading from the less to more evolved....Instead of filling the gaps in the fossil record with so-called missing links, most paleontologists found themselves facing a situation in which there were only gaps in the fossil record, with no evidence of transformational intermediates between documented fossil species (Jeffrey H. Schwartz).[13]

Despite the bright promise that paleontology provides a means of "seeing" evolution, it has presented some nasty difficulties for evolutionists, the most notorious of which is the presence of "gaps" in the fossil record. Evolution requires intermediate forms between species and paleontology does not provide them. The gaps must therefore be a contingent feature of the record (David B. Kitts).[14]

A large number of well-trained scientists outside of evolutionary biology and paleontology have unfortunately gotten the idea that the fossil record is far more Darwinian than it is. This probably comes from the oversimplification inevitable in secondary sources: low-level textbooks, semi-popular articles, and so on. Also, there is probably some wishful thinking involved. In the years after Darwin, his advocates hoped to find predictable progressions. In general, these have not been found; yet the optimism has died hard, and some pure fantasy has crept into textbooks....One of the ironies of the creation–evolution debate is that the creationists have accepted the mistaken notion that the fossil record shows a detailed and orderly progression (cited by David Raup).[15]

The record jumps, and all the evidence shows that the record is real: the gaps we see reflect real events in life's history—not the artifact of a poor fossil record (Niles Eldredge).[16]

The absence of fossil evidence for intermediary stages between major transitions in organic design, indeed our inability, even in our imagination, to construct functional intermediates in many cases, has been a persistent and nagging problem for gradualistic accounts of evolution (Stephen J. Gould).[17]

Now that many evolutionists and paleontologists note the lack of fossil evidence supporting gradual evolution, what have they proposed in its place?

Punctuated Equilibrium

Developed in 1972 by Niles Eldredge and Stephen Jay Gould as a criticism of traditional Darwinism (gradualism), the theory of *punctuated equilibrium* holds that evolution occurs in "fits and starts"—sometimes moving very rapidly, sometimes slowly, and sometimes not at all. (As we've seen, Darwinism views evolution as a slow, continuous process without sudden jumps.)

Eldredge and Gould described the mechanism for punctuated equilibrium like this: Groups of creatures were cut off from the rest of their species in inhospitable fringe areas, where they could more quickly evolve. Such small groups allowed for inbred selection pressure that theoretically would cause positive (or negative) mutations to appear and be preserved—whereas in a larger population they would disappear. Such a changed species, it was further proposed, could eventually move into a broader geographical area, where individuals would become fossilized—thus giving the appearance of an abrupt change in the species. (It was argued that the original "fringe area" would never be dug for fossils.)[18]

However, punctuated equilibrium is really more of an observation—based on the fossil record, which shows sudden appearance of new species (for example, the Cambrian explosion) than it is a theory in the usual sense. Essentially it is simply an attempt to explain the fossil problem and does not offer any scientific support. And it doesn't resolve the problems raised by the mutational process:

1. Mutations do not add information.

2. Even if mutations could add information, there is a statistical impossibility of a major macroevolutionary change.

3. Inbreeding has never been shown to do anything but *weaken* the long-term survivability of an organism.

But some evolutionists feel compelled to adopt the theory in order to account for the problem of the gaps:

> We seem to have no choice but to invoke the rapid divergence of populations too small to leave legible fossil records (S.M. Stanley).[19]

However, there has been a major ongoing debate among evolutionists themselves of the likelihood of the punctuated equilibrium model versus the traditional gradualistic one. It appears the traditional gradualism model still has strong support. The following cites a number of researchers whose writings have supported this view:

> It is now clear that among microscopic protistans, gradualism does seem to prevail (Hayami and Ozawa, 1975; Scott, 1982; Arnold, 1983; Malmgren and Kennett, 1981; Malmgren et al., 1983; Wei and Kennett,

1988, on foraminiferans; Kellogg and Hays, 1975; Kellogg, 1983; Lazarus et al., 1985; Lazarus, 1986, on radiolarians, and Sorhannus et al., 1988; Fenner et al., 1989; Sorhannus, 1990, on diatoms).[20]

Whichever model evolutionists choose to support, however, the lack of a single example of a real transition is evidence enough that the fossil record does not support evolution.

Other Evolutionist Speculation

As we've seen, the fossil record yields support for evolution only when it's combined with speculation—and with the preconceived notion that evolution is fact. So searching out the fossil "missing links" is like trying to find pieces to a puzzle—but it's a puzzle that exists only in the mind of those who hold to evolutionary theory. What has resulted from the attempts to plug the gaps in the proposed evolutionary progression from simpler species to more complex ones?

> Many committed paleontologists and evolutionists now readily admit the failure of fossils to support evolution.

The Archaeopteryx

Some evolutionists still point to a few unusual animals as missing links—for example, the archaeopteryx. This ancient creature has characteristics of both a bird and a reptile. For instance, it has wings covered with fully formed feathers. One of the discovered specimens has the type of sternum that would be necessary for wing-muscle attachment. Yet in addition, the archaeopteryx has teeth, claws on its wings, and a tail. Even the scientific community can't make up its mind exactly what the archaeopteryx is. Some view it as a missing link. Some view it as the first bird. Opinions vary.

However, we can be certain of one thing. It—along with other examples such as the Jurassic bird and *ichthyostega*, a type of ancient frog—doesn't fit the model of a true missing link, because all of its components are fully formed. Its wings are perfectly suited to flight, and the structure of its feathers is perfect to the smallest detail. Just because it contains some characteristics of different species means nothing. After all, humans share characteristics with crocodiles, such as the vertebrate eye—does that mean we are related to crocodiles? A true missing link should show partial development of something that appears fully formed later on.

A Recent Find Further Confuses Evolutionary Fossil Claims

On July 15, 2002, French paleontologist Michel Brunet officially announced his discovery of a hominid skull in Chad, Africa, dating to between 6 and 7 million years ago—nearly twice the age of the oldest current hominid fossil. The hominid was nicknamed "Toumai," meaning "tree of life." Henry Gee, paleontology editor of the magazine *Nature*, called the find the "most important fossil in living memory."[21]

What is causing enormous concern for evolutionists is that "Toumai" shows humanlike features much more "advanced" than several "intermediate" fossils in the supposed line of development of the human evolutionary tree. This find, along with many other hominid discoveries over the last ten years, has thrown out any clear path of human evolution, despite several decades of efforts to construct one. Daniel Lieberman, a Harvard specialist on human evolution, declared of Brunet's discovery, "This will have the impact of a small nuclear bomb."[22] In fact, some scientists say that these recent discoveries, especially that of "Toumai," may make it impossible to identify a true missing link.

Fascination with fossils is not a good reason to accept evolutionary claims about a progression of species development. As we've seen, the fossil record is one of the weakest parts of the theory of evolution and is actually more consistent with the Genesis account of creation.

Once we throw out preconceived ideas, these ancient specimens can open our minds to other alternatives that more reasonably explain the observations we make of them. Such an alternative is that different, independent species make use of similar, sometimes *very* similar, structures and parts—because they were *designed* that way.

Fascinating Facts

Dinosaur bones were readily available and actually studied by early humans—at least by 2000 B.C.—and were considered to have originated long before then. In fact, discovery of such bones led to the development of legends, including the griffin, as well as the dragons long revered in the area of India and China. Even emperors of Rome mentioned in the Bible were avid collectors of dinosaur bones. Emperor Caesar Augustus established the first known museum of paleontology. And Tiberius Caesar, who "grew up with dinosaur discoveries" became fascinated with Pliny's reports of ancient "monster remains." He retired on the Isle of Capri, where the museum was located.

This enthusiasm revealed itself in artwork of early mankind (as in the case of the griffin, dragons, and others). Like today, people imagined what the ancient creatures (sometimes legends) looked like. Hence, use caution in jumping to conclusions that attempt to place man and dinosaurs together. *There is no such scientifically acceptable evidence as yet.* Presenting unsupportable information can greatly damage Christian credibility in other, far more important areas. (See chapter 3 and also *Dinosaurs and the Bible*.)

Test Yourself

1. Apart from some noticeable extinctions like the dinosaurs, how different are the majority of fossilized species from today's creatures?

2. How complete do scientists estimate the fossil record of today?

3. What is a true transitional species? Why are transitions important? Is the archaeopteryx a transition? Support your view.

4. Did Darwin believe the fossil record supported evolution? What was his view?

5. What is the role of dinosaurs in the Bible? (See *Dinosaurs and the Bible.*)

Chapter 2 Group Study

Homework Preparation (do prior to group)
Read: Job 40:15-24; 41; chapter 2 of this text; and page 25 (insert) in *Creation vs. Evolution*✝, and *Dinosaurs and the Bible*✝. Familiarize yourself with appendix B. Also go to www.evidenceofgod.com and familiarize yourself with tools regarding creation vs. evolution.

Opening Prayer
Discussion: Bring *Dinosaurs and the Bible* to your group. Discuss where, if anywhere, dinosaurs appear in the Bible. Is it likely they were on the ark? Is it essential to salvation to place dinosaurs in the Bible or on the ark? Christians disagree about dinosaurs—what can be done to mitigate problems between Christians, and why is it important to do this?

Practical-Experience Game

TV interview: The "Christian" is rushed into a recording studio to comment on the new finding of the hominid "Toumai" as the missing link. The objective is to convince the TV audience that fossils actually do not support evolution at all.

Closing Prayer

Using Science as Powerful Evidence of God

Modern science should become one of the evangelists' (and apologists') greatest tools in spreading the gospel. From the complexity of the simplest living cell to our latest understanding of the cosmos (including the big bang and even ideas about an old universe), *science now provides some of the most compelling evidence about the God of creation—* the God of the Bible. *When nonbelievers discover that God exists and that the words of the Bible can be trusted, it leads to a credible presentation of the gospel.* The following sections will demonstrate how to effectively use science to help others know God.

Once we become involved in an analytical discussion about the origin of life, inevitably the issue of the age of the universe comes up—whether the discussion is between a Christian and non-Christian, or between Christians with differing viewpoints. Since this is often a needless stumbling block for nonbelievers, the issue of age of the universe and the best stance regarding it for the purpose of evangelism, warrants some consideration.

General Revelation and Special Revelation

Theologians define two ways in which God reveals himself to us. The first is *general revelation,* which is through his creation. The second is *special revelation,* which is through his Word—the Bible. Both of these are equally true. They are equally important. And they must be consistent since both are from God. Hence, there is nothing that is true in what we know about the universe that is false in the Bible, and vice versa.

Key Concept

General revelation *is God's communication to mankind through his creation.*

Special revelation *is God's communication to mankind through his Word (the Bible).*

Both *are equally true and valid and must be consistent with each other. God wants us to use our minds to test everything and to love him (1 Thessalonians 5:21; Mark 12:30).*

Because of a perceived conflict by some people between general-revelation facts (from modern science) and special-revelation words (in the Bible), one of the sharpest conflicts in all of Christianity has arisen regarding an aspect of God's creation—that of the age of the universe. Some Christians argue that the days indicated in Genesis 1 are strictly literal 24-hour days. Others argue they are intended to mean distinct, long periods of time. *This issue is important only because inflexibility that results from misunderstanding affects some people's ability to present the Bible's message to nonbelievers. It is not a salvation issue,* and as will be shown, it doesn't even matter in building a case for the evidence of God in creation. Hopefully the following discussion will allow Christians to set this issue aside and will also provide understanding why this text takes the approach it does regarding creation versus evolution. The age of the universe issue should *never* stand in the way of presenting the gospel.

There are those who maintain the universe must be only about 10,000 years old because the Bible has genealogical timelines that date back about 7000 years (with some generations omitted)—and then there were previously six literal "days" of creation as specified in Genesis 1. This interpretation is known as the "young-earth view." To reconcile its special-revelation (Bible) understanding with the general revelation from science (which believes in a multibillion year old universe), young-earth proponents attempt to demonstrate why commonly accepted scientific knowledge regarding age of the universe is in error.

Then there are Christians who believe the universe is about 14 billion years old (in agreement with science). They attempt to reconcile their general-revelation orientation with special revelation by demonstrating that the actual words of the original language of the Bible had sufficient latitude to allow for an interpretation that is confirmed by science. This interpretation is known as "old earth." One key example of latitude in the original biblical Hebrew is the word *yom*, which usually means "day." Ancient Hebrew was limited to only a few thousand words, and the only word for *era, epoch, age,* or a closed-end period of time was *yom.* Hence, argues the old-earth group, there would be no choice but to use the word *yom* to describe several distinct multimillion year periods of time. Besides, they argue, even in today's English with its many word options, we still occasionally use the word "day" to indicate an era—such as the phrase "in the *day* of the knights of old."

_____Key Concept_____

Young-earth Christians are those who believe that *the universe is only about 10,000 years old—because of the genealogies in the Bible and because they maintain a literal interpretation of the creation "days" in Genesis 1.*

Old-earth Christians are those who believe the uni*verse is billions of years old (in accord with present-day science)—and they believe that the original language of the Bible provides sufficient latitude for long periods of time for creation.*

Although the labels "young earth" and "old earth" are commonly used among Christians, another way to think of the two groups is that of a "special-revelation" orientation and a "general-revelation" orientation. This designation focuses on the two equally valid theological viewpoints, while merely describing an individual's *orientation—not to the exclusion of the other form of revelation.* The author believes that such a designation might help each side to better *respect* the other's point of view. Disrespect is divisive to the body of Christ and harmful to Christian testimony.

It is beyond the scope of this book to digress into in-depth arguments for either the young-earth or old-earth positions. Readers can learn more about either by going to this Web site for young earth—www.icr.org (Institute for Creation Research), or this one for old earth—www.reasons.org (Reasons to Believe).

It is within the scope of this book, however, to present evidence of God, Jesus, and the Bible to an unbelieving world in the most effective way. Therefore great consideration will be given to the knowledge and education of the world as a starting point. It is for this reason that an age-of-the-earth preface to this section is given, in hopes that those holding a young-earth position might understand the reasons why we will assume an old-earth position in reasoning with nonbelievers. Just as Jesus did, we will *start* talking to people *where they are,* not where we are (whether we are young- or old-earth believers). As will be seen, all creation arguments made for old earth are statistically even more valid for a young-earth position.

Why an Old-Earth Position Is Assumed for Nonbelievers

The age of the universe is a *major stumbling block* for many nonbelieving people, who think that *all* Christians believe the universe is only 10,000 years old. They think that considering the God of the Bible requires abandoning their education and accepting a belief that has men and dinosaurs roaming the earth together about 7000 years ago—something many people feel is intellectually unacceptable. Ironically, whether the universe is 7000 years old or 14 billion years old is moot (which will be demonstrated). Still, we are faced with an educated world—and many will never be receptive to the gospel message *unless they realize that many Christians agree with both the scientific estimate of the age of the universe and the Bible.*

The preponderance of scientific evidence, which is growing exponentially, indicates that the universe is about 14 billion years old (some now have refined it to 13.6 billion years). To many scientists whose life is devoted to this, including many steadfast Christians, certainty about the old age of the universe might be compared to our certainty of the spherical shape of the earth—before we could verify it with space probes.

It *is not* the author's goal to persuade Christians to either a young- or old-earth stand, but to let the evidence fall where it may for each individual. It *is* the author's goal to encourage love and tolerance on both sides, and to utilize the old-earth position in this text because it is 1) biblically supportable according to many leading scholars; 2) the most commonly accepted position in a nonbelieving world and hence tends to minimize roadblocks; and 3) the most conservative when applying statistical modeling. Again, the overall objective is to present the love and gift of the gospel of Jesus Christ in the most reasonable and effective manner, and encourage Christians not to divide over this issue.

> Many people reject listening to the Christian message outright because they believe *all* Christians think the universe is only 10,000 years old—which they view as an intellectually unacceptable position, given the conclusions of modern science.

The words of the Bible should always be viewed on a case-by-case basis, using care not to be inflexible, and using our best scientific knowledge to add to our general-revelation understanding. People haven't always been right. We should remember always that one of the ways God commands us to love him is with our mind—thereby using *all* the knowledge he reveals.

Some Observations About the Old-Earth Viewpoint

Because this book encourages all Christians to start with an old-earth position in presenting the faith to nonbelievers, some discussion will be given regarding the old-earth viewpoint. This should provide some assurance that latitude on the issue of "days" has valid theological, scholarly support.

In many faithful Christians' minds, we have reached a point of knowledge today regarding age of the universe allowing us to evaluate the word "day" in Genesis 1 using general revelation. These people (who feel there is overwhelming evidence of the old age of the universe) believe that we are at a point similar to that when we rejected the literal interpretation of "four corners of the earth" as meaning a flat earth (Revelation 7:1; 20:8). They believe "day" is simply a metaphorical indication of a closed-end period of time in the same sense that the Bible uses "four corners of the earth" metaphorically to represent "all over the earth." In such a case, like the discovery that the Earth is round (in clarifying Revelation 7:1), scientific knowledge forces us to recognize general revelation as clarifying special revelation of the "days" of creation.

An example of such a supporter of the certainty of the old age of the universe is Nobel Laureate physicist Murray Gell-Mann, who said it would be easier to prove that the earth is flat than to prove that the universe is only a few thousand years old.[1] Others don't even think it is necessary to consider Genesis 1 metaphorically, since they believe that the Hebrew word *yom* was always intended to mean *age* (this is the common day–age interpretation of Genesis 1).

It really comes down to this: Is it worth denying the gospel to nonbelievers because of an unyielding stand? We should remember that many of the top research astrophysicists with advanced degrees from MIT, Stanford, and the like are devoted Christians with exceptional biblical backgrounds. Can we in good conscience *deny a fellow human the gospel* based on a nonprofessional, personal understanding of a non-salvation matter? Is it right to make a judgment about special revelation at the expense of general revelation? We should not allow these issues to weaken our presentation of the Bible.

──────── Key Concept ────────

The age of the earth is not a salvation issue, and therefore it should not be made into a roadblock to nonbelievers.

As a final note on biblical hermeneutics (interpretation), there are many top biblical scholars who indicate that Genesis 1 allows for a day–age (old-earth) interpretation. Noted biblical scholar J.P. Moreland says,

You can maintain a personal belief in young earth yet still present evidence for God using creation and old-earth ideas (in order to avoid unnecessary conflict, and without compromising your beliefs). Simply stress that there are those who believe "just as strongly" in old earth as in young earth—yet in the end, the age of the universe is a moot point, as can be mathematically demonstrated.

Now...I'm not a Hebrew exegete. But I will tell you that two of the best-known exegetes of the Old Testament in the American evangelical community are Gleason Archer at Trinity Evangelical Divinity School and Walter Kaiser at Gordon-Conwell. Walter Kaiser and Gleason Archer are respected in the entire United States as being faithful expositors of the Old Testament. Both of them know eight to ten Old Testament languages, and they both have spent their entire lives in Hebrew exegesis. Both of them believe the days of Genesis are...vast, unspecified periods of time, and are in no way required to be literal twenty-four hour days.[2]

Basic Assumptions

So as we deal with the issue of creation versus evolution, this text (as do the reference text *Dismantling Evolution* and the evangelism reference *Creation vs. Evolution*) will assume that the hard-science major findings of science are accurate. It will assume that astrophysics is accurate in its measurement of the age of the universe at about 14 billion years. It will assume that the findings of molecular biology regarding DNA and life origin are accurate. It will assume that the disciplines of molecular biology, chemistry, and mathematical modeling, including radiometric dating, are valid.

However, this and the companion texts will not assume that soft-science claims are accurate regarding evolution—soft sciences such as geology, paleontology, and general biology. Soft science is the only hope of evolution, and it can be soundly refuted using the more reliable hard sciences.

Clearly, general revelation can and should be used as support for the Bible (special revelation)—but *correctly*. Later chapters using hard evidence in this book will provide Christians with adequate knowledge, accepted by the scientific com-

> Leading biblical scholars agree there is sufficient latitude in the Hebrew Old Testament for an old earth position. Therefore, young earth believers can in good conscience discuss creation using an old-earth framework.

munity, to soundly counter evolution and support the creation account in the Bible. Science supports creation. (Extensive use of the question checklist in appendix B is recommended, along with use of the primary references in this book.)

Fascinating Facts

History reveals that many accepted both old- and young-earth positions up until the "Scopes Monkey Trial" of 1925. William Jennings Bryan, defender of creation at the trial, was an "old-earth" advocate. When evolution effectively "won" (although Scopes technically lost), the Christian world went largely to a young-earth viewpoint. At the time it was not recognized that 1) the universe had a beginning—Einstein's general relativity was still far from proven, so many scholars believed in an infinite universe; and 2) there was no knowledge of cell complexity. Hence many thought "young earth" was necessary to refute evolution. However, now we know evolution is impossible either way.[3]

General Approach for Using Science with Nonbelievers (The Five "P's")

1. *Pray* for an open mind for the nonbeliever, and that you will have a mindset of presenting the love of Jesus with gentleness and respect (1 Peter 3:15).

2. *Prepare* yourself by memorizing some of the key facts in the following chapters that demonstrate the consistency of science with the Bible—in particular the creation account.

3. *Present* the evidence of the God of creation and tie the (statistical) miracle of the accuracy of the special revelation of the Bible with the general revelation of science. Be prepared to address the young-earth–old-earth question in a manner that is comfortable to you, if needed. This will help with the receptivity of the listener.

4. *Provide* a follow-up. Offer a booklet (the Examine the Evidence series is designed for this purpose) and schedule a time to get together again.

5. *Proceed* to present the gospel. Recognize that every nonbeliever is in a different stage regarding their receptivity to Jesus. Try to ascertain the correct time and place to present the good news. Being too "pushy" can dissuade nonbelievers. (See *How to Talk About Jesus with the Skeptics in Your Life.*)

Key Concept

The anthropic principle refers to the amazing, "perfect and precise" design of the heavens and earth for life. It shows that the "Big Bang" was anything but an "explosion"; but instead, a harmonious symphony of creation directed by God—*which is totally supported by the Bible (see chapter 4).*

Test Yourself

1. What does *general revelation* mean? What does *special revelation* mean?

2. What does young earth refer to? What does old earth refer to?

3. Is it necessary to believe either a young- or old-earth viewpoint to be a Christian?

4. Why is it recommended to be tolerant of an old-earth position when approaching a nonbeliever?

5. Do biblical scholars accept old earth as legitimate? Name at least two.

Chapter 3 Group Study

Homework Preparation (do prior to group)
Read: Psalm 19:1; chapter 3 of this text; and pages 16–17 of *Creation vs. Evolution* ✝. Familiarize yourself with appendix B. Also go to www.evidenceofgod.com and familiarize yourself with tools regarding creation vs. evolution.

Opening Prayer
Discussion: Review the history of the debate over creation. Discuss why the "Scopes Monkey Trial" was such a pivotal point. The Scopes Trial also was the key point when old earth versus young earth became an issue between Christians. Science at the time incorrectly believed in an infinite universe. How would this impact thinking?

Practical-Experience Game
Role-playing: The "Christian" encounters a "non-believer" who thinks that all Christians believe the universe is only 10,000 years old. The Christian should role-play as if he were really a young-earth Christian. After it is established that there are two points of view, the "non-believer" asks why there is such disagreement. How should the Christian respond?

Closing Prayer

Great theologians speak about general and special revelation:

Augustine (about 354–430):

"Usually, even a non-Christian knows something about the earth, the heavens, and the other elements of this world, about the motion and orbit of the stars and even their size and relative positions, about the predictable eclipses of the sun and moon, the cycles of the years and the seasons, about the kinds of animals, shrubs, stones, and so forth, and this knowledge he holds to as being certain from reason and experience. Now, it is a disgraceful and dangerous thing for an infidel to hear a Christian, presumably giving the meaning of Holy Scripture, talking nonsense on these topics; and we should take all means to prevent such an embarrassing situation, in which people show up vast ignorance in a Christian and laugh it to scorn....

If they find a Christian mistaken in a field which they themselves (the non-Christian) know well and hear him maintaining his foolish opinions about our books, how are they going to believe those books in matters concerning the resurrection of the dead, the hope of eternal life, and the kingdom of heaven, when they think their pages are full of falsehoods and on facts which they themselves have learnt from experience and the light of reason?"[4]

Thomas Aquinas (1225–1274):

"The truth of our faith becomes a matter of ridicule among the infidels if any Catholic, not gifted with the necessary scientific learning, presents as dogma what scientific scrutiny shows to be false."[5]

Creation, Science, and the Bible

How did everything come into existence? Either things were created, or they came about by some random process. Think about it. There is no other alternative.

In the broadest sense, "everything" includes all matter, energy, and life. We know these things are in existence now, but were they always in existence? Was there a beginning, as the Bible indicates? Was there an end to creation? What does science tell us? Does it differ with the Bible or support it? Can evolution and creation both be right (a kind of "theistic evolution")?

What the Bible Says About Creation and Evolution

1. The Bible indicates there was a beginning of everything (Genesis 1:1). This means that there was previously a time of nothingness, and that a God who transcends the space–time domain we perceive exists and created what was to come.

2. The Bible indicates that Creation took place in a series of orderly steps over several distinct periods of time. (These periods of time are the "days" of young earth or "ages" of old earth.)

3. The Bible indicates each separate species was created "according to its kind." Hence they did not evolve from one species to another as theistic evolution would indicate. They were created sequentially.

4. The Bible indicates that there was an end to creation ("God rested," Genesis 2:2).

What Science Says about Origins

1. Time, matter, and space had a beginning. General relativity, which was proposed as a theory by Albert Einstein in 1915, has now been proven by many scientific experiments. Essentially it is verified to the same degree as other laws of physics.

2. Life-forms appeared on this Earth at different points in time that scientists define as "ages" or "epochs."

3. Life-forms appeared in a sequence on this planet at different points in time. Evolution—species change through favorable mutation—is most often taught as the basis for this sequence of new species development.

4. There was a point after which no new creation took place.

It becomes apparent that science agrees with the Bible in regard to the general process of the development of the origin of life, with the exception that many scientists accept neo-Darwinian evolution of species over creation.

Creation in the Bible Agrees with Science

Some people are surprised to discover that the scientific record of the events of creation agrees completely with the Genesis account. To fully understand this, it is important to recognize the starting frame of reference of God—at the surface of the waters (Genesis 1:2). It is also important to recognize that the entire creation is not accounted for in Genesis, and that there are some life-forms (such as the dinosaurs) that are not mentioned. (See page 538 in part 6 for a chart noting the consistency of the Bible's account with the scientific account.) After all, the Bible was never intended to be a science book, but a book about mankind's relationship with God. The steps of creation in Genesis and the steps of development of the universe based on science are compared below.

Step 1 (Genesis 1:1-2)

In the beginning God created the heavens and the earth. Now the earth was formless and empty, darkness was over the surface of the deep, and the Spirit of God was hovering over the waters.

It is particularly important to recognize the presence of the "Spirit of God" at the "surface of the waters." This frame of reference will be important in considering the remaining steps of Genesis.

Science says: There was a beginning of time, space, and matter according to general relativity which was first proposed by Albert Einstein in 1915, and was ultimately verified by Penzias and Wilson, Smoot, and many other scientists thereafter. Science also indicates that the initial state for a planet such as Earth would be "empty and void."

Step 2 (Genesis 1:3)

God said, "Let there be light," and there was light.

Because the spirit of God was hovering over the "surface of the waters," this reference indicates that light became visible from the vantage point of God—in other words, at the surface of the ocean.

Science says: Light throughout the universe would have been available long before Earth developed. However, when considering the language of the Bible, science would agree to the point of Genesis 1:3—that the next development step, *from the vantage point of the surface of the earth,* would be that dense gases would become translucent—allowing a small amount of light to reach the earth. This step is vital for photosynthesis, necessary for plant life.

Step 3 (Genesis 1:6)

> God said, "Let there be an expanse between the waters to separate water from water." So God made the expanse and separated the water under the expanse from the water above it. And it was so.

Science says: The next step in development was that heated water would evaporate into clouds. This would set up the hydrological cycle, which is necessary for life.

Step 4 (Genesis 1:9-10)

> God said, "Let the water under the sky be gathered to one place, and let dry ground appear." And it was so. God called the dry ground "land," and the gathered waters he called "seas." And God saw that it was good.

Science says: The next phase of planetary development would be heavy seismic and volcanic activity, which would have caused creation of the continents and other land masses in a proportion of 30-percent land—ideal for life.

Step 5 (Genesis 1:11)

Then God said, "Let the land produce vegetation: seed-bearing plants and trees on the land that bear fruit with seed in it, according to their various kinds." And it was so.

Science says: Of all the life-forms mentioned in the creation account of the Bible, vegetation would be the next step. Light, water, and the large amounts of carbon dioxide that were all present on early earth would have set the stage for plant life.

Step 6 (Genesis 1:14-18)

God said, "Let there be lights in the expanse of the sky to separate the day from the night, and let them serve as signs to mark seasons and days and years, and let them be lights in the expanse of the sky to give light on the earth." And it was so. God made two great lights—the greater light to govern the day and the lesser light to govern the night. He also made the stars. God set them in the expanse of the sky to give light on the earth, to govern the day and the night, and to separate light from darkness.

Science says: As plant life gave off oxygen (along with other factors), the atmosphere became transparent to the point that the sun, moon, and stars were visible at the face of the Earth. (Prior to that time, dense gases allowed some light, but not visibility of the heavenly bodies.)

Again, it is important to remember that the frame of reference is at the surface of the waters.

Some believe a literal interpretation of the Bible would indicate that the sun, moon, and stars were made during this step (day 4). This would make little sense to a scientist. The earth had to have daylight and nighttime (and had to rotate) to have a day or evening and morning at all—all of this requiring a sun. A solution to this dilemma is to recognize that the Bible stated the heavens were made on day one. There is nothing in the day-four language that would require creation of these bodies on day four—they could have been previously "made."

We also find that the Hebrew word for "made" on day four—*asah*—which usually means to produce or manufacture, also could have meant "made to appear," which would fit the remaining context better. First, we need to remember that the Spirit of God's vantage point was the surface of the waters. Second, we should consider that the Bible tells us why the heavenly bodies were "made to appear"—it was to "mark the seasons and days and years."

Step 7 (Genesis 1:20-21)

> *God said, "Let the water teem with living creatures, and let birds fly above the earth across the expanse of the sky." So God created the great creatures of the sea and every living and moving thing with which the water teems, according to their kinds, and every winged bird according to its kind. And God saw that it was good.*

Science says: Next in the line of development listed in the Bible were the sea creatures, followed by birds.

Step 8 (Genesis 1:24)

> *God said, "Let the land produce living creatures according to their kinds: livestock, creatures that move along the ground, and wild animals, each according to its kind." And it was so.*

Science says: Next, of biblical creatures, came the land animals.

Step 9 (Genesis 1:26)

> *Then God said, "Let us make man in our image, in our likeness, and let them rule over the fish of the sea and the birds of the air, over the livestock, over all the earth, and over all the creatures that move along the ground."*

Science says: The final creature to appear upon the Earth was man.

Step 10 (Genesis 2:2)

> *By the seventh day God had finished the work he had been doing; so on the seventh day he rested from all his work.*

Science says: There can be no more creation (first law of thermodynamics).

The biblical creation process agrees with science—as far as the events discussed in the Bible go (considering again that the Bible is not intended as a science text and does not include all the steps). No culture on the face of the earth understood the events of development of the universe at the time. Yet, if we consider just the naming of the ten events of creation in the correct order, we find the odds of randomly

The ten steps of creation in Genesis agree with the listing of the order of those same events as defined by science. The odds of randomly "guessing" this order would be about 1 chance in 4 million, similar to the odds of winning a state lottery with a single ticket.

guessing the steps and their sequence are about 1 chance in 4 million—about the same odds as winning a state lottery with one ticket.

The Bible and the Big Bang

The *big bang* is a term coined at the time scientists were originally speculating on the origin of the universe based on Einstein's theory of general relativity. In a nutshell, Einstein's equations (along with the updates based on experimental physics) indicate that the universe started from nothing and burst into existence. Unfortunately, the term *big bang* makes it sound like a chaotic explosion. Nothing could be further from the truth. Rather, the development of the universe has the appearance of a harmonious unfolding of an environment precisely tuned for mankind.

Ironically, today some believe the big bang supports evolution, perhaps because it suggests an old-earth point of view. The misunderstanding comes from the idea that billions of years is adequate for evolution. *But in reality, the big bang proves that time has a beginning and a limit—not nearly "enough" to even start life.* The irony is that when it was first discovered to be true, atheistic *scientists* (not clergy) were "up in arms," denigrating the discovery on the basis that it implied the existence of God (one even lamented that scientists were "running off to join the First Church of Christ of the Big Bang"). Some scientists even published books attempting to refute it, fearing its Bible-supporting implications.

Such scientists recognized that the big bang agreed with the Bible in several ways—most notably Genesis 1, that there was a beginning of time and space. In addition, many savvy scientists recognized that the moment a time limit was set, the random development of life would be mathematically unreasonable no matter how many billions of years would be available.

In addition to the reference to the beginning of time in Genesis 1:1, there are several references in the Bible to the "stretching" of the universe, which implies the expanding that we observe and that was predicted by the big-bang model (Psalm 104:2; Job 9:8; Isaiah 40:22; 42:5; 44:24; 45:12; 48:13; 51:13; Jeremiah 10:12; 51:15; Zechariah 12:1).

How Reliable Are General Relativity and the Big Bang?

Several of the key breakthroughs of twentieth-century physics involved phenomena that affected the study of the origin of the universe. Experimentation throughout this time tended to support the big-bang model. Here are some of those developments.

Hubble's Discoveries

In the 1920s, a contemporary of Einstein, Edwin Hubble, documented that the most distant galaxies are moving away from the Earth. Furthermore, the farther away the galaxies are, the faster they are receding. His experimental finding that showed this is termed the *redshift*.

To illustrate, consider the way we experience the Doppler effect with sound. With, for instance, an approaching train, the pitch of its noise is higher because the train is coming toward you, in effect compressing the wavelength of the sound waves reaching your ear. After the train passes by, however, the reverse happens—the sound wavelength expands, and the pitch decreases suddenly.

Likewise, the redshift of distant galaxies implies that they are moving away from us since red is the longest wavelength of visible light. The "degree of redness" indicates speed. Even though Hubble was the first to document an expanding universe, a great number of experiments have been done since to confirm *Hubble's law,* as it is termed.[1] For example,

> In 1996 two teams at the Carnegie Observatories engaged in measuring Hubble's constant by different methods reported converging findings on the age of the universe. One team, led by Wendy L. Freedman, estimated the age at 9–12 billion years. The other, led by Allan Sandage, estimated the age at 11–15 billion years.[2]

Background Radiation

In 1964 and 1965, Bell Labs' Arno Penzias and Robert Wilson were working with a large space antenna located in Holmdale, New Jersey. They noted a 3° K. "background" radiation that came literally from all directions of the universe. (Ironically, other scientists had observed the same background radiation before, but had simply dismissed it as an anomaly.)

About the same time, Princeton University's Robert Dicke, looking for additional evidence of the big bang, had postulated that if the big bang had occurred, a remnant of very low-level radiation would be resonating throughout the universe. Penzias and Wilson's discovery thus provided strong confirming evidence for the big bang. (In 1978, Penzias and Wilson were awarded the Nobel Prize in Physics.)

Mapping the Background Radiation

The COBE (COsmic Background Explorer) space probe was launched in 1989 by a team under the leadership of George Smoot of the University of California at Berkeley. It was equipped with a great deal of sophisticated equipment, including instrumentation that could compare the spectrum of background radiation with that of a precise "blackbody." The probe was designed to confirm or deny the big bang as the origin event, and to map cosmic background radiation precisely.

On April 24, 1992, the news hit. The research team was heralded around the world for "discovering the edges of the universe." By then the COBE spacecraft had beamed back a tremendous number of data points confirming background radiation and mapping the universe.

Stephen Hawking, Cambridge University's Lucasian professor of mathematics, said, "It's the discovery of the century, if not of all time."[3] Michael Turner, astrophysicist at Fermilab and the University of Chicago, indicated that the discovery was "unbelievably important....The significance of this cannot be overstated. They have found the Holy Grail of cosmology."[4] Project leader Smoot exclaimed, "What we have found is evidence for the birth of the universe." He added, "It's like looking at God."[5]

Since 1992, there have been numerous independent experimental confirmations of results of the COBE breakthroughs. The data from other sophisticated information gathering tools has simply confirmed what Penzias and Wilson originally observed in 1965.

The Search for Helium

The big-bang model states that, by the time the universe was 20 seconds old, there would have been a high proportion of helium (estimated to be about 25 percent of all matter). One of the ways to examine the likelihood of the big bang is to determine the elements in existence in the universe at its very edges. These areas would have been the first to be formed, and if a high proportion of helium exists in them, this would support the big-bang model.[6]

In 1994, astronomers measured an abundance of helium in very distant intergalactic gas clouds. More confirmation of the high presence of helium in distant galaxies was later made by American and Ukrainian astronomers, as noted in the 1999 issue of the *Astrophysical Journal*. [7]

A Confirmed Model and a Confirmed Principle

In the years since the original COBE discoveries, millions of data points of the universe have been mapped annually, which continually adds experimental data to confirm Einstein's principle of general relativity. The big-bang theory has been tested by measuring the expansion speed of the most distant galaxies, and five independent methods have come up with extremely consistent indications that the universe is between 14.6 to 15.1 billion years old. (Note: Some have recently calculated a universe age of 13.6 billion years.) Today, virtually all physicists accept general relativity as an essential law of physics, and the big bang as the model of the origin of the universe. In a 2001 interview, astrophysicist Dr. Hugh Ross noted, "General relativity is as close to a law of physics as one gets."[8]

Elsewhere Ross further emphasizes the empirical support for general relativity:

> Over the last few decades numerous observational tests have been devised for general relativity. In each case general relativity has passed with flying colors.[9]
>
> General relativity predicts the rate at which two neutron stars orbiting one another will move closer together. When this phenomenon was observed and measured, general relativity proved accurate to better than a trillionth of a percent precision.
>
> In the words of Roger Penrose, this test result made general relativity "one of the best confirmed principles in all of physics."[10]

With its latest refinements, the big-bang construct is now admired even by atheists who understand the implications of a universe with a beginning. Physicist Lawrence Krauss, a self-described atheist, praises the model as one of *"the most exquisitely designed entities known to man."*[11]

The big-bang principle of physics is fully supported by the Bible. It provides very strong evidence that creation occurred because 1) there was a beginning of time and 2) there was a limited amount of time since the advent of creation—making it an impossibly short time for random development of even a single cell (as will be seen in a later analysis).

Test Yourself

1. In general, how does the Bible agree with science about origins?

2. What does Genesis 1:2 say about the location of God at creation? Why is this important in the reconciliation of Genesis with science?

3. If someone were to tell you that the sun was created on "day four" (Genesis 1:16)—after the creation of plants that need the sun—how would you respond?

4. What are the odds of "guessing" the steps of creation? Why is it significant?

5. In what way does the big bang support biblical creation?

Chapter 4—Group Study

Homework Preparation (do prior to group)

Read: Genesis 1–2:2; chapter 4 of this text, and pages 30-33 of *Creation vs. Evolution* ✝. Familiarize yourself with appendix B. Also go to www.evidenceofgod.com and familiarize yourself with tools regarding creation vs. evolution.

Opening Prayer

Discussion: Discuss Genesis 1 and how it relates to science. Discuss "Is Light Slowing Down?" on page 33 of *Creation vs. Evolution.* How can young-earth believers present creation to highly educated scientists without compromising their personal beliefs?

Practical-Experience Game

Debate: The "Christian" is pitted against a physicist who indicates the Bible is flawed. Specifically he claims that Christians think 1) the universe is only 7000 years old, 2) the sun was created after plants, and 3) dinosaurs lived with humans.

Closing Prayer

The Complexity of Living Things

The simplest life form is a single cell. However, a single cell is extraordinarily complex. And all this complexity fits within a minuscule space.

A reproducing cell is the smallest fully functional living creature. Cells can vary in size from the smallest—bacteria, which are about 1/50,000th of an inch across—to the largest, the yolk of an ostrich egg.[1] There is also a wide variety in the shape and function of living cells (for example, cells for plants, or for muscle, blood, nerves, and so on). We can put the size of a cell in perspective by noting that about 1000 "average" cells would fit within the period at the end of this sentence. (And 25,000 bacteria-sized cells would fit in the same space.)

Despite the vast differences between them, virtually all cells do certain functions. These functions are so complex that a single cell is far more complicated structurally than the most modern factory in the world. All cells "breathe," eat, get rid of waste, grow, reproduce, and eventually die. They are essentially miniature animals—in fact, there are many single-celled organisms. (One of the most well known is the amoeba, often studied in biology classes.)

A Multiplicity of Parts

The true complexity of a living cell cannot be well appreciated until the individual parts of its structure are considered. There are a number of parts that are common to most cells. Take a look at the diagram below, which is a highly simplified representation of how a cell might be likened to a typical factory.

A Simplified Schematic of a Very Basic Cell

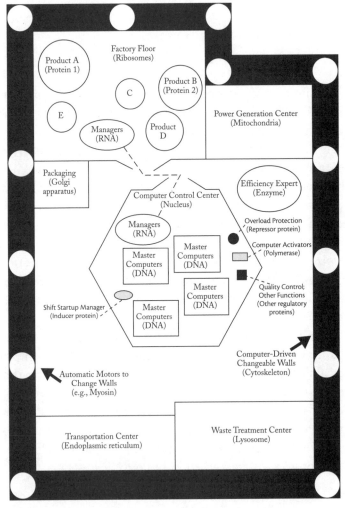

Below is a brief description of a few of the common parts of a cell. (Later in this chapter, we will illustrate how simplistic the factory illustration is when we review some of the intricacies of mitochondria, DNA, RNA, and protein chains.) Keep in mind, however, that all of this is packaged in a space usually a thousandth of the size of a period—sometimes less.

DNA is like the master computer—the essential part of every cell that dictates all its actions. Though an entire chain of DNA uses only six essential ingredients, the tiny chain is enormously long—often containing *billions* of parts. For example, if one were to take the amount of DNA in a single human body, straighten it out, and lay it end to end, it would extend for *50 billion kilometers* (from the Earth to beyond the solar system)![2] Obviously the amount of complex information on a single strand of DNA is enormous.

DNA is the primary element of chromosomes. Each species has a specific number of chromosomes per cell. For example, in humans, it's 23 chromosome pairs in "general" cells *(somatic cells),* or 46 total chromosomes. Sex cells (also called *germ cells*) differ, in that their chromosomes do not occur in pairs (in humans, they have 23 *single* chromosomes). The reproductive process combines the sex cells of a male and female—doubling the chromosomes upon fertilization and bringing the total back to the normal number (in humans, 23 pairs, or 46).

Mathematically, the process of sexual reproduction (as opposed to asexual reproduction) allows more diversification. In humans, 3.2 billion base pairs of DNA in a man combine with 3.2 billion base pairs in a woman. (Evolutionists claim that the enormous potential variation in gene sequencing through sexual reproduction can lead to other forms of creatures, though they admit that such an idea is speculation.)[3]

• At reproduction, the man and the woman each contribute 23 chromosomes to provide the new human being's standard 23 chromosome pairs (46 total) when they unite.

• While some other creatures have the same number of chromosomes as humans, the information contained in them is vastly different.

Though different species may have the same *number* of chromosomes as humans, the DNA will be different. *It is the information encoded in the DNA that separates a human being from a spider* (also, the DNA strands will be observably different).The ability of DNA genes (sections of DNA) to generate protein products also differs greatly from species to species. (All this raises an important issue confronting evolutionists: If species change from one into another, what mechanism changes—in fact, "improves"—the DNA?)

DNA manages an amount of information beyond human comprehension, doing an incredible number of things in a tiny fraction of a second. It gives instructions to each part of the cell about such typical factory functions as

1. generating power

2. manufacturing a great quantity and variety of products (proteins)

3. designating the function and relationship of these products

4. guiding key parts (molecules) to their final destination

5. packaging certain molecules in membrane-bound sacs

6. managing transfer of information

7. assuring a level of quality far beyond any human standard

8. disposal of waste

9. growth

10. reproduction

The makeup of the genes—that is, the grouping of the sections—of the DNA strand allows for 30,000 to 70,000 variations according to current estimates. There are also more complexity and more "splicing" alternatives than were once thought to exist. Hence, the available DNA information on the "production floors" (the *ribosomes*) is immense.

RNA is the substance that carries out the instructions of DNA. It is nearly the same as DNA, having six basic ingredients (more on this later). The easiest way to think of RNA is as a "reverse copy" of DNA that travels from the nucleus (the "computer center," where the DNA is) to the "production floor," where instructions for manufacturing a vast array of proteins are carried out.

The nucleus is like the "computer control room." It is where DNA is located and where the information is transferred from DNA to RNA. Within the nucleus occasionally there are found round structures called *nucleoli*. They surround sections of specific chromosomes and are believed to facilitate the production of *ribosomes*.

Ribosomes are essentially the "production floors"— where RNA instructions are received and various types of protein are "manufactured" depending on the RNA code. For instance, a human body requires literally thousands of different proteins to perform many tasks, from many needs within the cell to different types of protein to build hair, fingernails, muscles, and so on. In a single cell there may be many ribosomes, all producing vast numbers of different proteins.

Mitochondria are sites of energy production from cell respiration. A cell may contain hundreds of these sausage-shaped structures to provide all its energy needs.

Lysosomes process and rid the cell of destructive waste products. Essentially, they digest waste materials and food within the cell, using digestive enzymes (a protein produced within the cell) to break foods down into base elements.

The endoplasmic reticulum is like a transportation network for molecules within the *cytoplasm* (liquid substance of the cell). It transports the molecules to specific final destinations.

The Golgi apparatus is a form of "packaging center." It takes certain molecules and packages them into sacs, which are targeted to various locations within the cell "factory" or are even distributed outside.

Enzymes and regulatory proteins are produced by the cell for use in its own operation. Enzymes dramatically speed up certain activities of the cell. Some regulatory proteins (such as *polymerase*) in a sense turn genes "on" or "off"—permitting or preventing RNA replication depending on the needs of the cell. Many other regulatory functions are also accomplished by certain proteins, such as the built-in "proofreading" system. Without it, a cell might have a DNA copy error rate of 1 in 10,000. However, thanks to the error-control system, copy errors *(point mutations)* range only from 1 in 1 billion to 1 in 100 billion.[4]

The cytoskeleton is the amazing "scaffolding" inside the cell. A far cry from normal factory walls, it can change and adapt in many ways, based on DNA instructions. For example, one key role is the holding of the *organelles* (the "organs" of the cell) in place. But the cytoskeleton must also be able to move to accommodate growth and reproduction. Many types of proteins in the cytoskeleton enable this.

Atomic and Subatomic Structure

So far we've looked at only the tip of the complexity of molecular biology—just a small portion of the cell and its substructure. Consider further the vast complexity of an organism like a human being. There are as many as 100 trillion cells in the human body performing thousands of specific functions. Each cell contains about a trillion atoms.[5]

Fascinating Facts

- The human body contains 10^{28} atoms—more than all the stars in the universe.

- Isotope studies indicate that 90 percent of our atoms are replaced annually.

- Every five years, *100 percent* of our atoms are replaced.

- In the last hour, 1 trillion trillion of your atoms have been replaced.[6]

The sheer numbers of parts and changes and the amount of specialization seem almost incomprehensible. But scientists have learned about even more incredible instantaneous changes in our bodies at the subatomic level. For instance, a subatomic particle called the *xi* was found that has a life span of only one ten-billionth of a second. This means that, in only a few seconds, billions of xi particles have expended their life spans. *Essentially, our body is changing at a rate close to the speed of light.*

The Mystery of the Cell

Dr. Richard Swenson has brought together research by well-known scientists that gives even more evidence of the intricacy of the cell. He notes, "The mystery of the cell is both stunning and inspiring":

- Each cell is unimaginably complex. Each must live in community with its surrounding neighbors, doing its own specialized part in the whole.

- Each cell is surrounded by a membrane thinner than a spider's web that must function precisely, or the cell will die.

- Each cell generates its own electric field, which at times is larger than the electric field near a high-voltage power line.[7]

- Each cell contains specialized energy factories that synthesize *adenosine triphosphate* (ATP), which is the body's main energy source at the cellular level. Every cell contains hundreds of these factories, called *ATP motors,* embedded in the surfaces of the mitochondria. Each motor is 200,000 times smaller than a pinhead. At the center of each ATP motor is a tiny wheel that turns at about a hundred revolutions per second and produces three ATP molecules per rotation.[8]

- Cells don't stockpile ATP. Instead, they make it as needed from food consumed. Active people can produce their body weight in ATP every day.[9]

- Each cell has its own internal clock, switching on and off in cycles from 2 to 26 hours, never varying.[10]

Dr. Swenson goes on to say, "If after glimpsing the activity, intricacy, balance, and precision of life at this level you do not suspect a God [or intelligent designer] standing behind it all, then my best diagnostic guess is that you are in a metaphysical coma."[11]

Swenson's comment urges us to really think. How likely is it that such vast complexity and precision could have come about by chance? Those who support naturalistic evolution have a real problem here. The problem is to explain how such intricate cellular machines, far beyond what humans could design, could randomly come together. What mechanism could have caused it? What is the mathematical probability that it could have happened in the time frame of a 4.6-billion-year-old earth? Or even a 15-billion-year-old universe?

The obvious problems include the following:

1. How would any individual component "know" when to arrive?

2. How would all the components randomly "know" how to assemble properly?

3. How would the cytoskeleton—the amazing protective "shell"—"know" to cover the cell to allow it to work?

4. How would all this complexity happen at once? (For instance, just having a mitochondrion by itself would do nothing—without DNA, RNA, and protein.)

5. How would a mitochondrion with its numerous minute ATP motors—each producing 300 ATP molecules per second—come about?

6. Where would the information for cells to work individually or as a system come from in the first place?

7. Lastly, what would initially energize life?

The Role of DNA

In essence, any plant or organism's cells are directed by preprogrammed instructions contained in its DNA. DNA's role is central—it is like the master computer that orchestrates all of the information processing that makes an individual person who he or she is. Therefore, if we are to truly understand life, and in particular the origin of the first living cell, we should have a basic understanding of DNA; its structure and the process by which it creates the proteins that perform the actual functions of a living cell.

Structure

If we were to unravel a DNA helix, we would see a ladder-type structure with phosphates and sugars on each vertical column. The "rungs" attached to the sugar-phosphate sides are combinations of the bases: *thymine* (T) and *adenine* (A), or *guanine* (G) and *cytosine* (C). Those paired combinations are always TA, AT or GC, CG. No other combinations exist. The diagram on the following page illustrates the structure of an unraveled DNA molecule.

From its six basic components, DNA can produce many necessary proteins. Each protein chain is made up of a few hundred amino acids, from among the 20 kinds of "life-relevant" amino acids (out of more than 80 amino acids found on earth).[12] Any protein chain can have many of each different kind, so the order of the amino acids in a protein determines its function. The selection of 1) the right amino acids, along with 2) the right grouping of amino acid clusters, and 3) the right order are all extremely important. *None can be random in order for the protein to perform a function.* The bottom line is, the formation of the proteins needed is complex and precise.

The proteins in any multicelled life-form are the primary ingredients that determine what each cell is structurally, and

Stucture of DNA and RNA

How Protein Is Produced

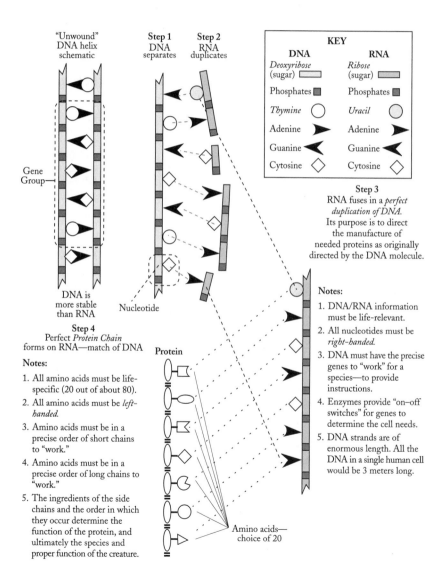

"Unwound" DNA helix schematic

Step 1 DNA separates

Step 2 RNA duplicates

Gene Group

KEY

DNA

Deoxyribose (sugar)

Phosphates

Thymine

Adenine

Guanine

Cytosine

RNA

Ribose (sugar)

Phosphates

Uracil

Adenine

Guanine

Cytosine

Step 3
RNA fuses in a *perfect duplication of DNA.*
Its purpose is to direct the manufacture of needed proteins as originally directed by the DNA molecule.

DNA is more stable than RNA

Nucleotide

Step 4
Perfect *Protein Chain* forms on RNA—match of DNA

Protein

Notes:

1. All amino acids must be life-specific (20 out of about 80).

2. All amino acids must be *left-handed.*

3. Amino acids must be in a precise order of short chains to "work."

4. Amino acids must be in a precise order of long chains to "work."

5. The ingredients of the side chains and the order in which they occur determine the function of the protein, and ultimately the species and proper function of the creature.

Amino acids— choice of 20

Notes:

1. DNA/RNA information must be life-relevant.

2. All nucleotides must be *right-handed.*

3. DNA must have the precise genes to "work" for a species—to provide instructions.

4. Enzymes provide "on-off switches" for genes to determine the cell needs.

5. DNA strands are of enormous length. All the DNA in a single human cell would be 3 meters long.

what each cell does. Since our bodies—and those of plants and animals—are made up of cells, we can conclude that it is protein, built according to the instructions of DNA, that determines what becomes hair, skin, bone, and all the organs of the body. It also determines whether we will be a plant, a human, or a toad.

Processes

The instructions built into the DNA molecule control the process of "telling" the ribosomes what proteins to manufacture. This process works essentially as indicated in the diagram on page 99. The DNA helix splits. Since the combinations are always in pairs (TA, AT or GC, CG), when "pieces" of RNA then attach to the single half of the DNA molecule, they always make an exact map. (In RNA, *ribose* is used as a sugar instead of *deoxyribose*—hence the "R" versus the "D"—and *uracil* takes the place of thymine.) The completed RNA molecule splits away and moves to the ribosome, where a protein is produced according to instructions carried by the RNA from the DNA. The DNA "knows" what the cell or organism needs next.

How? DNA is divided into groups of base-pair rungs we call *genes*. There are estimated to be somewhere between 30,000 and 100,000 genes on a DNA strand, and each gene "knows" how to make one type of protein. Therefore a DNA strand produces up to 100,000 proteins.[13] The genes direct all the traits of an individual, the order in which growth occurs, and feedback systems when repair or alterations are necessary.

Take, for example, the sequence of events from human conception, when a sperm and egg unite, through the process of differentiation. This is an issue no biologist understands. Yet, some facts are known. For instance, we know that, 30 hours after conception, the very first DNA molecule "commands" the very first cell division. The resulting cells each divide roughly twice per day. Since growth is exponential (each cell doubles twice a day), it doesn't take long for a couple billion cells to form. But what baffles scientists—especially evolutionists—is the stage when cells start to differentiate into arms, legs, toenails, retinas, and all the other parts of the body.[14] It's as if the DNA molecule is a highly designed supercomputer that knows exactly what to do, and when.

Key Concept

- DNA *is the "master molecule" that provides the unique controlling information for each person.*

- RNA *is essentially a DNA "copy" to allow protein development.*

- Proteins *(100,000-plus types) are amino-acid chains made according to DNA instructions depending upon the needs of the body.*

Functions

So what does all the microdesign in that single DNA molecule result in? The average human adult's body—every *second* of every day—is organizing about 150 quintillion (150×10^{18}) amino acids into carefully constructed chains.[15] What do these chains of proteins do? They carry out a vast array of bodily functions, most of which the average person never thinks about:

- In a lifetime, a heart beats 2.5 billion times, never stopping to rest.

- In a lifetime, 60 million gallons of blood are pumped through your body.

- A red blood cell runs around your body 200,000 times over 120 days, only to be destroyed in the spleen on the 200,001st trip.

- Your body has 60,000 miles of blood vessels—the equivalent of two-and-a-half times around the earth.

- The number of red blood cells in your body, if laid end to end, would circle the earth four times.

- Billions of white blood cells die every time you get a fever, so that you may live.

- You breathe about 23,000 times each day, and the quantity of air you breathe each day weighs about 22 pounds.

- The small air sacs in your lungs (the *alveoli*), if cut apart and laid flat, would cover half a tennis court.

- The lung cilia that sweep mucus up the trachea vibrate at a rate of about 1000 times per minute.

- The eye is so intricate and complex that there is only one chance in 10^{78} that any two humans would have the same characteristics.

Fascinating Fact

It would take a minimum of 100 years of Cray Super-computer time to simulate what takes place in your eye every second.[16]

- In the retina there are 120 million *rods* (for dim, night, and peripheral vision) and about 7 million *cones* (for color and detail vision).[17]

- The eye can distinguish millions of shades of color.

- The ear has a million moving parts.

- In addition to its complex hearing system, the ear has over a hundred thousand motion-detecting hair cells that allow us to maintain balance and motion.

- Your nose can determine 10,000 different smells.

- Your body has 450 "touch" cells per square inch.

- There are estimated to be 100 billion neurons in the brain.

- Each neuron is estimated to have 10,000 branching fibers connecting it with other neurons.

- The brain has the capacity to store the amount of information contained in 25 million books (8 million more than are now in the Library of Congress).

- The brain makes about a thousand trillion computations per second.[18]

All of the above—and much, much more—just from one tiny DNA molecule that somehow "knew" exactly how to build and what to do for a particular person. Your body is vastly more complex than all manufacturing facilities in the entire world together. The idea that the body's vast microbiological complexity could have evolved from a simple bacterium exceeds belief. Where did all the information come from?

The more we learn about molecular biology, from the complexity of cellular structure to the vast complexity of our own human bodies, the more obvious it is that all living things are designed. However, basic understanding of molecular biology only sets the stage for a more rigorous analysis of the origin of life. And with origin of life, we can determine that evolution is beyond reason and that the only alternative is intelligent design of life itself—or God.

Test Yourself

1. How large is the "average" cell? What does it do?

2. What is the DNA molecule? RNA? Protein?

3. Describe in general how the DNA is structured, and how it produces protein.

4. How many chromosome pairs does a human have? Is it the number of chromosomes that separates humans from animals?

5. Name three fascinating facts about our body that would indicate design.

Chapter 5 Group Study

Homework Preparation (do prior to group)
Read: Psalm 139:13-16; chapter 5 of this text; and pages 26-27 of *Creation vs. Evolution* ✝. Familiarize yourself with appendix B. Also go to www.evidenceofgod.com and familiarize yourself with tools regarding creation vs. evolution.

Opening Prayer
Discussion: Read Psalm 139:13-16 and discuss the relationship of God's creation of human beings to the wondrous

complexity of the human body as reviewed on pages 101-103. Review the process of how DNA directs the manufacture of protein.

Practical-Experience Game

Role-playing: The objective of the "Christian" is to inform the "nonbeliever" of the amazing complexity of the human body and discuss how it relates to the high probability of a designer (God).

Closing Prayer

Calculating the Impossibility of the Random Origin of Life

Even with a rudimentary view of a single living cell and the everyday functions of living things, we can still have a sense of the overwhelming complexity of life at its smallest level. Now, with advanced microscopy techniques that can peer into living DNA, even to the extent that specific DNA is being mapped for many creatures, we can use mathematical modeling to calculate the probabilities of random creation of life (evolution). Since randomness is something that by its very nature lends itself to statistical analysis and laws of probability, new knowledge gained from microbiology and cosmology allows us to evaluate the likelihood of a random-origins theory.

With respect to the first created living cell, creation and evolution are independently exclusive events. If one happened, the other couldn't have. And if one didn't happen, the other must have happened. So with new knowledge about the vast complexity and requirements for life (from molecular biology), and with constraints placed on the available time for random events to occur (from cosmology), scientists can now analyze requirements for the random origin of life (neo-Darwinian evolution). The result is virtual certainty that random origin of life is impossible—thereby proving the only alternative, the existence of a Creator (God).

Hard Science Involves Probabilistic Proof

There is a limit beyond which something is for all practical purposes impossible. For probabilistic purposes, scientists generally regard anything with less than 1 chance in 10^{50} of occurring randomly as essentially impossible or absurd (without supernatural input). So when we look at the odds of evolutionary events taking place, we will use the same standard.

Fascinating Facts

One hundred and fifty people attempting to flip 150 heads in a row at a rate of one attempt per second for 15 billion years would still yield a probability of only 1 chance in ten thousand, trillion trillion. The simplest life-form would require 110,000 such coin flips, not just 150!

The hard sciences use mathematics, experimentation, and statistics as a foundation for determining a highly probable outcome. Evidence that is consistent with mathematical calculations based on proven formulas and data is the best, most solid evidence—and reasonable, useful assumptions can be based on it. Hard, empirical evidence leaves little room for speculation and interpretation. It can eliminate a lot of "fanciful thinking" by demonstrating that some theories based on observation alone are unreasonable.

The complexity of living cell-systems was briefly reviewed in chapter 5. Apart from understanding the microbiology required for life, we also have the hard science of astrophysics, which has now defined limits for the age and size of our universe. These and similar hard sciences provide important boundaries in evaluating what is possible in regard to the origin of life.

Once we break down the most fundamental, simplest living cell that can be imagined to start any random evolutionary process, we can begin listing biochemical requirements and each one's statistical probability. We know, for example, that the first living cell had to have a minimal number of building blocks, including at least a minimally sized DNA molecule, and life-specific amino acids. (While there would be other requirements as well, simply analyzing these alone will adequately prove the point.)

Chirality

Previously we looked at the development of a human being from the information in a single tiny DNA molecule. But what about the very first organism of life? Certainly it was far simpler than a human being. Are there any major obstacles for the theory of the random origin of the very first cell of life?

Most evolutionists believe that the very first cell of life was a simple bacterium. Current bacteria cells have about 128 million base pairs (the "rungs" of DNA—see page 99) of DNA.[1] However, scientists have found ancient fossils of bacteria with only 500,000 base pairs. Some speculate further that it may have been possible for the earliest bacterium to have survived with as little as 100,000 base pairs of DNA.

Likewise, in the very first simple bacterium, there was a minimum limit to the number of amino acids for protein production. The accepted number is a bare minimum of 10,000 amino acids comprised of at least 100 functional protein chains (although each would likely contain a few hundred amino acids). Why are these numbers of DNA base pairs and amino acids so important? Because of chirality.

Chirality is the term given to the necessity that all nucleotides (sugars) in a DNA or RNA chain be of a certain molecular orientation ("right-handed," technically *dextroform*) for the chain to work.

Likewise, nearly all of the 20 different amino acids (actually 19) used in cellular protein chains must also be of a specified orientation ("left-handed," technically *levoform*) for a protein to work. Not one can be defective. If these chirality requirements are not met, the entire process of manufacture from DNA to RNA to "working protein" fails. Hence, for the first bacterium, a perfect mix of both nucleotide orientation (right-handed) and amino-acid orientation (left-handed) had to occur. Even if we consider the simplest bacterium, we also need to keep in mind that both the DNA and protein chains are extremely long.

Chirality

Example 1: *Acceptable*
All perfectly oriented amino acids *and* nucleotides

Example 2: *Unacceptable*
One mistake in any of the amino acids *or* nucleotide orientations

The Problem Presented by Chirality

In nature, however, we find that all amino acids occur randomly, in equal proportions of right- and left-handed (a *racemic mixture*). After years of study, scientists have not found a single means of adequately *purifying* the mixture—that is, increasing substantially the proportion of left-handed amino acids. (The same problem, though more complex to explain, exists for nucleotides, which must be right-handed.) To create the first cell, *all of the thousands of amino acids in the hundred-plus functional proteins required for the first cell would have to suddenly show up—the right types at exactly the right place at exactly the right time—all left-handed.* This is the only way they would have been able to properly bond as instructed by the DNA.[2]

Likewise, all 100,000-plus nucleotides would have to show up at exactly the right time in exactly the right way—all right-handed—to form a functioning DNA molecule.

In other words, to just get the 100,000 correctly oriented nucleotides together in the first place would be like flipping a coin and getting 100,000 heads in a row. To get the 10,000 correctly oriented amino acids together would be like flipping 10,000 tails in a row. To do both, which is necessary, would be like correctly getting 110,000 specified flips in a row. Of course there are other problems of random assembly, but we need not go beyond the chirality problem to make the point.

The Coin-Flip Analogy

Let's consider further the example of a coin flip, which will help us relate to these truly large numbers. What is the probability of flipping 150 heads in a row? The math is fairly simple—just multiply ½ times itself 150 times. The bottom number of the fraction becomes so large that straight calculation is difficult for some computers. Using logarithms, this number can be calculated as follows:

$h = 2^{150} \log_{10} (h) = 150 \times \log_{10} (2)$ [because log
$(h^n = n \times \log(h))$]

$\log_{10} (h) = 4.5$ so...

$h = 10^{45}$

In other words, the probability of flipping heads 150 times in a row is 1 chance in 10^{45}—or 1 chance in a billion trillion trillion trillion!

A skeptic might say, "Well, the probability is still not zero—it *could* happen." Let's try to understand how unlikely the event of flipping 150 heads in a row really is. Assume you could convince 150 friends to join you in a gym for a coin-flipping experiment. Assume further that each of you would flip a coin a second—all together, 150 flips per second. Of course this is no small feat. The time it takes to flip a coin, look at it, and see what everyone else has would certainly take far more than a second. However, let's consider it possible. Even if you and your friends could start flipping at the time the universe began (according to most scientists, 14 billion years ago), you would still only be able to flip 10^{17} times. After all that time what is the probability that you would have succeeded in having one coordinated flip be all heads? It would still be only 1 chance in ten thousand trillion trillion. Statisticians would deem this "impossible."

Scientists Recognize the Problem

Some scientists have proposed ways around the chirality problem. Christian de Duve, of the Institute of Cellular Pathology in Brussels, Belgium, proposed a certain form of molecular modeling. Yet he went on to say,

> The proposed explanation does not entirely solve the chirality problem.

Later he says,

> Molecular modeling could not possibly help clarify this issue.[3]

Others have attempted to prove that chirality is not necessary and have failed. Dr. Alan Schwartz of the Evolutionary Biology Research Group at the University of Nijmegen in the Netherlands describes such an attempt:

> In an experiment designed to test the requirement for chiral purity, it was demonstrated that incorporation of even a single mononucleotide of opposite chirality into the end of a growing chain in template-directed oligomerization is sufficient to terminate the reaction (Joyce et al., 1984).[4]

Esteemed evolutionists clearly recognize chirality as a major problem.

A Mathematical Comparison

As indicated earlier, randomly getting the correctly oriented compounds for the very first, simplest organism would be like correctly predicting 110,000 coin flips in a row. The probability of each flip being correct is of course 1 out of 2. One bad flip and the game is over. A direct calculation would simply be multiplying ½ x ½ 110,000 times. What are the odds that result? Very straightforward: $\frac{1}{2}^{110,000}$. Converted to base-ten, the odds are a staggering 1 in $10^{33,113}$!

This number is so large, it's like the chance of winning more than *4700* state lotteries in a row with a single ticket for each! Or, if we counted all the subatomic particles in the entire universe (10^{84})—in fact, in nearly 400 universes—it would be the same as the odds of selecting a single, predesignated particle from that number. Is it understandable why chirality alone is such a stumbling block for evolutionary science?

─────── Key Concept ───────

The odds of evolution, considering the need for correct chirality alone, are 1 chance in $10^{33,113}$. It would be like winning 4700 state lotteries in a row with the purchase of a single ticket for each. Or it would be like properly selecting a predesignated subatomic particle from 400 universes the size of ours.

Evolutionists' Struggle with Chirality

Notice what is being said about the problem of chirality by evolutionists:

> A recent world conference on "The Origin of Homochirality and Life" made it clear that the origin of this handedness is a complete mystery to evolutionists.[5]

The Web site of the University of California at Davis observes,

> Obviously, the origin of chirality is linked with the origin of life as we know it, so that same sorts of problems arise....There are several theories for the origin of chirality, none of them obviously superior to the others.[6]

Since no scientist can refute the mathematical impossibility of a random solution to the chirality problem, attention has been given to a means of *optically purifying* the particles (sorting them by orientation) and grouping the correct sorted particles together. This is where theories start to appear that suggest purification in outer space with some kind of transfer to earth. But such unsupported notions bring up their own problems, such as, where and how do the molecules get together? Can they really be purified 100 percent? How are they transported to earth? And, most important, where is the evidence?

At this point, unfortunately, some thinking begins to depart the scientific realm entirely. For instance, one Web site goes to great lengths in its attempt to give rational reasons for the random origin of DNA. But then the author stumbles:

> This [chirality] was discovered as long ago as 1848 by Louis Pasteur, and modern science calls it biological homochirality. Science has no explanation for this.[7]

This becomes such a problem for the author's theories that he later muses,

> What could cause a pre-organic engineer [alien] to create organic life using only half of the available amino acids? Why would he restrict himself to creating designs that were limited in this way?
>
> One possibility is that local conditions were such that only organic molecules of a particular handedness were available....
>
> If the first cell was created off-world, then this place is our best guess to start looking.[8]

In seriousness, this sort of thing is what even such esteemed evolutionary theorists as John Maynard Smith and Eors Szathmary (authors of the standard work *The Origins of Life*) are considering.

Other suggestions have also been made, as an article in *Science* magazine reported:

Origin of life researchers are attempting to look for weak forces that might explain how life consists of left-handed amino acids and right-handed sugars. Some of the "classic" mechanisms, such as circularly-polarized light from supernovae and other explosive astronomical events, have now been eliminated.

Researchers have shown that such [circularly polarized] light can skew chemical reactions toward producing one particular chiral molecule at the expense of its twin. But supernovae and other astronomical sources would generate both the left- and right-spinning forms equally and so would be unlikely to produce an imbalance in organic molecules.

Even these problems ignore the more fundamental problem of high radiation levels that would be produced by these astronomical sources that are incompatible with living organisms or even complex organic chemicals.[9]

> There is no hard evidence supporting any reasonable solution to the chirality problem. Evolutionists recognize this.

Scientists have struggled with chirality for more than a century. The problem is essential to our understanding of the origin of life. And, at least from the evolutionary viewpoint, no satisfactory answer has been found.

Experts Acknowledge Other Random-Origin Problems

Here's what some experts in the field are saying about the probability of the random origin of the very first cell:

- Marcel Schutzenberger of the University of Paris declared, "There is no chance (<10^{-1000}) to see this mechanism appear spontaneously; and if it did, even less for it to remain."[10]

- Molecular biologist Harold Morowitz calculated that, if every chemical bond were broken in the simplest living cell, the odds of it reassembling under ideal conditions would be $10^{-100,000,000,000}$.[11]

- Astrophysicist Edward Argyle observes that a simple E. coli bacterium, with an information content of about 6 million bits, would have required about $10^{1,800,000}$ cases, or "states," to occur on the early Earth for its inception to occur.[12]

- John Horgan stated in a *Scientific American* article, "Some scientists have argued that, given enough time, even apparently miraculous events become possible—such as the emergence of a single-cell organism from random couplings of chemicals. Sir Frederick Hoyle, the British astronomer, has said such an occurrence is about as likely as the assemblage of a 747 by a tornado whirling through a junkyard. Most researchers agree with Hoyle on this point."[13]

> Stephen C. Meyer, who holds a PhD in the history and philosophy of science from Cambridge University, states, "While many outside origin-of-life biology may still invoke 'chance' as a causal explanation for the origin of biological information, *few serious researchers still do.*"[19]

- The odds that all the functional proteins necessary for life might form in just one place by random events (not including all the other problems such as chirality) were calculated by Hoyle and his associate Chandra Wickramasinghe to be 1 chance in $10^{40,000}$.[14]

- Thomas Huxley, an ardent supporter and contemporary of Darwin, once supposedly stated that six monkeys typing randomly for millions of years could type out all the books in the British Museum. David Foster, a cyberneticist, concluded that "Huxley was hopelessly wrong in stating that six monkeys allowed enormous time would randomly type all the books in the British Museum when in fact they could only type half a line of one book if they typed for the duration of the universe."[15]

- Hoyle and Wickramasinghe provided calculations for a slightly different version of the Huxley claim—that instead of all the books in the British Museum, monkeys could type out the complete works of William Shakespeare. Their calculations indicated that the world was not large enough to hold the hordes of monkeys and typewriters (let alone the wastebaskets) required for such a feat. They indicated this was analogous to the unlikelihood of the random creation of living material.[16]

- Gerald Schroeder continues the monkey analogy by stating that the chance of their randomly typing out any sentence at all, only a few words in length, is on the order of 1 in 10^{120}. He goes on to say, "*Randomness just doesn't cut it when it comes to generating meaningful order out of chaos. Direction is required. Always.*" The odds with a world of monkeys and typewriters and a universe of time pale in comparison to the odds of just the chirality problem. And the problem becomes far greater when other factors are considered.[17]

Noted atheists Carl Sagan and Francis Crick were attempting to build a case for extraterrestrials (to gain research funding in that field). In the process, they estimated the difficulty of evolving a human by chance alone as $10^{-2,000,000,000}$. This would be in the same range as the estimate of Harold Morowitz.[18]

Some Other Origin Factors and Their Approximate Probabilities

Below is a listing of some of the critical factors—a few of which we've already touched on—that are causing hard scientists, such as those above, to discard the notion of the naturalistic origin of the first cell.

Factor	*Probability*[20]
Chirality	$1/_{10}{}^{33,113}$
Life-specific amino acids in the right place	$1/_{10}{}^{6021}$
Correct specific amino acids in the right place	$1/_{10}{}^{13,010}$
Correct material in the right place for each gene	$1/_{10}{}^{60,155}$
Correct sequencing of genes	$1/_{10}{}^{528}$
Total odds for the naturalistic origin of the most simple conceivable bacterium (conservatively figured)	$1/_{10}{}^{112,827}$

This would be like winning 16,119 state lotteries in a row (with one ticket each).

Or it would be like picking a single predesignated electron out of more than 1300 universes as large as ours, assuming all matter was broken into subatomic particles.

Key Concept

The odds of the random origin of life (the first simple bacterium) would be the same as those of selecting one randomly marked subatomic particle out of 1300 universes the size of ours—all broken apart into subatomic particles. It is impossible.

Test Yourself

1. Describe the probability of flipping 150 heads in a row. How does this relate to the chirality problem of the first cell of life?

2. What is chirality? Why is it important in showing why evolution is impossible?

3. Beyond chirality, name three other critical molecular factors for origin of life.

4. Illustrate the probability of random origin using the examples of the lottery or the universe.

Chapter 6 Group Study

Homework Preparation (do prior to group)

Read: Chapter 6 of this text and pages 10–15, 28–29, and 34–37 of *Creation vs. Evolution* ✝. Familiarize yourself with appendix B. Also go to www.evidenceofgod.com and familiarize yourself with tools regarding creation vs. evolution.

Opening Prayer

Discussion: Discuss what chirality is. What techniques might be used in showing others that evolution is statistically unreasonable? Spend a few minutes seeing if the group can flip only ten heads in a row. Have everyone flip as fast as they can for five minutes. How many in a row did the "best" consecutive "flipper" get?

Practical-Experience Game

Press conference: The Christian is attempting to use the press to persuade the public to pressure schools into teaching statistical problems with evolution.

Closing Prayer

Mutations:
A Faulty Mechanism
for Evolution

Many evolutionists do not want to discuss the mathematical–statistical problems presented previously regarding evolution as it relates to origin of life. Stephen C. Meyer's quote from the previous chapter is worth repeating: "While many outside origin-of-life biology may still invoke 'chance' as a casual explanation for the origin of biological information, few serious researchers still do."[1] Evolutionists do, however, still love to theorize how the simplest forms of life evolved into more complex forms. Although we have demonstrated that neo-Darwinian process could not have reasonably even started, we will move on and further demonstrate that evolution after the initiation of life is impossible as well.

The Claim

The touchstone of evolutionary theory is the claim that mutations in DNA will eventually lead to improved species. To put it in perspective: First, a simple 100,000-base-pair bacterium mutated into slightly more advanced organisms. Exponentially, over time each organism then mutated into more and more organisms, until we arrived at the more than 1.7 million species we see today. (Actually, the rate of development would have to be much higher because species have been going extinct all along—presently, at an estimated rate of three species per hour).[2]

Virtually all biology and science textbooks base evolution upon mutation. For example, some evolutionists state,

> Biology textbooks are liable to say that mutations—that is, new heritable variants—are random....Can it really be true that mutations...led to the evolution of the wonderfully adapted organisms we see around us? This book [*The Origins of Life* by Maynard Smith and Szathmary] is an attempt to answer that question.[3]

> Scientists realize that mutations—changes in genes—are what produce new genetic characteristics (as well as inherited diseases). They further realize that without mutations, there can be no evolution.[4]

> Although mutation is the ultimate source of all genetic variation, it is a relatively rare event.[5]

> Beneficial mutations—if they are germinal [take place in the sex cells]—are the basis of evolution.[6]

All the above quotes indicate the assumption that favorable mutations, as they are passed on, can lead to vastly different species. We'll look at this assumption from several perspectives.

What Is a Mutation?

A mutation is a random change in the nucleotides of a DNA molecule. It occurs during reproduction, when the DNA is being doubled in preparation for cell division.

Several things can cause a mutation. First there are random copying errors. These are extremely rare because DNA actually has its own "proofreading" system. Second, there are external effects, like radiation, that can cause a DNA molecule to mutate.

For mutations to be passed on to offspring, they must occur in the sex *(germ)* cells. Otherwise the mutation exists solely within the individual organism itself. However, it's rare that mutations spread through an entire population unless there is significant inbreeding. This is because in sexually reproducing populations, an organism's characteristics are made up from both the male and female parent. Therefore, the odds are 50 percent or less that a mutated gene will be passed on.

Virtually all mutations are harmful. They tend to create problems rather than provide an advantage. (More on the statistics of this later.) Populations with heavy inbreeding—therefore, more preserved mutations—tend to have more defects and more frequent health problems.

The sources referred to above all recognize the harmful effect of mutations:

> In general, new mutations are more likely to be harmful to survival than adaptive.[7]

> The altered information [mutation] shows up in the offspring, usually as a defect.[8]

> Mutations that give rise to substantial changes in the physical characteristics of the organism, however, are unlikely to be advantageous.[9]

> Most mutations that cause a visible change are harmful.[10]

Evolutionists, though recognizing that most mutations are harmful, still embrace them as the mechanism for evolution. Why? As mentioned above, *mutations are the only hope for change from one species to another.*

_____Key Concept_____

Virtually all mutations are harmful.

Real Change Between Species?

As noted previously, recent data shows that about three species are becoming extinct every hour. There is good evidence that the rate of extinction has rapidly increased lately, but extinction does raise a question: If mutational change is so effective in creating new species, why is there evidence throughout the past that we are losing some but gaining none?

Some evolutionists do point to what they call new species. However, it seems clear that those populations have simply experienced microevolutionary changes. An environmental impact has led to a change in the gene pool, and a visible change has resulted. This is the case with the peppered moth and the polar bear, both of which have been cited as examples of new species.

Noted astrophysicist Fred Hoyle agrees with this conclusion:

> My impression is that some evolutionists have sought to speed things up by wrongly considering cases where species are only coping with environmental conditions they experienced before, so that memory is being misinterpreted as discovery.[11]

Hoyle goes on to cite the peppered moth as an example of the way many evolutionists misinterpret adaptation as development of a new species. After extensively using differential equations to evaluate the potential of positive mutations to develop new and different species, he concludes,

Rarer advantageous mutations are swamped by more frequent deleterious mutations. The best that natural selection can do, subject to a specified environment, is to hold the deleterious mutations in check. When the environment is not fixed there is a slow genetic erosion, however, which natural selection cannot prevent.[12]

Changes Within Species

Before we delve into whether DNA mutations can actually make a change between species, let's look at an easier issue: mutations *within* existing species. As far back as the mid-1830s, the concept of natural selection was being discussed. For instance, the naturalist Edward Blyth (1810–1873), a contemporary of Darwin, reasoned that, if species could evolve to a greater extent through genera, families, orders, and classes, then why couldn't they evolve to a lesser extent when their environmental boundaries are threatened?

Blyth's reasoning was natural, but the facts are that when a species has a significant environmental change, its tendency is not to adapt, but instead to become extinct.[13] This supports Hoyle's observation of the failure of positive mutational change to outweigh negative mutational change. So does the fact that extinctions outpace the supposed development of new species.

Other mathematicians have also analyzed the effect of mutations. One of the world's great experts on the mathematics of evolution, Sir Ronald Fisher (1890–1962), who was also an architect of neo-Darwinian theory (and one of the founders of the field of population genetics), made one of the first mathematical studies on how natural selection works. Essentially he looked at offspring in populations, noting which offspring had a positive survival value because of a positive mutation or a negative survival value because of a negative mutation. After considerable analysis, he concluded that

> most mutants, even if they have positive survival values, will be wiped out by random effects.
>
> *...A single mutation, even if it is a positive one, has only a small chance of survival. As a result, a single mutation is unlikely to play much of a role in evolution.*

He summed up,

> If positive mutations are to play a role in evolution, many of them must occur.[14]

It's important to keep in mind that these observations came from an architect of neo-Darwinism.

Fisher's calculations, checked and recalculated by Dr. Lee Spetner (who holds a degree in physics from MIT), indicate that evolutionists are wrong to conclude that only a small number of positive mutational changes will take over a population. *The number must be massive.* And at this point we're talking only about *improving* a population, not about turning a lizard into a bird.

Mutations Are Like Typing Mistakes

One of the easiest ways to understand why mutations are almost always negative is to look at them like typing mistakes. Essentially that's exactly what they are: errors in conveying information. When a DNA molecule is copied and an error is made, that would be like typing a message and suddenly hitting the wrong key. What are the odds it will make an improvement? The following is a simple example:

The fox runs wild	The foi runs wild
The for runs wild	The foa runs wild
The foj runs wild	The fos runs wild
The fob runs wild	The fok runs wild
The fot runs wild	The foc runs wild
The fol runs wild	The fou runs wild
The fod runs wild	The fom runs wild
The fov runs wild	The foe runs wild
The fon runs wild	The fow runs wild
The fof runs wild	The foo runs wild
The fog runs wild	The fop runs wild
The foy runs wild	The foh runs wild
The foq runs wild	The foz runs wild

It's difficult to improve a sentence with a mistake, isn't it? The same is true of DNA, which is pre-programmed for a specific purpose. A mistake *takes away* information.

Mutations Don't Add Information

Assuming that mutation is the mechanism for evolutionary change, then mutations must be able to add information in order to develop more sophisticated organisms. If the first organisms were single-celled, with perhaps only 100,000 base pairs of DNA, and now we have humans, who are vastly more complex, with 3.2 billion base pairs of DNA, information had to be added somehow over time. As has been said, "Without mutation, there could be no evolution." Put another way, if mutations can't add information, there can be no evolution.

> But so far as known, or at least so far as I know, there are no such examples [of mutations adding information].[15]

In this statement, Dr. Lee Spetner is not claiming that there aren't mutations that help a creature survive. But he does indicate that these mutations simply change the function of a gene—they don't add anything.

Key Concept

Mutations don't add information—they cause it to be lost.

Examples of Information Loss

All point mutations that have been studied have shown that not only is no information gained, information is *lost*. Let's evaluate some individual cases:

- *Bacteria resistant to streptomycin.* Some bacteria have built up a resistance to the antibiotic streptomycin through mutation. Normally, a molecule of the drug attaches to a matching site on a bacterium's ribosome, thereby interfering with its ability to make necessary protein. (Mammals don't have the same site on their ribosomes, so the drug doesn't hurt them.)

  The bacterium's mutation changes the shape of the site so the drug can't attach any longer. This mutation adds survival value to the bacterium and is inheritable, but it doesn't add any information. In addition, the loss of specificity (information) in the ribosome degrades the general performance of the bacterium.[16]

- *DDT-resistant insects.* Likewise, some insects have developed mutations that allow a resistance to DDT. DDT works by attaching poisonous molecules to matching sites on the insect's nerve-cell membranes. The mutations spoil the match, making the poison ineffective. Again, no new information is added; there is only a change. However, the cost of surviving DDT is losing specificity in the protein of the nerve cells.[17]

- *Polar bears' resistance to cold.* The polar bear has adapted superbly to its frigid environment. However, the mutations for adaptation lessen its survivability should the environment change.

- *Grains and vegetables with increased yields.* The yields of many edible plants have been increased through changes in the regulatory genes. Though the cells make more food protein, the cost is a loss of specificity in the plant's regulatory protein. Again, no new information is added.[18]

- *Dairy cattle with increased production.* Cattle bred for greater milk production turn out to be less fertile. Again, there is an overall loss of information.[19]

A 20-year series of experiments by evolutionary researchers originally suggested that cultures of bacteria could actually add information, thus forming a possible basis for macroevolution. However, evaluating the experiments in detail,

> We see that no new information got into the genome. Indeed, it turns out that each of those mutations actually lost information. They made the gene less specific. Therefore, none of them can play the role of the small steps that are supposed to lead to macroevolution.[20]

Summarizing our initial points, if mutations don't add information, and if addition of information is also necessary, then macroevolution cannot possibly occur.

A Statistical Analysis of the Probability of
Mutations Leading to Macro Change

Dr. Lee Spetner has analyzed the likelihood of development of new species through mutation.[21] He selected horses for his analysis because they are very often used as examples of evolution.

In order to calculate the odds of mutation creating a new species, we need to know

1. what the chance is of getting a mutation

2. what fraction of the mutations have a selective advantage

3. how many replications there are in each step of the chain of selection

4. how many of those steps there have to be to achieve a new species

What is the chance of getting a mutation? Considerable research has been done on the chance of obtaining a mutation. Studies indicate that the probability of a mutation varies according to the species. For example, bacteria have the most mutations, with a rate of between .1 and 10 per billion transcriptions. (To return to our typing example, this would equate to one error in 50 million pages of typing—the lifetime output of about 100 professional keyboarders.) However, other organisms have a mutation rate of 1 in 10 billion (10^{-10}).[22] So we'll use a mutation rate of 10^{-10}.

What fraction of mutations have an advantage? In order to cause a selective advantage that can lead forward to a new species, a mutation must have two components:

• It must have a positive selective value ("help" the species).

• It must add a little information to the genome.

As we have already seen, this second point is a problem. We have no evidence whatsoever that mutations have added information to the genome of an organism. However, for the sake of this analysis, let's assume it's possible and continue.

The first point also presents a problem. How many mutations must happen to have a positive selective value adequate to improve a given population? Sir Ronald Fisher admits it would take "many," as we noted earlier. A minimum mutation would be that of one nucleotide, and some biologists (for example, Richard Dawkins) assume that even the most minimal mutation can trigger macroevolutionary change. At this point, let's assume we don't know how many mutations would be required to get an adequate selection value for a macro change so we can continue with the analysis.

How many replications are necessary to make a new species? The smaller the change in each step, the more steps are needed. Another architect of neo-Darwinism, the late G. Ledyard Stebbins, estimated that it would take about 500 steps to create a new species.[23] The question then becomes, how many births would be required for a small evolutionary step to occur? Paleontologists who have studied horses over their theorized 65-million-year development have provided information to Dr. Spetner that leads him to conclude it would take about 50 million births.

Returning to the problem of advantageous mutations. What fraction of mutations must be advantageous (adaptive) in order to create a selective advantage? No one really knows, except that, as Fisher pointed out, there would have to be "many." So in order to continue, let's turn the question around and see how many advantageous mutations it would take to cause evolution to "work." This way, we can judge whether or not the number is actually realistic.

We need to start by giving a "value" to the "typical" mutation. This value indicates the contribution the mutation makes to favorable species change. The late George Gaylord, generally acknowledged as the "dean of evolutionists," indicated a "frequent value" is about a tenth of a percent.[24] Spetner uses that in his calculations.

Survival of mutations. "Next," says Spetner, "We move to evolutionist and population genetics expert Fisher's calculations that for only one mutation with a tenth of a percent selective value, the odds are 500 to one against its survival....There would have to be 1100 of them to have a 90% chance of survival."[25]

Here we begin to see the problem with mutations causing one of the steps assumed to be necessary for the evolution of horses. First, the positive mutation has to occur (with an adequate selective value), then it has to survive, then it has to take over the population. The chance that such a mutation will appear in the population is 1 in 600 ($\frac{1}{600}$). If it has as high a selective value as one-tenth of a percent, the chance that it will survive is 1 in 500 ($\frac{1}{500}$). Thus, the chances of it appearing, surviving, and taking over the population would be $\frac{1}{600}$ x $\frac{1}{500}$ = $\frac{1}{300,000}$. But there's a further statistical problem for evolutionists when we use their own numbers in our calculations. The above 1 chance in 300,000 is simply for *one* step of the *500* said to be necessary to effect an evolutionary change. In order to calculate what it would take for all 500 steps to take place, assuming no errors, we would have to multiply $\frac{1}{300,000}$ by itself 500 times. Our result is $2.7/10^{2739}$.

This is a probability that a statistician would call impossible. It would be like winning 391 lotteries in a row with a single ticket for each one. And keep in mind the following:

- This is only *one change* in the evolutionary ladder.

- We used *numbers supplied by evolutionists.*

- We *yielded on contentions that we believe to be false,* such as the assertion that a mutation can add information.

When we place the evolutionary idea of mutation under critical analysis, we discover that there is no evidence of mutations adding information. Using numbers and assumptions from evolutionists to estimate the probability of mutation achieving only one improved species, we get an impossible result.

Test Yourself

1. Evolution required mutating from the first cell to how many species today?

2. What are the requirements for a mutation to be passed on?

3. Name two of the critical problems in the theory that mutations can create new, superior species.

4. What are some commonly misunderstood examples of mutations producing "new, superior species" that in actuality are examples of microevolution?

5. What is the statistical probability of only one evolutionary change?

Chapter 7 Group Study

Homework Preparation (do prior to group)
Read: chapter 7 of this text and page 24 of *Creation vs. Evolution* ✝. Familiarize yourself with appendix B. Also go to www.evidenceofgod.com and familiarize yourself with tools regarding creation vs. evolution.

Opening Prayer
Discussion: Discuss Spetner's analysis of one evolutionary change (pp. 132–135). Attempt to have everyone understand the mathematics and be able to explain, in general terms, how mutations—even if they could add information—would be impossible.

Practical-Experience Game
Role-playing: The Christian is talking to a knowledgeable high school biology teacher who teaches evolution. The objective is to create doubt in the nonbeliever's mind that mutations are a viable mechanism for evolution.

Closing Prayer

Irreducible
Complexity: A Major
Transitional Problem

Afundamental prerequisite for neo-Darwinian evolution is that infinitesimal changes in an organism's system must take place over long periods of time. This raises a question: What happens when a large number of very complex changes must happen all at once—for an "improved system" (such as an eye) to work? A system requiring several concurrent major changes to function at all is termed an "irreducibly complex" system.

From Darwin to evolutionist Richard Dawkins, evolutionary claims have been made based on looking at just the exterior of organisms—the "macro" portions. They may look easily designed on the outside, but it's an entirely different story on the inside.

Take an automobile as an example of an irreducibly complex system. If we took just a typical automobile's engine alone, it could be broken down into hundreds of parts vital to the function of the car. The drive train likewise. But living systems, at the cellular level, are infinitely more complex than just a car body, an engine, and a drive train. Not only would we need to throw in the equivalent of gas tanks, spark plugs, engine seals, radiators, fuel lines, pistons, electronic ignition systems, fuel pumps, exhaust systems...we'd have to throw in a few trillion other parts as well—all put together in the right way at the same time. This makes many living systems *irreducibly complex* to an extreme degree.

Michael Behe, well-known molecular biologist and author of the book *Darwin's Black Box*—and the champion of the concept of *irreducible complexity*—describes it this way:

> What type of biological system could not be formed by "numerous, successive, slight modifications" [the premise of evolutionary theory]?
>
> Well, for starters, a system that is irreducibly complex. By irreducibly complex I mean a single system composed of several well-matched, interacting parts that contribute to the basic function, wherein the removal of any one of the parts causes the system to effectively cease functioning.[1]

As with the car example above, *if the proposed macroevolution of a system cannot happen gradually, and if the system is necessary to increase the survival value of a species, then the system could not have been brought about by evolutionary processes.*

A Basic Illustration of Irreducible Complexity

Behe explains the basic premise of his model in terms of a simple mousetrap.

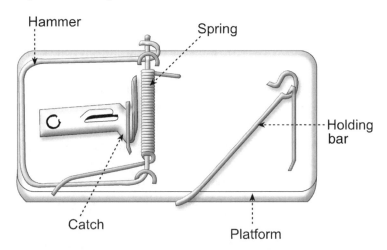

Notice that the components of the mousetrap include

1. platform

2. hammer

3. spring

4. catch

5. holding bar

If we put the mousetrap into the context of gradualistic evolution, we might imagine just the platform evolving and remaining in a population. However, it by itself has no survival value, so in all likelihood it would disappear. It certainly wouldn't catch any mice. Likewise, the hammer might evolve within a population for a while, but again, since it has no survival value by itself, it also would probably disappear from the population. The same could be said for each one of the components of the mousetrap. In order for any one part to have any mouse-catching value, *all the parts must be available at one single time*—not to mention the necessary information, and the energy to set the trap.

Yet even this very basic illustration oversimplifies things. If the platform were not strong enough, it wouldn't work— it couldn't withstand the tension of the spring–hammer combination. If the spring were not strong enough, it wouldn't work—it couldn't project enough force to kill a mouse. If the catch were too short, it wouldn't reach the hammer...and so on.

Cellular Systems Are Much More Complex than a Mousetrap or Car

Consider a macro change involving a system of cells. The cellular system's complexity is vastly greater than all of the manufacturing facilities in the world put together. Think of just the ATP motors in mitochondria—let alone all the other functions cells need to perform—and the complexity of DNA instructions that we saw earlier.

In Darwin's day, it may have been understandable to look at beak types in finches and, in the macro sense, assume that one finch had evolved from another. Even in the mid-twentieth century, it was perhaps justifiable to hold that apes and humans, because of their appearance, were related. Today, with molecular biology, it's not. With the electron microscope, X-ray crystallography, and nuclear magnetic resonance imaging, we can peer into the actual makeup of genes and the function of living cells.

Michael Behe makes a relevant observation. When, toward the beginning of the twentieth century, neo-Darwinian theory was being synthesized, there was one important group that was absent—the molecular biologists. Why? Because neither the discipline nor its tools existed! As in the example below, much of the criticism of irreducible complexity is made by biologists who haven't learned to "think small" enough yet.

- *The premise* regarding the human eye, as argued by Francis Hitching:

  It is quite evident that if the slightest thing goes wrong en route—if the cornea is fuzzy, or the pupil fails to dilate, or the lens becomes opaque, or the focusing goes wrong—then a recognizable image is not formed. The eye either functions as a whole or not at all. So how did it come to evolve by slow, steady, infinitesimally small Darwinian improvements? Is it really plausible that thousands upon thousands of lucky chance mutations happened coincidentally so that the lens and the retina, which cannot work without each other, evolved in synchrony? What survival value can there be in an eye that doesn't see?[2]

- *A response* by zoologist Richard Dawkins to Hitching's argument:

> [Hitching] also states, as though it were obvious, that the lens and the retina cannot work without each other. On what authority? Someone close to me has had a cataract operation in both eyes. She has no lenses in her eyes at all. Without glasses she couldn't even begin to play lawn tennis or aim a rifle. But she assures me that you are far better off with a lensless eye than with no eye at all. You can tell if you are about to walk into a wall or another person. If you were a wild creature, you could certainly use your lensless eye to detect the looming shape of a predator, and the direction from which it was approaching.[3]

Why is Dawkins' remark out of date? It's because of its implication that the eye could have evolved in partial macro steps (for instance, without a lens). It also implies that the remainder of the eye—the incredibly complex retina and its light-sensitive cells—is a whole and that it all could have developed at once. This old way of thinking can no longer be supported by the molecular biochemical evidence. If evolution is going to work, it must work at the cellular level or not at all.

Key Concept

An irreducibly complex system *is one that requires several major changes to occur all at once in order for the system to function at all. Since evolution requires gradual change, and since many systems in living organisms are irreducibly complex, it follows that evolution is not possible.*

Getting Down to the Real Analysis

In order to have macro value in a population, mutations need to be positive, they need to survive, and they need to have a high enough selective value—about .1 percent. (We analyzed this in chapter 7.) With a system as useful as the eye, we should be able to assume that the selective value would be high enough.

The problem would arise with the enormous number of mutations it would take to have all of the necessary subsystems mutate at the same time. After all, with the human eye, we're considering more than just the easily seen parts—the cornea, the iris, the pupil. We also have to account for the lens, the muscles attached to the lens, the retina with its 120 million rods and 7 million cones, and many other parts, not to mention a brain that has to know how to process the information. Every one of these subsystems is made up of countless cells—each cell being a miniature "factory."

Let's consider the simplest, most basic part—the light-sensitive cell (a single rod or cone). We'll review it from a modern biochemical model. The following is a paraphrase of Michael Behe's description, found in his landmark book, *Darwin's Black Box.*[4]

The Biochemical Cycle of a Light-Sensitive Cell

1. Light strikes the cell, and a photon interacts with a molecule called *11-cis-retinal.*

2. This rearranges within picoseconds (the time it would take light to travel the width of a hair) to turn into *trans-retinal.*

3. The change in the shape of the retinal molecule forces a change in the shape of the protein *rhodopsin,* to which the retinal is tightly bound.

4. The protein's metamorphosis alters its behavior— it's now called *metarhodopsin II*.

5. The altered protein sticks to another protein called *transducin*.

6. Before bumping into metarhodopsin II, transducin had been tightly bound with a small molecule called *GDP*.

7. When the transducin interacts with metarhodopsin II, the GDP falls off, and a molecule called *GTP* binds to the transducin.

8. *GTP-transducin-metarhodopsin II* now binds to a protein called *phosphodiesterase*, located in the inner membrane of the cell.

9. When attached to the metarhodopsin II group, the phosphodiesterase acquires the chemical ability to "cut" molecules called *cGMP* in the cell. The phosphodiesterase lowers the concentration of cGMP, just as a pulled plug lowers the water level in a bathtub.

—∿— —∿— —∿—

Another membrane protein that binds cGMP is called an *ion channel*. It acts as a gateway to regulate the number of sodium ions in the cell. Normally the ion channel allows sodium ions to flow into the cell, while a separate protein actively pumps them out again.

The dual action of the ion channel and the "pump" keeps the level of sodium ions in the cell within a narrow range.

—∿— —∿— —∿—

10. When the concentration of cGMP is reduced because of cleavage by the phosphodiesterase, the ion channel closes, causing the cellular concentration of positively charged sodium ions to be reduced.

11. This causes a current to be transmitted down the optic nerve to the brain.

12. The result, when interpreted by the brain, is vision.

—◊◊◊— —◊◊◊— —◊◊◊—

If the reactions mentioned above were the only ones that operated in the cell, the supply of 11-cis-retinal, cGMP, and sodium ions would quickly be depleted. Something has to turn off the proteins that were turned on and restore the cell to its original state.

In the dark, the ion channel, in addition to sodium ions, also lets calcium ions into the cell. The calcium is pumped back out by a different protein so that a constant calcium concentration is maintained.

—◊◊◊— —◊◊◊— —◊◊◊—

13. When cGMP levels fall, shutting down the ion channel, the calcium ion concentration decreases too.

14. The phosphodiesterase enzymatic reaction, which destroys cGMP, slows down at a lower calcium concentration.

15. A protein called *guanylate cyclase* begins to resynthesize cGMP when calcium levels start to fall.

16. While all of this is going on, metarhodopsin II is chemically modified by an enzyme called *rhodopsin kinase*.

17. The modified rhodopsin then binds to a protein known as *arrestin*, which prevents the rhodopsin from activating more transducin. (Thus we see that the cell contains mechanisms to limit the amplification of the signal started by a single photon.)

18. Trans-retinal eventually falls off rhodopsin and must be reconverted to 11-cis-retinal. It must be re-bound to rhodopsin to get back to the starting point for another visual cycle.

19. To accomplish this, trans-retinal is first chemically modified by an enzyme to *trans-retinol*—a form containing two more hydrogen atoms.

20. A second enzyme then converts the molecule to *11-cis-retinol*.

21. Finally, a third enzyme removes the previously added hydrogen atoms to form 11-cis-retinal, and the cycle is complete.

All of this process takes only a few picoseconds—*and it takes place in 127 million rods and cones in each eye.*

Immediately, we observe that the process is far more complex than Darwin or any soft-science biologist ever dreamed of. It's hard enough to conceive of how evolution could assemble the overall structure of the rods and cones. But the real difficulty comes when we dig into the individual cells and analyze specifically what they do. The omission of any single step of the 21 listed above would result in lack of vision. So the mutations that must occur to create a light-sensitive spot can be generalized into four stages:

1. *Accumulation of the necessary base molecules* for the process in a single location in the first place

2. *Assembling the structural elements* in a mechanical system that will allow the chemical system to work

3. *Developing the complex process* outlined above that results in electronic impulses to the brain

4. *Teaching the brain* how to interpret such signals

The concept of irreducible complexity indicates that all of the above would have to happen simultaneously because any partial light-sensitive spot would have absolutely no survival value. If it had no survival value, the mutation(s) would die out.

Facing the Data

How realistic is it that mutations would actually randomly produce such a light-sensitive spot in a population? We might argue that the necessary base molecules could be assembled in a single location randomly.

But the minute we move to stage 2, the problem becomes substantially greater. Now we are asking the mutations to add considerable information—how to structure something simultaneously with all the other things that must come together at once.

The problem is taken to a further extreme once we move to stage 3. Now enormous amounts of mutational information are necessary (just review the complexity of the system's 21 steps listed above). At this point we need the molecules, the correct structure, and a highly complex chemical system to all have mutated at exactly the same time. Then the final straw is the necessity of the brain's sudden realization of how to use this new neural input.

In reality, 127 million such light-sensitive cells had to come together in each eye. But for the eye to work, many other parts are needed, each with its own microbiological irreducible complexities: the optic nerve, the contents of the eyeball, the lens, the cornea, the muscles, and so on. And if all of these individual irreducibly complex parts can't come together at once through simultaneous mutations, the survival value of the eye is worthless. (Again, you can't catch many mice with just a block of wood.)

Logically, it doesn't seem conceivable that the necessarily immense number of highly complex, integrated mutations could possibly take place simultaneously in order to form entire sophisticated systems. Further, we have to keep in mind what we saw in the previous chapter:

- Positive mutations are very rare.

- Mutations generally don't survive in a population.

- Mutations don't add information.

- For the development of a complex system, a large number of simultaneous positive mutations would have to survive and take over a population.

As we saw from Dawkins, the necessity of irreducibly complex components has not been accounted for in biochemical models of naturalistic evolution. This is another question that has not been answered by neo-Darwinists. In summary, irreducible complexity seems to point us toward the alternative to evolution again—toward intelligent design (God).

Test Yourself

1. Define *irreducible complexity,* and then give some examples to explain it.

2. Why would a simple mousetrap be irreducibly complex?

3. In general, describe how vastly more irreducibly complex a human eye would be than a mousetrap.

4. What do you think Darwin would think about irreducible complexity? Why?

5. How does the problem of mutational change combine with the problem of irreducible complexity to make an extraordinarily large problem?

Chapter 8 Group Study

Homework Preparation (do prior to group)
Read: Chapter 8 of this text and appendix B. Also go to www.evidenceofgod.com and familiarize yourself with tools regarding creation vs. evolution.

Opening Prayer
Discussion: As a group, make a list of systems in the human body that are irreducibly complex. Discuss each one and review how you might explain the concept to people who believe in evolution.

Practical-Experience Game
TV interview: The reporter brings the Christian into the studio for an interview about the "new" concept of irreducible complexity. Explain how it works in a way that the majority of listeners can understand.

Closing Prayer

Part 1

Evidence of God's Existence in Creation: Summary and Conclusion

1. Creation and naturalistic macroevolution are mutually exclusive, independent scenarios of how things came to be. If something came about by random chance, it couldn't have been created, and vice-versa. Therefore if one can be proven to be true—or untrue—it would verify the veracity of the other.

2. We now know (by Einstein's theory of general relativity) that there was a beginning of time, space, and matter. Since the first law of thermodynamics indicates that matter and energy can not be created (or destroyed), the original cause of existence had to be outside of the time–space dimensions.

3. We know that if things in existence were not randomly formed—in particular, life—they must have been created by an intelligent designer. Through observation alone, we can marvel at the intricacy of design that is apparent in all of life. One "name" for such an intelligent designer is "God."

4. We can reason that the basis for evolution as it is being taught in schools is strictly theoretical soft science that might just as well be a basis for creation as evolution. In many cases myths are intentionally used to mislead

people, as in the cases where microevolution is used to try to support macroevolution.

5. We know that the fossil record does nothing to support evolution. Even top paleontologists recognize its short-comings. If anything, the fossil record, in particular the Cambrian explosion, is more indicative of creation as described in the Bible.

6. We find that the account of creation as indicated in the Bible is consistent with scientific knowledge. Likewise, other references in the Bible are consistent with science.

7. We now can determine the vast complexity of the events required for any proposed random development of a living cell. Just the problem of chirality alone makes the concept of random origin of life untenable.

8. Beyond the mathematical problem of chirality are many other structural problems, such as selection of the "right" amino acids and DNA components, gene sequencing, amino-acid placement, and others. The odds against random assembly of the cell's components are astronomical, and its occurrence would certainly be impossible within a time frame of a mere 14 billion years or so.

9. Mutational change as a mechanism for species development is unreasonable. Mutations take away information; and to be successful they must add information (consider the information increase from a single-cell creature to a human being). Mutations are virtually always destructive, and the small portion of positive mutations would mathematically, almost always, die out in a population. Mutations are not the same as genetic variations, which are built into a species to improve its survivability.

10. Irreducible complexity makes the idea of the transition of one species into a new species with a dramatic improvement (such as the addition of an eye) unreasonable.

    Finally, even the evolutionists who write the books and journal articles on how evolution works indicate that every step of the evolutionary process is filled with uncertainty and problems. If evolutionists can't verify their own theories, and if they admit to problems throughout the proposed system, how is anyone to believe it is true? On the other hand, there is enormous evidence that evolution is mathematically and statistically (using hard sciences) impossible.

11. Conversely, evidence does support the creation account of the Bible. First, the scientific record supports the steps of creation in the Bible.

12. The soft-science discovery of the Cambrian explosion supports creation.

13. The amazing intricacy of the design of living systems—far beyond statistically reasonable naturalistic processes—supports creation.

14. The presence of many irreducibly complex systems in living organisms supports creation.

15. The fact that nonliving matter has become "alive," in and of itself supports creation (given that "spontaneous generation" is a nonscientific myth).

Part 2

Evidence of the Reliability of the Bible

The Bible's self-proclamation that all of the Scripture is inspired by God is of profound importance. In essence, the Bible claims it is the ultimate authority for "righteousness" (this means a "right" relationship with God, which would include eternal salvation) and also for our life on earth. If we are to grant the Bible such divine authority, we should expect it to be accurate in all respects—regarding the account of creation (see part 1); historically (see this part); scientifically (see chapter 9); and prophetically (see part 3).

We also need to be certain that the original manuscripts—which would have been the original "inspired" version—have been accurately copied and handed down to us through the ages. Furthermore, if the ancient prophecies regarding Jesus Christ are to be considered of value, we must be certain that they were in fact prophesied *before* his birth and not just written after the fact. These issues regarding the reliability of the Bible will be reviewed in this part.

The Importance of a Theocracy in Regard to Scripture

The people of Israel were to be a nation governed by God. In fact, they were governed by God until the time of Samuel (1 Samuel 8:6), when they complained they had no king like other nations. Soon, Saul became Israel's first king, in 1050 B.C. (or shortly thereafter).

It's difficult for us today to fully appreciate what it would mean to be a nation governed by God, without human laws. But several things must be considered:

- All laws and rules came from holy Scripture provided by God. Specifically, these laws were contained primarily in the first five books of the Bible given to Moses—otherwise known as the *Torah,* the *Pentateuch,* or the *Law.* This is very unlike today, when there are a variety of governmental laws for each state and nation, along with various laws for every religion. In the case of the Israelites, the laws were one and the same.

- Governance was through religious leaders—all chosen by God. These leaders were sometimes priests (always from the tribe of Levi), as in the case of Moses and Aaron. At other times they were selected "judges," as in the case of Samson, Gideon, and Deborah. And sometimes they were prophets, as in the case of Samuel.

- God's laws were unchangeable, and there was no "vote" by the people regarding any of the laws, rules, or penalties.

- Holy Scripture was regarded as so important that specially trained people (scribes) were designated, and special rules were defined, for making copies. In addition, there were ceremonial rites during the copying process, and when the holy scrolls had reached the end of their useful life, they were often given a "ceremonial burial."

• The Israelites were taught holy Scripture from early in their youth. Vast amounts of Scripture were memorized.

• People deemed as prophets of God, who wrote (or had their scribes write) a great deal of holy Scripture, were highly esteemed, but critically monitored. If they made a *single mistake* in prophecy, they were to be stoned to death (Deuteronomy 18:20).

• Penalties for breaking of the laws contained in holy Scripture were often very strict. For example, anyone "cursing" his mother or father had to be put to death (Leviticus 20:9). Certainly, Israelites would want and need to be knowledgeable of Scripture.

So given that the nation of Israel was a theocracy, and that all laws and rules—both religious and political—came from holy Scripture, there would be extreme attention to detail in maintaining a consistently accurate set of documents.

Moreover, since so much holy Scripture was memorized, was read every Sabbath (heard by virtually the entire populace), and was strictly enforced on a legal basis, there would be little opportunity for errors to creep in undetected. In essence, with the degree of knowledge and scrutiny of the Jewish nation, any mistake would have been discovered and corrected immediately. In fact, in the copying of master scrolls, even a single-letter mistake was not tolerated.

Scriptural Copy Rules

The scribes were required to adhere to very precise rules. Their discipline was ingrained into them through their years of training. The many rules used by Old Testament scribes included the following:[1]

1. A synagogue roll must be written on the skins of clean animals,

2. prepared for the particular use of the synagogue by a Jew.

3. These must be fastened together with strings taken from clean animals.

4. Every skin must contain a certain number of columns, equal throughout the entire codex.

5. The length of each column must not extend over less than 48 or more than 60 lines; and the breadth must consist of thirty letters.

6. The whole copy must be first-lined; and if three words be written without a line, it is worthless.

7. The ink should be black, neither red, green, nor any other color, and be prepared according to a definite recipe.

8. An authentic copy must be the exemplar, from which the transcriber ought not in the least deviate.

9. No word or letter, not even a yod, must be written from memory, the scribe not having looked at the codex before him....

10. Between every consonant the space of a hair or thread must intervene;

11. between every new parashah, or section, the breadth of nine consonants;

12. between every book, three lines.

13. The fifth book of Moses must terminate exactly with a line; but the rest need not do so.

14. Besides this, the copyist must sit in full Jewish dress,

15. wash his whole body,

16. not begin to write the name of God with a pen newly dipped in ink,

17. and should a king address him while writing that name he must take no notice of him.

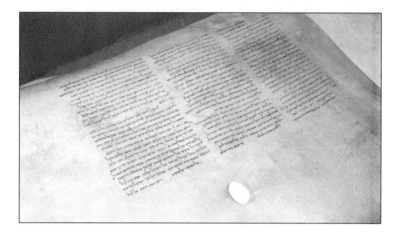

Apart from these special requirements were the basic scribal rules. The word *scribes* literally means *counters*. To verify the accuracy of every scroll that was copied, they had several items that were counted. They counted every letter and compared it to the master scroll. They counted the number of words. And as a final crosscheck, they would count through each scroll to the halfway point and compare the letter with the "halfway letter" of the master scroll.

Hence, the precision of the Old Testament scribes (and even a few New Testament "professional" copyists) was enormous. It is far different than we might expect in today's world.

Memorization of Scripture Increases Reliability

Imagine attempting to alter history and the words of holy Scripture. Succeeding would have required changing a high percentage of all written Scripture to assure that contradictions didn't exist and that the "change" would be passed on to future generations. (We know from the Dead Sea scrolls that this did not happen.)

However, if someone really wanted to change holy Scripture, changing all the written scrolls would still not be enough. Virtually all of the Jews memorized vast amounts of Scripture. It was a vital part of their education. Hence, if someone wanted to change Scripture (for some unknown ulterior motive), they would have to not only change the many copies, but would have to change the memories of tens of thousands of Jews as well. This was certainly not likely in a theocracy, where the very words of God were taken so seriously.

The Bible Is
Scientifically Accurate

For the Bible to be regarded as the inspired word of God, it must be scientifically accurate...since God would certainly know the facts about his creation. A word of caution, however, as we seek to evaluate the claim of scientific accuracy. Over time, science has often discovered new facts that confirmed a revised understanding of the truth, previously unknown. These discoveries have always been consistent with the Bible—however, at times a careful consideration of the words and (importantly) the context of the words must be made. In many cases science has discovered facts that the Bible had contained far in advance of the discoveries. And in a few cases, scientific discoveries have helped with a better understanding of the Bible's message.

For example, at the time of Galileo, science thought that the Earth was at the center of the universe and that the sun revolved around it. The Bible seemed to theologically support this view—with the interpretation that if mankind were "special," it would be at the center of the universe. Moreover, certain verses in the Bible seemed to indicate that a rising and setting sun meant that the earth was stationary (see Ecclesiastes 1:5). Anyone challenging this view at this time faced potential death as a heretic at the hands of the Roman Catholic church.

Galileo's predecessor, Copernicus, who advanced the idea that the planets revolved around the sun, dared not publish his works for fear of persecution by the Inquisition. Galileo supported the views of Copernicus and faced the threat of torture, even death. He was imprisoned and declared a heretic by the Church for his beliefs—a charge that was maintained even until 1992—when he was finally exonerated.

Notwithstanding that the Bible does contain certain metaphorical or phenomenological statements (as the above example in Ecclesiastes 1:5 demonstrates when it speaks of the rising and setting of the sun), the Bible is scientifically accurate and even contains an enormous number of insights far in advance of their discovery by humans. In evaluating the Bible from a "scientific standpoint" we must keep in mind that the Bible is not a science textbook—it is a book to define human beings' proper relationship with God. Therefore, one would not expect a great deal of discussion of science. However, as the summary below indicates, when there is a reference in it about a fact of nature, it is accurate—and in many cases there are insights provided thousands of years in advance of their understanding by science.

The account of creation (the Bible: 1450 B.C.; science: 1900s). As part 1 indicated, the account of creation as given in the Bible (Genesis 1) is accurate according to the steps understood by science. Written down originally by Moses, they were not fully recognized by science until the 1900s, using modern astronomy, physics, chemistry, paleontology, and geology.

The hydrological cycle (the Bible: 3000 B.C.; science: 1700s). The hydrologic cycle was first written about in the book of Job, about 3000 B.C. It states,

*He draws up the drops of water, which distill as
rain to the streams; the clouds pour down their
moisture and abundant showers fall on mankind*
(Job 36:27-28).

In addition, Solomon described the hydrological cycle in
about 935 B.C., saying,

*All streams flow into the sea, yet the sea is never
full. To the place the streams come from, there
they return again* (Ecclesiastes 1:7).

Science, however, did not understand the hydrological
cycle until Perrault and Marriotte correctly identified the
process in the 1700s.

The Earth hangs in empty space (the Bible: 3000 B.C.; science: 1543). Ancient cultures believed many things, yet virtually all thought of the earth as being some type of flat,
unmovable object. Many myths were associated with the
various beliefs. The Bible correctly indicated that the earth
was suspended in space:

*He spreads out the northern [skies] over empty
space; he suspends the earth over nothing* (Job
26:7, brackets in original).

Science did not discover this until Copernicus in 1543.

Air has weight (the Bible: 3000 B.C.; science: 1643).
Although ancient people widely believed air to be weight-
less, the book of Job indicated that it in fact had weight:

*To establish a weight for the wind, and apportion
the waters by measure* (Job 28:25 NKJV).

Torricelli, an Italian, discovered barometric pressure in
1643.

Time, space, and matter had a beginning (the Bible: 1450 B.C.; science: 1916). The Bible's first words are "in the beginning." And elsewhere, including the New Testament, there are references to the beginning of time (2 Timothy 1:9; Titus 1:2; 1 Corinthians 2:7). In 1915, Albert Einstein's equations of general relativity proposed a beginning of time, matter, and space. Later these equations were confirmed by repeated experiments.

Key Concept

The confirmation by science that time had a beginning is one of its most important consistencies with the Bible. Not only is it a dramatic change in thinking that confirms the relationship of the Bible with general revelation, but it is foundational to disproving evolution. Once a limit is placed on time, be it 10,000 or 100 trillion years—it makes evolution impossible (see part 1).

The first law of thermodynamics (the Bible: 1450 B.C.; science: 1842). The law of conservation of energy indicates that matter and energy can neither be created nor destroyed (just converted). There are many biblical references to God's *completion* (that is, there was no more creation), going as far back as Genesis (2:2-3), and also in several other books (Psalm 148:6; Isaiah 40:26; 2 Peter 3:3-7; Hebrews 4:3-4,10). Joule and Mayer both independently discovered this in the same year (1842)—what is now known as the first law of thermodynamics.

The second law of thermodynamics (the Bible: 1000 B.C.; Science: 1850). Commonly known as entropy, this law states that all things progress from a state of order to a state of disorder (within a closed system) without a purposeful input of energy. Common illustrations: things decay, springs unwind, stars burn out, heat dissipates, and materials become mixed over time. There are many references to the principle of entropy in the Bible, for example,

> *In the beginning you laid the foundations of the earth, and the heavens are the work of your hands.* They will perish, *but you remain;* they will all wear out like a garment (Psalm 102:25-26).

Other similar references include Isaiah 51:6; Matthew 24:35; Romans 8:20-22; 1 John 2:17; and Hebrews 12:27. In 1850, Clausius discovered this second law of thermodynamics.

The Earth is a sphere (the Bible: 700 B.C.; science: 1543).

Most of the world thought that the earth was flat until after the time of Copernicus in 1543. However, the Bible referenced the Earth in the form of a "circle" (or implied it to be a sphere, using a broader definition of the original Hebrew word *khug*):

> *He sits enthroned above the circle of the earth, and its people are like grasshoppers* (Isaiah 40:22).

The universe is expanding—(the Bible: 1000 B.C.; science: 1916). The motion of the heavens is predicted by the general-relativity equations first proposed by Albert Einstein and since confirmed many times. Experimental physicists, such as Edwin Hubble, verified the predicted expanding universe as early as the early 1900s. However, the Bible indicated that the universe is expanding far earlier than that. As early as about 1000 B.C., the writer of Psalm 104 wrote,

> *He wraps himself in light as with a garment; he stretches out the heavens like a tent* (verse 2).

Many other verses indicate that the heavens were (and are being) stretched out by God (Job 9:8; Isaiah 40:22; 42:5; 44:24; 45:12; 48:13; 51:13; Jeremiah 10:12; 51:15; Zechariah 12:1).

The stars are uncountable (the Bible: 600 B.C.; science: 1920s). Ancient people thought the stars were countable. In fact, in about 100 A.D., Ptolemy was actively cataloguing the stars—estimated to number 1100 at that time. Of course, modern science, starting in about the 1920s with new high-powered telescopes, realized that the number of stars was in the billions. Later they recognized that there are about a billion galaxies, each with about a billion stars. However, the Bible recognized this when it proclaimed the stars "uncountable" in about 600 B.C.:

> *I will make the descendants of David my servant and the Levites who minister before me as countless as the stars of the sky* (Jeremiah 33:22).

The accuracy of the literal biblical statement can now be easily verified. If stars were "counted" at a rate of ten per second, it would take more than 100 trillion years to "count" the stars...which is clearly impossible.

Currents in the ocean (the Bible: 700 B.C.; science: 1855). Archaeologists often use the Bible as a trusted historical document that leads to the discovery of ancient cultures and cities. One person who used the Bible as a trusted "scientific document" was Matthew Fontaine Maury, the father of oceanography. Maury read the statement that there are "pathways in the sea":

> *This is what the LORD says—he who made a way through the sea, a path through the mighty waters...*(Isaiah 43:16).

Taking this verse literally, he searched the oceans of the world and discovered and mapped major currents that have been used ever since for sea travel. (Another reference to "paths of the seas" is in Psalm 8:8.)

Global wind patterns (the Bible: 1000 B.C.; science: 1960s). It took satellite technology to fully recognize the global wind patterns that exist. However, the Bible indicated existence of such patterns in the book of Ecclesiastes, written by Solomon in about 1000 B.C.:

> *The wind blows to the south and turns to the north; round and round it goes, ever returning on its course* (1:6).

Principle of allowing land to lie fallow (the Bible: 1450 B.C.; science: 200 B.C.). Today agriculturists realize the importance of "giving the land a rest" every seven years or so to allow for replenishment of nutrients. The first recorded history of ancient men doing this (apart from the Israelites) is the Romans in about 200 B.C. Some historians believe the Romans learned this practice from the Israelites. The Bible commanded that the land be given a rest every seventh year:

> *In the seventh year the land is to have a sabbath of rest, a sabbath to the LORD. Do not sow your fields or prune your vineyards. Do not reap what grows of itself or harvest the grapes of your untended vines. The land is to have a year of rest* (Leviticus 25:4-6).

Engineering of Noah's ark (the Bible: 1450 B.C.; science: 1900s). The Bible defines the dimensions and building specifications for Noah's ark (Genesis 6:15). Modern engineering has calculated that for a barge-type design best-suited for rough seas, the design of Noah's ark is optimum.[1]

The genetic code (the Bible: 1450 B.C.; science: 1735). We had little understanding of the basic classification of species until Carolus Linnaeus developed an organism classification system in 1735—still used in part today. The most fundamental component of this system is the basic reproducing species. The Bible referred to such a basic genetic classification system when it refers to creatures "according to its kind" (Genesis 1:21-31; 7:14).

Circumcision on the eighth day (the Bible: 1450 B.C.; science: 1947). No one really knows for sure why God specifically chose circumcision as the sign of his covenant with Abraham (Genesis 17:11). Though it seems like an odd practice, research has indicated that it does have medical value. A study in the mid-1900s showed that Jewish women had a lower rate of cervical cancer. The smegma bacillus has been shown to be a major cause of cervical cancer. It can be easily carried in the foreskin of uncircumcised males and transferred to females through abrasions of the cervix (as those occurring in childbirth).

Interestingly, God specified that newborns be circumcised on the eighth day after childbirth (Genesis 17:12). Research shows that infants are particularly susceptible to hemorrhaging from the second day after birth to the fifth. A small cut can be deadly. Vitamin K, necessary for the production of prothrombin (the body's blood-clotting substance) is not present sufficiently until days five through seven. It skyrockets to 110 percent of normal on day eight, and then levels off. The Bible specifies the best possible day.

Quarantine (the Bible: 1450 B.C.; science: 1500s). When the Black Plague was killing much of Europe prior to the Renaissance, desperate nations turned to the Church for guidance. Germs and infections were not understood at the time. The clergy went back to the books of Moses for guidance and instituted the laws of Moses as taught to the

Israelites, including those for dealing with infectious diseases like leprosy. Leviticus 13 stressed separating people with infectious disease from others. This, combined with the other laws of Moses, helped bring the Black Plague under control.

Proper waste disposal (the Bible: 1450 B.C.; science: 1500s). Like the lack of quarantine, poor waste disposal methods led to the spread of the Black Plague. The laws of Moses clearly specified the proper method (Deuteronomy 23:12-14), which aided in stopping the spreading of the disease.

Proper handling of the dead (the Bible: 1450 B.C.; science: 1500s). The Bible also was specific regarding the proper handling of the dead (Numbers 19). When this procedure was implemented, along with the other laws of Moses, it also helped stop the spread of the Black Plague.

Sterilization (the Bible: 1450 B.C.; science: 1800s). It is easy to take our understanding of germs and disease for granted. However, germs and sterilization were not understood until the time of Joseph Lister (1865)—near the end of the Civil War. The Bible required sterilization for many things: infectious disease (Leviticus 13), childbirth (chapter 12), bodily discharges (chapter 15), and handling of the dead (Numbers 19).

Test Yourself

1. Where in the Bible is the hydrologic cycle mentioned?

2. Why was the discovery by science that time had a beginning so important?

3. What are the first and second laws of thermodynamics? List one location for each in the Bible.

4. Name three key medical principles provided in advance in the Bible.

5. Where in the Bible did God promise the Hebrews they would have "none of the diseases of the Egyptians"?

Chapter 9 Group Study

Homework Preparation (do prior to group)
Read: Deuteronomy 7:12-15; 2 Timothy 1:9; Titus 1:2; 1 Corinthians 2:7; chapter 9 of this text; and pages 5, 21, 24, and 25 in *Science: Was the Bible Ahead of Its Time?* †.

Opening Prayer
Discussion: Have everyone in the group select the biblical scientific insight that has the most personal impact on them. Let each person review their selection and why it was so important.

Practical-Experience Game
Debate: The "Christian" will debate a "scientist." The issue is whether or not the Bible is scientifically accurate. (Make sure the "scientist" has time to prepare.)

Closing Prayer

The Structure of
the Bible

The Bible is a series of 66 books (39 in the Old Testament and 27 in the New Testament) that were written by at least 40 different authors, in many different lands and under many different circumstances. Yet it is entirely consistent on many highly controversial issues. This alone indicates miraculous inspiration from God.

The Bible can be confusing to the new reader who doesn't understand that it is generally not in chronological order. The Old Testament is grouped into the topics of 1) the Torah, 2) the other books of history, 3) literature, and 4) prophecy; it is "subgrouped" by chronological order within these categories and in the order of the canonization by the Jews.

The New Testament starts with the three synoptic (similar) gospels, followed by the book of John. The historical book of Acts (of the apostles) follows and is believed to have been an addition to the book of Luke. The letters of Paul are next in the New Testament, followed by letters of other apostles. And the New Testament closes with the book of Revelation.

A simple summary of the Bible and its structure follows. Every reader is encouraged to use a good study Bible, a reputable Bible handbook, or both to add depth. It will be helpful to refer to part 6 for historical context in order to envision how the books of the Bible fit with the events of world history. (Dates for biblical manuscripts are from the Life Application Bible.)

Although the historical portion of the Old Testament provides much important teaching, fundamental to its overall message is the promise of a Messiah (Jesus), along with the promises of greatness to Abraham (Genesis 12) and God's covenant promising the land of Israel to Abraham's descendents (Genesis 15).

The Torah

The first five books of the Bible are grouped together and known as the *Torah*, the *Pentateuch* or the *Law*. These books—Genesis, Exodus, Leviticus, Numbers, and Deuteronomy, were all "given" to Moses by God during the wandering of the Hebrews in the wilderness following their deliverance from bondage in Egypt.

The books of the Torah form a vital foundation for both Judaism and Christianity. Many orthodox Jews focus almost solely on the Torah and devote themselves to daily reading to ensure that it is read cover to cover every year. For Christians, the Torah introduces the nature of a perfectly loving, holy, and just God, through his relationship with the early Israelites. And the greatest commandments referred to by Jesus (Mark 12:30-31) are first mentioned in the Torah:

> *Love the* LORD *your God with all your heart and with all your soul and with all your strength* (Deuteronomy 6:5-6).

> *Love your neighbor as yourself. I am the* LORD (Leviticus 19:18).

The book of **Genesis** introduces an omnipotent God by describing the power of his creation. It shows that the process of creation was done in a planned, orderly manner. Next, Genesis reviews the important relationship of human beings with God—starting with the desired relationship and then describing how that relationship was broken due to mankind's choice to disobey God. The remainder of Genesis provides a historical account of various individuals and their relationship with God and other humans, eventually leading the chosen descendents of Noah's son Shem (who became the Hebrew nation of the Israelites) into Egypt.

Exodus is an account of how God called Moses to deliver the Hebrews from bondage in Egypt. In the process of deliverance, God performed many miracles, including the parting of the Red Sea (or Sea of Reeds) when it blocked the Hebrews' passage. Exodus describes the 40 years of wandering in the wilderness, during which time the Ten Commandments were given to the fledgling nation, within the books of the Torah. Exodus concludes with the introduction of the tabernacle, where the Israelites were exposed to the glory of God and called to worship him.

The book of **Leviticus** is a detailed account of many laws given to the Israelites. Of primary importance were the spiritual laws required in the sacrifice, offering, and worship of God. In addition there were laws of health and general holiness, along with special instructions for the tribe of Levi (the Levites), who were to serve as the priests.

The book of **Numbers** describes events that took place in the wilderness, including the taking of a census, a rebellion against the leadership selected by God (Moses and Aaron), the process of wandering, and some initial attempts to enter the promised land of Canaan. During the process of 40 years of wandering, God was preparing a new generation to enter the Promised Land.

The book of **Deuteronomy** describes Moses' addresses to the Israelites prior to entry into the Promised Land. It starts with reviewing some of the mighty acts of God, including God's relationship to his chosen people. The Ten Commandments are again reviewed, along with other laws that God required of his people. And it called for a lasting commitment to God. The book ends with the death of Moses prior to the crossing of the Jordan River into Palestine.

Other Books of History

Other books of history in the Bible include Joshua, Judges, Ruth, 1 and 2 Samuel, 1 and 2 Kings, 1 and 2 Chronicles, Ezra, Nehemiah, and Esther.

Joshua covers the period from the exodus, when the leadership of the Israelites was transferred from Moses to Joshua. It focuses primarily on the initial conquest of the land promised to Abraham, demonstrating God's power and fulfillment of his promises. While generally very sucessful, the Hebrews initially settled in the Promised Land without fully conquering it.

Judges picks up where Joshua leaves off by reviewing the history of the Israelites in Palestine during the period after Joshua's leadership, when there was no preordained line of leadership. Instead, God raised up a sequence of judges, who were given authority to deal with situations that threatened the land. The book shows that even when the people were not in strict obedience with God's wishes, he still cared for their needs.

The book of **Ruth** is a four-chapter story of the relationship of a peasant Moabite girl, Ruth, and her commitment to her Israelite mother-in-law, Naomi, and later to her "kinsman–redeemer" husband, Boaz. This short book has several purposes: 1) to show how three people from different cultures remained strong in character and devoted to God even when society around them was collapsing; 2) to model the role of a kinsman–redeemer (the concept that one person can redeem another, much like the blood of Christ redeemed sinners); and 3) to show that the lineage of Jesus was made up of a variety of people (including Rahab, a prostitute, and Ruth the Moabite).

1 and 2 Samuel cover the time in the history of Israel transitioning from the period of the judges, when "everyone did as he saw fit" (Judges 21:25), to the period of the kings. God had selected Samuel the prophet as the primary leader over the nation, and the one to select the first king. 1 Samuel reviews Samuel's birth and early childhood, the point that he selected Saul as king, David's growth and favor due to his slaying of Goliath, Saul's jealousy of David, and Saul's eventual death. 2 Samuel records the history of David's reign and shows its effectiveness under God. It also reveals the personal qualities that please God (along with those that displease God) and shows David as an ideal leader (despite his failings) of an imperfect kingdom.

1 and 2 Kings cover the historical period of leadership by kings of Israel following David. 1 Kings starts with King Solomon, a son of David and Bathsheba. Solomon was the last of the kings ruling over the united kingdom of northern and southern Israel. Due to Solomon's falling away at the end of his life, the kingdom was taken away from his heirs and was divided between the ten tribes in the north ("Israel") and the two tribes in the south ("Judah"). 1 Kings focuses mostly on the life of Solomon and the early years of the kings of the divided kingdom, along with the prophets Elijah and

Elisha. 2 Kings covers the many kings of both nations that followed.

1 and 2 Chronicles can be puzzling because it covers much of the same historical period as 2 Samuel and the two books of Kings. Jewish tradition has it that the scribe, Ezra, wrote 1 and 2 Chronicles, possibly after exile to Babylon. 1 Chronicles covers virtually the same timeframe as 2 Samuel and serves as a commentary on it, stressing the life of David. 2 Chronicles covers the period beginning with Solomon's reign to the destruction of Jerusalem by the Babylonians (586 B.C.).

Ezra is believed to have been written about 450 B.C, perhaps by the scribe Ezra, and covers the period following 2 Chronicles, when King Cyrus of Persia allowed the Jews to return from exile. It deals with the return of the Jews, the rededication of the Temple's foundation, opposition from the Jewish enemies, and the ultimate faith and action of the people.

The book of **Nehemiah** is another post-exile book. It was written after Ezra and discusses Nehemiah's concern over the walls of Jerusalem lying in ruin. The book outlines how God provided Nehemiah as a leader to allow the rebuilding of the walls protecting Jerusalem in spite of severe opposition.

The book of **Esther** (about 483 to 471 B.C.) is believed to have been written after the time of the Jewish exile. Taking place in Persia, it outlines the sovereignty and love of God towards his people, even while they are in a foreign land. The drama of the book shows the courage of a single woman, Esther, who risked her own life in efforts that eventually resulted in the saving of the Jews.

Books of Literature

The books of literature in the Bible include Job, Psalms, Proverbs, Ecclesiastes, and Song of Songs (sometimes called Song of Solomon).

Job is believed to be the oldest writing in the Bible. Scholars think it was written by a man named Job, who lived in the area of Mesopotamia. It's interesting to think that the oldest book of the Bible might have come from Mesopotamia, which is known to be the cradle of civilization; it is where the Garden of Eden is believed to have been, along with the landing of Noah's ark (Mount Ararat, in the north), and the tower of Babel (near Babylon). Job philosophically addresses the issues of suffering by the righteous, the attacks of Satan, and the ultimate goodness of God.

Psalms is a collection of 150 "songs," or "psalms," written by various people between 1440 B.C and 586 B.C. The most prolific writer of the psalms was David, who wrote dozens around 1000 B.C. The psalms serve many purposes. Some express anguish and suffering. Others cry for help or confess sin. Many praise and worship God. Embedded in many of the psalms are prophecies of the Messiah to come.

Proverbs is a book of short, concise sayings that convey moral and practical truths (or wisdom). It is broken down into sections that impart wisdom to young people, to the general populace, and to leaders. Written by King Solomon in the early years of his reign (starting about 970 B.C), these memorable verses are applicable to general living.

Ecclesiastes was written by Solomon late in his life (probably about 935 B.C) and looks back on his years of learning, including those apart from God. The book's purpose is to help future generations avoid a meaningless existence without God.

Song of Songs (or Song of Solomon) is believed to have been written early in King Solomon's reign. The book is a love story between a bridegroom and his bride. It affirms the sanctity of marriage, and many scholars believe the book also serves as an allegory of God's love for his people.

Books of Prophecy

The books of prophecy are broken into the "major prophets"—Isaiah, Jeremiah, Lamentations, Ezekiel, and Daniel; and the "minor prophets"—Hosea, Joel, Amos, Obadiah, Jonah, Micah, Nahum, Habakkuk, Zephaniah, Haggai, Zechariah, and Malachi. The major prophets are not considered more significant, the books are simply longer. The minor prophets were grouped as "the Twelve" in the original (and current) Jewish Scripture. The prophetic books (Scripture) were extremely important to the Israelites since prophets were believed to be spokespeople for God if, and only if, prophecy was 100-percent accurate (Deuteronomy 18:20-22). When they were proven accurate as prophets of holy Scripture, their words and writings were taken as direction from God himself.

The book of **Isaiah** was written about 700 B.C. It is one of the most significant books of prophecy because it contains more prophecy about Jesus Christ than any other. In particular, chapter 53 provides an accurate and vivid description of the suffering savior to come—contradicting the common belief among many Jews that the prophesied Messiah was to be a military conqueror.

Fascinating Fact

The most surprising author in the Bible is King Nebuchadnezzar, the tyrant of Babylon who forced the Jews into exile (586 B.C.). He "authored" the beginning of the fourth chapter of Daniel, which provides indication that even the most unlikely people can be changed and used by God.

The prophet **Jeremiah** is believed to have written both the books of Jeremiah and **Lamentations**. Both were written in the period 627–586 B.C. in the southern kingdom of Judah. They urged God's people to repent from their sin before it was too late.

The book of **Ezekiel** was written to the Jews in captivity in Babylon in about 571 B.C. It foretold the eventual salvation of God's people.

Daniel was one of the most significant prophets of the Old Testament. He wrote in about 605 to 535 B.C. and gave a historical account of the captivity in Babylon. His prophecies indicated the enormous power and control God has over heaven and earth. Perhaps his most significant prophecy was foretelling the precise date when the Messiah would enter Jerusalem (Palm Sunday, the first day Jesus allowed himself to be publicly honored as the Messiah–king).

Hosea (about 753 to 715 B.C.) wrote to the northern kingdom to illustrate God's love for his people. **Joel** (about 835 to 796 B.C) warned Judah of impending judgment due to sin, while **Amos** (about 760 to 750 B.C.) likewise warned the northern kingdom of similar judgment.

Obadiah (about 853 to 841 B.C.) focused on the Edomites, an enemy of the Jews in Judah. The book demonstrated God's judgment on those that harm his chosen people. **Jonah** (about 785 to 760 B.C.) was written to God's people everywhere to demonstrate the extent of God's grace and to indicate that the message of salvation is for all people.

Micah (about 742 to 687 B.C. to Israel), **Nahum** (about 663 to 612 B.C. to Nineveh and Judah), and **Zephaniah** (about 640 to 621 B.C to Judah) all wrote to proclaim God's judgment on sin and call people to repentance. In the case of

Nahum, comfort was offered to Judah since judgment was proclaimed on Assyria.

Habakkuk (about 612 to 588 B.C.) was written to the people of Judah to reveal that God is in control despite a world that is seemingly out of control. **Haggai** (about 520 B.C.) called for a rebuilding of the Temple. **Zechariah** (about 520 to 518 B.C.) was written to the exiles who had returned to provide hope of a coming Messiah. And **Malachi** (about 430 B.C.) was a call to people everywhere to repent and restore their relationship with God.

The Gospels and Acts

The New Testament begins with four individual accounts of the ministry of Jesus Christ: Matthew, Mark, Luke, and John. While these books are historical, they are referred to as the Gospels (meaning "good news") because the purpose is to introduce Jesus in the way that is most important to humanity—his restoration of people's relationship with the living God.

The first three, Matthew, Mark, and Luke, are called the *synoptic* Gospels (meaning "from the same point of view") because they contain a number of verses that are identical (or almost identical). John covers many of the same events but has few actual verses that are identical to the other three. It is believed that Mark was the first Gospel written (about A.D. 55), and Matthew and Luke were believed to have drawn heavily from its content. There are also many verses in Matthew and Luke that are not found in Mark. Scholars believe these may have arisen from some as-yet-unidentified common source (it is referred to as "Q" in scholarly circles).

Despite the similarities of the Gospels (especially the synoptic Gospels), all present the ministry of Jesus from a different vantage point. Both the differences and the similarities are important in giving them credibility. Naturally the Gospels should be in agreement—if really from four eyewitnesses to the events—to verify the essence of the events. However, they should also have some degree of difference since every witness would remember different things and have a different idea of priority. If we were to think of it in terms of today's courts of law, witnesses with the same basic information to an event corroborate the event itself, while the differences each witness remembers add depth to the understanding of what really happened.

Each of the Gospel accounts deals with the ministry of Jesus, providing a vivid description of his perfect character, his miracles, his mission, and his teaching. All focus especially on the final passion week—the death and resurrection of Jesus—with some 25 percent to 35 percent devoted to this part of Jesus' time on earth. Matthew and Luke are unique in that they deal with Jesus' ancestry and the events surrounding his birth. John is unique in that it stresses the deity of Jesus, including his pre-existence and role in co-creating the universe as part of the Trinity (John 1).

Each Gospel author quoted Jesus extensively. Jesus' words make up the following percentages of the books: Matthew—60 percent; Mark—42 percent; Luke—50 percent; and John—50 percent.[1] As would be expected, there are multiple reports of significant events in Jesus' ministry in the different Gospels. For example, of the 35 miracles of Jesus, 18 of them are reported in more than one account. John's Gospel seems to have the intention of reporting important information that was omitted in the other Gospels. Of the eight miracles John discusses, only the feeding of 5000 people and Jesus' walking on water are in other Gospel accounts. Most significant of John's unique miracles is the raising of Lazarus from the dead, which certainly led to the intensity of the hatred of the Jewish leaders in the week of Jesus' death and resurrection.

Each of the Gospels has a different emphasis regarding the four roles that Jesus was to fulfill as foretold in the Old Testament.

Matthew (about A.D. 55 to 63) emphasizes the kingship of Jesus. He was portrayed as "lion-like"; the Gospel was clearly written for the Jews. Matthew's basic theme is that Jesus is the Messiah because he fulfilled the Old Testament prophecies. Hence, the tone of the Gospel is prophetic. Extensive use of Old Testament prophecy was made, with Matthew quoting 53 times directly from the Old Testament, more than any other Gospel. In accordance with the kingship, the Davidic line of Jesus was stressed, even through the genealogy.

Mark (about A.D. 55 to 60) focused more on Jesus as a servant (as prophesied in Isaiah 53). Mark stressed the obedience of Jesus in executing the will of the Father. Mark's theme is that Jesus backed up his words with action. The tone of the Gospel is practical, apparently slanted somewhat toward the Romans.

Luke (about A.D. 60) presented Jesus as the perfect man. Everything from the birth of Jesus throughout his life, ministry, death, and resurrection was indicative of his humanity. Hence, Luke's theme is that Jesus was God, but also human. The Gospel seemed to be written to the Greeks and described Jesus as the Son of Man. Its tone is historical.

John (about A.D. 85 to 90) portrayed Jesus as the divine son of God—and God himself (John 1). Jesus was described as the Word of God who pre-existed creation. John's essential theme is that belief in Jesus is required for salvation. John's Gospel was written to the church. Its tone is spiritual. Although John has fewer direct quotes from the Old Testament than any Gospel, it alludes to the Old Testament more than any.

The book of **Acts** (about A.D. 60 to 63) appears to be a continuation of the historical events after the resurrection given by Luke (for example, both books begin with addressing the account to "Theophilus"). It provides historical insight into the early development of the church. The book of Acts provides an important connection between the life and ministry of Jesus and the Christian church. It reviews the ministry of the apostles, paying particular attention to the early church leaders Paul and Peter. This is of considerable importance since the credibility of Paul regarding his connection with Jesus is essential (Paul wrote at least 13 books of the New Testament, which the Christian church relies upon as holy Scripture).

> The book of Acts helps lend credibility to the acceptance of Paul by the original disciples of Jesus, during the time of the eyewitnesses to the resurrection. This is extremely important because Paul wrote many books of the New Testament.

The Letters (Epistles)

The epistles represent the 21 books of the New Testament written by the apostles. The first 13 were written by Paul, almost all to the churches he helped establish. The book of Hebrews is of unknown authorship (some believe it was written by Paul). And the books of James; 1 and 2 Peter; 1, 2, and 3 John; and Jude were written by the authors whose names they bear. Although each epistle had a different purpose, in general they served as encouragement and guidelines for instructing the early church.

The book of **Romans** (about A.D. 57) was written to the Christians in Rome to introduce Paul and provide a summary of his teaching prior to his arrival in the city. Romans is considered to be the first great writing of Christian theology and is thought by many to be Paul's most significant book, having a vast impact on the development of the church. It focuses on the sin of mankind and the sinner's justification through the sacrifice on the cross by Jesus; it discusses the sanctification of the believer. Romans goes further to review God's purposes for Israel and to provide practical instruction to the church through service.

1 Corinthians (about A.D. 55) was the second letter written to the church Paul had established in Corinth (the first letter, and the one after 1 Corinthians, had been lost). It was written to identify and offer solutions to the problems the church there was encountering. It stressed the importance of unity in the church versus division, and the order and morality of the church versus disorder and immorality. Furthermore, the book reviews the gifts and doctrines of the church and condemns their abuse.

2 Corinthians (about A.D. 55 to 57—actually the fourth letter written to the church there) was intended to affirm Paul's ministry and authority and refute false teaching within the Corinthian church. It defended the glory of the Christian ministry and stressed the glory of the ministry of giving.

Galatians (about A.D. 49) was written to the churches Paul had founded on his first missionary trip to the region of Galatia. Its primary purpose was to refute those who taught that Gentiles must obey Jewish laws in order to be saved. In that sense Galatians taught personal revelation, justification, and sanctification.

Ephesians (about A.D. 60) was written to the church Paul founded in Ephesus to strengthen the believers' faith by explaining the nature and purpose of the church as the body of Christ.

Philippians (about A.D. 61) was written to the church in Philippi to thank them for the gift they had sent to Paul and to express to them that true joy comes through Jesus Christ alone. Such joy in Christ is expressed through our life, example, goal, and sufficiency.

Colossians (about A.D. 60) was written to the church in Colosse (never visited by Paul). The intent of this letter was to combat errors that had been introduced to the church by some believers who had attempted to combine elements of paganism and secular philosophy with Christian doctrine. The book stressed the glory of Christ, Christ's answers to doctrinal errors, and how union with Christ is the basis for Christian living.

1 Thessalonians (about A.D. 51) was written to strengthen the Thessalonians in their faith and to assure them of Christ's return.

2 Thessalonians (about A.D. 51 to 52) was written to the Thessalonians to clear up confusion regarding the second coming of Christ.

1 Timothy (about A.D. 64) was written to Paul's protégé Timothy and to young church leaders everywhere to provide encouragement and instruction. It reviewed the disciplines of sound doctrine, worship, church government, and local pastoral leadership.

2 Timothy (about A.D. 66 to 67) was written just prior to Paul's execution under Nero. It provided final instructions and encouragement to Timothy and other church leaders.

Titus (about A.D. 64) was written to a Greek named Titus, who had probably become a Christian through Paul's ministry. The book was to advise Titus in his responsibilities in supervising churches on the island of Crete.

Philemon (about A.D. 60) was written by Paul to Philemon to convince him to forgive his runaway slave and accept him as a brother in the faith.

Hebrews (before A.D. 70) was written to present the sufficiency and superiority of Christ. The author of Hebrews is unknown, although some verses suggest it may have also been Paul (Hebrews 13:23—Timothy was known to be a dear friend and brother of Paul; 2 Peter 3:15—which may have referred to the book of Hebrews). Hebrews is a pivotal book in defining the relationship of Christianity with Judaism. It discusses Christ's superiority to the prophets, angels, Moses, Joshua, and the priests. It also reviews the superiority of the New Covenant to the Old Covenant.

James (about A.D. 49) is the first letter of the New Testament that was definitely not written by Paul. The author, James—the brother of Jesus and a leader of the Jerusalem church—was writing to first-century Christians worldwide. The purpose of the letter is to expose hypocritical Christian practices and to encourage proper behavior.

1 Peter (about A.D 62 to 64) was written by the apostle Peter, probably while in Rome under the persecution of Nero. It was written to Christians driven out of Jerusalem to offer encouragement to them to endure their suffering.

2 Peter (about A.D. 67) was written by Peter to Christians everywhere to warn them of false teaching and to exhort them in their faith. Christians are encouraged to grow in their knowledge of Christ.

1 John (about A.D. 85 to 90) was written by the apostle John as a pastoral letter to several Gentile congregations, with the intention of teaching believers everywhere. Its purpose was to reassure Christians in their faith and to counter false teaching.

2 John (about A.D. 90) was written to a "chosen lady," which may have been a metaphor for a church, but the message was clearly intended for believers everywhere. This short letter was to emphasize the basics of following Christ and to warn about false teachers.

3 John (about A.D. 90) was written by John to the church leader Gaius and to Christians everywhere. The letter's purpose is to commend Gaius for his hospitality and to encourage him in his Christian life.

Jude (about A.D. 65) was written by Jesus' and James' brother Jude to Jewish Christians and to Christians everywhere. Its purpose was to remind the church to remain on guard—to oppose heresy and be strong in the faith.

The final book of the Bible is **Revelation,** written in about A.D. 95 by the apostle John while he was in exile on the island of Patmos. The letter is specifically addressed to seven churches in Asia, but clearly was intended to teach believers everywhere. Although written in a highly symbolic manner, perhaps partly to disguise the writer from the threat of persecution, the purpose of the book is to reveal the full identity of Christ, to give a warning, and to provide hope to believers.

Test Yourself

1. What are the books of the Torah, and about when were they written?

2. What are the main sections of the Old Testament?

3. What are the five books of the major prophets? How were the prophets determined?

4. About when were the Gospels written? What significance does the date of authorship have?

5. What is the primary purpose of the epistles? Who wrote the most?

Chapter 10 Group Study

Homework Preparation (do prior to group)
Read: 2 Timothy 3:16-17; chapter 10 of this text; and pages 8–15 in *Can You Trust the Bible?* ✝.

Opening Prayer
Discussion: Read 2 Timothy 3:16-17. Discuss the significance of these verses. Review pages 8 and 9 in *Can You Trust the Bible?* and discuss the timing of the books of the Bible relative to world history.

Practical-Experience Game
Role-playing: The issue between the "Christian" and the "nonbeliever" is the structure of the Bible. Be prepared to explain the structure and purpose of each major part, answering questions the nonbeliever may have.

Closing Prayer

The Dead Sea Scrolls, the Septuagint, and Their Validation by Jesus

Perhaps the single most important religious archaeological find ever is the discovery of about 800 scrolls in the caves at Qumran on the northwest shore of the Dead Sea. These scrolls were written from about 250 B.C. to about A.D. 65 and were discovered by accident in 1947. They varied in condition from complete, nearly perfect scrolls to others that were heavily damaged and broken into thousands of fragments. In addition to many scrolls relevant to the Essene culture, every book of the Old Testament except Esther was represented at Qumran (either in its entirety or in part). The number of Old Testament books and fragments found at Qumran is listed below:[1]

Book *(in order of Hebrew canon)*	Number of Copies (? = possible fragment)
Genesis	18 + 3?
Exodus	8
Leviticus	17
Numbers	12
Deuteronomy	31 + 3?
Joshua	2
Judges	3
1–2 Samuel	4
1–2 Kings	3
Isaiah	22
Jeremiah	6
Ezekiel	7
Twelve (minor prophets)	10 + 1?
Psalms	39 + 2?
Proverbs	2
Job	4
Song of Songs	4
Ruth	4
Lamentations	4
Ecclesiastes	3
Esther	0
Daniel	8 + 1?
Ezra–Nehemiah	1
1–2 Chronicles	1

Key Concept

The Dead Sea scrolls represent every book of the Old Testament except Esther (either in entirety or in part).

The scrolls found at Qumran had been buried deep in caves when the Romans were advancing to crush the Jewish revolt that started in A.D. 66. (Jerusalem and the Temple were totally destroyed in A.D. 70, and Jews were expelled from the city.) The Essenes were a sect of pious Jews who had chosen to live in seclusion from the religious mainstream in Jerusalem. They developed a home at an enclave in the city of Qumran on the northwest side of the Dead Sea. Here they practiced strict adherence to the Jewish religion and engaged in devoted copying of holy Scripture. Copies of Scripture and of important Essene documents were stored in pottery jars and then placed in cave libraries. When news of the advancing Romans was received by the Essenes, the caves at Qumran were abandoned (A.D. 68) and remained untouched for nearly 1900 years.

In March 1947 a Bedouin shepherd boy named Muhammad was looking for a lost goat in the hills around Qumran. He tossed a rock into a cave and was surprised to hear the shattering of pottery. Investigating the noise, he entered the dark cave and climbed down. He discovered a number of clay jars that contained leather scrolls wrapped in linen cloth. Because the scrolls had been so carefully prepared and sealed in the clay jars, they were in excellent condition. In the following years, other caves were found containing additional scrolls, bringing the final number to several hundred, with thousands of fragments that are still being analyzed and pieced together.

The importance of the discovery of the Dead Sea scrolls cannot be overstated in regard to corroborating the accuracy of the biblical manuscripts. For example, a scroll of Isaiah written in 150 B.C., found in nearly perfect condition, was compared to a Masoretic Hebrew text dated A.D. 916 and found to be consistent after more than 1000 years! In fact, of the 166 *words* in chapter 53 of the scroll of Isaiah, only 17 *letters* show any possible signs of change. And in the case of the letters in question, the changes represent matters of spelling and stylistic changes, such as conjunctions, which would have no bearing on the meaning of the text.[2]

The discovery of the Dead Sea scrolls and the comparison of the text with later copies have verified beyond a shadow of a doubt that the Old Testament has accurately been handed down for centuries. This is of immeasurable importance in evaluating the truth and relevance of Jesus because the Old Testament contains many prophecies about the Messiah that were precisely fulfilled by Jesus.

The Dead Sea scrolls, containing prophecies made hundreds of years before Jesus, were themselves written decades, and in some cases centuries, before Jesus. Thus we know the prophecies were not written "after the fact." This means we can know conclusively that the prophecies were not contrived. This is essential in evaluating the significance of fulfillment of the prophecies by Jesus. When we analyze the statistical odds of so many prophecies coming true in any one man, we find it to be virtually impossible except for divine intervention (see part 3). This leads us to the critical conclusion that Jesus was the Messiah prophesied in the Old Testament.

The Septuagint

It didn't take long after the conquest of Palestine by Alexander the Great in 331 B.C. before the people in Judea exchanged their native language of Hebrew in favor of Greek. When this happened, only scribes and a select group of other educated people had the capability to read holy Scripture. Recognizing this problem, the Jews appointed a group of 70 elders (hence the name Septuagint, or LXX) to translate the Old Testament into Greek, sometime during the third and second centuries B.C.

The Septuagint was the Scripture in common usage at the time of Jesus. Most of the quotations of the Old Testament in the New Testament are from the Septuagint. It would have been the Scripture that Jesus used to teach the common person. In fact, Christians adopted the Septuagint so whole-heartedly that the Jews ultimately lost interest in it and regarded it to be the "Christian Old Testament." Even now, it is regarded as the "official Old Testament" version by the Greek Orthodox Church. Today we have fragments of the Septuagint that date back to before 200 B.C. Some fragments of the Septuagint were found among the Dead Sea scrolls, though the majority of the scrolls were in Hebrew. There are several reasons why the Septuagint translation is especially important:

- As mentioned, it was the Old Testament version commonly available at the time of Jesus and therefore commands special consideration.

- Like the Dead Sea scrolls, the Septuagint establishes the prophecies about Jesus at a point in time *predating* Jesus. We can be certain that the prophecies were not contrived to fit the life circumstances of Jesus.

- The Septuagint was translated from Hebrew Scripture concurrent to or slightly earlier than the earliest Hebrew Scripture we have today (the Dead Sea scrolls). Consequently, it is useful for clarifying any points of contention.

Jesus Confirmed the Jewish Scriptures

When considering the reliability of the Bible, many overlook the confirmation of Jesus. First, we must remember that Jesus in effect confirmed the entire Old Testament. As noted, the holy Scripture that was in common usage during his time was the same Septuagint that we have available at our disposal to read today. Additionally, the Dead Sea scrolls represent the Hebrew Scripture of that time.

In other words, there was no question in Jesus' mind as to the selection of scrolls ("books") recognized as holy Scripture—called the *Tanakh* by the Jews. The Tanakh used by Jesus was identical to today's Old Testament, except that the Jewish scrolls *combined* some books (for example 1 and 2 Samuel, 1 and 2 Kings, 1 and 2 Chronicles, Jeremiah and Lamentations, and others) so the 39 books of the Protestant Old Testament were contained in 20 books.

The Apocrypha

The 11 apocryphal books included in the Bible of the Roman Catholic Church were not considered holy Scripture at the time of Jesus. They were usually found at the same location as holy Scripture and were regarded as good references for teaching. However, they were simply not deemed "God-breathed." Interestingly, because the books were virtually always together with the Bible, even when the Bible was placed in codex (book) form, the Apocrypha was generally included. Even the Bible produced by Martin Luther, the leader of the Protestant Reformation, contained the Apocrypha.

It wasn't until the Protestant Reformation that the Roman

> The Apocrypha was not recognized by Jesus—nor by the New Testament authors or church fathers—as holy Scripture until the 1500s, when the Roman Catholic Church declared it "equal to Scripture" and made it part of their Bible. It was, however, always regarded as "edifying," and even Martin Luther included it as part (a "non-God-breathed" part) of his Bible. Later, Protestants dropped the Apocrypha from their Bible.

Catholic Church infallibly declared the Apocrypha to be holy Scripture. The Protestant church disagreed and continued to hold that the apocryphal books were merely "good teaching" and not inspired by God. Eventually, due in large part to the cost of printing extra pages in a Bible for readers who were more interested in God's inspired Word, the Apocrypha was dropped from Protestant Bibles.

Jesus Preconfirmed the New Testament

Jesus actually preconfirmed the development of the New Testament and its inspiration by the Holy Spirit. While on earth, Jesus gave the apostles the authority to write it. He then further prophesied and confirmed it.

First, authority was granted. The Holy Spirit was to guide the very words of the apostles:

The Counselor, the Holy Spirit, whom the Father will send in my name, will teach you all things and will remind you of everything I have said to you (John 14:26).

When he, the Spirit of truth, comes, he will guide you into all truth. He will not speak on his own; he will speak only what he hears, and he will tell you what is yet to come (John 16:13-14).

The Holy Spirit will teach you at that time what you should say (Luke 12:12).

Second, the gospel was prophesied. Jesus prophesied 17 times that the gospel would be spread. For instance,

This gospel of the kingdom will be preached in the whole world as a testimony to all nations, and then the end will come (Matthew 24:14).

I tell you the truth, wherever this gospel is preached throughout the world, what she has done will also be told, in memory of her (Matthew 26:13).

Heaven and earth will pass away, but my words will never pass away (Luke 21:33).

Third, Jesus confirmed the gospel during the period in which it was being preached on three separate occasions:

One night the Lord spoke to Paul in a vision: "Do not be afraid; keep on speaking, do not be silent" (Acts 18:9).

I fell into a trance and saw the Lord speaking. "Quick!" he said to me. "Leave Jerusalem immediately, because they will not accept your testimony about me" (Acts 22:17-18).

The following night the Lord stood near Paul and said, "Take courage! As you have testified about me in Jerusalem, so you must also testify in Rome" (Acts 23:11).

Though the New Testament was written after the extensive appearance of Jesus on earth prior to the resurrection, we find that Jesus foretold of its coming. Furthermore, he confirmed the writing of the New Testament during the period in which it was being recorded and later compiled.

> Jesus confirmed the Old Testament (Tanakh) when he was on earth. He also preconfirmed the New Testament.

Knowing that the Holy Spirit guided the writing of the New Testament, and knowing that Jesus himself foretold and confirmed it, we can be confident of its words.

Test Yourself

1. What is the only Old Testament book not included in the Dead Sea scrolls?

2. Why is it important to know the Dead Sea scrolls were actually written before the birth of Christ?

3. What is the Septuagint? Why is it important?

4. In what ways did Jesus confirm the Bible?

5. What is the Apocrypha? Who includes it as part of the Bible? Who doesn't? Why?

Chapter 11 Group Study

Homework Preparation (do prior to group)
Read: Matthew 24:14; chapter 11 of this text; and pages 20, 21, 28, 29 in *Can You Trust the Bible?* ✝.

Opening Prayer
Discussion: Discuss why the Dead Sea scrolls are probably the single most important archaeological discovery of all time—especially in regard to the Bible. Pay particular attention to the prophecies of Jesus.

Practical-Experience Game
TV interview: The "Christian" is on a secular show that is dealing with the question of whether or not the prophecies of Jesus were written after the fact.

Closing Prayer

The New Testament
Manuscript Explosion

The early Christian church exploded onto the scene more quickly than any major theological or philosophical phenomenon before or since. The Bible indicates that about 3000 people were added to the group of believers on a single day—50 days after the resurrection (on the day now known as Pentecost). Presumably these were all men, since that is the way "people" were counted at the time. Adding women, children, and existing believers, this could have brought the total number to approximately 6000 to 10,000. A few days later, when Peter and John were seized by the temple guard and placed in jail for preaching about the resurrection of Jesus (Acts 4:1-4), the number of Christians had grown to about 5000 men. Again, adding women and children, this could have equated to perhaps 10,000 to 15,000 within days of the resurrection!

The rapid chain-reaction expansion of the church required some controls to ensure accuracy and consistency of the message. For that reason, the account of the ministry of Jesus and his death and resurrection was recorded by several different authors.

In addition to accurate accounts of Jesus for distribution in a rapidly expanding church, also necessary were guidance and organization for growth. The letters of Paul were designed for such a purpose. Like the Gospels, they were widely copied and distributed. *The Gospels, the letters, and the book of Revelation* (all of the New Testament) *were accepted by many people as inspired by God* at the time of the writing of the autographs. The church fathers had agreed on the confirmation of the writings of the New Testament by the early 200s, and it was officially canonized in 397.

The Old Testament was copied for centuries by trained scribes, with detailed scriptural copy rules that resulted in precision recording without error (see pages 156–157). Dr. Norman Geisler writes,

> Even though not all of the New Testament copyists were professionally trained scribes, nevertheless, they transcribed it with such care that the accuracy of the process is demonstrated by our ability to determine the original text with a higher degree of accuracy than any other book in the ancient world.[1]

Ancient New Testament Manuscripts

Today, nearly 2000 years since the time of Jesus, we have an extraordinary number of ancient manuscripts still in existence for the New Testament (about 5700). This is truly remarkable, considering the early persecution that sought to destroy the New Testament records. These copies exist in several forms and languages:[2]

Extant Ancient Manuscripts by Language	Number in Existence
Greek	5700
Latin Vulgate	8000 to 10,000
Ethiopic, Slavic, Armenian	8000
Other	About 1000
Total	**About 24,000**

Also important is the proximity of New Testament records to the resurrection. The earliest of them are even within the time of the eyewitnesses. Many more are within a generation or two. Two important criteria help to ensure the trustworthiness of the text: 1) a large number of consistent manuscripts; and 2) the dating of early manuscripts in close proximity to the events. This compares very favorably to other ancient documents that we commonly regard as history:[3]

Work	Number of Extant Manuscripts	Years Since Original
Homer—*Iliad*	643	400
Herodotus—*History*	8	1350
Thucydides—*History*	8	1300
Plato	7	1300
Demosthenes	200	1400
Caesar—*Gallic Wars*	10	1000
Livy—*History of Rome*	19 + 1 partial	1000; 400
Tacitus—*Annals*	20	1000
Pliny Secundus—*History*	7	750
New Testament	5700	**50 to 225**

It is apparent that the New Testament stands head and shoulders above all other major books of antiquity in 1) the number of corroboratory copies and 2) the proximity of the copies to the original writing. This is of great significance. We readily accept other books of history written by such authors as are listed above even though documentary confirmation is far less substantial and the copies are much further removed from the original autographs. We should have significantly greater confidence in the accuracy of the transmission over time of the New Testament.

Finally, regarding the consistency of the vast number of New Testament copies themselves, we find substantial agreement and no doctrinal disagreement. As mentioned, New

Testament copyists for the most part were not scribes trained in the classical sense. An example of an insignificant inconsistency between two New Testament documents might be transposition of word order. In English, it makes a great deal of difference if we write "man eats chicken" or "chicken eats man." In Greek it does not. Each sentence in Greek has a defined subject, verb, and predicate based on the form of the word. Hence the order of words makes no difference.[4] Biblical scholars who have analyzed New Testament documentation proclaim it far "purer" than any other book of antiquity. Scholars Norman Geisler and William Nix conclude that the New Testament has survived in a "form that is 99.5% pure."[5]

Fascinating Fact

Voltaire, the famous French writer and philosopher, boasted in the 1700s that within 100 years, Christianity and the Bible would disappear—implying that his works would remain much longer. Of course, few know much about Voltaire's works today, while the Bible is a perennial bestseller. Ironically, Voltaire's house and printing press are now used by the Geneva Bible Society to publish Bibles.[6]

Key Concept

Some 5700 ancient copies of the New Testament are in existence today, with some portions estimated to be within 50 years of the original. This is far superior to any other ancient text, most of which have less than a dozen copies written at least 1000 years after the autographs.

Ancient Manuscripts Confirm Accuracy

As indicated above, there was such an explosion of manuscripts of the New Testament that even today we have a vast number of ancient copies—far surpassing all other books of ancient history.

Apart from the New Testament copies, there are even several documents from non-Christian sources that corroborate some key facts about Jesus, such as the crucifixion, the belief in the resurrection, his great following, and his miracles.

Examples of Extant New Testament Copies

While ancient New Testament copies number in the thousands, there are several that are especially significant.

The John Rylands papyrus. John 18:31-33, and also John 18:37-38, appear on what is known as the John Rylands papyrus:

> *Pilate said, "Take him yourselves and judge him by your own law."*
>
> *"But we have no right to execute anyone," the Jews objected. This happened so that the words Jesus had spoken indicating the kind of death he was going to die would be fulfilled.*
>
> *Pilate then went back inside the palace, summoned Jesus and asked him, "Are you the king of the Jews?"* (John 18:31-33).
>
> *"You are a king, then!" said Pilate. Jesus answered, "You are right in saying I am a king. In fact, for this reason I was born, and for this I came into the world, to testify to the truth. Everyone on the side of truth listens to me."*
>
> *"What is truth?" Pilate asked. With this he went out again to the Jews and said, "I find no basis for a charge against him"* (John 18:37-38).

The John Rylands papyrus, dated back to A.D. 125, is the oldest known commonly accepted fragment of the New Testament in existence today. (Although some scholars believe portions of the New Testament have been found among the Dead Sea scrolls, others believe such finds are merely from the nonbiblical book of Enoch.)

The Rylands papyrus is important in its dating and location. Found in Egypt—hundreds of miles from the suspected place of the autograph in Asia Minor—it seems to indicate that the original Gospel of John may well have been written as early as the A.D. 40s.[7] The famous Bible scholar F.F. Bruce, who was Rylands Professor at the University of Manchester, says that the Gospel of John—the latest of the Gospels—was written in A.D. 90.[8]

Whether the original Gospel of John was written as early as the 40s or as late as 90, we know that it was present at the time of many eyewitnesses to the crucifixion and resurrection of Jesus. This provides assurance that it was available for examination regarding accuracy.

The Codex Sinaiticus. The Codex Sinaiticus is one of the most important ancient biblical manuscripts ever found because it is one of the earliest nearly complete copies of the Bible. Even the story of the discovery of the Codex is interesting:

> The fire burned warmly, casting flickering shadows off the walls of the monastery at the base of Mount Sinai. The monks huddled around it in quiet conversation about the day's events. A young man of 30, Tischendorf from the University of Leipzig had arrived early in the day in search of manuscripts of the Bible. The monks were fascinated by his enthusiasm, yet smiled privately, wondering why finding old Bibles mattered so much to him.

Tischendorf was near the fire and reached over to a wastebasket full of paper used to keep the fire going. As he was about to toss a sheet into the blaze, he stopped in disbelief at what he was holding in his hand. To his amazement, it was part of an ancient copy of the Septuagint version of the Bible. The monks laughed when Tischendorf told them what he had found, saying that they had already burned two wastebaskets full of the same manuscript. The young man begged them to give him any other sheets of the manuscript and asked them not to burn any others that they may have.

Tischendorf returned to his home and had the portions of the Bible he had retrieved published, naming them the codex Frederico–Augustanus. Later he returned a second time to the monastery, and later, yet a third time. By now he had gained the confidence and friendship of the monks. He brought a copy of a published version of the Septuagint, which he gave to the steward of the monastery. Later that evening the steward pulled Tischendorf aside.

"I have something to show you," he said as he reached into his closet and pulled out a manuscript that was meticulously wrapped in a red cloth. Slowly he opened it. Tischendorf couldn't believe his eyes. It was a nearly complete Bible, obviously of ancient origin. Tears streamed down his face. That evening, Tischendorf stayed up all night poring over the words of the manuscript. He wrote in his journal at the time, "It really seemed a sacrilege to sleep." Something truly important had been discovered.[9]

Dr. Constantin von Tischendorf's discovery of the manuscript, now known as the Codex Sinaiticus, was made in 1859. It contains nearly all of the New Testament and over half of the Old Testament. The manuscript was eventually presented by the monastery to the Russian czar, and was later bought by the British government for 100,000 pounds on Christmas Day in 1933.

The Codex, written in Greek, was copied primarily from a master scroll sometime around A.D. 350. Experts have concluded that three scribes were involved in the writing, and as many as nine "correctors" had made some notations over the centuries. The Codex consists of 148 14-inch x 15-inch pages written in brown ink in four columns, 48 lines per column, per page. It is consistent with the many early copies of portions of the New Testament that have been found (some of these portions of the Bible date back to the early second century). Today the Codex Sinaiticus resides in the British Museum.

The Codex Sinaiticus, written only a few generations after the eyewitnesses of Jesus, provides corroboration that the text of the New Testament is an accurate representation of Jesus' life, death, and resurrection.

The Codex Vaticanus. According to author and historian Eusebius, Constantine requested 50 "official" copies of the Bible be made to be held by Rome in the early 300s. Some scholars contend that the Codex Vaticanus, which has been held for centuries at the Vatican in Rome, is one of the actual 50 copies requested by Constantine.

Of this we can't be certain. We can be sure, however, of the importance of the manuscript due to its early origin and completeness.

The Codex Vaticanus was written about A.D. 325. It is a nearly complete edition of today's Bible. It contains all of the Old Testament except for most of the book of Genesis. It contains the New Testament including the Gospels, Acts, and the Pauline letters through a portion of Hebrews. The pastoral letters and the book of Revelation are missing. The missing portion (most of Genesis and the end of the Bible) is because both the beginning and the end of the Bible had been damaged and were lost.

The Codex Vaticanus was written in Greek uncial—meaning in all capital letters with no punctuation. The Old Testament consists of 617 leaves (pages) and the New Testament consists of 142. Each leaf is about 11 inches by 11 inches, and is formatted with three columns of 40, 44 lines per column. Scholars believe one scribe copied the Old Testament from a master, and another copied the New Testament likewise. One "corrector" is believed to have worked on the manuscript shortly after its writing and a second one hundreds of years later—probably about the tenth or eleventh century.

The significance of the Codex Vaticanus is enormous. It is the earliest, nearly complete Bible we have available today, and it was written only 250 years after the time of the apostles. It is identical to the Bible we read today, with only a few exceptions that are often noted in many study Bibles.

The Codex Vaticanus provides evidence that the story of Jesus as we read it today is identical to the beliefs that were widely accepted near the time of Jesus.

Test Yourself

1. Why do large numbers of consistent manuscripts matter for reliability?

2. Why does having copies closer to the autographs help ensure reliability?

3. Approximately how many copies of somewhat complete ancient manuscripts of the Bible are in existence today? Compare that to another ancient manuscript.

4. How many years since the autograph of the book of John was the John Rylands papyrus written? Is it conceivable the copyist ever met the apostle John?

5. What are the Codex Sinaiticus and Codex Vaticanus, and about when were they written?

Chapter 12 Group Study

Homework Preparation (do prior to group)
Read: chapter 12 of this text and pages 24–27 in *Can You Trust the Bible?* ✝.

Opening Prayer
Discussion: Discuss the statement by Norman Geisler and William Nix that the Bible is "99.5%" accurate textually (page 200). How do the number of manuscripts, the proximity to autographs, and the degree of variation let them determine this?

Practical-Experience Game
Press conference: The "Christian" will be addressing concerns from the press regarding the assurance that the Bible is reliable. How do we know it wasn't changed by the Catholic Church (or other parties) over the years, as is often claimed?

Closing Prayer

Non-Christian Documents About Jesus

The sun was setting, and the cool dry air was blowing in over the Nile. The men carried their precious treasure with them to hide for safekeeping for future generations. Finally they reached the place where the documents would be safe. It was the east bank of the Nile. Cliffs towered above. The heavy jar they carried contained 45 texts in 13 papyrus books (codices), most of which were Gnostic writings (a copy of Plato's *Republic* was also included). The books were carefully packaged in a jar, protected with "packing material," and topped with a bowl. Slowly, the jar was lowered into the hole, was covered with dirt, and a boulder was placed on top. Constantine had recently made Christianity the prominent religion of the Roman Empire. Now, the basics of Gnosticism would be preserved despite any persecution that might occur as a result of its being regarded as heretical by the leaders of the Christian church.

The "Gospel of Thomas" was among the documents that were discovered buried beneath a boulder in a large jar at the base of the cliffs on the east side of the Nile River in Egypt. This important discovery was made in 1945. Although the document bears the name "gospel," it is not canonical, nor is it even consistent with New Testament biblical teaching. The importance of the document is strictly as one of several

nonbiblical sources that corroborate the existence and the
words of Jesus.

Scholars consistently believe that the Gospel of Thomas
was written sometime in the early to mid-second century.
The most commonly cited date is about A.D. 140. Essentially,
it is supposedly an anthology of 114 obscure sayings of Jesus,
which the prologue states were collected and transmitted by
St. Didymus Jude Thomas. It was written in Coptic using an
expanded Greek alphabet. Although it is a heretical source,
the following list[1] of parallels between the New Testament
Gospels and the Gospel of Thomas (GTh) helps corroborate
the existence of the widespread teachings of Jesus.

Gospel of Thomas	Matthew	Mark	Luke
9	13:3-8	4:3-8	8:5-8
10			12:49
16	10:34-36		12:51-53
20	13:31-32	4:30-32	13:18-19
26	7:3-5		6:41-42
34	15:14		6:39
35	12:29	3:27	11:21-22
41	25:29		19:26
45	7:16-20		6:43-46
46	11:11		7:28
54	5:3		6:20
64	22:3-9		14:16-24
65	21:33-39	12:10	20:17
73	9:37-38		10:2
86	8:20		9:58
89			11:39-40
93	7:6		
94	7:7-8		11:9-10
100	12:13-17		20:22-25
103	24:43		12:39
107	18:12-13		15:3-7*

* Source: www.sacred-texts.com/chr/thomas.htm

The Gospel of Thomas clearly contradicts biblical teaching in important areas. It does not include any of Jesus' words regarding salvation or the ultimate historical revelation of his second coming and creation of a "new heaven and a new earth" (salvation for the Gnostic is through self-knowledge).

> The Gospel of Thomas is *not* a Gospel, nor is it even consistent with Christian doctrine. It does, however, provide additional non-Christian corroboration of the historical existence of Jesus, and of his well-known sayings.

Although found in Egypt, the Gospel of Thomas has also been found in Syria. At this point we can't be certain where it originated or where it may have been more popular.

While the Gospel of Thomas has no canonical theological value and is from a sect regarded as heretical, it does have historical value as a corroborative document written by those familiar with the teaching of Jesus, near the time of Jesus. It also supports much, although certainly not all, of the teaching of the New Testament.

References to Jesus in the Jewish Talmud

The Babylonian Talmud consists of 63 books of legal, ethical, spiritual, theological, ritual, and historical insight. Written and edited over many centuries, the part of the Talmud of most interest regarding Jesus is that portion that was written during the Tannaitic Period, from A.D. 70 to 200. A particularly significant text is in Sanhedrin 43a:

> On the eve of Passover they hanged Yeshu [Jesus—one version of this text actually says "Yeshu the Nazarene."]. And an announcer went out in front of him for forty days, saying: "He is going to be stoned, because he practised sorcery and enticed and led Israel astray. Anyone who knows anything in his

favor, let him come and plead in his behalf." But not having found anything in his favor, they hanged him on the eve of Passover.[2]

This passage is important in that it was written by Jews that not only denied Jesus, but were actively proselytizing against Christians. Courts of law have long maintained that some of the most powerful testimony is corroborative testimony from hostile witnesses (in this case Jews testifying about Jesus). What can be deduced from the Talmud's words is

1. that Jesus existed

2. that Jesus was crucified ("hanged") on the eve of Passover

3. that he performed miracles (the Jews referred to this as sorcery)

4. that he led many people away from legalistic Jewish teaching (as indicated in the New Testament—Matthew 15:3-9)

5. that the Jewish leaders were plotting to kill Jesus

In summary, the evidence of Jesus written in the Talmud, by the very Jews who despised him, is strong testimony of his existence and acts. It is very significant that it is in total agreement with the account of Jesus in the New Testament, including references to miracles, to the crucifixion, and to other details.

―――――Key Concept―――――

Key facts of history, including the miracles of Jesus, are confirmed in the Jewish Talmud—by the very people bent on stopping him.

References to Jesus by the Jewish Historian Josephus

Flavius Josephus is widely recognized as one of the greatest first-century historians. He himself has a colorful history.

Born in A.D. 37, only a few years after the death of Jesus, he spent his youth in Israel. During his early 20s he was sent to Rome to negotiate the release of several priests held hostage by Emperor Nero. Upon returning home, the Jewish revolution had begun. Josephus was drafted into becoming the commander of the revolutionary force in Galilee. When the Roman general Vespasian captured the city of Jotapata, he found Josephus alone, with his group of followers all dead. At Josephus' direction, they had made a suicide pact, and oddly enough only Josephus did not take the deadly poison. Josephus proclaimed himself a prophet. Because Josephus flattered Vespasian into thinking that Vespasian was the messiah the Scriptures talked about, Vespasian spared Josephus' life. Later, when Vespasian became emperor of Rome, Josephus was brought into the royal family of the Flavians. For the remainder of the war, Josephus assisted the Roman commander Titus with his knowledge of the Jewish culture. However, since Jerusalem regarded Josephus as a traitor, he had no luck in negotiating with the revolutionaries and, instead, became a witness to the destruction of Jerusalem and the Temple.

Josephus began writing the history of the war between the Romans and the Jews in the 70s. The book was apparently factually correct; however, it also was written to flatter the Romans and warn other provinces of the folly of opposing Rome. Later Josephus wrote a massive work about the history of the Jews *(Jewish Antiquities)*, which was published in 93 or 94.[3]

Josephus wrote about Jesus in his *Antiquities* as follows:

> Now there was about this time Jesus, a wise man *if it be lawful to call him a man,* for he was a doer of wonders, *a teacher of such men as receive the truth with pleasure.* He drew many after him *both of the Jews and the gentiles. He was the Christ.* When Pilate, at the suggestion of the principal men among us, had condemned him to the cross, those that loved him at the first did not forsake him, *for he appeared to them alive again the third day, as the divine prophets had foretold these and ten thousand other wonderful things about him,* and the tribe of Christians, so named from him, are not extinct at this day (Antiquities 18:63-64).[4]

Josephus is one of the best-known early Jewish historians, and he corroborated many things about Jesus, including his historicity, his crucifixion, and his miracles.

This writing is an extremely powerful statement by a non-Christian writing within the period of the eyewitnesses. Although there is some doubt regarding all of the words—some of which are believed to have been added (those that are italicized above are in question)—even if we consider only the words regarded by scholars as historically certain, we find corroboration of the historicity of Jesus, his miracles, his loyal followers, and his crucifixion by Pilate.

References to Jesus by the Historian Tacitus

Born only 22 years after the death of Jesus, Cornelius Tacitus was an energetic substitute consul and later proconsul in Asia Minor. Little is known about his life, but he was friends with the Roman consul Pliny the Younger.

Tacitus was known to be an eloquent, effective speaker. He tended to encourage his audiences to maintain a high moral standard. In his governing roles, he at times was in charge of government policy and even the army.

Tacitus is most famous for his important historical works, written at a time when very little history has survived. He wrote five *Histories,* of which four have survived (and part of the fifth). *Histories* covers only the history of the emperor Galba (A.D. 68–69) and the beginning of the reign of Vespasian (A.D. 70). He also wrote a 12-volume set called the *Annals,* which spans the historical period from the reign of Tiberius (from a point predating the ministry of Jesus) to the reigns of Claudius and the beginning of Nero's (the last years of Paul's ministry). Writing in about 115, Tacitus states in his *Annals* 15.44:

> But not all the relief that could come from man, not all the bounties that the prince could bestow, nor all the atonements which could be presented to the gods, availed to relieve Nero from the infamy of being believed to have ordered the conflagration of the fire of Rome. Hence to suppress the rumor, he falsely charged with the guilt, and punished Christians, who were hated for their enormities. Christus, the founder of the name, was put to death by Pontius Pilate, procurator of Judea in the reign of Tiberius: but the pernicious superstition, repressed for a time broke out again, not only through Judea, where the mischief originated, but through the city of Rome also, where all things hideous and shameful from every part of the world find their center and become popular. Accordingly, an arrest was first made of all who pleaded guilty; then, upon their information, an immense multitude was convicted, not so much of the crime of firing the city, as of hatred against mankind.[5]

It is very significant that Tacitus, who was clearly anti-Christian, treated the existence of Jesus and his many believers in a matter-of-fact way. In addition, he indicated the belief the early Christians had in the resurrection (the "novel superstition"), and also provided extrabiblical support of many other details of the account in the New Testament writings.

Reference to Jesus by Historian Pliny the Younger

Pliny the Younger began practicing law in A.D. 79 at the age of 18. He very quickly developed a stellar reputation in civil law that led to demand for his services in political courts that tried officials for extortion. Major victories that stand out as indications of his skill include the condemnation of a governor of Africa, and also of a group of officials in Spain.[6]

Pliny the Younger was also an avid writer. He published ten major books containing a variety of letters. The letters were quite diverse in content. Many contained historical information relating to his relationship with people such as Emperor Trajan. Yet others contain advice to young men, letters of inquiry, and descriptions of various natural settings.

His letters mark the first time the Roman government recognized Christianity as separate from Judaism. As governor of Bithynia (in Asia Minor), he was caught in what seemed to be a quandary. Christians who were brought before him seemed to be harmless, yet were refusing to worship the Roman emperor (the Roman population regarded emperors as gods) and were harming the local idol trade because of their denunciation of idols. Pliny the Younger decided to execute several Christians who were brought before him if they did not recant their faith. Unsure of his action, he wrote to his friend Emperor Trajan for advice:

Sir,

It is my constant method to apply myself to you for the resolution of all my doubts; for who can better govern my dilatory way of proceeding or instruct my ignorance? I have never been present at the examination of the Christians [by others], on which account I am unacquainted with what uses to be inquired into, and what, and how far they used to be punished; nor are my doubts small, whether there be not a distinction to be made between the ages [of the accused]? And whether tender youth ought to have the same punishment with strong men? Whether there be not room for pardon upon repentance? Or whether it may not be an advantage to one that had been a Christian, that he has forsaken Christianity? Whether the bare name, without any crimes besides, or the crimes adhering to that name, be to be punished?

In the meantime, I have taken this course about those who have been brought before me as Christians. I asked them whether they were Christians or not? If they confessed that they were Christians, I asked them again, and a third time intermixing threatenings with the questions. If they persevered in their confession, I ordered them to be executed; for I did not doubt but, let their confession be of any sort whatsoever, this positiveness and inflexible obstinacy deserved to be punished.

There have been some of this mad sect whom I took notice of in particular as Roman citizens, that they might be sent to that city. After some time, as is usual in such examinations, the crime spread itself and many more cases came before me. A libel was sent to me, though without an author, containing many names [of persons accused]. These denied that they were Christians now, or ever had been. They called upon the gods, and supplicated to your image, which I caused to be brought to me for that purpose, with frankincense and wine; they also cursed Christ; none of which things, it is said, can any of those that are ready Christians be compelled to do; so I thought fit to let them go. Others of them that were named in the libel, said they were Christians, but presently denied it again; that indeed they had been Christians, but had ceased to be so, some three years, some many more and one there was that said he had not been so these twenty years. All these worshipped your image, and the images of our gods; these also cursed Christ. However, they assured me that the main of their fault, or of their mistake was this:— That they were wont, on a stated day, to meet together before it was light, and to sing a hymn to Christ, as to a god, alternately; and to oblige themselves by a sacrament [or oath], not to do anything that was ill: but that they would commit no theft, or pilfering, or adultery; that they would not break their promises, or deny what was deposited with them, when it was required back again; after which it was their custom to depart, and to meet again at a common but innocent meal, which they had left off upon that edict which I published at your command, and wherein I had forbidden any such conventiclers. These examinations made me think it necessary to inquire by torments what the truth was; which I did of the two servant maids, who were called Deaconesses; but still I discovered no more than that they were addicted to a bad and to an extravagant superstition.

Hereupon, I have put off any further examinations, and have recourse to you, for the affair seems to be well worth consultation, especially on account of the number of those that are in danger; for there are many of every age, of every rank, and of both sexes, who are now and hereafter likely to be called to account, and to be in danger; for this superstition is spread like a contagion, not only into cities and towns, but into country villages also, which yet there is reason to hope may be stopped and corrected. To be sure, the temples, which were almost forsaken, begin already to be frequented; and the holy solemnities, which were long intermitted, begin to be revived. The sacrifices begin to sell well everywhere, of which very few purchasers had of late appeared; whereby it is easy to suppose how great a multitude of men may be amended, if place for repentance be admitted.[7]

It is most interesting to go back in time and actually feel the events taking place at the time of Christian persecution. Here we see the result of a letter to the emperor of Rome that describes the judgmental process and capital punishment of those proclaiming Christianity. While we are aware that there are many Christians who chose death over cursing Jesus, the letter also describes in vivid detail those who *did* recant their faith to save their lives—in other words those who "sold out" Christ to worship Emperor Trajan. One wonders how committed they were to Jesus in the first place.

The letter also points out the strength of the belief in the resurrection (the "bad" superstition was probably a reference to the resurrection). According to the letter, the believers in Jesus spanned a broad group of people—young, old; male, female; and of every social class. And it references how quickly it was spreading throughout the region.

References to Jesus by the Historian Suetonius

Caius Suetonius Tranquillus was the private secretary of Emperor Hadrian. We know that Hadrian was very concerned about the spread of Christianity. He was so concerned that he covered up the holy sites of the crucifixion and the resurrection with pagan statues in an attempt to "help" Christians forget them. Obviously there was discussion of Jesus and the Christians between Hadrian and Suetonius.

Suetonius was a historian who lived from about A.D. 69 to 140. Apart from his relationship to Hadrian, little is known about his life. He did write many ancient historical works that we still have today, including *De vita Caesarum* ("about the lives of the Caesars," translated into English in 1957 by Robert Graves as *The Twelve Caesars*) and the much larger collection of biographies *De viris illustribus* ("concerning illustrious men").

The actual words Suetonius wrote about Jesus Christ and the Christians are:

> Because the Jews at Rome caused constant distur-bances at the instigation of Chrestus (Christ), he (Claudius) expelled them from the city of (Rome) (*Life of the Emperor Claudius*, chapter 25—excerpt.)[8]

> During his reign many abuses were severely punished and put down, and no fewer new laws were made; a limit was set to expenditures, the public banquets were confined to a distribution of food, the sale of any kind of cooked viands in the taverns was for-bidden, with the exception of pulse and vegetables, whereas before every sort of dainty was exposed for sale. Punishment was inflicted on the Christians, a class of men given to a new and mischievous super-stition. He put an end to the diversions of the chariot drivers, who from immunity of long standing claimed the right of ranging at large and amusing themselves by cheating and robbing the people. The pantomimic actors and their partisans were banished from the city (*Life of the Emperor Nero*, chapter 16—excerpt).[9]

Suetonius reaffirms the historicity of the belief in the resurrection, calling it, like other ancient historians that were nonbelievers, a "superstition."

Reference to Jesus by the Historian Phlegon

The early church father Origen was seeking ancient writings by non-Christian historians about the events of the crucifixion and resurrection. He was told of writings by Phlegon, who wrote about the events of the earthquakes and darkened sky at the time of the crucifixion.

Phlegon blamed the darkness at the time of the crucifixion on a solar eclipse, which Origen refutes. Ironically, we know that scientifically a solar eclipse would be impossible at Passover (the time of Jesus' crucifixion) because Passover is timed when there is a full moon. It would be scientifically impossible for a solar eclipse to occur then because the moon would be on the wrong side of the earth.

Origen (A.D. 184–254) references two works by Phlegon: 1) *Chronicles* and 2) *Olympiads*. Unfortunately both originals have been lost. Only the references to them by Origen remain. The citations in which Origen addresses the mistaken solar eclipse at the time of the crucifixion, are as follows:

> And with regard to the eclipse in the time of Tiberius Caesar, in whose reign Jesus appears to have been crucified, and the great earthquakes which then took place...(*Origen against Celsus*).[10]

> Phlegon mentioned the eclipse which took place during the crucifixion of the Lord Jesus and no other (eclipse); it is clear that he did not know from his sources about any (similar) eclipse in previous times and this is shown by the historical account of Tiberius Caesar (*Origen and Philopon, De. Opif. Mund.*, II21).[11]

Phlegon also referred to Jesus' prophecy and indicated that the prophecies came true:

> Now Phlegon, in the thirteenth or fourteenth book, I think of his Chronicles, not only ascribed to Jesus a knowledge of future events…but also testified that the result corresponded to his predictions *(Origen against Celsus).*[12]

Phlegon's extrabiblical writing provides support of the events as described in the Bible. Although he was not a Christian, he did not deny the events, and he even supported the prophetic accuracy of Jesus.

References to Jesus by Lucian of Samosata

The satirist Lucian had a passion for history and the truth. This passion is recorded in some of his writings:

> History…abhors the intrusion of any least scruple of falsehood; it is like the windpipe, which the doctors tell us will not tolerate a morsel of stray food.[13]

> The historian's one task is to tell the thing as it happened.[14]

> [The historian] must sacrifice to no God but Truth; he must neglect all else; his sole rule and unerring guide is this—to think not of those who are listening to him now, but of the yet unborn who shall seek his converse.[15]

This conviction about history and the truth is important when we consider his writings regarding Jesus (especially considering that he is a satirist who would tend to poke fun at things).

Lucian was born in Samosata, and lived from about 125 to 180. He was the son of a sculptor, but quickly decided not to pursue the same career and chose instead a career of rhetoric and later public speaking in such locations as Ionia, Greece, Italy, and even Gaul. His speaking was self-proclaimed to simply amuse, not to establish any moral truths or philosophize. He was, however, a lover of historical accuracy and truth, as the previous quotes indicate.

Lucian frequently poked fun at the Christians, whom he regarded as simple and gullible. He wrote,

> The Christians...worship a man to this day—the distinguished personage who introduced their novel rites, and was crucified on that account....[It] was impressed on them by their original lawgiver that they are all brothers, from the moment that they are converted, and deny the gods of Greece, and worship the crucified sage, and live after his laws.[16]

Although making fun of Christians in this statement, several points are worth noting: 1) that Jesus is referred to as a man, 2) that his "novel rites" are noted, 3) that he was crucified, 4) that his followers thought highly of him, 5) that the followers were *converted from the gods* of Greece to 6) *worship the "sage."*

References to Jesus by Emperor Hadrian

Hadrian, the emperor of Rome from 117 to 138, had a significant impact on the Jewish and Christian world. In an attempt to rid Christians of any memories of holy sites of Jesus, he built a pagan temple over the site of the crucifixion and placed statues of Venus on the place of the crucifixion and Jupiter on the place of the resurrection.[17] Far from causing

Christians to forget these sites, they only served as markers, allowing them to be revered as holy sites later on.

Hadrian's abhorrent actions—forbidding several Jewish customs, building pagan monuments, and taxing the Jews and Christians in the name of pagan gods—led to a Jewish revolt, which was put down in 132. Once the revolt was over, Jews were not permitted back into the city of Jerusalem—and most Christians in the region were Jews.

Hadrian seemed to be more tolerant of Christians than other Roman leaders during persecution, and in a letter written to the proconsul of Asia in 124 he warns against false accusation:

> I do not wish, therefore, that the matter should be passed by without examination, so that these men may neither be harassed, nor opportunity of malicious proceedings be offered to informers. If, therefore, the provincials can clearly evince their charges against the Christians, so as to answer before the tribunal, let them pursue this course only, but not by mere petitions, and mere outcries against the Christians. For it is far more proper, if anyone would bring an accusation, that you should examine it.

Hadrian further explained that if Christians were found guilty they should be judged "according to the heinousness of the crime." If the accusers were only slandering the believers, then those who inaccurately made the charges were to be punished.[18]

However, that we not be misled, during organized massacres such niceties didn't apply. Also, like at other times, Christians were required to worship Roman gods (especially Jupiter), and refusal to renounce their faith and bow down to Roman gods resulted in execution.

Hadrian's policies (even to the extent of attempting to obliterate the holy sites) and writings provide non-Christian evidence contemporary with some eyewitnesses to Jesus of the rapid spread of Christianity and of the strong belief in the resurrection.

Test Yourself

1. Why are non-Christian writings about Jesus valuable?

2. Some people claim the Gospel of Thomas is a legitimate biblical Gospel. What would you tell them? Why is it an important historical document anyway?

3. What did Jewish leaders record in their ancient holy documents about Jesus?

4. Who was Josephus? What did he say about Jesus?

5. Name at least three other ancient non-Christian authors who wrote about Jesus.

Chapter 13 Group Study

Homework Preparation (do prior to group)
Read: Chapter 13 of this text and pages 30, 36 in *Can You Trust the Bible?* ✝.

Opening Prayer
Discussion: Some non-Christian writers confirmed important historical facts, such as the crucifixion of Jesus. But others spoke of hard-to-believe events like his miracles and the "superstition"—that is, his resurrection. Discuss both, with emphasis on the latter.

Practical-Experience Game

Role-playing: Credibility of the Bible is an issue with the "nonbeliever." The "Christian" should use what he or she has learned, including the miraculous, consistent authorship (see page 30 in *Can You Trust the Bible?*) to help resolve this issue.

Closing Prayer

The Early Church
Fathers Confirm
the Bible

It didn't take long for the early church to commit the story of Jesus to writing. By A.D. 64 persecution was in full swing—only about 30 years after Jesus' death. And the Christian church was exploding, seeming out of control to those wishing to suppress it. Many scholars believe that three of the four Gospels had been recorded by then in order to ensure that trustworthy, standardized accounts could be passed on to others. By the end of the first century, all of the Gospels, the book of Acts, the letters, and the book of Revelation—all of the books making up the New Testament—had been completed.

In addition to writing down the New Testament shortly after Jesus' death, the leaders of the first-century church (and in the beginning of the second century) committed large sections to memory. This memorization helped guard against errors since anyone wanting to intentionally distort the gospel message would have to contend with the memories of the church leaders as well.

Early church fathers also included verses and sections of the New Testament in other writings and teachings on a vast scale. Literally all books of the New Testament were cited! In fact, nearly every verse can be found in nonbiblical writings.

So extensive was this early recognition and reference to the New Testament, that scholars analyzing it proclaim that if all of the copies of the New Testament were destroyed, it could be reconstructed solely from external references by others. The vast number of quotes by early church leaders is summarized below:[1]

New Testament Quotes from Early Church Leaders

Author	Dates	Gospels/Acts	Letters	Revelation	Total
Justin Martyr	100–165	278	49	3	330
Irenaeus	120–202	1232	522	65	1819
Clement of Alexandria	150–216	1061	1334	11	2406
Origen	185–253	9580	8177	165	17,922
Tertullian	155–220	4324	2729	205	7258
Hippolytus	170–236	776	414	188	1378
Eusebius	260–340	3469	1680	27	5176
Total		**20,720**	**14,905**	**664**	**36,289**

In addition to this list, the well-known martyr Ignatius (30–107), in his seven epistles, quoted from the books of Matthew, John, Acts, Romans, 1 Corinthians, Galatians, Ephesians, Philippians, Colossians, 1 and 2 Thessalonians, 1 and 2 Timothy, James, and 1 Peter. Ignatius was personally acquainted with some of the apostles and had every opportunity to verify the accuracy of the life of Jesus through the eyewitnesses themselves.

The Early Church Creeds

Priscilla looked up at the priest with tears in her eyes as he asked the most important questions of her life: "Do you believe in God, the Father Almighty...in Jesus Christ, the Son of God, who was born of the Holy Spirit and the Virgin Mary...in the Holy Spirit, in the holy church, and the resurrection of the body?" Her husband and two young children looked on, with an approving smile.

"Yes, I believe," she said, her voice deep with emotion. With that Priscilla was dipped in water and then anointed with oil. "This I do as a sign of your baptism with the Holy Spirit," the priest continued. Overjoyed, Priscilla started weeping and tightly hugged her husband while thinking about her new relationship with the Lord Jesus Christ.

Only 180 years had passed since Jesus had walked the face of the earth.

An early church leader, Hippolytus, wrote about baptisms in the early 200s. The words selected as a statement of faith were foundational to what Jesus himself regarded as fundamental to Christian belief. We can be assured of this because those crafting such statements of faith were within a few generations of Jesus. The doctrine was discussed by Christian leaders such as Ignatius and Clement of Rome (A.D. 95), who both had actual contact with the apostles themselves. Ignatius and Clement then passed it on to other early leaders, including Polycarp (70–156), Justin Martyr (about 100 to 165), Irenaeus (120–202), Tertullian (155–220), and Hippolytus (170–236).

There was unbroken continuity between the teachings of Jesus and the apostles and the Christian church's defined statements of faith (see page 555).

The Apostles' Creed, which is a fundamental statement of faith actively used by many denominations today, is believed to have its roots in the "Interrogatory Creed of Hippolytus" (about 215).[2] The Apostles' Creed is especially significant because it affirms

- Jesus' "oneness" with God, the Creator of the universe

- Jesus' virgin birth

- Jesus' bodily resurrection

- The triune nature of God (Father, Son, and Holy Spirit)

- The forgiveness of sin

The Apostles' Creed was specifically intended to combat Gnosticism—the heretical belief of opposing spiritual realms of good and evil, with the material world aligned with evil. Gnosticism was philosophical in origin, and it rejected the redemption and bodily resurrection of Jesus.

The Apostles' Creed

I believe in God, the Father Almighty,
    the Creator of heaven and earth,
    and in Jesus Christ, His only Son, our Lord:
Who was conceived of the Holy Spirit,
    born of the Virgin Mary,
    suffered under Pontius Pilate,
    was crucified, died, and was buried.
The third day He arose again from the dead.
He ascended into heaven
    and sits at the right hand of God the Father
        Almighty,
    whence He shall come to judge the living and the
        dead.
I believe in the Holy Spirit, the holy catholic church,
    the communion of saints,
    the forgiveness of sins,
    the resurrection of the body,
    and life everlasting.
    Amen.

Another early creed of significance was the Nicene Creed, adopted about 325 (later revised by the First Council of Constantinople, 381). This creed was developed at the First Council of Nicaea, convened by Roman Emperor Constantine. The creed's purpose was to counter the heresy of Arianism, which rejected the deity of Jesus.

The Nicene Creed

We believe in one God,
the Father,
the Almighty,
maker of heaven and earth,
of all that is, seen and unseen.

We believe in one Lord, Jesus Christ,
the only Son of God,
eternally begotten of the Father,
God from God, Light from Light,
true God from true God,
begotten, not made,
of one Being with the Father.
Through him all things were made.
For us and for our salvation
he came down from heaven:
by the power of the Holy Spirit
he became incarnate from the Virgin Mary,
and was made man.
For our sake he was crucified under Pontius Pilate;
he suffered death and was buried.
On the third day he rose again
in accordance with the Scriptures;
he ascended into heaven
and is seated at the right hand of the Father.

He will come again in glory to judge the living and the
dead,
and his kingdom will have no end.
We believe in the Holy Spirit, the Lord, the giver of life,
who proceeds from the Father and the Son.
With the Father and the Son he is worshiped and glorified.
He has spoken through the Prophets.
We believe in one holy catholic and apostolic Church.
We acknowledge one baptism for the forgiveness of sins.
We look for the resurrection of the dead,
and the life of the world to come.
    Amen.

The Canon of the Bible

"Canon" simply means "standardized." In biblical understanding, it has the special importance of implying Scripture
is from God, or "God-breathed." There is substantial evidence from historical writings that indicates the canon of the
Old Testament was essentially "closed" (determined) no later
than 167 B.C. Jesus referred frequently to the Scriptures as a
preordained collection of words from God. No room for
variance was ever suggested.

There were three sections of the Bible that were canonized
at different points in time: the Torah, or first five books of the
Bible; the Tanakh, or Old Testament; and the entire Bible,
including the New Testament.

The Canon of the Torah

The first five books—the Torah—were immediately
regarded as Holy Scripture ("God breathed"), and for good
reason:

1. God commanded Moses to write down his laws both
   on large rocks and on scrolls for future generations.

Write on them all the words of this law when you have crossed over to enter the land the LORD *your God is giving you, a land flowing with milk and honey, just as the* LORD, *the God of your fathers, promised you* (Deuteronomy 27:3-4).

You shall write very clearly all the words of this law on these stones you have set up (Deuteronomy 27:8).

2. God's presence was easily observable through his glory. We find the glory of God on almost a daily basis as the "cloud by day" and "the pillar of fire by night" guides the Hebrews through the wilderness (Exodus 13:21). Likewise, the glory of God was seen over the Tabernacle (40:34-35), and upon Mount Sinai.

   When Moses went up on the mountain, the cloud covered it, and the glory of the LORD *settled on Mount Sinai. For six days the cloud covered the mountain, and on the seventh day the* LORD *called to Moses from within the cloud. To the Israelites the glory of the* LORD *looked like a consuming fire on top of the mountain* (Exodus 24:15-17).

3. God's inspiration was seen on Moses himself. When Moses went to speak to God to receive the law, he returned with a "radiance" upon his face—indicative of his interaction with God. At first, this frightened the people. Moses even placed a veil over his face after addressing the people, until the next time he would see God.

   When Moses finished speaking to them, he put a veil over his face. But whenever he entered the LORD's *presence to speak with him, he removed the veil until he came out. And when he came out and told the*

Israelites what he had been commanded, they saw that his face was radiant. Then Moses would put the veil back over his face until he went in to speak with the LORD (Exodus 34:33-35).

4. God's presence was apparent through great and highly visible miracles. Things like the parting of the Red Sea, the daily provision of manna, and the defeat of the Amalekites (Exodus 17:8-14) were obvious indications of God's direct interaction.

Despite the fact that there was no need to verify the holy Scripture of the Torah, the Jewish exile to Babylon (586 B.C.) created some concern over having the written records of Moses "officially" canonized. Hence, shortly after the time of the return of the Jews to Israel (around 500 B.C.), the Torah was officially canonized.

Jesus directly supported the words of the Torah, indicated by his frequent quoting of it. Seven times he referred to it as the authoritative Word of God (Matthew 4:4,7,10; 19:18-19; 22:32,37-39.) And 16 times he referred to events recorded in it (Matthew 8:4; 10:15; 11:23; 17:3; 23:35; 24:37; Luke 16:29,31; 17:28,32; 20:37; 24:27; John 3:14; 6:31; 8:17,56).

Jesus also confirmed all the major events in the first half of Genesis, which are some of the most controversial historical facts in biblical criticism. Nonetheless, Jesus confirmed them as history.

The Old Testament Canon

As the Old Testament (or Tanakh as referred to by the Jews) was recorded, it was guided by several tests of inspiration from God. The most important test of something being from God was the test of 100-percent perfect prophecy. Prophecy was designated as a "test" by God through Moses in the Torah. We discover some of the background behind this when the Israelites were requesting not to hear the voice of God, or see his "great fire" any more, or they would "surely die" (Deuteronomy 18:16). God indicated through Moses that future prophets would be raised up that could be tested through 100-percent perfect prophecy (verse 22):

> *The nations you will dispossess listen to those who practice sorcery or divination. But as for you, the LORD your God has not permitted you to do so. The LORD your God will raise up for you a prophet like me from among your own brothers. You must listen to him. For this is what you asked of the LORD your God at Horeb on the day of the assembly when you said, "Let us not hear the voice of the LORD our God nor see this great fire anymore, or we will die."*
>
> *The LORD said to me: "What they say is good. I will raise up for them a prophet like you from among their brothers; I will put my words in his mouth, and he will tell them everything I command him. If anyone does not listen to my words that the prophet speaks in my name, I myself will call him to account. But a prophet who presumes to speak in my name anything I have not commanded him to say, or a prophet who speaks in the name of other gods, must be put to death."*
>
> *You may say to yourselves, "How can we know when a message has not been spoken by the LORD?" If what a prophet proclaims in the name of the LORD does not take place or come true, that is a message the LORD has not spoken. That prophet has spoken presumptuously. Do not be afraid of him* (Deuteronomy 18:14-22).

God further defines his uniqueness and the importance of prophecy in his words through the prophet Isaiah:

> *Remember the former things, those of long ago;*
> *I am God, and there is no other;*
> *I am God, and there is none like me.*
> *I make known the end from the beginning,*
> *from ancient times, what is still to come.*

—Isaiah 46:9-10

God makes it known that he is unique (there is "no other" and "there is none like me"); furthermore, that no one else "makes known the end from the beginning." Consequently, the Old Testament is filled with prophecy throughout all books. As one would expect, short-term prophecy (fulfilled within the same time frame and in the same book as recorded) was a primary tool in discovering if someone was a prophet worthy of being included in holy Scripture. Part 3 reviews the important issue of biblical prophecy in depth. In addition to long-term prophecies found in Part 3, others can be found in Appendix C.

So the books of Old Testament Scripture were in general determined using prophecy as a primary test, soon after they were written (using the short-term prophecies of the writer as verification). Yet it wasn't until 167 B.C. (the year that the Seleucid ruler Antiochus Epiphanes IV sacrificed a pig on the Temple altar, sparking the Jewish revolt by the Maccabees— with Hanukkah representing the revolt's end exactly one year later) that a consensus was made by the Israelites regarding the books and completeness of the Old Testament.

As mentioned earlier in this part, Jesus confirmed the Old Testament since this was the official Bible (the Septuagint) used during his time on earth.

Even though the canon of the Old Testament was unofficially recognized by 167 B.C., it was not until the Jews faced the second exile in A.D. 70 that it was officially recognized.

The New Testament Canon

The Christian church had essentially affirmed a canon (an accepted collection of books) for the entire Bible by 200. Early church fathers Irenaeus (about 130) and Origen (about 180) both listed all 27 books of the New Testament (although some were listed as suspect: 6 by Irenaeus, and 5 by Origen).[3] However, final confirmation of the canon did not occur until the Council of Carthage in 397.

As mentioned above, Jesus actually preconfirmed the New Testament when he indicated that it would come following his resurrection (see pages 193–194). He authorized it, he prophesied it, and confirmed it while it was being preached.

It is significant that the canon came under scrutiny shortly after the time of the writing of the books of the New Testament and remained so for many years before its final approval. This way, the books of the New Testament had substantial time for critics to voice potential concerns and for those who had the best, closest knowledge to review them.

It is also significant that each canon of the Bible—the Torah, the Tanakh, and the New Testament—all enjoyed general acceptance 200 years or more prior to official acceptance. There would have been ample time for any substantial claim to authenticity to be challenged by those still close to the time of the writing of the autograph.

Test Yourself

1. Why was it important that there be an unbroken chain of documentation from the apostles through the early church fathers to today?

2. If we lost all copies of the New Testament, what could the church fathers' quotes do for us?

3. What is Gnosticism? What creed was established to refute it?

4. What was the purpose of the Nicene Creed? Who convened the council?

5. List all six canons (official and unofficial) and approximately when they were established.

Chapter 14 Group Study

Homework Preparation (do prior to group)
Read: chapter 14 of this text and pages 16, 17, 32, and 33 in *Can You Trust the Bible?* ✝.

Opening Prayer
Discussion: Discuss the continuity of communication from the apostles through the early church fathers to the many documents of the New Testament (see pages 226-227). Why is this unbroken chain from the apostles important in demonstrating reliability of the Bible?

Practical-Experience Game
TV interview: The "TV spokesperson" interviews the "Christian" about the early church fathers and their role in the developing New Testament. Discuss how we know it wasn't changed at this time, and how in fact these leaders helped ensure reliability.

Closing Prayer

Archaeological Evidence of the Old Testament

The question often is asked, "Does archaeology prove the Bible?" The answer, of course, is no. Archaeology usually cannot prove details of the events that happen and especially can't prove what is in the mind of the people in existence at the time (for example, it can't prove motives). But it can *suggest* things, including motives.

What archaeology can also do, however, is verify existence of certain things such as cities, cultures, and things. For example, it can prove the *existence* of the Temple—just as outlined in the Bible. Events can also be strongly suggested, and in some cases (especially where there are inscriptions) virtually confirmed. Hence, many things that are discussed in the Bible can be examined using archaeology, and can either be strongly supported, or dismissed. To date, archaeology has dramatically supported the Bible, far beyond most people's original expectations.

Note: The information in chapters 15 and 16 is taken from one or more of the following sources (in most cases multiple sources address the same findings):

• Finegan, Jack. *The Archeology of the New Testament: The Life of Jesus and the Beginning of the Early Church,* rev. ed. Princeton, NJ: Princeton University Press, 1992.

• Free, Joseph P., and Howard F. Vos. *Archaeology and Bible History.* Grand Rapids, MI: Zondervan Publishing House, 1992.

• McDowell, Josh. *Evidence That Demands a Verdict—Volumes I and II.* Nashville, TN: Thomas Nelson, Inc., 1993.

• ——. *The New Evidence That Demands a Verdict.* Nashville, TN: Thomas Nelson Publishers, 1999.

• McDowell, Josh, and Bill Wilson. *A Ready Defense.* San Bernardino, CA: Here's Life Publishers, Inc., 1990.

• McRay, John. *Archaeology and the New Testament.* Grand Rapids, MI: Baker Book House, 1991.

• Millard, Alan. *Illustrated Wonders and Discoveries of the Bible.* Nashville, TN: Thomas Nelson, Inc., 1997.

• Packer, J.I., Merrill C. Tenney, and William White Jr. *Illustrated Encyclopedia of Bible Facts.* Nashville, TN: Thomas Nelson, Inc., 1980.

• Pritchard, James B. *The Harper Atlas of the Bible.* New York: Harper & Row, 1987.

• Unger, Merrill F. *The New Unger's Bible Handbook.* Chicago: Moody Press, 1984.

• Youngblood, Ronald F. *New Illustrated Bible Dictionary.* Nashville, TN: Nelson, 1995.

What Is Archaeology?

It's natural to think of archaeology as an "old science." After all, it involves old things. Most people are surprised to learn that archaeology is relatively new, whether or not it is really a "science." (Some people define *science* as only the disciplines using the scientific method. Others, including the Webster dictionary definitions, broaden the word *science* to include any method of systematic study.)

Archaeology is the systematic study of things that cultures have left behind. It was not a subject of professional interest until the 1700s. At that time it focused primarily on "valuable" objects (mainly gold and silver artifacts). The systematic (scientific) approach wasn't widely used until the 1900s—years after some critics blindly (and incorrectly) assumed the Bible lacked any evidence to support it. In the late 1800s, "higher criticism" (popular at the time) suggested the Bible might be full of myths and errors. Some archaeologists sought to "prove" the Bible to be inaccurate. Others took the opposite approach and attempted to find evidence for it. The archaeologists working in the Middle East were surprised at their discoveries, which supported the Bible in virtually all details (see pages 268 and 274 regarding great archaeologists who switched from Bible critics to believers).

Archaeologists who were using the Bible as a guide began finding parts of history they didn't know existed. Ancient cultures thought to be nonexistent were discovered. Ancient cities thought to be myths were found. And events thought to be "legends" were confirmed. Today the Bible is regarded as a fundamental archaeological reference.

We should realize, however, that most of this archaeological evidence has appeared in the *last 50 years*. Only during that relatively short period of time have archaeologists uncovered such things as the existence of Sodom and Gomorrah, people as prominent as King David, or cultures such as the early Hittites. Now museums are filled with archaeological evidence supporting the Bible.

Archaeology Refutes "Higher Critics" of the Bible

Many textbooks and much public opinion are still based on remnants of the inaccurate period of "higher criticism" from the late 1800s to the early 1900s. These "critics" believed that the Bible was in error, yet they had no hard evidence upon which to back such criticism. Now, archaeology has embarrassed former "higher critics" of the Bible with facts. Here are some examples of mistakes made:

- "Higher critics" believed the Hittite culture of the time of Abraham could not possibly have existed as reported in the Bible (Genesis 10:15; 15:20; 23:3,7-20; 25:10; 49:32). Now, archaeology has uncovered numerous artifacts of the early Hittites. So numerous are these artifacts that they fill an entire museum in Israel.[1]

- The Bible speaks of Tubal-Cain (a descendent of Cain, Adam and Eve's son) as forging "all kinds of tools out of bronze and iron" (Genesis 4:22). Science dated the beginning of the Iron Age at about 1200 B.C., much later than the estimated time of Tubal-Cain. Yet an iron blade has been found just northwest of Baghdad—not far from the probable site of the Garden of Eden—that dates back to no later than 2700 B.C., long before the previous estimate.[2]

- It was believed that domesticated camels did not exist at the time of Abraham (as indicated in Genesis 12:16). Then archaeologists discovered paintings of domesticated camels on the walls of the temple of

Hatshepsut (near the city of Thebes, Egypt), which date back to that period.[3]

- It was once argued that the account of the strong, bolted doors of Lot's house (Genesis 19:9-10) was illogical because at that time cities were in a state of decline. Then archaeologists discovered the biblical city of Kiriath Sepher in the same area, with evidence of walls and strong doors. The construction dates from 2200 to 1600 B.C., the time of Lot.[4]

- It was insisted that the laws of the Old Testament (the Torah, the first five books written by Moses) could not possibly have been written as far back as 1450 B.C. No culture was thought to be that advanced. Then in 1902, archaeologists found an artifact from Babylon with similar laws—the Code of Hammurabi, which dated before the time of Moses.[5]

- The existence of the Philistines was once doubted. The Bible reports them as active enemies of Israel during the time of the judges. Now, many Philistine cities are just beginning to be uncovered. To date, more than 28 sites and 5 major centers have been uncovered in Palestine. Even the burning of the city of Gibeah, as indicated in Judges 20:8-40, has been confirmed.[6]

- It was thought that David could not have been a musician, since the instruments the Bible says he played were not developed until later. Then, archaeologists discovered the types of instruments used by David in the city of Ur (Abraham's hometown)—including lyres, flutes, harps, and even a double oboe, dating back to 2500 B.C. Additional discoveries of musical instruments were made in Egypt (dating back to 1900 B.C.) and in Palestine (dated about 2000 B.C.), both long before the time of David (which was about 1000 B.C.)[7]

Unfortunately, it takes time to correct long-standing misconceptions.

How Archaeology Is Conducted

Modern archaeology—highly organized and meticulous—keeps records in depth, and is *very* slow. Long ago "treasure hunters" obliterated many sites in search of quick riches. Today, archaeologists value most writings and artifacts more than gold or gems.

Archaeology is a relatively new science. Even so, it has already refuted many older beliefs that the Bible was incorrect (especially those of "higher criticism" of the Bible—popular in the late 1800s).

In the Middle East, the common form of a site for excavation is a large mound, called a *tell*, which is essentially a buried city. The original locations of cities (where *tells* later developed) were carefully selected, based on such things as water supply and natural defense. When a city was destroyed, it was typical to rebuild on top of the old city. As time passed, this cycle of destruction and rebuilding resulted in a large manmade hill. Of course, the uppermost level represented the most recent civilization, the lower ones earlier cultures. Occasionally pits were dug through several strata.

As excavation takes place, the precise location and relationship of various artifacts is lost forever. Therefore, digs are systematically divided into square areas and frequently photographed. Each artifact is thoroughly documented. Digging may start with shovels, which, as critical areas are approached are quickly replaced with small hand tools—even spoons and toothbrushes. Due to the enormous time and expense required, only a small dent has been made to date in the tens of thousands of potential sites.

How Archaeological Dates Are Determined

Occasionally archaeologists find coins or inscriptions of dates to verify the time of a city or culture. Such finds are extremely rare. However, the vast amount of pottery left behind—with obvious style changes that can be referenced to dates—provides an abundant and reliable source of dating. As an example, the oil lamps below show a very distinct progression of style readily recognizable by archaeologists. Such lamps are very commonly found in the Holy Lands.[8]

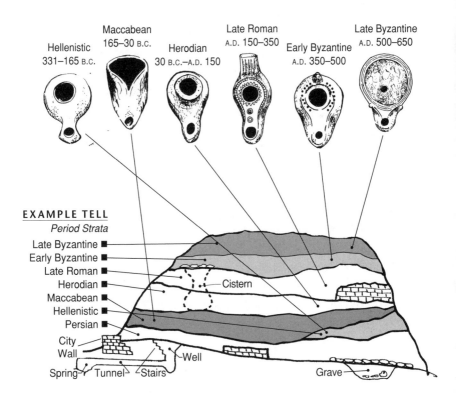

Does Absence of Evidence Mean Evidence of Absence?

Some people say, "No evidence means it didn't exist." For example, so far, no patriarch name inscriptions previous to Moses have been found on any clay tablets. But we should not expect to find such records. The patriarchs were nomads of little or no world acclaim; they were not kings building pyramids.

Skeptics may question why Egyptians, for example, would not record the mass exodus of the Hebrews. It is naive to think that Egyptian (or other) pagan rulers would document their major failures and defeats (the Bible is unique in that it readily points out the failures of its leaders). However, in fact we do find evidence in Egyptian art and inscriptions that the Hebrews *did exist as slaves that assisted in great building projects,* just as the Bible indicates. Therefore, they were there—and then they left—so there had to have been some form of "exodus," whether one accepts the Bible or not. Even so, many other ancient writings do cite biblical events and people (for example the Qur'an of Islam cites many biblical characters).

In addition, we find that as time goes on, archaeology often eventually uncovers evidence.

Archaeology Improves Biblical Understanding

At times sections of the Bible don't seem to make sense. Scholars who believe the Bible is the inerrant Word of God are confident that eventually all seemingly inconsistent sections will be made clear. Archaeology has assisted in aiding hermeneutics (interpretation) in a number of areas. An example follows:

How Many Quail Were in the Desert?

Some people believe the number of quail God provided to the wandering Israelites seems unrealistic if they were in fact piled three feet high upon the ground. Note the King James translation:

> *There went forth a wind from the* LORD, *and brought quails from the sea, and let them fall by the camp, as it were a day's journey on this side, and as it were a day's journey on the other side, round about the camp, and as it were two cubits high upon the face of the earth* (Numbers 11:31 KJV).

However, the Hebrew word for "upon" was the same as the word for "above" (Hebrew was the original language).[9] Of course, if the intent of the word was to state that the quail were flying three feet above the ground, it would indicate that they would be easy to capture. Archaeology has found ancient writings in Sinai that record the catching of quail in nets as they fly three feet above the ground. In fact, the same practice is used in the region even today.

Some more modern biblical translations have, therefore, changed the language to reflect this:

> *Now the* LORD *sent a wind that brought quail from the sea and let them fall into the camp and all around it! For many miles in every direction from the camp there were quail flying about three feet above the ground* (Numbers 11:31 NLT).

There are other such examples in the Bible as well.

Old Testament Archaeology Examples

The Garden of Eden (Genesis 2:11-14). The Bible provides some clues to the location of the Garden of Eden with its description. (See *Can Archaeology Prove the Old Testament?* page 24).

Old Testament Sites Confirmed by Archaeology

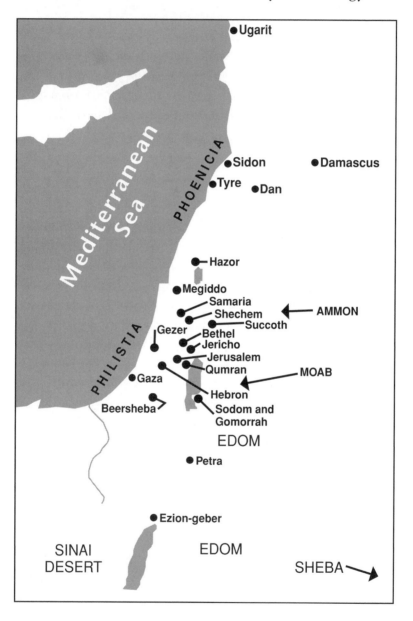

Cain and Abel (Genesis 4). Early wind and string instruments and an iron blade (from about 2700 B.C.) were discovered near the proposed site of the Garden of Eden.[10] (See *Can Archaeology Prove...*, page 24.)

The Flood (Genesis 6). Archaeology has uncovered *more than 200 accounts* from cultures all over the world of a major flood that destroyed humanity and animals. (See *Can Archaeology Prove...*, page 25.)

The Tower of Babel (Genesis 11). Many structures, called *ziggurats*—very high brick towers containing a shrine at the top, have been found near Babylon. One fragment of a clay tablet found in Babylon tells of one temple that so "offended the gods" that it was destroyed one night, and the people were scattered with their "speech made strange." (See *Can Archaeology Prove...*, page 25.)

Abraham in Egypt (Genesis 12:10-20). Archaeologists now support two details of Abraham's sojourn in Egypt that were once thought inaccurate. (See *Can Archaeology Prove...*, page 26.)

Sodom and Gomorrah (Genesis 19). The cities of the plain may be under shallow water at the south end of the Dead Sea (it fluctuates greatly in depth—37 feet in a few decades). Another site, Bab edh-Dhra, appears to be a possible location of Sodom or Gomorrah. It's located adjacent to a large graveyard showing mass simultaneous burial. Also, a thick layer of ash covers the ruins. Josephus, the first-century historian, records that "traces" of all five cities of the plain were visible at that time.

Early Hittites (Genesis 15:20; 23:10; 26:34). Many discoveries provide proof of a large Hittite empire in Syria, with tribal areas extending southward into Canaan. So vast is the amount of evidence today that many museums contain Hittite artifacts; and in some universities a PhD can be earned in Hittite studies alone. (See *Can Archaeology Prove...*, page 27.)

Fascinating Facts

Rocks of iron and hills of copper: God told Moses that the promised land would have "rocks of iron and copper that could be dug from the hills" (Deuteronomy 8:9). Twenty miles south of the Dead Sea, a large area is dotted with ancient furnaces. The vast region is covered with heaps of copper slag, and some copper veins are still visible above ground.[11]

Sarah's grave (Genesis 23). A cave in Hebron is believed to be the actual grave of Sarah (and of Abraham, Isaac, and Jacob—Genesis 25:9; 49:29-30). Now a Muslim mosque has been built over it (Abraham and Sarah are revered by most Muslims). Although access to the cave has generally been forbidden, at least twice the cave has been entered by non-Muslims (one of whom did not realize its significance). Shortly after the Six-Day War of 1967, a 12-year-old girl was lowered into the cave, some 12 feet underground. A 57-foot corridor led to a blocked entrance,

> Much of the archaeological information we have from before and during the time of the patriarchs helps define the culture but, understandably, does not name specific people. This is still of great importance, as it corroborates the biblical account.

presumably leading to other underground areas. Three large stones, one appearing to be a tombstone, were in front of it. And during World War I, a British officer, looking for other soldiers, slid down an incline into a 20-foot by 20-foot room. He reported a stone object measuring six feet long, three feet wide, and three feet high. Only later did he realize it might have been Sarah's tomb.

The Laws of Moses. For years, "higher criticism" of the Bible claimed the laws of Moses (in Leviticus) were far too advanced for the period and could not have been written until 500 B.C. or later. Then in 1902, the Laws of Hammurabi were found carved into a seven-foot tall black *stele* from Babylon—discovered in Susa in Elam—radically changing scholars' views. (See *Can Archaeology Prove...*, page 31.)

Joshua's conquest (Joshua 12:9-24). A group of letters, the Amarna Tablets, were written by kings of Palestinian and Syrian cities to kings of Egypt about 1400 B.C. (Joshua's time). These tablets confirm the conditions and many events of the time of Joshua. Seven of the letters were written by kings of Jerusalem, and others were from kings of the important seaports of Tyre and Sidon, along with letters from many of the 31 kings that Joshua conquered. Several mention an invasion by the *Habiru* (apparently a derivative of the word "Hebrew").[12]

King David; King Saul's death (1 Samuel, 1 Chronicles, 1 Kings). Archaeology has found extensive support for the biblical account of David. (See *Can Archaeology Prove...*, page 34.)

Some people once even argued that King David was a myth—until 1993. In that year, a stone monument fragment was discovered at Tel Dan, near the border of Israel and

Syria. The monument, believed to be a victory *stele*, mentions King David and the "House of David," along with words implying a victory by the king of Damascus, Ben-Hadad, who "smote Ijon, and Dan, and Abel-beth-maachah" (1 Kings 15:20).[13]

Dating of the kings of Israel. Thanks to the Assyrians, archaeology can confirm the precise dates of the kings of Israel back to the time of Solomon. Excavations have uncovered lists of *all kings of Assyria from 893 to 666 B.C.* and the dates they took office (the "eponym lists"). The exact years for each can be established by using an eclipse in the capital city of Nineveh (May–June 763 B.C.—confirmed by astronomers) as a benchmark. The archaeological records of King Shalmaneser III (858–824) discuss the great battle of Qarqar (853) and mention King Ahab of Israel. The battle was in the last year of King Ahab's reign. Since the Bible specifies the succession of kings of Israel and the lengths of their reigns, it is easy to establish the dates of each.

King Ahab. Evidence of Ahab's reign exists outside of Israel (in neighboring Moab) on a black victory *stele* set up by Moab's King Mesha, recording his victory over Ahab in about 860 B.C. (See *Can Archaeology Prove...*, page 38.)

King Jehu. The Black Obelisk of Shalmaneser II, which mentions Jehu, was discovered in Nimrud, a city just south of Nineveh. (See *Can Archaeology Prove...*, pages 38-39.)

God's protection of Jerusalem (2 Kings 19:20-36). Isaiah prophesied that God would protect Jerusalem against attack by Sennacherib of Assyria. An angel of the Lord killed 185,000 Assyrians the night after the prophecy (Isaiah 37:35-36). Excavation of two separate cylinders (the Taylor cylinder from ancient Nineveh and the Oriental Institute cylinder) both confirm this unusual event, stating with great pride the defeats of many cities in Palestine, yet acknowledging the failure to conquer Jerusalem.

Hezekiah's tunnel (2 Kings 20:20; 2 Chronicles 32:30). Hezekiah built an 1880-foot-long, 6-foot-high tunnel that ended at the Pool of Siloam, where an inscription was found that described how workers started at each end and "could hear each other digging" as they finally met in the middle (without the benefit of modern engineering). (See *Can Archaeology Prove...*, page 41.)

The Exile (2 Kings, Daniel, Ezekiel). There is substantial archaeological evidence of three separate phases in the exile of Judah to Babylon. The first (605 B.C.), when Daniel was deported, is confirmed by the "Babylon Chronicle," found in the court records of Babylon. The second (597), when Ezekiel was captured, is confirmed by the "Chronicles of the Chaldean Kings." And the third and final deportation, following the fall of Jerusalem (586), is supported by the "Lachish Letters."

The Dead Sea scrolls. The most important religious archaeological find in history is the Dead Sea scrolls. About one-third of the hundreds of scrolls are of the Old Testament (copies, often multiples, of every book except Esther), many written at least a century or two before Christ. The remaining scrolls contain a vast amount of information about the culture of the period. Hidden in jars in caves up to A.D. 70 and then forgotten until 1947, the scrolls are like a time capsule, showing virtually no difference from today's Masoretic text.

King Jehoiachin. Archaeology has uncovered interesting evidence for Jehoiachin, king of Judah for only three months, including a clay tablet "receipt" listing payment for rations of oil, barley, and other food to captives in Babylon, and listing King Jehoiachin and his five sons as recipients (2 Kings 25:27-30).[14] (See *Can Archaeology Prove...*, page 42.)

Ezekiel the prophet (book of Ezekiel). Stone tablets have been uncovered in recent years that contain a nearly complete text of the book of Ezekiel. Study of the specific form of Hebrew used in the inscriptions indicates the tablets were written during the time of Ezekiel—600 to 500 B.C. Some scholars have suggested they may have been chiseled by the prophet Ezekiel himself (which the Talmud seems to indicate).[15]

The return from the Exile (Ezra, Haggai, Zechariah). Archaeology confirms many important biblical prophecies. One of the most amazing is the confirmation of the prophecy that the person responsible for the Jewish return from the first exile would be a man named "Cyrus." The Cyrus cylinder, found in Babylon, records this proclamation along with other historical facts in the Bible, including the takeover of Babylon by the Persians without violence and the return of the treasures of the temple (Ezra 1:1-6).

Key Concept

The "Cyrus cylinder" is an important archaeological find that confirms the decree by Cyrus to allow the Jews to return to Jerusalem from the first exile to rebuild the city and the Temple—exactly as prophesied in Isaiah 44:28 more than 100 years in advance.

Tyre: fulfilled prophecy. Although the Bible is silent between the Old and New Testament (400 B.C. to Jesus' time), archaeology continues to document fulfillment of many prophecies given earlier. Among them is the double destruction in 586 and 330 B.C. of Tyre, the greatest seaport of Ezekiel's time (Ezekiel 26:3-16). (See *Can Archaeology Prove...*, page 44.)

Summary of More Old Testament Archaeology Examples

For further study and reference, here are some additional Bible events and people whose occurrence or existence is supported by archaeology. (All page numbers refer to *Can Archaeology Prove the Old Testament?*)

- *Laban's idols,* Genesis 31 (page 28).

- *Jacob and Joseph,* Genesis 37–50 (page 29).

- *From leaders to slaves,* Genesis and Exodus (page 29).

- *Hebrew slaves build cities,* Exodus 1:11; 5:13-18 (page 30).

- *The Tabernacle* (page 31).

- *The fall of Jericho,* Joshua 6 (page 32).

- *Cities of the time of the Judges,* book of Judges (page 32).

- *Dagon, god of the Philistines,* 1 Samuel 5:2-7 (page 33).

- *King Solomon's anointing,* 1 Kings 1:5-7, 41-50 (pages 35–36).

- *King Jeroboam,* 1 Kings 12:20 and elsewhere (page 37).

- *Rehoboam, Shishak,* 1 Kings 14:25-26 (page 37).

- *Omri's dynasty* (page 38).

- *Samaria* (page 38).

- *Amos' prophecies,* book of Amos (page 39).

- *Sargon,* Isaiah 20:1 (pages 39–40).

- *Nebuchadnezzar,* Daniel 2–4 (page 42).

- *Jeremiah's prophecy,* Jeremiah 42:8-12 (pages 42–43).

- *Suza (Sushan) and other details about Nehemiah,* Nehemiah 1–2 (pages 43–44).

Test Yourself

1. What is a *tell?* How are dates in archaeology determined?

2. What is higher criticism of the Bible? Give some examples of higher criticism that were later proven unfounded by using archaeology.

3. What evidence is there that David existed?

4. What is the archaeological evidence that provides a reliable point of reference for the dating of the kings of Israel?

5. What is the Cyrus cylinder? Why is it important?

Chapter 15 Group Study

Homework Preparation (do prior to group)
 Read: chapter 15 of this text and *Can Archaeology Prove the Old Testament?* ✝.

Opening Prayer

Discussion: What does archaeology "prove"? What can it tell us, and what are its limitations? Discuss as a group.

Practical-Experience Game

Debate: The "Christian" is facing the "nonbeliever," who still accepts "higher criticism" of the Bible (still found in some books).

Closing Prayer

Archaeological Evidence of the New Testament

The vast majority of Jesus' time was spent in the region of Galilee. Yet his influence was felt throughout the region. Jesus visited the Gentile areas of Tyre and Sidon (Matthew 15:21), the Transjordan area (the area east of the Jordan, also heavily Gentile), Samaria (John 4:5), and a few selected cities near Jerusalem in Judea.

Also, many people, including religious leaders, came to see him. We know that "many people came to him from Judea, Jerusalem, Idumea, and the regions across the Jordan and around Tyre and Sidon" (Mark 3:8). This was an extensive travel commitment in ancient times. The trip from Jerusalem to Nazareth took about four to five days. Travel from areas further south (for example, Idumea) took several days longer. And there was no schedule—no guarantee Jesus would be in town when people arrived. All this shows that Jesus made an enormous impact on the region.

Sites of Jesus' Life and Ministry

All of the following New Testament sites have been located using archaeology.

Bethany—site where Jesus apparently lived during his last week of ministry (Matthew 21:17). Jesus was anointed there (26:6).

Bethlehem—birthplace of Jesus (Matthew 2:1). Magi visited Jesus there (2:9). Herod slaughtered children (2:16).

Bethphage—site where Jesus sent disciples to retrieve a donkey for his final entrance into Jerusalem (Mark 11:1).

Bethsaida—village in which Jesus healed a blind man (Mark 8:22). Site where Jesus fed 5000 (Luke 9:10).

Caesarea (Maritima)—important port. Site of conversion of centurion by Peter (Acts 10:1) and Paul's trial (Acts 23:33).

Caesarea Philippi—city where Peter first proclaimed Jesus as the Messiah, the son of the living God (Matthew 16:16).

Cana—city where Jesus performed his first miracle—turning water into wine (John 2:1).

Capernaum—headquarters of Jesus' ministry (Matthew 4:13). Many miracles performed. The home of Peter is located there.

Emmaus—an early appearance of Jesus after the resurrection occurred on the road to this town (Luke 24:13).

Gadara—demon-possessed man came from the region bearing this city's name (Luke 8:26).

Gennesaret—Jesus arrived here after calming the seas. People brought sick people to be healed by him (Matthew 14:35).

Gergesa—actual site on Sea of Galilee where the demon-possessed pigs ran down a steep bank into the sea (Matthew 8:28).

Jericho—just outside of this city, Jesus healed blind Bartimaeus (Mark 10:46).

Jerusalem—most important Jewish city. Site of temple. Jesus was crucified, buried, and resurrected there.

Magdala—fishing village on the Sea of Galilee. Believed to be the home of Mary Magdalene.

Nain—site where Jesus raised a widow's son from the dead (Luke 7:11).

Nazareth—important trade crossroads. Home of Jesus during his youth. Site of limited number of miracles (Mark 6:5).

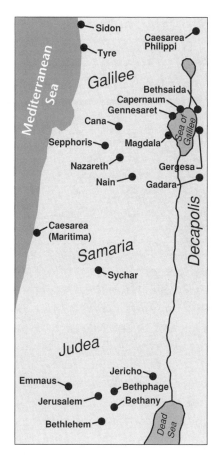

Sepphoris—capital city of Herod Antipas, very close to Nazareth. It's possible Jesus worked there as a carpenter.

Sidon—important Mediterranean port city. Jesus visited to minister to Gentiles (Matthew 15:21).

Sychar—city in Samaria where Jesus met the woman at the well, promising her "living water" (John 4:5).

Tyre—important Mediterranean port city. Jesus visited to minister to Gentiles (Matthew 15:21).

Historical Tradition

It's common to venerate important sites of history. For instance, Americans revere historical sites such as Independence Hall, Mount Vernon, and Lincoln's birthplace. If a catastrophe destroyed any of these structures, no doubt the sites would continue to be well-known.

> Most of the sites of Jesus' ministry mentioned in the New Testament have been discovered.

Likewise, the sites of New Testament archaeology were well known in their own time. First, nonbiblical historical documents *reveal a clear lineage of relatives of Christ extending into the third century.*[1] Relatives would know the sites of the birth and death of Jesus and of the important events of his life. Second, the followers of Jesus had an amazing passion for the truth of the gospel—a truth worthy of dying for. So it's not surprising that in spite of persecution many sites of the Gospel accounts were recorded in early church tradition. These traditions about sites are not always accurate, but when they are substantiated by early historians, their reliability is strengthened. Ironically, even the attempts to end reverence of those sites by erecting pagan memorials on them only served to mark the sites until the Roman Empire's acceptance of Christianity in the fourth century, after which the sites could be openly recognized.

Historical Tradition Versus Legend

How do we separate the legend of George Washington throwing a silver dollar across the Potomac River from the tradition that Washington's home was at Mount Vernon? We can test the evidence by the following criteria:

1. Is there *early* evidence of *belief* in the place or event as historical fact?

2. Is the early evidence from a *reliable source?*

3. Is there early evidence that the place or event was *widely accepted* as fact?

Valid historical traditions can pass these tests, while legends can't. The reason is that *legends take time to develop into belief.* Obviously if a ridiculous statement is made (for example, that Elvis Presley rose from the dead), the contemporary audience will reject it as nonsense. Little documentation, if any, would survive, and there would be virtually no contemporary followers of the belief. *The opposite happened with the biblical events.* There was a *vast explosion* of belief *in spite of persecution* and the attempts to eradicate those beliefs about the events surrounding Jesus. In the case of the ridiculous, only time can allow it to seem plausible. It took centuries for people to deify Buddha or Confucius (which, by the way, ran counter to their own teachings). As another instance, some people now deify Mary, Jesus' mother—many centuries after the fact. However, the sites and events surrounding *Jesus himself* were quickly believed and recorded *by contemporaries.*

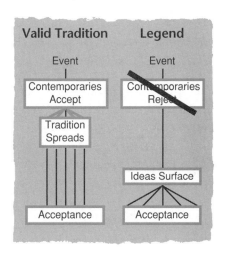

Jesus' Relatives Were in Nazareth

Nonbiblical sources reveal that relatives of Jesus resided in the area of Nazareth at least until the third century (and perhaps much longer). Julius Africanus (about 200) writes of relatives of the Lord who came from both Nazareth and nearby Cochaba and who kept "records of their descent with great care."

> Historical tradition is far from perfectly reliable as history. However, it is also far from worthless—unlike legends. Tradition is often based on a reliable, unbroken chain of communication, and many times can be supported by early archaeology.

Eusebius (about 300) writes of two grandsons of Jude, half-brother of Jesus, who were brought before the emperor Domitian in the fifteenth year of his reign (the year 95) and were freed when they admitted to being from the house of David. They then started several churches in the area "because they were relatives of the Lord." Eusebius also mentions Symeon, son of Clopas (who was thought to be Joseph's brother), who succeeded James as church leader and was martyred at the age of 120.[2]

Jesus' Brothers, Sisters, and Relatives

The Bible clearly distinguishes between Jesus' "blood" brothers and sisters (actually half-brothers and half-sisters) and his disciples (Matthew 12:46-50). Archaeology reveals that the early church of Rome (later to evolve into the Roman Catholic Church) acknowledged Jesus' relatives, including his brothers James and Jude, the grandsons of James and Jude, his cousin Symeon, and other descendant relatives such as Conon. *Early documents, mosaics, inscriptions, and monuments all attest to this.* The existence of Jesus' relatives was also confirmed by eyewitnesses and non-Christian historians.

Stones May Not Talk—but People Do!

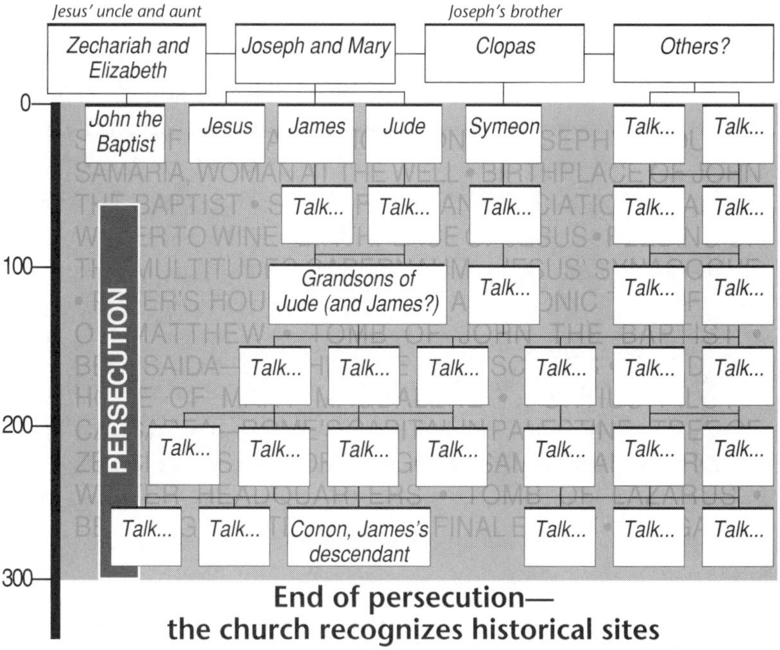

Jesus' uncle and aunt				Joseph's brother		
Zechariah and Elizabeth	Joseph and Mary		Clopas		Others?	

John the Baptist	Jesus	James	Jude	Symeon	Talk...	Talk...
		Talk...	Talk...	Talk...	Talk...	Talk...
		Grandsons of Jude (and James?)		Talk...	Talk...	Talk...
	Talk...	Talk...	Talk...	Talk...	Talk...	Talk...
Talk...	Talk...	Talk...	Talk...	Talk...	Talk...	Talk...
Talk...	Talk...	Conon, James's descendant		Talk...	Talk...	Talk...

(left axis: 0, 100, 200, 300 — vertical label: PERSECUTION)

End of persecution—
the church recognizes historical sites
—

Centuries later, the evolved Roman Catholic Church denied the same people it had earlier memorialized, after redefining Mary as a perpetual virgin. Therefore the concept that Mary was a perpetual virgin does not fit the criteria for tradition (it would have had to have been conceived of, and supported, very early).

___Key Concept___

Roman Catholic theology now proclaims "perpetual virginity" of Mary. This doctrine was conceived in the 1500s. Protestants and most scholars believe that Jesus had natural brothers and sisters (Matthew 12:46-50).

New Testament Archaeological Examples

The birthplace of Jesus. The Church of the Nativity in Bethlehem marks the traditional spot of the birth of Jesus. The construction of the original church was ordered by Constantine's mother, Helena. (Constantine was the emperor who ended the persecution of Christians and made Christianity the official church of the Roman Empire). As with many Christian sites, attempts were made to stop the worship of Jesus by destroying this site; but an indication of restored worship—a church—always seemed to reappear. Excavation at the site of the Church of the Nativity reveals evidence of earlier churches, including columns and capitals actually dating to the time of Constantine. Early writers indicated that Jesus was born in a cave, which was a common site for a stable during that time. The exact location of the cave of Jesus' birth is thought to be under an altar that marks the spot in the present day Church of the Nativity.

The Church of the Nativity.

Capernaum: Jesus' synagogue. The Capernaum synagogue in which Jesus preached has been located underneath the ruins of later synagogues. The lower-level floors that were excavated contained early pottery and a coin dated to about 146 to 116 B.C. (the reign of Ptolemy VIII of Egypt), indicating the synagogue's likely presence during Jesus' time. (See *Can Archaeology Prove the New Testament?* page 32.)

Synagogue in Capernaum.

Capernaum: Peter's house. A dwelling in Capernaum has been revered for centuries as the house of Peter. The style of architecture precisely matches the type of home mentioned in the Bible, from which the roof was partially removed to let down a paralytic (Mark 2:4). In addition, the house is located close to the shore of the Sea of Galilee and even contains fishhooks on the floor. It was obviously the house of a fisherman. Most important is the evidence that supports the long-standing

Early churches were often established on traditional sites within 300 years of Jesus. Although the original churches were destroyed by successive invaders, they were usually rebuilt. Archaeology frequently uncovers a history of churches on sites.

tradition of the house being Peter's. Aetheria, a pilgrim in the area from 381 to 384, wrote about the existence of the house of the first of the apostles, "where the paralytic was healed."

> The existence of the "house church" in what is believed to be the home of the apostle Peter is good evidence that it was believed by second-century Christians to be authentic.

In addition, there is evidence that the site was venerated by many people from early in the Christian era. A substantial amount of early graffiti dating back to the second century has been found (124 fragments in Greek, 15 in Hebrew, and 18 in Syriac). The graffiti speak of the apostle Peter, of Jesus, and of requests for Jesus' help. The house of Peter was converted early into a place of worship and was significantly changed at least three times. The earliest evidence of its use as a place of worship dates back to the first century, a time contemporary with Peter. (See *Can Archaeology Prove...*, page 33.)

The apostle Peter's house in Capernaum.

A fishing boat used on the Sea of Galilee. A fishing boat used in the time of Christ was discovered near Bethsaida. It was 26 ½ feet long, 7 ½ feet wide, and 4 ½ feet high. This was the type of boat that was probably used to cross the Sea of Galilee, including the time Jesus calmed the storm (Matthew 8:23-27) and the time he walked on water (Matthew 14:22-33). (See *Can Archaeology Prove...*, page 35.)

First-century fishing boat.

Caesarea: evidence of Pontius Pilate found. During the excavation of the Roman theater at Caesarea, a stone was found in the landing of a flight of steps. It bears the inscription "To the people of Caesarea Tiberium Pontius Pilate Prefect of Judea." Another line seems to indicate the word meaning "dedication." It is likely that the stone was originally placed on an outside wall to commemorate the theater's construction.

Pontius Pilate Stone.

Fascinating Facts

William Albright (1891–1971). Once a director of the School of Oriental Research at Johns Hopkins University, William Albright wrote more than 800 books and articles, mostly on the validity of biblical manuscripts. He is best known for his work in confirming the authenticity of the Old Testament, and especially the authentication of the Dead Sea scrolls.

Albright also researched and confirmed the dating of the writings of the New Testament. His conclusion was that there was "no longer any solid basis for dating any book of the New Testament after about A.D. 80." Early in his professional life, Albright had some doubts about the validity of biblical claims about Jesus. These, however, were answered conclusively in favor of the authenticity of the Bible as he conducted his research.

Bethany: the tomb of Lazarus. One of the most significant events of Jesus' ministry was his raising of Lazarus from the dead (John 11). Not surprisingly, the location of this event has been venerated since early times. Several early writers record the existence of the crypt of Lazarus, and archaeologists believe they have discovered it. Several things lead many archaeologists to believe it is authentic. First, the identification of the village and the general site is accepted. Second, the artifacts found are consistent with the period. Third, there is substantial evidence that contemporaries to the event believed this to be the actual site of the tomb. The evidence includes early graffiti written by Christians. The graffiti refer to Lazarus being raised from the dead there and request similar mercy for the writers themselves. (See *Can Archaeology Prove...*, page 38.)

The "Tomb of Lazarus."

The Temple in Jerusalem. The most important place by far to Jews from the time of Solomon was the Temple. The original Temple, built by Solomon in about 974 B.C., was destroyed at the time of the exile to Babylon and then was later rebuilt. King Herod the Great significantly expanded the size of the Temple during his reign. Referred to by some people as the "third Temple," it was destroyed in A.D. 70.

Jesus spent a significant amount of time at the Temple. He was brought there to be circumcised and was blessed by prophets (Luke 2:21-38). He returned as a child for Passover celebrations (Luke 2:41). And during his ministry, Jesus certainly worshiped there and twice drove out the money-changers from the its outer court. (See *Can Archaeology Prove...*, page 39.)

The Western (Wailing) Wall of the Temple.

Gethsemane. The Gethsemane Church of All Nations marks the site revered for centuries as the place where Jesus went before being betrayed. In the center of the eastern nave is a rock, identified as the very rock on which Jesus prayed (Matthew 26:36). It is built on the foundation of an earlier Byzantine church. Eusebius identified the site in 330.

The Garden of Gethsemane.

The trials of Jesus: Caiaphas and Pilate—Jesus went through a series of trials centering around the house of Caiaphas, the high priest (John 18:24), and the palace of

The proposed site of Jesus' scourging.

Pilate. Although sites for both have been suggested, neither has been confirmed yet. However, first-century stone steps leading from the place of the Last Supper to Gethsemane, and from Gethsemane to the general location of the house of the high priest, have been excavated. These steps are almost certainly authentic.

The site of Jesus' death and resurrection. The Church of the Holy Sepulcher marks the site most archaeologists agree is the place of Jesus' crucifixion and resurrection. Such a site would certainly be remembered by early Christians. So important was the site that the emperor Hadrian placed a statue of the pagan god Venus on the site of Golgotha (where Jesus was crucified) and a similar statue of Jupiter on the tomb of the resurrection, hoping that Christians would forget their holy sites. Instead it helped them mark and remember the locations. (This same approach was tried by Hadrian in Bethlehem.)

Later, when Constantine ended persecution by making Christianity the state religion of Rome, his mother Helena helped erect a church over the two sites. A large gathering of bishops was held in Jerusalem to consecrate the church in the year 335. Eusebius was present and wrote about its significance. Later, in 348, Cyril of Jerusalem gave a famous series of lectures in the church, repeatedly mentioning the historical significance of the site. It was recorded that even wood from the three crosses and the

> Many scholars consider the sites of the crucifixion and resurrection as two of the most reliable sites for Jesus. Constantine's mother, Helena, marked the sites in about 326 based on tradition. And the marking of the sites by Hadrian—who had tried to hide them with pagan statues—lends credibility to the tradition.

sign in three languages above Jesus' head were in existence in the church at that time. Cyril also gave a vivid description of the tomb in which Jesus lay, before Constantine's workmen started construction of elaborate buildings to honor the site. (Cyril had been born early enough to see the site both before and after the church was built.)

> Never be too quick to accept "sensational major archaeological finds" as genuine. However, always be receptive to learning more about them as scholars analyze them to confirm more evidence about the past.

Several other early writers also mentioned the church, Golgotha, and the tomb. Although the church suffered the destruction common to most Christian landmarks, it was repeatedly rebuilt and stands today as a silent reminder of the most important event in history.

The site of the crucifixion in the Church of the Holy Sepulcher.

The ossuary of Caiaphas (Matthew 26:3-4,63-66). In November 1990, construction workers in a section south of Jerusalem's Old City broke through a burial cave that had been sealed since Rome had destroyed the city in A.D. 70. Inside they found an ornately decorated ossuary—a box that contained the bones of a deceased person. But this ossuary was no ordinary find. Etched on the side, in ancient Aramaic, was the name "Caiaphas." That inscription, along with other inscriptions of family members in the tomb, made it clear that this was the actual ossuary of Caiaphas, the high priest who first sought to kill Jesus.

Christian ossuaries in Jerusalem. The discovery of two ossuaries outside of Jerusalem in 1945 by Eleazar L. Sukenik provided interesting insights about first-century Christians. The ossuaries were marked with graffiti and four crosses. The words *Iesous iou* were found, which essentially meant "Jesus, help." Also found were the words *Iesous aloth*, which essentially meant "Jesus, let him arise."

Experts date the ossuaries to about A.D. 50, which would have been within 20 years of Jesus' death and resurrection. It is even conceivable that they were eyewitnesses to the resurrection.

Ossuaries in Jerusalem said to be those of Mary, Martha, and Lazarus.

Fascinating Facts

Sir William Ramsay (1852–1916). Sir William Ramsay was, arguably, the greatest archaeologist of his day. He had rejected much of the written New Testament account and was determined to prove it false based on other writings of the day that contradicted the Bible. Ramsay believed that the books of Luke and Acts were actually written in about A.D.150 and therefore did not bear the authenticity that a first-century document would. His archaeological journeys took him to 32 countries, 44 cities, and 9 islands.[3] Throughout some 15 years of intensive study, he concluded that "Luke is a historian of the first rank—this author should be placed along with the very greatest of historians."

What Critics Thought—What Ramsay Discovered:

- There was no Roman census (as indicated in Luke 2:1).
  There was a Roman census every 14 years, beginning with Emperor Augustus.

- Quirinius was not governor of Syria at the time of Jesus' birth (as indicated in Luke 2:2).
  Quirinius was governor of Syria in about 7 B.C.

- People did not have to return to their ancestral home (as indicated in Luke 2:3).
  People did have to return to their home city—verified by an ancient Egyptian papyrus giving directions for conducting a census.

- The existence of the treasurer of the city of Corinth, Erastus (Romans 16:23), was incorrect.
  A city pavement in Corinth bearing the inscription "Erastus, curator of public buildings, laid this pavement at his own expense."

- Luke's reference to Gallio as proconsul of Achaia was wrong (Acts 18:12).
  The Delphi inscription that reads, "As Lucius Junius Gallio, my friend and proconsul of Achaia."

Time and time again Ramsay's search to find evidence that Luke's writing was in error turned up evidence that it was, in fact, accurate. As a result, Sir William Ramsay eventually converted to Christianity and proclaimed Luke as "one of the greatest historians" of all time.

Summary of More New Testament Archaeology Examples

For further study and reference, here are some additional Bible events and people whose occurrence or existence is supported by archaeology. (Unless otherwise noted, all page numbers refer to *Can Archaeology Prove the New Testament?*)

- *The site of the annunciation of Jesus' birth,* Luke 1:26-28 (page 28).

- *The second site of annunciation,* Luke 1:29-38 (page 28).

- *The birthplace of John the Baptist,* Luke 1:65 (page 29).

- *Joseph's house,* Matthew 13:55; Mark 6:3; Luke 4:16 (page 30).

- *The site of the baptism of Jesus* (page 31).

- *Cana: Jesus changes water into wine,* John 2:1-11 (page 31).

- *Samaria: the woman at the well,* John 4:1-41 (pages 31–32).

- *The feeding of the multitudes with five loaves and two fish,* Mark 6:32-44 (page 33).

- *The tax office of Matthew,* Matthew 9:9 (page 33).

- *The healing of the demoniac: demons cast into pigs,* Matthew 8:28-34 (page 34).

- *The tomb of John the Baptist,* Matthew 14:12 (page 34).

- *Caesarea: the praetorium where Paul was guarded,* Acts 23:35 (page 36).

- *Bethphage: Jesus begins the final entry,* Matthew 21:1-2 (page 38).

- *The Mount of Olives: Jesus reveals end-time events,* Matthew 24:3 (page 39).

- *The Mount of Olives: Jesus weeps over the city,* Luke 19:41-44 (page 39).

- *The Last Supper* (page 40).

- *The ascension of Jesus,* Luke 24:50-53; Acts 1:9 (page 41).

- *Deception by Sapphira,* Acts 5:1 (page 42).

- *The Synagogue of the Freedmen,* Acts 6:9 (page 42).

- *The Ethiopian eunuch,* Acts 8:26-40 (page 42).

- *Confirmation of the existence of Sergius Paulus,* Acts 13:6-12 (page 42).

- *John Mark's sudden return to Jerusalem,* Acts 13:13; 15:38-39 (page 43).

- *Correction of information about Iconium, Lystra, and Derbe,* Acts 14:6 (page 44).

- *Confirmation of the "district" of Macedonia,* Acts 16:12 (page 44).

- *Confirmation of the word "rulers,"* Acts 17:6,8 (page 44).

- *Inscription naming Erastus,* Romans 16:23 (page 45).

- *The controversial ossuary of James (Evidence for Jesus,* page 144).

Test Yourself

1. What is the difference between tradition and legend? Are traditions valuable?

2. What evidence is there that the site of Jesus' birth is authentic?

3. Where are the sites of the crucifixion and the resurrection? Why might we believe them to be valid?

4. What do we know about relatives of Jesus after his crucifixion? How does that relate to the information we have concerning him?

5. Name some archaeological finds about other key New Testament characters, such as Pilate, Caiaphas, and others.

Chapter 16 Group Study

Homework Preparation (do prior to group)
Read: chapter 16 of this text and *Can Archaeology Prove the New Testament?* ✝.

Opening Prayer
Discussion: Read the biblical passages relating to the discoveries made by Sir William Ramsey (see page 274). Discuss the discoveries and how they changed Ramsey's life. How can this information be used to help others trust the Bible's claims?

Practical-Experience Game

TV interview: A "TV host" is interviewing a "Christian" for recommendations of possible New Testament sites to visit. Be prepared to discuss where to go and why.

Closing Prayer

Part 2

Evidence of the Reliability of the Bible: Summary and Conclusion

There is virtually no reasonable basis for questioning the validity of the biblical manuscripts. As indicated, the foundation for the writings—starting with the importance of the theocracy and the scriptural copying care provided by the scribes—provides a solid basis for accurate manuscripts for the Old Testament manuscripts to begin with. Evidence provided by the Dead Sea scrolls and the Septuagint corroborate our expectations of virtual perfection in accuracy.

Furthermore, we find incredible scientific accuracy of information foretold in the Bible, but not discovered by science until centuries later. This adds to the evidence that the Bible was divinely inspired, in much the same way that the imbedded 100-percent perfect prophecy (see part 3) proves the divine inspiration of the Bible.

Confirmation by Jesus of the Old Testament and his pre-confirmation of the New Testament is additional strong support that the Bible is reliable.

The existence of thousands of consistent ancient copies of the New Testament, some written shortly after the time of Jesus, provides an enormous base of evidence that the historical record of Jesus and the early Christian church was widely circulated and believed by early Christians. Hence, there would have been adequate opportunity for errors to be challenged. And if the account were not accurate, it would not have survived.

There are a number of specific ancient manuscripts that confirm the biblical account. Not only are there virtually complete examples of the Bible itself, but there are extra-biblical sources, some even written by non-Christians and enemies of the church, which provide evidence of accurate historicity.

Even writings and quotes from early church fathers extensively support the 100-percent accuracy of the Bible—so much so that the entire New Testament is believed to be contained in these nonbiblical writings.

Finally, the entire Bible was canonized in three stages: the Torah, the Tanakh, and the New Testament. In each case, they were popularly accepted rather quickly after being written as Holy Scripture and confirmed officially at least 200 years later.

The Bible is a book defining man's relationship with God. However, it is based on history. And the foundation of Christianity is based on history—the facts of the crucifixion and resurrection of Jesus Christ. Therefore the reliability of the historical account of the Bible is vital to Christianity. As can be seen, the available evidence supporting the Bible far surpasses any other book of history whatsoever.

Part 3

Evidence of God, the Bible, and Jesus in Prophecy

A Verse to Memorize

I am God, and there is no other; I am God, and there is none like me. I make known the end from the beginning, from ancient times, what is still to come (Isaiah 46:9-10).

The most important questions any human being can ever ask are

1. Is God real? How do we know?

2. If God is real, how do we know what to trust regarding his message to us? In other words, what religions, books, and people are truly from God?

3. Is the Bible inspired by God?

4. Is Jesus God?

The reason these questions are so vital are that they deal with our position in eternity (not to mention a better life on Earth) if, in fact, God is real and the Bible and Jesus are what they claim to be. Making an informed decision about God, the Bible, and Jesus certainly should have precedence over any other human activity—over a person's golf game, vacation, or even job and family. (Unfortunately, in some cases, even forsaking one's family is necessary to know the true God.)

The Bible does not mince words in stating its claim and the eternal importance of a decision to accept or reject Jesus (note about the verse below—the fuller meaning of the word "believes" is to intellectually believe and accept—in this case the sacrifice of Jesus):

A Verse to Memorize

Whoever believes in the Son has eternal life, but whoever rejects the Son will not see life, for God's wrath remains on him (John 3:36).

This makes the alternatives in eternity very clear. Either 1) believe and accept Jesus in order to claim eternal life; or 2) reject Jesus and not see life—instead facing the wrath of God. The Bible further gives an indication of the wonderful nature of eternal life (with God) versus the alternative of eternity away from God (no 'life').

The Kingdom of Heaven for the Believer

The kingdom of heaven is like treasure hidden in a field. When a man found it, he hid it again, and then in his joy went and sold all he had and bought that field (Matthew 13:44).

Again, the kingdom of heaven is like a merchant looking for fine pearls. When he found one of great value, he went away and sold everything he had and bought it (Matthew 13:45-46).

Now the dwelling of God is with men, and he will live with them [believers accepting Jesus—in heaven]. *They will be his people, and God himself will be with them and be their God. He will wipe every tear from their eyes. There will be no more death or mourning or crying or pain, for the old order of things has passed away* (Revelation 21:3-4).

The Fate of the Nonbeliever

The devil, who deceived them, was thrown into the lake of burning sulfur, where the beast and the false prophet had been thrown. They will be tormented day and night for ever and ever (Revelation 20:10).

If anyone's name was not found written in the book of life [those receiving life through acceptance of Jesus], *he was thrown into the lake of fire* [where Satan, the beast, and the false prophet were thrown—see above verse] (Revelation 20:15).

This is how it will be at the end of the age. The angels will come and separate the wicked from the righteous and throw them into the fiery furnace,

where there will be weeping and gnashing of teeth
(Matthew 13:49-50).

Given the Bible's very clear description of the consequences for either accepting or rejecting Jesus Christ, one
would be foolish not to very carefully consider this decision.
It would be like knowing with absolute certainty that a tornado was going to hit your house (like approaching death)
and not preparing for it.

So the key issues are the questions posed at the outset of
this section. If God, Jesus, and the Bible are *not* valid, then
the decision to heed the words of the Bible and follow Jesus
are moot. However, if they *are* valid, then ignoring Jesus
would be the most costly decision one could make. So how
can we test to see if God, Jesus, and the Bible are real?

Prophecy:
The Test of God

Some people wrongly believe having faith in God means simply accepting him without putting the religions, people, holy books—and especially the Bible—to the test. Sometimes they will even quote the Bible to justify this position:

> *Without faith it is impossible to please God* (Hebrews 11:6).

Unfortunately, reading this portion of this verse by itself can lead people into accepting a God that is not the true God. Sometimes it is an ecumenical god that people believe in—an all-pervasive god that is somehow part of all religious thought. These people sometimes say things like "My god works for me." However, if the "god" they follow is not the one true God, it could be deadly. And the Bible doesn't want people to have such "blind faith." Continuing with the verse we can analyze its totality:

A Verse to Memorize

And without faith it is impossible to please God, because anyone who comes to him must believe that he exists and that he rewards those who earnestly seek him (Hebrew 11:6).

Notice that the end of the verse clearly states a process: 1) To earnestly *seek* God, 2) at which time we will be *rewarded,* 3) with a rational *belief* in God that leads us to 4) well-founded *faith* in something unseen.

In addition, the Bible commands us to test everything. And upon reading its admonition, we should notice that it doesn't exclude itself. In other words we should test everything—including the Bible:

A Verse to Memorize

Test everything. Hold on to the good (1 Thessalonians 5:21).

What test would the God of the universe require to determine if something would be from him? Certainly it would be a test that no person, or thing (including Satan), could accomplish except God. Certainly it would be something that human beings could understand.

One-hundred-percent perfect prophecy is such a test. As the verse introducing this part indicated (Isaiah 46:9-10), God is unique ("there is no other") in his ability to know the "end from the beginning."

We also find prophecy commanded in the Law of Moses when the Jews were asking not to be forced to "hear" or see the glory of God—instead prophets would be provided (Deuteronomy 18:15-16).

The seriousness of prophecy was further indicated in Deuteronomy when false prophets (one single mistake) were ordered to be put to death:

> *If anyone does not listen to my words that the prophet speaks in my name, I myself will call him to account. But a prophet who presumes to speak in my name anything I have not commanded him to say, or a prophet who speaks in the name of other gods, must be put to death.*
>
> *You may say to yourselves, "How can we know when a message has not been spoken by the* LORD?*" If what a prophet proclaims in the name of the* LORD *does not take place or come true, that is a message the* LORD *has not spoken. That prophet has spoken presumptuously. Do not be afraid of him* (Deuteronomy 18:19-22).

Moreover, the Bible frequently uses prophecy as a test, as in the case where the prophet Elijah courageously prophesied that God would produce sacrifice-consuming fire—a test against 450 prophets of the pagan god Baal provided by the hated "prophet-murderers" Jezebel and Ahab.

> *Elijah said to them, "I am the only one of the* LORD's *prophets left, but Baal has four hundred and fifty prophets. Get two bulls for us. Let them choose one for themselves, and let them cut it into pieces and put it on the wood but not set fire to it. I will prepare the other bull and put it on the wood but not set fire to it. Then you call on the*

*name of your god, and I will call on the name of
the LORD. The god who answers by fire—he is
God."*

*Then all the people said, "What you say is
good"* (1 Kings 18:22-25).

After hours of praying, the 450 prophets of Baal produced no fire. Then Elijah, confident of his prophecy,
directed his altar to be soaked three times with water. The
Bible records the results of his prophecy:

*At the time of sacrifice, the prophet Elijah stepped
forward and prayed: "O LORD, God of Abraham,
Isaac and Israel, let it be known today that you
are God in Israel and that I am your servant and
have done all these things at your command.
Answer me, O LORD, answer me, so these people
will know that you, O LORD, are God, and that
you are turning their hearts back again."*

*Then the fire of the LORD fell and burned up
the sacrifice, the wood, the stones and the soil, and
also licked up the water in the trench.*

*When all the people saw this, they fell prostrate
and cried, "The LORD—he is God! The LORD—he
is God!"* (1 Kings 18:36-39).

The prophet Isaiah indicates another example using
prophecy as a test:

*Present your case," says the LORD.
"Set forth your arguments," says Jacob's King.
"Bring in [your idols] to tell us
what is going to happen.
Tell us what the former things were,
so that we may consider them*

and know their final outcome.
Or declare to us the things to come,
tell us what the future holds,
so we may know that you are gods.

—Isaiah 41:21-23

Indicative of the importance placed on prophecy in determining if something was from God, even when Jesus was being mocked, prophecy was demanded:

> *They spit in his face and struck him with their fists.*
> *Others slapped him and said, "Prophesy to us,*
> *Christ. Who hit you?"* (Matthew 26:67-68).

Types of Prophecy

The three primary types of prophecy are short-term prophecy, long-term prophecy, and end-times prophecy. Each of these forms serves a vital role in helping us understand God, Jesus, and the Bible and our eventual relationship with God.

Short-Term Prophecy

Short-term prophecy is prophecy that was recorded in the Bible and fulfilled a very short time thereafter. Generally, the prophecy was recorded in the same book it was fulfilled. These prophecies were very important to the Jews because they were one of the primary means by which prophets were validated. In other words, if significant short-term prophecy was consistently made and fulfilled, it would confirm that a prophet was truly speaking from God. However, one single mistake would not only discredit the "prophet," it would also be grounds for immediate execution.

Take, for example, the short-term prophecies by Nathan of the consequences to King David after his sin of adultery with Bathsheba (and the murder of Uriah).

> *Nathan said to David, "You are the man! This is what the LORD, the God of Israel, says: 'I anointed you king over Israel, and I delivered you from the hand of Saul. I gave your master's house to you, and your master's wives into your arms. I gave you the house of Israel and Judah. And if all this had been too little, I would have given you even more. Why did you despise the word of the LORD by doing what is evil in his eyes? You struck down Uriah the Hittite with the sword and took his wife to be your own. You killed him with the sword of the Ammonites. Now, therefore, the sword will never depart from your house, because you despised me and took the wife of Uriah the Hittite to be your own.'*
>
> *"This is what the LORD says: 'Out of your own household I am going to bring calamity upon you. Before your very eyes I will take your wives and give them to one who is close to you, and he will lie with your wives in broad daylight. You did it in secret, but I will do this thing in broad daylight before all Israel.'"*
>
> *Then David said to Nathan, "I have sinned against the LORD."*
>
> *Nathan replied, "The LORD has taken away your sin. You are not going to die. But because by doing this you have made the enemies of the LORD show utter contempt, the son born to you will die"* (2 Samuel 12:7-14).

This passage from the Bible contains four major prophecies: 1) that David's child would be a son, 2) that the child would die, 3) that the "sword would not depart from David's house," implying continuing family strife, and 4) that someone close to David would "lie with [David's] wives ...in broad daylight before all Israel."

Later in the same book (2 Samuel), we find fulfillment of all of these prophecies. Bathsheba gave birth to a son that died. David's son Absalom obtained an army and fought David for the throne, and eventually, Absalom "lay with David's concubines (wives)" on the roof of the palace—in "view of Israel" (2 Samuel 16:22).

We can see that these four very specific prophecies would provide strong credibility to Nathan as a prophet. It would lead to the inclusion of this story in holy Scripture in spite of its embarrassment to King David.

Although short-term prophecies were extremely important to the Jews at the time, they are of limited importance to us (particularly skeptics) today, since one might suggest that ancient authors could have had mixed motives that might cause them to incorrectly claim prophecies after the fact.

Long-Term Prophecy

Other prophecies in the Bible were made at one point in time and in one book of the Bible, and are fulfilled at a later time or are recorded in a different book of the Bible by a different author, or both. These prophecies provide greater assurance for today's skeptics of the miracle of God's inspiration of prophecy—especially when the prophecies and fulfillment can be supported by objective history and archaeology. Several selected long-term prophecies are reviewed below in this part, with many others listed in appendix C.

End-Time Prophecy

The final primary category of prophecy in the Bible is prophecy relating to the end times—to things beyond this world, including life after death, heaven, and hell. The importance of such prophecy is obvious—it provides indication of what is to eventually come—whether after death, or at the end of time.

The problem with end-time prophecy is that it can't be proven until the end of time... when it's too late to react to the prophecy. But confidence gained from perfect short-term and long-term prophecy should lead us to have confidence in end-times prophecy.

> The three types of prophecies work together. Short-term prophecies helped people acknowledge the true prophets of God, so they could include only their writings in holy Scripture. Long-term prophecies provide today's skeptic proof that the Bible is inspired by God, and that Jesus is who he claimed to be—God incarnate. And 100-percent perfect short- and long-term prophecies provide confidence that end-time prophecies will be accurate as well.

Test Yourself

1. Recite the verse that sets God apart from all other things, stating that he alone knows the "end from the beginning."

2. What is the verse that defines the consequences of life with and without Jesus?

3. Describe heaven. Describe hell.

4. Define short, long, and end-time prophecy. What is the role of each?

5. What does the Bible say about prophets who make one mistake? Where does it say this?

Chapter 17 Group Study

Homework Preparation (do prior to group)

Read: Isaiah 46:9-10; Deuteronomy 18:20-22; Hebrews 11:6; John 3:36; 1 Thessalonians 5:21; chapter 17 of this text; and pages 4–7 in *Does the Bible Predict the Future?* ✝.

Opening Prayer

Discussion: Read the biblical passages above that relate to prophecy. Discuss how important it is that God provides us an absolutely "foolproof" method of testing that something is from him. Discuss the role of short-term, long-term, and end-time prophecy.

Practical-Experience Game

Role-playing: The "Christian" must attempt to set the stage for future prophecy discussion by reviewing the need for a foolproof test of something "being from God." The seriousness of the subject, and the consequences, should be conveyed.

Closing Prayer

Why Prophecy Is a
Reliable Test

The Bible tells us that God is unique and that only he knows the end from the beginning (Isaiah 46:9-10). This establishes prophecy as a test of something being "from God." Logically, we know that humans can't prophesy without God, otherwise certain people would consistently win at gambling. Likewise, we can rest assured that Satan can't predict the future, otherwise he would use prophecy to lead people away from God—such as giving certain people the knowledge of how to consistently win fame or fortune. (Note that this does not preclude Satan from giving certain people knowledge of *historical* events—such as "psychics" who appear to have knowledge of locations of previously murdered victims.) Prophecy, or predicting the future, is a particularly good test of something being from God because human beings are familiar with it and are capable of understanding the point at which prophecy is beyond human reason and is obviously from God.

Consider the fact that every minute of every day people are attempting to predict the future. Not only does this involve gambling in casinos and on the stock market, people are attempting to predict the future of their relationships, their health, their finances, and other things. While people may not be particularly good at predicting the future, especially if it involves a *highly specific* prediction, they nevertheless *understand* what future prophecy involves. What they usually don't understand is the extent to which probability plays a part of our everyday lives. Nor do most people understand completely the dramatic mathematical odds associated with many prophecies (otherwise fewer people would play the lottery).

Prophecy Can Be "Hard Evidence" of God, Jesus, and the Bible

Hard evidence inevitably involves mathematics that either defines a truth by definition (often as an equation) or as a highly probable statistical event. Prophecy can provide hard evidence of God, Jesus, and the Bible because it can be evaluated using "absurdly conservative" assumptions and still prove (statistically) the supernatural inspiration of the Bible. More on that later, but first let's outline how prophecy in the Bible can most effectively be evaluated by the skeptic.

The value of prophecy in "proving" the existence of God, the deity of Jesus, or the inspiration of God of the Bible, is directly related to 1) the degree of improbability of random occurrence of a specific event(s) prophesied without God; and 2) the number of consecutive correct prophecies made without error.

First, the *specificity* of any prophecy plays a large part in its significance. For instance, proclaiming that someone will meet a "tall, dark, handsome stranger" doesn't say much. One example of such a prophecy was Jeane Dixon's supposed "prediction" about John F. Kennedy's election and assassination.[1] In reality, her prediction in *Parade* magazine in 1956 said that "a Democrat" would win the election and would "die in office." This was far less specific than predicting "John F. Kennedy would be assassinated," as some later retold the "prophecy." Just how amazing was this prediction?

First, the odds of a Democrat winning that presidential election were about 50 percent. Second, the odds of a president dying in office—as of 1960—were about 40 percent. The combined probability of both events happening was 50 percent times 40 percent—20 percent. In other words, there was a 1 in 5 chance that the events would have occurred anyway. So was the prophecy remarkable? No. Yet it catapulted Jeane Dixon into a successful career as a "psychic." But her career also included many mistakes, such as

1. the prediction that World War III would occur in 1954

2. the prediction that Jacqueline Kennedy would never get married again (ironically, this prediction was made the day before she married Aristotle Onassis)

3. the prediction that the Vietnam conflict would end in 1966 (it continued until 1975)

If Jeane Dixon had made those prophecies in God's name in the Israel of biblical times, she would have been stoned to death! On the other hand, if just those four prophecies had all come true without error, it would have been very impressive.

An extremely spectacular prophecy with insurmountable odds can provide prophetic proof of God just by itself (such as the prophecy of Jesus' resurrection). However, a large number of 100-percent-correct prophecies without error can statistically also provide certainty that something is "from God." Often a person or thing (for example, a holy book) claiming to be "from God" combines several prophecies of varying specificity. For example, suppose one prophesied that the next president of the United States would be a Republican female, aged 51, from the state of Rhode Island, with a first name Zora, who married a man named Blake who was born in Woodstown, New Jersey. She was born in the city of Big Bear Lake, California, with a foot-wide birthmark on her back, stands five feet, two inches tall, weighs 111 pounds, has 11 letters in her last name, has a father from Grenada, a mother from Panama, and has blue eyes—and oh, one more thing…the prophecy predicts the *exact fingerprint pattern* of the new president. This is a pretty impressive prophecy. For sake of the example, let's assume the following estimated odds:

Specification	1 Chance in...
Republican	2
Female	50
Age 51	20
From Rhode Island	165
First name Zora	2011
Married Blake	1000
Born in Woodstown	1000
Born in Big Bear Lake	1000
Foot-wide birthmark	100,000
Five feet, two inches tall	15
111 Pounds	10
11 letters in last name	9
Father from Grenada	20,000
Mother from Panama	7000
Blue eyes	2
Correct fingerprints	64,000,000[2]
Total odds	**1 chance in 1.6 x 10^{45}***

---

* 2 x 50 x 20 x 165 x 2011 x 1000 x 1000 x 1000 x 100,000 x 15 x 10 x 9 x 20,000 x 7000 x 2 x 64,000,000.

Certainly this would be an amazing prophecy if made by an individual (with nothing being wrong). As absolutely remote as this incredible prophecy is, for a person (or holy book) it might be just as impressive to simply predict a *large number* of events accurately in a row without error. Let's compare the above prophecy to someone predicting *many correct elections in a row*—simply predicting the winning party. Assume the "prophet" predicted a Republican and he wins. The person was correct, but how significant is it? Not very, since the odds are roughly 50 percent. Now let's assume the "prophet" correctly predicts two such elections in a row. The dual prediction is a bit more interesting. It would be like flipping heads in a row twice, or $\frac{1}{2} \times \frac{1}{2} = \frac{1}{4}$, or 1 chance in 4. Let's continue the example for 150 elections.

The odds of correctly predicting 150 events with a random probability of 50 percent each is easy to calculate mathematically. It is $\frac{1}{2}$ multiplied by itself 150 times. We find the odds of correctly making 150 perfect prophecies (none wrong) with a 50-percent chance of each is 1 chance in 10^{45}, or 1 chance in a billion trillion trillion trillion! We can see that the probability of predicting all 150 "simple-to-prophesy" events is as amazing as prophesying one incredibly unlikely event (such as the election of one very specific person as president). And as demonstrated in part 1 (pages 111–112), the likelihood of flipping 150 heads in a row is beyond reason.

When evaluating biblical prophecy, we will use the above two principles to conservatively determine the proof of the existence of God, whether he inspired the Bible, and the deity of Jesus, the two key principles of prophecy evaluation being

1. specificity of prophecy
2. number of consistently correct prophecies

Probabilistic Prophecy Standards

Human beings have developed standards using statistics to "prove" something is certain. For example, scientists have essentially proven that gravity exists. I doubt anybody will be able to refute this. Many other laws of physics have also been proven, based on tests that indicate the probability of the law is so high (regarding cause and effect) that any other explanation is deemed virtually impossible. Scientists generally regard any event with a probability of less than one chance in 10^{50} as being impossible (without God).

> The specificity and the number of consistently correct prophecies are the two criteria that will be used in analyzing the statistical significance of the Bible.

On the other hand, do we know for *absolute* certainty that these laws are true? No! But as a result of massive experimentation, we know that the odds of denying the laws of physics are absurdly small. Many experiments involving dropping things have determined that gravity exists beyond any doubt. People accept it as fact. Scientists commonly accept statistical experiments as proof. And nobody (at least no sane person) would jump off a cliff trying to prove that the law of gravity is wrong. All laws of physics that we commonly accept today, on which are based everything from the design of airplanes to the safety of our bridges, are founded on statistical proof.

In a sense, everyone's daily actions are also based on statistical, or "probabilistic," proof. Becoming acquainted with such everyday proofs teaches us to avoid doing ridiculous things like jumping in front of speeding trucks (force = mass times acceleration, a Newtonian law of physics); standing in a bathtub and sticking our finger in an electrical socket; or remaining in the path of an advancing tornado. All of these situations carry a very high probability of a disastrous consequence based on proof of the laws of physics. *None* are proven to 100-percent certainty. Yet all key laws of physics are proven to a degree of certainty under 1 chance of nonoccurrence in 10^{50}. That means that there is less than 1 chance in 100,000,000,000,000,000,000,000,000,000,000,000,000, 000,000,000,000 of any of them *not* being right.

In other words, the odds of gravity *not existing* are absurdly small. Gravity is essentially an absolute fact. Yes, a hardcore skeptic might claim that gravity is "still unproven." However again, I have yet to find a skeptic willing to challenge the proof of gravity by jumping off a cliff.

Statistical proof is probably the most common proof we use in the daily course of our lives:

- Every time we enter a freeway we have some probability of suffering a fatal auto accident.

- Every minute we have some probability of being hit by a meteorite.

- Every time we eat we have some probability of choking to death.

- We depend on the proof of gravity for the stability of everything from our homes to large buildings and bridges.

- We depend on the proof of the laws of physics for such things as heating and refrigeration, electricity, and the structural soundness of, for example, dams.

- We depend on the proof of chemistry findings for medicines and thousands of other substances.

Statistical proof is not 100-percent certain. But it is *highly reliable* through repeated observation and experimentation. Again, the standard benchmark is that anything with a probability of less than 1 in 10^{50} is impossible or absurd (without God); therefore humans accept such probability as "proof."

> We live our lives by probability on a daily basis. From a human standpoint, there is a point at which probability can be effectively used as "proof."

Key Concept

Scientists generally accept a standard that anything with a probability of less than 1 chance in 10^{50} is regarded as impossible.

Prophecy Criteria

As noted, the specificity of any prophecy would determine, in large part, its significance along with the number of perfectly correct prophecies. Also, the verification that the prophecy was actually made *before* the fulfillment would be of vital importance. And verification of the reliability of the information regarding both the original prophecy and the fulfillment would be critical. Such verification issues are addressed in part 2.

Criteria for statistical evaluation of prophecy includes that a prophecy would be

1. *Of sufficient specificity, and unlikelihood, that a cursory examination would lead a reasonable person to conclude that fulfillment would yield a probability of*

1 in 10 or smaller. This criterion eliminates the "tall, dark, handsome" generalities and the "Democrat dying in office" prophecies that are not very remarkable. While 1 chance in 10 by itself is not that spectacular either, as demonstrated above, several 1-in-10 prophecies strung together—with none being wrong— would be. (For example, just *eight* correct 1-in-10 prophecies in combination would equate to 1 chance in 100 million.)

2. *Authenticated by one source and confirmed by a separate source that would receive no net benefit from the confirmation of the prophecy.* This would eliminate contriving prophecies for someone's benefit. "Net benefit" is important because in some cases there may be some perceived benefit that might prejudice the confirmation of the prophecy. While there is no indication of the Jewish historians of the Bible ever falsely recording anything, the elimination of any potentially suspect prophecy strengthens any conclusion.

3. *Based on reliable source.* The sources of both prophecy and confirmation must be reliable, or the prophecy becomes just speculation. Part 2 demonstrates that the holy Scripture upon which the Bible was written is reliable. In particular, both the Dead Sea scrolls and the Septuagint provide powerful evidence that all Old Testament prophecies about Jesus were written prior to his birth.

Test Yourself

1. Why does prophecy, in particular, lend itself to probability analysis?

2. What are the two criteria that should be evaluated in determining the probability of a string of consistently correct biblical prophecies?

3. Give an example of how, mathematically, a string of many 100-percent-correct prophecies can be of the same importance as one extremely amazing prophecy.

4. What is the probability of flipping "just" 150 heads in a row?

5. What standard do scientists use for defining something as impossible?

Chapter 18 Group Study

Homework Preparation (do prior to group)

Read: chapter 18 of this text and pages 8–11 in *Does the Bible Predict the Future?* ✝.

Opening Prayer

Discussion: Humans have used probability to define things as "proven," such as gravity and many laws of physics used by engineers. Discuss the simple "coin flip" example (see pages 111–112) and discuss the probability numbers as "proof."

Practical-Experience Game

Debate: The "Christian" is opposing a "nonbeliever skeptic" who argues that nothing is provable. The objective is to convince him otherwise.

Closing Prayer

Sample Prophecies of Major Historical Events

In 722 B.C., Samaria, the capital city of the ten northern tribes, was captured by the Assyrians, who proceeded to take the Jews into captivity. Although some attempts were made by Assyria to conquer Judah (the Southern Kingdom), they never succeeded. Later, the Babylonians, under King Nebuchadnezzar, conquered the Assyrians and began expanding their empire. They successfully attacked Judah and began exiling Jews in 606 to 605 B.C. However, the first exile was not complete until the successful siege of Jerusalem by Nebuchadnezzar, in 587 to 586 B.C.

Prophecies About the First Jewish Exile

At that time the exile of the Jews of the Southern Kingdom was completed. *Eight* prophets correctly predicted this along with many specific details.

Moses (Deuteronomy 28:49-57). Moses prophesied about this exile in about 1450 B.C. (As a reference point, Lamentations was written by Jeremiah soon after the fall of Jerusalem in 586 B.C., confirming Moses' prophecy almost 900 years later.)

Prophecy	Fulfillment
A foreign nation would defeat the Hebrew nation.	History
Everything would be destroyed.	History
The invaders would have no respect for the elderly and no pity for the young.	Lamentations 2:21
They would lay siege to cities.	Lamentations 3:5
The Hebrews would resort to cannibalism.	Lamentations 2:20

Amos (Amos chapters 3; 5–9). Almost 40 years before the Assyrian conquest and almost 200 years before the Babylonian conquest, Amos (about 760 B.C.) prophesied that Israel would be devastated for her sins. *Fulfillment:* History.

Hosea (Hosea 1:2-8). Hosea (about 753 B.C.) likens Israel to an adulterous wife who will be punished by God, then eventually restored. He prophesies that Judah will be temporarily spared. *Fulfillment:* History. Israel—the Northern Kingdom—was exiled by the Assyrians in 722 B.C. Judah was spared for another 130 years.

Micah (Micah 1:2–3:12). Micah (about 742 B.C.) prophesied judgment against Samaria (the capital of the Northern Kingdom) and Jerusalem. Many details were given, including a later reuniting of Israel. *Fulfillment:* History. When Samaria fell, the capture of the Northern Kingdom by the Assyrians was complete. Later Jerusalem was besieged and captured.

Isaiah (Isaiah 7:18-25; 9:8–10:4). Isaiah (about 740 B.C.) prophesied the defeat of Israel at the hands of the Assyrians and the captivity of the Northern Kingdom. He also prophesied a later defeat of Judah, the Southern Kingdom. *Fulfillment:* History.

Habakkuk (Habakkuk 1:1-11). Habakkuk (about 612 B.C.) prophesied that the Babylonians would sweep through and defeat Judah. Details given include the siege of various cities. *Fulfillment:* History.

Jeremiah (Jeremiah 5:1-19; 6:1-30; 7:30-34). Jeremiah (about 627 B.C.) prophesied many details about the judgment of the exile, including the devastation to come. He also predicted that the Ben Hinnom Valley would be named the "Valley of Slaughter." *Fulfillment:* History.

Ezekiel (Ezekiel 6:1-14; 7:1-27; 8:17-18). Ezekiel actually became a prophet in 593 B.C. after he was in exile (along with Daniel and others). He made many specific exile prophecies. *Fulfillment:* History.

The many specific prophecies of the first exile of the Jews, confirmed by history and archaeology, had a probability of coming true randomly of *much smaller than 1 in 10—each.*

Prophecies of the Exact Timing of the First Exile

Jeremiah specifically prophesied that King Nebuchadnezzar would begin the exile of the Israelites to servitude in Babylon. The prophecy was made in the first year of Nebuchadnezzar's reign, prior to his defeat of Judah (Jeremiah 25), and it specifically limited the time of the servitude in exile to 70 years (verse 12). *Fulfillment:* We find in history that the exile began in 607 to 606 B.C. and that the Jews were allowed to start returning in 537 B.C., 70 years later.

Later Jeremiah prophesied a second 70-year period of exile—the time from the total destruction of Jerusalem until the final return was completed—when the Temple would be rebuilt (Jeremiah 29:10-14). *Fulfillment:* The exile was complete after the capture of Jerusalem in 587 to 586 B.C., exactly 70 years later.

The prophecies of the exact length of the Jews' exile—
over two different periods, and as confirmed by history and
archaeology—would likely have a probability of *far less than
1 in 100* of being fulfilled randomly.

Key Concept

*The exact length of the first exile was prophesied by
Jeremiah.*

A Prophecy Naming the Person Who Would Allow the Return of the Jews

Isaiah prophesied in about 700 B.C. that a leader named
"Cyrus" would allow the Jews to return to rebuild Jerusalem
and the Temple:

> [The LORD] *says of Cyrus, "He is my shepherd
> and will accomplish all that I please; he will say of
> Jerusalem, "Let it be rebuilt," and of the temple,
> "Let its foundations be laid."*
>
> *This is what the LORD says to his anointed, to
> Cyrus, whose right hand I take hold of to subdue
> nations before him and to strip kings of their
> armor, to open up doors before him so that gates
> will not be shut: I will go before you and will level
> the mountains; I will break down gates of bronze
> and cut through bars of iron. I will give you the
> treasures of darkness, riches stored in secret
> places, so that you may know that I am the LORD,
> the God of Israel, who summons you by name*
> (Isaiah 44:28–45:3).

This is a very specific prophecy naming a future leader, "Cyrus," whom God would enable to defeat the Babylonians and whom God would summon by name to allow Israel to return to the land and rebuild Jerusalem and the Temple. Isaiah made this prophecy more than 100 years before Jerusalem and the Temple were even destroyed—about *160* years before Cyrus was born! *Fulfillment:* The Persians conquered Babylon. Cyrus became king and allowed the Jews to return to rebuild the city and the Temple precisely as prophesied.

Modern archaeology has even located an ancient artifact, the "Cyrus cylinder," which shows the actual decree Cyrus gave that allowed the Israelites to return to their land and rebuild (see page 252).

> The precise name of the person allowing the return of the Jews to rebuild Jerusalem and the Temple was prophesied more than 100 years in advance. This amazing prophecy is backed up by the discovery of the Cyrus cylinder.

This prophecy of the exact name of the person who would allow the Jews to return to their homeland—confirmed by history and archaeology—would likely have a probability of vastly less than 1 in 100 of being fulfilled by chance.

We can notice the extreme specificity of the above prophecies of the first exile of the Jews. What were the odds of these prophets correctly predicting by chance

- the total destruction of two capital cities

- exile of the Northern Kingdom by the Assyrians

- exile of the Southern Kingdom 130 years later at the hand of the Babylonians

- the exact length of the exile

- the name of the person who would overthrow Babylonia and decree the return of the Jews to their homeland?

The statistical odds against just these prophecies all coming true in one source (the Bible) is staggering.

Prophecies of the Second Jewish Exile, and the Survival and Return of the Jews

Several key prophecies indicate that the Jews would be exiled a second time, that their identity would be maintained, and they would later return to their homeland. In A.D. 70 the Jews were removed from Jerusalem and scattered over the face of the Earth—the *second* exile.

> *In that day the* LORD *will reach out his hand a second time... He will raise a banner for the nations and gather the exiles of Israel; he will assemble the scattered people of Judah* from the four quarters of the earth (Isaiah 11:11-12).

> *Say to them, "This is what the Sovereign* LORD *says: I will take the Israelites out of the nations where they have gone.* I will gather them from all around and bring them back into their own land. *I will make them one nation in the land, on the mountains of Israel. There will be one king over all of them and they will never again be two nations or be divided into two kingdoms"* (Ezekiel 37:21-22).

> *To your offspring I will give this land* (God speaking to Abraham in Genesis 12:7).

*I will make you into a great nation and I will bless
you; I will make your name great, and you will be
a blessing. I will bless those who bless you, and
whoever curses you I will curse; and all peoples
on earth will be blessed through you* (God to
Abraham in Genesis 12:2-3).

Fulfillment: History. In 1948, Israel became a nation,
nearly 2000 years after the Jews had been dispersed from
their homeland. *Never before in the history of the world has
an ethnic group been separated from its homeland for more
than a few generations and yet maintained its identity.* Not
only did the Jews maintain
their identity, as indicated in
Genesis 12:2-3, but against all
odds, they returned to the land
God had promised Abraham
through his son Isaac. And
since that time—against great
odds—Israel has survived several attempts to destroy it.

> The prophecies about the
> Jewish exiles—especially
> the return from the
> second exile, which is
> confirmed by history and
> events that we can
> observe today—are
> among the most amazing
> prophecies ever. The
> probability of their
> coming true without
> divine inspiration is small
> beyond reason.

Concerning the prophecy
that the name of Abraham—
the father of the Jews—would
become great, consider this:
The Jewish population represents about three-tenths of 1
percent of the world popula-
tion—in other words, 34 people out of 10,000. Yet we hear
far more about the Jews than we do about many cultures,
races, and religions of dramatically greater population size.

Dating Considerations

Sometimes ancient dating varies by a year or two. The
reason is that ancient dates were usually defined based on

the time of a particular ruler's reign, and different systems were used in recording when a particular king's reign started. What formed the most accurate basis for the dating of the kings of Israel (893–666 B.C.) was a very accurate account from Assyria that was discovered—the eponym lists (see page 250). Then multiple references in different books of the Tanakh allow us to relate the Jewish prophets to the kings of their time.

Archaeology also has confirmed *many* details of the exile period, right down to finding an ancient receipt for goods provided to the family of Judah's king Jehoiachin in Babylon (where he was kept in exile). The Bible had precisely indicated that Jehoiachin was given a daily ration (see pages 251–252 and 2 Kings 25:27-30).

Four Hundred Years of History Prophesied

In about 550 B.C., while in captivity in Babylon, Daniel made an extraordinarily detailed prophecy. He accurately prophesied the next 400 years of history that involved Israel. The prophecy uses vivid imagery of a "ram" with two "horns"—one horn being longer—raging east and west and defeating everyone. Then a "goat" with a single large horn suddenly appeared, furiously attacking the ram and breaking off his two horns and trampling him (Daniel 8:1-14). The images continue with the goat's large horn breaking off at the height of its power and then being replaced with four smaller horns. A small horn came from one of these horns, and it grew in power to the south and east toward the "beautiful land," where it would take over the daily sacrifice from the "Prince of the host" and take over the sanctuary.

If the prophecy stopped there, it would be of little value since its imagery is vague and nondescript. However, the angel Gabriel precisely interpreted the vision. All this was written down in the time of Daniel, long before the events took place.

In Daniel 8, virtually 400 years of history were precisely foretold:

1. The Babylonian Empire was in power in the region at the time (Daniel was in exile in Babylon when this prophecy was made).

2. The ram with two horns was the kings of Media and Persia, with the longer horn being the ruler of Persia (Cyrus) who grew in prominence. *Fulfillment:* History indicates that the Medo-Persian Empire overthrew the Babylonian Empire. Cyrus became the dominant king.

3. The goat with one large horn represented the Greek Empire, with the large horn representing its first ruler, Alexander the Great. This is particularly amazing, because at the time of the prophecy, 200 years before Alexander, Greece was a very weak country. No one would have thought it would become a world power.

   The goat's "crossing the whole earth without touching the ground" (8:5) indicates great speed of conquest. The speed with which Alexander conquered that portion of the world had never been seen before. *Fulfillment:* Starting in 326 B.C., it took Alexander only three years to establish the Greek Empire's control over much of the civilized world.

4. At the height of its power, the large horn would be broken off. *Fulfillment:* Alexander the Great died suddenly at age 33, in 323 B.C.

5. The four horns represented four kingdoms that would arise from the Greek nation, but would "not have the same power" (verse 22). *Fulfillment:* After his death, Alexander's conquests were divided between four of

his generals, none of whom would attain the same power. The empire was split into the areas of Macedonia and Greece; Thrace, Bithynia, and most of Asia Minor; Syria and the territory east of Syria (including Babylon); and Egypt and Palestine.

The small horn was described by Daniel as growing in power to the east and south toward the "beautiful land" (Israel) and eventually setting itself up to be as great as the "Prince of the host"; taking away daily sacrifice and "bringing low" the sanctuary (verses 9-11).

Later in the chapter Daniel identifies the small horn as a "stern-faced king" who would take power in the latter part of the reign of "wicked rebels" in the land. This king would consider himself superior and would set himself up against the "Prince of princes" (that is, a heavenly authority—verses 11,25). He was described as destroying "the mighty men and the holy people." In the end, this king would "be destroyed, but not by human power" (verse 25).

Fulfillment: In history, these specific events were fulfilled precisely as well. The Seleucids (from the north) took control of Palestine. A particularly wicked king emerged, Antiochus IV Epiphanes (the "small horn" of verse 9), who put an end to Jewish worship and daily sacrifice. Jews were put to death for possessing the Scriptures.

Antiochus killed thousands of Jews who attempted to maintain their worship of God in spite of his decrees (destroying "the mighty men and the holy people"). He considered himself superior to all others, as reflected in the name "Epiphanes," which means "God manifest," and eventually rededicated the Jewish Temple to the Greek god Zeus and sacrificed a pig on the altar (detestable to the Jewish people)—thus fulfilling Daniel's prophecy about the "sanctuary."

This enraged the population and was the catalyst for the Maccabean revolt that ended up in defeat of that hated ruler, and the erection of a new altar and rededication on the 25th of Kislev, 164 B.C., exactly three years later. The success of the Maccabean revolt against the superior power of Antiochus could be viewed as "not by human power" (verse 25).

All the points of Daniel's prophecy have been confirmed by history—ancient writings and archaeology. All together, they have a probability of coming about randomly of *vastly* less than 1 in 1000.

Test Yourself

1. When did the first exile of the Jews begin? Who exiled the Jews? Who prophesied it?

2. How long was the first exile prophesied to be? Who made the prophecy?

3. What is the name of the ruler prophesied to allow the Jews to return from exile?

4. Why is the prophecy of the second exile return significant?

5. Name the empires that Daniel prophesied in his 400-year prophecy in Daniel 8.

Chapter 19 Group Study

Homework Preparation (do prior to group)

Read: Daniel 8; chapter 19 of this text; and pages 34–39 in *Does the Bible Predict the Future?* ✝.

Opening Prayer

Discussion: Review Daniel 8 and as a group attempt to estimate the odds that all parts of this prophecy would come true as indicated. Determine, as a group, what range of odds is realistic that the prophecy of a second exile and return would come true.

Practical-Experience Game

TV interview: Because of its many prophecies, the "TV interviewer" is interested in claims that the Bible is divinely inspired. The "Christian" being interviewed should use prophecies to persuade the interviewer that the Bible is inspired by God.

Closing Prayer

20

Prophecy Proof of the God of Judaism

The Bible contains scores of prophecies about cities, nations, and people, providing surprising detail about the future. Here are examples of two such prophecies:

Assyria and Its Capital, Nineveh

- *The defeat of Assyria and Nineveh* (Isaiah 10:5-34). Isaiah made this prophecy in about 735 B.C.

- The King of Assyria would be punished for "willful pride" (verse 12). *Fulfillment:* The historical fall to Babylon in 612 B.C.

- Although destruction of the ten northern tribes of Israel by Assyria had been assured (Isaiah 7:18-25), Jerusalem was to be spared (10:32-34). Even Assyria's route to the intended conquest of Jerusalem was predicted (verses 28-32). *Fulfillment:* History, exactly as prophesied. Despite the odds, which favored the Assyrians considerably, Jerusalem was spared from destruction at their hands.

- A remnant of Israel (the ten northern tribes) would return (verse 21). *Fulfillment:* History. A remnant of Jews returned from captivity following the destruction of Nineveh.

- Destruction was decreed upon the whole land of the Assyrians (verse 23). *Fulfillment:* History. The Babylonians entirely destroyed the Assyrian kingdom.

The Future of the City of Tyre

Tyre was among the mightiest Mediterranean trading ports of Ezekiel's day (his prophecy, in chapter 26 of his book, was made about 586 B.C.). It was a New York or Hong Kong of its time. Tyre rejoiced in the destruction of Judah, with the notion that perhaps further business would come to them (verses 1-2). Many details of Tyre's destruction were predicted—the destruction of both its mainland stronghold and the island portion of the city.

- Nebuchadnezzar of Babylon would be brought from the north to lay siege to Tyre and destroy it (verses 7-9). *Fulfillment:* History. The mainland city was conquered by Babylonian siege, but not the island city.

- Many nations would attack Tyre (verse 3). *Fulfillment:* History.

- Its walls and towers would be destroyed, and the rubble would be scraped away, making it a "bare rock" (verse 4). *Fulfillment:* History. The rubble of the mainland city was scraped away into the sea—by the Greeks under Alexander the Great in order to make a causeway to lay siege to the previously unreachable island portion of the city. Evidence of this is still apparent today.

- Fishermen would spread their nets where there was commerce before (verse 5). *Fulfillment:* History. The island part of the city is beneath the sea.

- Tyre would "never be rebuilt" (verses 7-14). *Fulfillment:* History. There is a city named Tyre, but much smaller and in a different location. The great island city itself is underwater.

- Nearby rulers would surrender without a fight (verse 16). *Fulfillment:* After the amazing conquest of the island portion of Tyre by Alexander the Great, nearby rulers surrendered.

> The prophecies about cities, nations, and people and their fulfillment provide additional undeniable evidence of the inspiration of the Bible. These prophecies are easily testable using history and archaeology.

Very detailed prophecies about Nineveh and Tyre were both fulfilled precisely as indicated. (About 80 additional significant non-Messianic prophecies, provable through history and archaeology, are contained in appendix C.)

Statistical Analysis of Old Testament Prophecy

The Old Testament passes the test of perfect prophecy, and therefore the Jews would believe it to be divinely inspired. But how would it stack up to the human standard set by scientists—that the random occurrence of anything with a probability of less than 1 chance in 10^{50} is essentially impossible—without God?

To answer such a statistical question, we must estimate how likely it would be to have each of these individual prophecies come true randomly. Then we can estimate the multiple probability of their all coming true simply by using statistical conventions.

It is not possible to know with certainty the odds of specific events happening. Opinions could vary widely. However, the number of correct prophecies in the Old Testament is so large that a statistician could assign just about any probability to any specific one and arrive at the identical conclusion.

For example, if someone wanted to estimate that the odds of the exiled Jews surviving as an ethnic group and returning to Israel was 1 in 10 rather than 1 in 10,000,000, this might be an absurdly conservative estimate, but it would be okay. Or say that the odds that the name of Cyrus would be prophesied years before he was born were also 1 in 10 rather than 1 in 1,000,000—again, this might be absurdly conservative, but it would be okay too. In other words, the Bible contains so many correct prophecies that it makes little difference what odds are assigned to a particular prophecy. (Any skeptic can feel free to change probabilities in the analysis of prophecies or throw out entire prophecies if desired.)

Fascinating Fact

Because of the large number of correct prophecies in the Bible, we can use an absurdly conservative estimate of probability for each individual prophecy and still obtain the same overall conclusion.

So let's do some very simple statistical calculations using extremely conservative assumptions. In fact, let's assume that each prophesied event has a chance of *only 1 in 10* of occurring randomly. What would the real odds of the Jews surviving as a people after their exile—then returning to their homeland 2000 years later—realistically be? The odds of this alone are surely one out of millions. Or Daniel's prophecy of 400 years of history, the predictions of the exact timing of the first exile, or the naming of Cyrus? The odds of any of these prophecies coming true is certainly extremely remote. However, for the purpose of the analysis below, the absurdly conservative estimate of odds for all of these is just 1 chance in 10.

There are so many fulfilled biblical prophecies that a proof of God and of the divine inspiration of the Bible can be made even by allowing absurdly conservative odds. Adding the prophecies we've previously examined to the historically verifiable prophecies in appendix C (which exclude short-term and other "non-historically-verifiable" ones), we come up with 118 total non-Messianic historical prophecies. Mathematically, the probability of all 118 of these prophecies coming true randomly, if we assign the probability of only 1 in 10 to each, is calculated by multiplying the one in ten odds by itself 118 times. The result is 1 chance in 10^{118}.

In other words, $\frac{1}{10}$ x $\frac{1}{10}$ x $\frac{1}{10}$, and so on, 118 times.

How large is this number? Here are some comparisons:

1. It would be like winning 17 state lotteries in a row with a single ticket for each,

2. It would be like dividing all time since the beginning of the universe (an estimated 15 billion years) into seconds, randomly "marking" 7 of those seconds, then correctly guessing by chance every one of the 7 designated seconds.

3. It would be like being struck by lightning 24 times in one year.

From the above extremely conservative model, we can see that the biblical prophetic results *would be regarded as impossible by science* (that is, without God) because the odds of their random occurrence are far, far less than 1 chance in 10^{50}. Therefore we might "scientifically reason" that a supernatural God must 1) exist, and 2) have inspired the prophets and original writings. A logical extension of this would be that the God who provided the information in the Old Testament must be the real God. Later, we will expand the prophetic test to that of testing the claims of Jesus to be divine.

Key Concept

Taking only 118 verifiable Old Testament prophecies and applying an extremely conservative probability of 10-percent chance for each still indicates only 1 chance in 10^{118} that they could, taken together, be fulfilled without God.

Another way to analyze such prophecies is to select only the prophecies whose fulfillment occurred centuries later and which were confirmed by history outside the Bible, then to assign them reasonable odds and calculate the probabilities.

Another Prophecy Estimate of Odds

1. Isaiah's naming of Cyrus nearly two centuries in advance (Isaiah 44:28–45:3).　　$\frac{1}{10,000}$

2. Daniel's 400 years of precisely predicted history (Daniel 8).　　$\frac{1}{1,000,000}$

3. Prophecies by five prophets of the total destruction of Ammon, Edom, and Moab.　　$\frac{1}{10,000,000}$

4. The detailed prophecy of the destruction of Tyre, hundreds of years in advance (Ezekiel 26).　　$\frac{1}{100,000}$

5. The prophecy of the destruction of Nineveh more than 100 years in advance (Isaiah 10:5-34).　　$\frac{1}{1,000,000}$

6. The destruction of the Amalekites predicted 450 years in advance (Exodus 17:14). $\frac{1}{10,000}$

7. Jerusalem to be rebuilt from the "Tower of Hananel to the Corner Gate" (Jeremiah 31:38-40). $\frac{1}{1000}$

8. Detailed prophecies of the first Jewish exile by seven prophets—some more than a century in advance. $\frac{1}{100,000}$

9. The Jews' ultimate survival of their dispersion and their return to their homeland in 1948 (Isaiah 11:12; Ezekiel 37:21-22). $\frac{1}{100,000}$

10. Israel's survival since 1948 despite being heavily outnumbered during many conflicts (Amos 9:14-15). $\frac{1}{1,000,000}$

The cumulative probability of just the prophecies above all coming true randomly is 1 chance in 10^{53}. Again, this falls outside of what is regarded as randomly possible by scientists.

From this we can conclude statistically that

1. God exists—proven statistically by the 100-percent fulfilled prophecy in the Jewish Bible (the Tanakh).

2. The Old Testament was inspired by God.

Test Yourself

1. What are some of the prophecies made about Nineveh and Assyria?

2. What are some of the prophecies made about Tyre?

3. What evidence is there of the fulfillment of the prophecies about Tyre?

4. Think up an example of ridiculously conservative odds, then take the 118 non-Messianic prophecies listed in this chapter and appendix C, and calculate the probability.

5. How remote are the odds of the random fulfillment of the above prophecies? Why can we use absurdly conservative estimates of odds and still demonstrate God's existence?

Chapter 20 Group Study

Homework Preparation (do prior to group)
Read: Ezekiel 26; chapter 20 of this text; and pages 40–41 in *Does the Bible Predict the Future?* ✝.

Opening Prayer
Discussion: Review the prophecies made about the city of Tyre in Ezekiel 26, then discuss all of the things that God is demonstrating to the world and those reading them.

Practical-Experience Game
Role-playing: A "nonbelieving skeptic" challenges the importance of prophecy by indicating he doesn't agree with the odds that Christians use in calculating the prophecy miracle. The "Christian" should effectively address this concern.

Closing Prayer

Prophecy and Jesus

Prophecy is of paramount importance in validating the identity of Jesus and his role. First, it is important in the establishment of the Bible as an authority in its statements about Jesus. As was already seen, Old Testament prophecy statistically proves the divine inspiration of the holy Scriptures. However, prophecy about Jesus, if shown to be historically verifiable, could also validate that its claims of Jesus are true.

Again, the reason for the importance of prophecy is that *only* God knows the end from the beginning (Isaiah 46:9-10). Therefore if God's Word (the Bible), verified through prophecy, proclaims Jesus as the divine Messiah—and Jesus proclaims himself to be God in the Bible through prophecy—it follows that Jesus must be God (or a liar...but a divine Messiah could not lie). Other more specific claims of Jesus—in particular, that he came to Earth to be a sacrifice and redeemer for the sins of man (John 3:16-17), and that the only way to heaven is through him (John 14:6)—would also be verified if prophecy could prove Jesus to be God.

Furthermore, we should look for evidence of prophecy from Jesus himself. This is because if he is really who he claims to be—God incarnate—then he would certainly be able to prophesy accurately, and one should expect him to prove himself through prophecy.

The Jews accused Jesus of blasphemy several times due to his indications that he was divine. Below are examples of the things Jesus said or did that so inflamed the Jews because of his claim to be God.

Claims of Jesus to Be God

Jesus' claim to be God is reported throughout the New Testament, which also reports the Jewish religious leaders as very upset by it.

- "I and the Father are one" (Jesus, in John 10:30).

- "Anyone who has seen me has seen the Father. How can you say, 'Show us the Father'? Don't you believe that I am in the Father, and that the Father is in me?" (Jesus, in John 14:9-10).

- "I tell you the truth," Jesus answered, "before Abraham was born, I am!" (John 8:58). The statement "I am" was tantamount to a claim to be God (see Exodus 3:14).

- Jesus acknowledged several times that he was the Messiah (Mark 14:61-63; John 4:25-26; Luke 9:20). Mark 14:61-63 implied that a claim to deity was included in Jesus' claim to be the Christ (the Messiah).

- Jesus referred to himself as the Son of God and, more often, Son of Man, both of which spoke of his deity—something the Jewish leaders would have clearly understood from a prophecy by Daniel:

  In my vision at night I looked, and there before me was one like a son of man, *coming with the clouds of heaven. He approached the*

Ancient of Days and was led into his presence. He was given authority, glory and sovereign power; all peoples, nations and men of every language worshiped him. His dominion is an everlasting dominion that will not pass away, and his kingdom is one that will never be destroyed (Daniel 7:13-14).

At a critical point in Jesus' trial, before his crucifixion, he was asked a question he was required to answer by law:

The high priest said to him, "I charge you under oath by the living God: Tell us if you are the Christ, the Son of God."

"Yes, it is as you say," Jesus replied (Matthew 26:63).

Many times, Jesus referred to himself as the Messiah, or God incarnate—in every Gospel.

Analyzing Prophecies About Jesus

The entire Old Testament (the Jewish Bible) is filled with prophecies that match Jesus—including many details about his life, death, and resurrection. Whole chapters of books contain considerable numbers of prophecies about Jesus.

Key to accepting these prophecies, of course, is to ascertain that they were in fact written before the time of Jesus—not afterwards, in a fraudulent attempt to deify him.

Evaluating Basic Assumptions

Any test of prophecies about Jesus for today's skeptic relies on two important questions:

1. Was there adequate time distance between the recording of the prophecies in the Old Testament and the record of the fulfillment in the New Testament?

2. Were the New Testament accounts of Jesus accepted as accurate and as fulfillment of prophecy by the early Jews who were close to the events?

Several things help establish credibility of the prophetic records. As a foundation, there was a 400-year period between the final prophecies of the coming of a Messiah (recorded in the Jewish Scriptures) and their fulfillment through Jesus. During this time some important things happened, which we've previously discussed. As they are so critical, let's review the issues.

1. The *Tanakh* (Jewish Scripture) canon was popularly recognized.

2. The *Dead Sea scrolls* were written, including many complete copies and fragments of every book in the Tanakh except the book of Esther.

3. The *Septuagint* (the Greek translation of the Tanakh, also designated as the LXX) was made.

4. *Other translations* of the Tanakh were made.

These events of the 400-year period were important for the following reasons:

- The *Tanakh* canon (those books recognized as divinely inspired Scripture) had been popularly established by about 167 B.C. So by the time Jesus was teaching, there was widespread knowledge among his thousands of hearers of what was meant by "Scripture." There were no doubts about which books were and were not included. In A.D. 70, exactly the same books of Scripture used by Jesus and others were recognized as the official canon by the Jewish religious authorities—the same books in use today by both Jews and Christians.

- The *Dead Sea scrolls* consist of some 800 manuscripts and representing all books of the Old Testament except Esther (with multiple copies of most books). A substantial portion of the Tanakh copies were written more than 200 years before Jesus—as indicated by both radiometric dating and paleography (the study of ancient writing). The scrolls were stored in a cave by a Jewish religious sect, the Essenes, just prior to the Roman conquest in A.D. 70 and remained untouched until about 1947, when the first ones were discovered in Qumran by the Dead Sea (not far from Jerusalem). Hence, they were like a "time capsule."

  The scrolls have been compared to the modern copies and have been found to agree, virtually letter-for-letter. (Most of the differences are in the spelling of names.) The point is, the Dead Sea scrolls essentially "froze in time" the prophecies about Jesus—long before he was born.

- The *Septuagint* is a translation from Hebrew into Greek of the Tanakh made by an appointed team of 70 scholars ("Septuagint" comes from the word for "seventy"). Since many Jews of the time (about 280 B.C.) spoke Greek, this official translation was intended to enable everyone to read holy Scripture. (The earliest manuscript portions now in existence are parts of the Torah, copied before 200 B.C.)

  The Septuagint is especially important in verifying prophecy, because some scholars contend in retrospect that translations of the original Hebrew made after Jesus' time may have not adequately reflected the original meaning. However, the Septuagint clearly demonstrates the Jewish understanding of the Scriptures at a time *well* before Jesus arrived! It was translated by 70 of the best scholars of the time—scholars who were placing their best understanding of the Hebrew meaning into Greek and who used ancient Hebrew on a daily basis. Furthermore, the Hebrew texts from which they worked were much closer to the originals than the ones we have today.

- *Other translations* of the Tanakh—into several different languages—were made before Jesus' time. All of these also help to document the detailed prophecies of a coming Messiah.

Key Concept

We know that the Old Testament prophecies predate Jesus because of 1) the unofficial Tanakh canon, which was established and later verified by Jesus; 2) The Dead Sea scrolls; 3) the Septuagint; and 4) other translations.

There is a substantial body of evidence that any prophecies in the Old Testament about a coming Messiah and other future events were reliably recorded. They were clearly written before the fact, before Jesus of Nazareth was born. Scholars can see, touch, and study these documents. The credibility of the prophetic record is firmly established.

The Prophecies with Substance

In order to objectively evaluate prophecy about Jesus, it is important to isolate the prophecies made with substance versus those that are not provable or are unclear. For example, who could ever prove today that Jesus was born of a virgin?

Nobody. We should ignore unprovable prophecies, including this one, in order to be as objective as possible to determine the validity of God, Jesus, and the Bible.

Some skeptics argue that Christians try to stretch the words of the Old Testament prophecies to fit Jesus. One example sometimes cited is Genesis 3:15:

> *I will put enmity between you and the woman,*
> *and between your offspring and hers; he will crush*
> *your head, and you will strike his heel.*

Christians say this is a prophecy about Jesus. The serpent (Satan) strikes at the heel of the woman (through Jesus' crucifixion), and her offspring (Jesus) crushes Satan's head. Although this interpretation is possible, to a skeptic the words from Genesis reveal nothing that is specific or provable.

There is nothing specific that identifies Jesus with the offspring of Eve. The claim that striking at the heel was a symbol of crucifixion and crushing the head was Satan's final defeat by Jesus is ambiguous. The snake certainly represents Satan, but in regard to undeniably provable prophecies for a skeptic, this and other similar ambiguous prophecies are excluded from statistical analysis in this text.

However, by applying basic logic, it is quite easy to find many Old Testament prophecies about Jesus. For instance, in the Bible's oldest book, Job (from about 2000 B.C.), there is the first prophecy written about a "redeemer" who lives eternally (at both the time of Job and at the "end"). This redeemer was apparently identified as God, who would come to earth.

> *I know that my Redeemer lives, and that in the*
> *end he will stand upon the earth. And after my*

skin has been destroyed, yet in my flesh I will see
God; I myself will see him with my own eyes—I,
and not another. How my heart yearns within me!
(Job 19:25-27).

While these words aren't definitely specific to Jesus, they are specific to a Redeemer—one like Jesus, as described in many places in the Old Testament (for example, Isaiah 53) and in the New Testament.

Isaiah 53

Isaiah 53 is highly descriptive of the future Messiah. It contains many very specific prophecies that reflect directly on Jesus' life. (See numbered points within the following)

Who has believed our message and to whom has the arm of the LORD been revealed? He grew up before him like a tender shoot, and like a root out of dry ground. He had no beauty or majesty to attract us to him, nothing in his appearance that we should desire him ①. He was despised and rejected by men ②, a man of sorrows, and familiar with suffering ③. Like one from whom men hide their faces he was despised, and we esteemed him not ④.

Surely he took up our infirmities and carried our sorrows ⑤, yet we considered him stricken by God, smitten by him, and afflicted ⑥. But he was pierced for our transgressions ⑦, he was crushed for our iniquities; the punishment that brought us peace was upon him, and by his wounds we are healed ⑧. We all, like sheep, have gone astray, each of us has turned to his own way; and the LORD has laid on him the iniquity of us all ⑨.

He was oppressed and afflicted, yet he did not open his mouth ⑩; he was led like a lamb to the slaughter ⑪, and as a sheep before her shearers is silent, so he did not open his mouth ⑫. By oppression and judgment he was taken away ⑬. And who can speak of his descendants? For he was cut off from the land of the living; for the transgression of my people he was stricken ⑭. He was assigned a grave with the wicked ⑮, and with the rich in his death ⑯, though he had done no violence, nor was any deceit in his mouth ⑰.

Yet it was the LORD*'s will to crush him and cause him to suffer, and though the* LORD *makes his life a guilt offering ⑱, he will see his offspring and prolong his days, and the will of the* LORD *will prosper in his hand ⑲. After the suffering of his soul, he will see the light [of life] and be satisfied ⑳; by his knowledge my righteous servant will justify many, and he will bear their iniquities ㉑. Therefore I will give him a portion among the great ㉒, and he will divide the spoils with the strong ㉓, because he poured out his life unto death, and was numbered with the transgressors ㉔. For he bore the sin of many, and made intercession for the transgressors ㉕* (brackets in original).

These 25 prophecies are very specific to Jesus:

1. Jesus came to human beings in a fashion that would seem unattractive—as a baby. He worked as an ordinary carpenter.

2. He was despised and rejected.

3. He knew much suffering.

4. He was not esteemed.

5. He carried mankind's sorrows (sins).

6. People considered him "stricken by God," or afflicted.

7. He was "pierced" for man's transgressions.

8. His injuries brought healing.

9. He spoke of himself as giving his life for the "sheep." All human sin was borne by him.

10. When he was oppressed at his trial, he would not open his mouth except as legally required.

11. He was led to his crucifixion like a lamb to slaughter.

12. "As a sheep before her shearers is silent," Jesus did not defend himself at his trial.

13. He was taken away "by oppression and judgment."

14. He was "stricken" for the transgression (sin) of many.

15. He was crucified with two criminals and was supposed to have been buried with them.

16. A rich man, Joseph of Arimathea, asked for Jesus' body and placed it in his (Joseph's) tomb.

17. Jesus neither resisted by force, nor did he lie in his testimony before the Roman governor Pilate.

18. God the Father accepted Jesus' life as a "guilt offering."

19. God's will "prospered" through Jesus.

20. After suffering, Jesus again saw the light—upon his resurrection.

21. Jesus justified "many" and bore their sins.

22. God exalted him to greatness.

23. He divided the "spoils" with the "strong" (believers would prosper eternally).

24. He poured himself out to the point of death and was considered a sinful man (transgressor).

25. He carried the sins of the many and interceded with God for transgressors (sinners).

Key Concept

Isaiah 53 is one of the most important prophetic chapters since it contains 25 individual prophecies that accurately describe the person and role of Jesus.

Fascinating Fact

Some Jewish groups have actually cut Isaiah 53 out of their Bibles because it so closely matches Jesus. Yet anyone visiting the Shrine of the Book in Jerusalem—the home of the Dead Sea scrolls—can clearly see this passage in the scroll of Isaiah, precisely as it was originally written.

Test Yourself

1. Quote at least three places where Jesus claimed deity.

2. List four ways we can be certain that the prophecies of Jesus weren't contrived after the fact.

3. When were the earliest Dead Sea scrolls written? What books are included?

4. What is the Septuagint? And why is it important?

5. What is the significance of Isaiah 53? How many prophecies does it contain?

Chapter 21 Group Study

Homework Preparation (do prior to group)
Read: All biblical claims by Jesus to be the Messiah (see pages 355–357); chapter 21 of this text; and pages 28-29 in *Does the Bible Predict the Future?* ✝.

Opening Prayer
Discussion: Discuss Jesus' claims to be the Messiah, Son of God, and Son of Man, and all allusions to deity. In addition to these claims, what actions did Jesus or others take that indicate he claimed to be God? Why is his accurate prophecy so important?

Practical-Experience Game
Debate: A "Christian" will debate a "nonbeliever" over the reliability of prophecy in defining the deity and role of Jesus.

Closing Prayer

Old Testament Prophecy Completely Describes the Messiah

Athorough review of prophecies about Jesus in the Old Testament reveals that a complete picture of Jesus is given, which includes specifically that a plan for the Messiah was preconceived by God and fulfilled by Jesus. So complete is this information that one can analyze it in much the way a newspaper reporter would—seeking the "who, what, when, and where" of Jesus.

Who

According to the Scriptures, the Messiah would come from the line of descent running through

- Shem (Genesis 9–10)
- Abraham (Genesis 22:18)
- Isaac (Genesis 26:4)
- Jacob (Genesis 28:14)
- Judah (Genesis 49:10)
- Jesse (Isaiah 11:1-5)
- King David (2 Samuel 7:11-16)

The New Testament indicates fulfillment of these prophecies as reported in the accounts of Matthew (Matthew 1) and Luke (Luke 3:23-28). Luke investigated history by talking to eyewitnesses and by reviewing other accounts of Jesus (Luke 1:1). Matthew investigated the legal claim of Jesus to the kingship of Israel, which would have been of paramount importance to the Jews. The kingship of Jesus came from David through the line of Joseph, his stepfather (as recorded in Matthew), while his physical descent from David came

Fascinating Fact

The Curse of Jehoiachin. At the time of the Babylonian captivity (586 B.C.), God said that the king of Judah, Jehoiachin (in the line from David to the Messiah), would be cursed:

This is what the LORD says: "Record this man as if childless, a man who will not prosper in his lifetime, for none of his offspring will prosper, none will sit on the throne of David or rule any more in Judah" (Jeremiah 22:30).

This clearly states that none of Jehoiachin's offspring (the seed of his body) would inherit the throne of David, in apparent contradiction to the prophecy that the Messiah would come from the line of David (2 Samuel 7:11-13). However, the Gospels' accounts of Jesus satisfy both of these prophecies and also the prophecy of a "virgin birth." Matthew reports that the *line of kingship* was passed on to Jesus, who was the legal heir of Joseph (identified as "the husband of Mary"), but not his physical "offspring." (Joseph didn't inseminate Mary—the Holy Spirit "overshadowed" her—Luke 1:35.)

On the other hand, Jesus' physical descent through Mary, as recorded by Luke, still qualified him as the "son of David." Both accounts are consistent with prophecy. Both are consistent with both the divine nature and human nature of Jesus.

through the line of Mary (as recorded in Luke). The difference in their perspectives was not surprising, since Matthew was a tax collector and had to be very aware of legal affairs, whereas Luke was a doctor.

Isaiah 7:14

Isaiah records that the Messiah would be called *Immanuel*—meaning "God with us." This is precisely how Jesus was described by Matthew at the time of his birth (Matthew 1:23). He has been called Immanuel ever since. And if Jesus' statements in the Gospel accounts were accurate, he was indeed "God with us."

What
The Messiah's Life Was Vividly Described

Apart from Isaiah 53, there are many other prophetic references to the Messiah's activities, including

- teaching in parables (Psalm 78:2)
- riding into Jerusalem as a king, but on a donkey (Zechariah 9:9)
- being betrayed by a friend (Psalm 41:9)
- earning 30 pieces of silver that were then thrown in the Temple to a potter (Zechariah 11:12-13)
- being rejected by Israel (Isaiah 8:14)
- being mocked with lots cast for his clothing (Psalm 22:18)
- having his hands and feet pierced (Psalm 22)
- being given gall and wine (Psalm 69:21)
- being pierced (Zechariah 12:10)

- being buried in a rich man's grave (Isaiah 53:9)

- being raised from the grave (Psalm 16:10)

The Gospels report these events and assert that Jesus fulfilled these prophecies.

The Messiah Would Perform Certain Miracles

Ancient Israel believed that some miracles could be done *only by God*, including these prophesied by Isaiah:

> *Say to those with fearful hearts, "Be strong, do not fear; your God will come, he will come with vengeance; with divine retribution he will come to save you." Then will the eyes of the blind be opened and the ears of the deaf unstopped. Then will the lame leap like a deer, and the mute tongue shout for joy* (Isaiah 35:4-6).

The Gospel accounts report that the blind, deaf, lame, and mute were healed by Jesus (Matthew 9:27-30; 11:5; 15:30-31; 21:14; Mark 7:32-37; 10:51-52; Luke 7:22; John 5:3-15; 9:13-25).

Jesus also asked some disciples to report the miracles they had seen in order to verify his deity to John the Baptist, who was imprisoned.

Jesus replied, "Go back and report to John what you hear and see: The blind receive sight, the lame walk, those who have leprosy are cured, the deaf hear, the dead are raised, and the good news is preached to the poor" (Matthew 11:4-5).

Miracles, by definition, seem impossible—especially in today's world. It is interesting to note that even some non-Christian sources known to be enemies of Jesus also commented on them. For example, writings in the Jewish Talmud called Jesus a "sorcerer."

The Role of the Messiah Was Explained

Old Testament prophecies that described the Messiah indicated he was to be

- a redeemer—one who would save people from their sins (Isaiah 53).

- a prophet and a teacher (Deuteronomy 18:15).

These prophecies were made more specific by other requirements set forth in the Old Testament, which tied directly into Jesus, who as the Messiah described in Isaiah 53, was to be "led like a lamb to the slaughter":

- A *blood sacrifice* was needed because of mankind's sin: "Sacrifice a bull each day as a sin offering to make atonement" (Exodus 29:36-37).

- *Perfection* was required in the sacrifice: "When anyone brings from the herd or flock a fellowship offering to the LORD to fulfill a special vow or as a freewill offering, it must be without defect or blemish to be acceptable" (Leviticus 22:21).

- *God himself* would provide the sacrifice: "Abraham answered [Isaac], 'God *himself will provide the lamb* for the burnt offering, my son.' And the two of them went on together" (Genesis 22:8).

The near-sacrifice of Isaac by Abraham is a model of the Christian claim about God providing Jesus as the perfect sacrificial "lamb."

The Death of the Messiah

Psalm 22 was written about 600 years before crucifixion was even invented. Nonetheless, it is a vivid portrayal of a death by crucifixion and matches the events of Jesus' death on the cross. (Corresponding points are numbered.)

My God, my God, why have you forsaken me? ① *Why are you so far from saving me, so far from the words of my groaning? O my God, I cry out by day, but you do not answer, by night, and am not silent.*

Yet you are enthroned as the Holy One ②*; you are the praise of Israel. In you our fathers put their trust* ③*; they trusted and you delivered them. They cried to you and were saved; in you they trusted and were not disappointed.*

But I am a worm and not a man, scorned by men and despised by the people ④*. All who see me mock me; they hurl insults, shaking their heads: "He trusts in the* LORD*; let the* LORD *rescue him* ⑤*. Let him deliver him, since he delights in him."*

Yet you brought me out of the womb; you made me trust in you even at my mother's breast. From birth I was cast upon you; from my mother's womb you have been my God ⑥*. Do not be far from me, for trouble is near and there is no one to help* ⑦*. Many bulls surround me; strong bulls of Bashan encircle me. Roaring lions tearing their prey open their mouths wide against me* ⑧*. I am poured out like water, and all my bones are out of joint* ⑨*. My heart has turned to wax; it has melted away within me. My strength is dried up like a potsherd, and my tongue sticks to the roof of my mouth* ⑩*; you lay me in the dust of death* ⑪*. Dogs have surrounded me; a band of evil men has encircled me* ⑫*, they have pierced my hands and my feet* ⑬*. I can count* *all my bones* ⑭; *people stare and gloat over me* ⑮. *They divide my garments among them and cast lots for my clothing* ⑯.

But you, O LORD, *be not far off; O my Strength, come quickly to help me. Deliver my life from the sword, my precious life from the power of the dogs. Rescue me from the mouth of the lions; save me from the horns of the wild oxen.*

I will declare your name to my brothers; in the congregation I will praise you. You who fear the LORD, *praise him! All you descendants of Jacob, honor him* ⑰*! Revere him, all you descendants of Israel! For he has not despised or disdained the suffering of the afflicted one; he has not hidden his face from him but has listened to his cry for help.*

From you comes the theme of my praise in the great assembly; before those who fear you will I fulfill my vows ⑱. *The poor will eat and be satisfied; they who seek the* LORD *will praise him—may your hearts live forever* ⑲....*All the ends of the earth will remember and turn to the* LORD, *and he rules over the nations* ⑳.

All the rich of the earth will feast and worship; all who go down to the dust will kneel before him— those who cannot keep themselves alive ㉑. *Posterity will serve him; future generations will be told about the Lord. They will proclaim his righteousness to a people yet unborn* ㉒*—for he has done it* ㉓.

Though written by David some 1000 years prior to Jesus' time, this one psalm (often called the "crucifixion psalm") provides many details about the death of Jesus as recorded by the Gospel authors. These authors even point out Jesus' fulfillments of Psalm 22. Here are the 23 prophetic details numbered above, as they correspond with the New Testament accounts:

1. With the first words he spoke on the cross—"My God, my God, why have you forsaken me?"—Jesus called the onlookers' attention to this prophetic psalm. It was an indication that prophecy in God's Word was going to be fulfilled (Matthew 27:46; Mark 15:34).

2. Jesus acknowledged that God was the One enthroned (Revelation 3:21; 4:2-11; 7:15).

3. Jesus acknowledged that God was the God of the Jewish forefathers (Matthew 22:31-32; Mark 12:26).

4. Jesus was scorned and despised (John 15:18,24-25).

5. Jesus was mocked (Matthew 27:41-43).

6. Jesus was steadfastly committed to God.

7. Jesus relied on God as always near, even when others ran away (Matthew 26:56).

8. His enemies encircled him—both when he was mocked with a crown of thorns on his head and at the foot of the cross (Matthew 27:29,41-43).

9. Bones coming out of joint is typical of crucifixion.

10. Jesus was thirsty during the crucifixion (John 19:28).

11. Jesus died physically (Mark 15:37).

12. Evil men encircled Jesus (Matthew 27:28-31).

13. Jesus' hands and feet were nailed to the cross. (The Psalm 22 prophecy was made 600 years before crucifixion was invented—see John 20:25).

14. Crucifixion causes extreme dehydration and wasting of the body (John 19:28).

15. The onlookers gloated over Jesus' death (Matthew 27:29,41-43).

16. The Roman soldiers gambled for Jesus' clothing (John 19:23-24).

17. Jesus gave honor and praise to God.

18. Jesus gave continued praise and reverence to God.

19. Jesus declared that those who sought and found God would live forever (John 3:16,36).

20. At the end of the earth, all peoples will bow down to God (Revelation 4:10; Romans 14:11).

21. Everyone will ultimately bow down and worship God (Revelation 4:10; Romans 14:11).

22. Future generations will hear of Jesus and God (Mark 13:10).

23. "It is finished," Jesus' final words on the cross, convey essentially the same message as the close of the crucifixion psalm, "For he has done it" (John 19:30).

Psalm 22 is consistent from beginning to end in describing the crucifixion of Jesus. Perhaps Jesus' opening remarks on the cross were to draw future generations to this prophetic psalm. While some skeptics may claim that Jesus actually set out to fulfill these and other prophecies, we can then simply ask how Jesus fulfilled the many prophecies beyond his control (such as the actions of the Romans).

_____Key Concept_____

*Psalm 22 is one of the most important prophecy
chapters in the Bible because it so completely prophesied the crucifixion—the focal point of Jesus' role
on earth.*

When

The Timing of Jesus' Birth Was Defined

Genesis prophesied that the scepter would not "pass"
from Judah until "he comes to whom it belongs"(that is, the
Messiah):

> *The scepter will not depart from Judah,*
> *nor the ruler's staff from between his feet,*
> *until he comes to whom it belongs*
> *and the obedience of the nations is his.*

—Genesis 49:10

By Jewish definition, the "scepter" referred to the control
of the administration of the death penalty. The Jewish nation
maintained this control even through the first exile—until
the Romans took over in A.D. 11.[1] At that time, the Jewish
religious leadership "tore their garments" in mourning that
the scepter had passed and no messiah had arrived. Unfortunately, these leaders did not realize that the messiah had
already come—in the form of a baby born in Bethlehem.

The Coming of the Messiah to Jerusalem

> *From the issuing of the decree to restore and*
> *rebuild Jerusalem until the Anointed One, the*

ruler, comes, there will be seven "sevens," and sixty-two "sevens." It will be rebuilt with streets and a trench, but in times of trouble. After the sixty-two "sevens," the Anointed One will be cut off and will have nothing. The people of the ruler who will come will destroy the city and the sanctuary (Daniel 9:25-26).

This prophecy requires some understanding of Jewish culture and historical events. However, once it is understood, it is one of the most amazing and important prophecies about Jesus. It literally defines the exact day that he would ride into Jerusalem on a donkey, allowing himself (for the first time) to be hailed as king (Palm Sunday).

First, "Anointed One" is the literal translation of the word "Messiah"—the one anointed by God. Second, "Seven 'sevens'" plus "sixty-two 'sevens'" equals an important time frame of 69 "sevens." To the Jews, "seven" could be any period of seven—days, months, or years. Assuming 69 periods of seven years, and multiplying those 483 years by the Jewish standard year of 360 days, we obtain the result of 173,880 days. (It is important to note that the Jews considered 360 days as a year and that prophetic "years" would be stated in this 360-day time frame.)

This relationship was most famously recognized by Sir Robert Anderson, in his book *The Coming Prince*. Harold Hoehner, in his book *Chronological Aspects of the Life of Christ,* came up with exactly the same number of days as Anderson. Within a time period of 173,880 days from the decree by Artaxerxes to rebuild Jerusalem and the Temple, the Messiah would arrive at Jerusalem as "the ruler."[2]

Amazingly, the 173,880-day period from Artaxerxes' decree ends exactly at the day of the entry of Jesus into Jerusalem on Palm Sunday (the tenth of Nisan by the

Jewish calendar), which both scholars recognized. Daniel's prophecy exactly identifies Jesus as the perfect lamb of the Jewish Passover, which was always selected on the tenth of Nisan as prescribed in the Tanakh (Exodus 12:3). We can note many references to Jesus as the Passover lamb—by prophets like Isaiah (Isaiah 53), by John the Baptist (John 1:29), and ultimately in the book of Revelation (Revelation 5:6). All of these references precisely fit the entry of Jesus into Jerusalem and his being hailed on the same day the Passover lamb was selected (and crucified on the day the lamb was slaughtered).

Hoehner explains the precision of the prophecy thus:

> Multiplying the sixty-nine weeks by seven years for each week by 360 days gives a total of 173,880 days. The difference between 444 B.C. and A.D. 33 then is 476 solar years. By multiplying the 476 by 365.24219879 or by 365 days, 5 hours, 48 minutes, 45.975 seconds [there are 365 ¼ days in a year], one comes to 173,855 days, 6 hours, 52 minutes, 44 seconds, or 173,855 days. This leaves only 25 days to be accounted for between 444 B.C. and A.D. 33. By adding the 25 days to March 5 (of 444 B.C.), one comes to March 30 (of A.D. 33) which was Nisan 10 in A.D. 33. This was the triumphal entry of Jesus into Jerusalem.[3]

A few points that further help us understand Daniel's prophecy are:

- An actual solar year has 365.24219879 days. (This is the exact length of time required for the earth to make one circuit around the sun.) Understanding the prophecy requires adjusting the Hebrew year to an exact solar year (the God of the universe would know the solar year).

- Although several "decrees" were made by Persian kings about Jerusalem, the only decree that completely fits with Daniel's words is the decree by Artaxerxes in 444 B.C. ("in the twentieth year of King Artaerxes"—Nehemiah 2:1-8) that was made for a complete restoration of the city. (Other decrees were focused on the Temple or fell short in restoration of the city.)

The timing of Jesus' entry into Jerusalem on Palm Sunday—the first time he allowed himself to be called "King of Israel"—was precisely predicted by Daniel, to the day. This is unimaginable by random chance. And the prophecy continues on to describe the destruction of the city and the Temple, which happened in A.D. 70 under the Romans.

Where

The "Ruler's" Place of Birth Was Prophesied

But you, Bethlehem Ephrathah, though you are small among the clans of Judah, out of you will come for me one who will be ruler over Israel, whose origins are from of old, from ancient times (Micah 5:2).

Two things make the prophecy of the Messiah's birthplace particularly interesting: 1) that it was in a specific, very small town, and 2) that it would be a ruler "from ancient times," which seems to refer to something supernatural. In fact, the *precise*

The two time prophecies about Jesus are among the most amazing and important in the Bible. First, they are incredibly specific and therefore indicate divine inspiration. And second, they define both his physical birth and the "birth" of Jesus' ultimate kingship on Palm Sunday.

town indicated in the prophecy was a small town outside of Jerusalem—Bethlehem Ephrathah, in Judea, not the Bethlehem closer to Joseph and Mary's hometown of Nazareth.

But the "origins" of the ruler over Israel were to be "from of old, from ancient times." This indicates a more significant claim. The Messiah would need to preexist his birth in a supernatural way. This claim is made of Jesus by the apostle John (John 1, especially verses 1-2 and 14; Revelation 1:8). The apostle Paul also declares that Jesus has been in existence since before the beginning of time (2 Timothy 1:9).

Test Yourself

1. What ancestors of Jesus were prophesied?

2. List at least five things that were prophesied about "what" Jesus would be.

3. What two prophecies concerning the "when" of Jesus were made? Where can they be found in the Bible? Why are they important?

4. Explain the "Palm Sunday" prophecy in a way that an average person can understand it.

5. What is the "where" prophecy? And where is it located in the Bible?

Chapter 22 Group Study

Homework Preparation (do prior to group)
Read: John 2:4; Luke 19:37-40; chapter 22 of this text; and pages 22–25 in *Does the Bible Predict the Future?* ✝.

Opening Prayer
Discussion: Read John 2:4 and Luke 19:37-40. What did Jesus mean when he said his time had not yet "come," in speaking to his mother? How was this different in Luke 19:37-40? Discuss the prophecy of Jesus' entry on Palm Sunday so everyone understands it.

Practical-Experience Game
Debate: A "Christian" will debate a "nonbeliever" over the reliability of prophecy in defining the deity and role of Jesus.

Closing Prayer

Statistical Prophecy
Proof of Jesus
Compared to Others

Many specific prophecies about Jesus have been reviewed. We know that the Old Testament manuscripts were made before the time of Jesus (part 2). Likewise the New Testament manuscripts, widely circulated during the time of Jesus (also see part 2), provide evidence that the fulfillment of prophecies was accurate.

So the essential question is, what does this mean? Are the prophecies statistically reliable enough to draw conclusions about Jesus and his claims? To answer these questions, let's start with an estimate of only 30 of the prophecies about Jesus.

Messianic Prophecy	A "Guesstimate" of Odds
1. Shem an ancestor (Genesis 9–10)	1/3
2. Abraham an ancestor (Genesis 22:18)	1/1000
3. Isaac an ancestor (Genesis 26:4)	1/10,000
4. Jacob an ancestor (Genesis 28:14)	1/100,000
5. Judah an ancestor (Genesis 49:10)	1/1,000,000
6. Jesse an ancestor (Isaiah 11:1-5)	1/10,000,000
7. King David an ancestor (2 Samuel 7:11-16)	1/100,000,000

8. Bethlehem Ephrathah as birthplace
   (Micah 5:2)   1/100,000

9. Star connected with birth
   (Numbers 24:17)   1/100,000

10. Called "God with us" (Isaiah 7:14)   1/100,000

11. Calming the sea (Psalm 107:29)   1/10,000,000

12. "Special" miracles (Isaiah 35:4-6)   1/100,000,000

13. Names given (Iaiah 9:6)   1/10,000

14. Use of parables (Psalm 78:2)   1/10

15. Ultimate king over all
    (Isaiah 45:23; Psalm 22)   1/10

16. Sin offering and Passover lamb
    (Isaiah 53)   1/100

17. Will die with "wicked men"
    (Isaiah 53:3-9)   1/10

18. Will be buried with a rich man
    (Isaiah 53:3-9)   1/10

19. Timing of entry into Jerusalem
    (Daniel 9:20-27)   1/10,000,000

20. Entering Jerusalem as a king on
    a donkey (Zechariah 9:9)   1/100

21. Betrayed by a friend—for 30 pieces
    of silver (Zechariah 11:12-13)   1/1000

22. Rejection by Israel; will say
    nothing at his trial (Isaiah 8:10; 53)   1/10,000

23. Hands and feet pierced (Psalm 22)   1/10,000

24. Identifying the place of crucifixion
    (Genesis 22)   1/1,000,000

25. Will thirst while being put to death
    (Psalm 69:20-22)   1/10

26. No bones broken (Psalm 22)   1/10

27. Identification of words at the
    beginning and end of execution
    (Psalm 22)   1/1000

28. Lots cast for clothing (Psalm 22)   1/1000

29. Will be given gall and wine
    (Psalm 69:20-22)   1/10

30. Will be "pierced"
    (Isaiah 53:5; Zechariah 12:10)   1/100

The cumulative probability of all these prophecies randomly coming true in one person would be 1 chance in 10^{110}. This would be like winning about 16 lotteries in a row. Even if a skeptic were to substantially reduce some of the above estimates, the result would still be deemed impossible. For example, let's very conservatively assume the above estimates are off by a factor of a trillion trillion! This would still result in the "impossible odds" of all prophecies coming true in one man—Jesus—of one chance in 10^{86}! How remote are these odds? They would still be like taking all of the matter in the entire universe (that is, one billion billion stars and solar systems) and breaking it all down into subatomic particles, and randomly selecting one marked electron! Truly the prophecies made about Jesus in the Old Testament alone verify his divinity because they verify the Bible's claims about him, and his claims about himself.

Prophecies Made by Jesus Himself

Old Testament prophecies provide powerful evidence about Jesus. However, there is also evidence that Jesus himself is a divine prophet. Although he prophesied many things, by far the most significant were his multiple prophecies that he would be betrayed, crucified, and on the third day *rise from the dead*:

> *Now as Jesus was going up to Jerusalem, he took the twelve disciples aside and said to them, "We are going up to Jerusalem, and the Son of Man will be betrayed to the chief priests and the teachers of the law. They will condemn him to death and will turn him over to the Gentiles to be mocked and flogged and crucified. On the third day he will be raised to life!"* (Matthew 20:17-19).

Fascinating Fact

Jesus prophesied his death and resurrection numerous times, in all four Gospels:

- Matthew 12:40; 16:21; 17:22-23; 20:17-19; 26:61; 27:40; 27:63
- Mark 8:31; 9:30-32; 10:32-34; 14:58; 15:29-30
- Luke 9:21-22,44-45; 18:31-34
- John 2:13-22; 3:14-16; 12:32-34

If there was ever an unusual and amazing prophecy, it would be one with the specific details of the prophesier's death, and far more, that he would rise from the dead in three days! Out of all kinds of prophecy, this one is phenomenal and would be beyond any odds imaginable!

So central was this prophecy to Jesus' life that he stated it many times; it was recorded in the Gospel accounts in 18 places (see above)! It is a prediction that only an all-knowing God could make and fulfill.

In addition to this, Jesus also prophesied specifically about other things as well:

- One of his disciples would betray him (Matthew 26:21; Mark 14:17-21; Luke 22:21-22).

- His disciples would desert him (Matthew 26:30-31; Mark 14:26-27).

- Peter would disown him three times (Matthew 26:33-34; Mark 14:29-30; Luke 22:31-34).

- He would meet the disciples in Galilee after he had risen (Mark 14:28).

Key Concept

Jesus' prophecy of himself that he would be betrayed, crucified, and raised from the dead was made by him 18 times in the New Testament. Its fulfillment is ultimate proof that he is who he claimed to be—God.

Other People Believed That Jesus Was God

An obvious question is, with all the prophetic evidence, did the Jews of the day, who certainly would be aware of the prophecies in the Tanakh, think that Jesus was God?

In fact, the Jews in Jerusalem were very rapidly accepting Jesus as Messiah in the months after his death. The Bible reported that the number who immediately believed in the resurrection (presumably the eyewitnesses) was at least 120

(Acts 1:15) before the Feast of Pentecost—which was 50 days after the resurrection. (It could have been more since this verse refers only to believers present at that setting.) When Peter spoke on the Day of Pentecost, immediately 3000 men were added to the group of believers (Acts 2:41). Why was Peter's message so compelling? Because it was based on the prophecies the Jews knew and the events they had witnessed or had heard about. The Bible further reports that the number increased daily (2:47).

With additional study of the biblical record we find that when Peter and John were speaking before the people and the Sanhedrin (the ruling religious council), the number of followers had already grown to 5000 men. Adding in women and children, the count could easily have approached 15,000 people—in a city of a little over 100,000 at the time. Within days, believers in Jesus had become nearly 15 percent of the local population! No wonder the religious leaders were extremely concerned! And of course the great persecution of Jesus' followers was soon underway.

There is also other evidence from biblical writings that the early Jews believed Jesus was God. First, let's consider the Jewish Gospel writers (Matthew, Mark, and John). After all, they not only were with Jesus and knew him well, but they also took the time to write the accounts while the eyewitnesses to the events were still alive. All of them faced persecution and risked death, based on the truth of what they had written in the Gospel accounts.

One of the most striking indications of the early belief that Jesus was God is in the Gospel of John. John himself was an eyewitness to all the events of Jesus' life, and his account was both written and circulated during the lifetime of other eyewitnesses:

In the beginning was the Word, *and the Word was with God, and the Word was God. He was with God in the beginning.*

Through him all things were made; without him nothing was made that has been made. In him was life, and that life was the light of men. The light shines in the darkness, but the darkness has not understood it.

There came a man who was sent from God; his name was John. [This is speaking of John the Baptist.] *He came as a witness to testify concerning that light, so that through him all men might believe. He himself was not the light; he came only as a witness to the light. The true light that gives light to every man was coming into the world.*

He was in the world, and though the world was made through him, the world did not recognize him. He came to that which was his own, but his own did not receive him. Yet to all who received him, to those who believed in his name, he gave the right to become children of God—children born not of natural descent, nor of human decision or a husband's will, but born of God.

The Word became flesh and made his dwelling among us. *We have seen his glory, the glory of the One and Only, who came from the Father, full of grace and truth* (John 1:1-14).

John's words clearly show that he believed that Jesus was God. And others who were close to him also believed that he was God.

- Peter worshiped him (Luke 5:8). A Jew would worship no one other than God.

- Likewise, Thomas worshiped him (John 20:28).

- Peter, James, and John witnessed and reported the "transfiguration" (Matthew 17), a visible demonstration that Jesus possessed the same glory as God the Father.

- Elizabeth, Jesus' relative, believed that he was God (Luke 1:41-55).

- Simeon, a devout Jewish prophet, believed that Jesus was God (Luke 2:25-35).

- Anna, a prophetess, believed he was God (Luke 2:36-38).

- Even Jesus' half brothers James and Jude eventually believed that Jesus was God (see the books of James and Jude).

- A Roman centurion and others who were at the crucifixion believed Jesus to be God:

> *At that moment the curtain of the temple was torn in two from top to bottom. The earth shook and the rocks split. The tombs broke open and the bodies of many holy people who had died were raised to life. They came out of the tombs, and after Jesus' resurrection they went into the holy city and appeared to many people.*
>
> *When the centurion and those with him who were guarding Jesus saw the earthquake and all that had happened, they were terrified, and exclaimed, "Surely he was the Son of God!"* (Matthew 27:51-54).

The high priest and others at Jesus' trial believed that Jesus was claiming to be God incarnate:

The high priest said to him, "I charge you under oath by the living God. Tell us if you are the Christ, the Son of God."

"Yes, it is as you say," Jesus replied. "But I say to all of you: In the future you will see the Son of Man sitting at the right hand of the Mighty One and coming on the clouds of heaven."

Then the high priest tore his clothes and said, "He has spoken blasphemy! Why do we need any more witnesses? Look, now you have heard the blasphemy" (Matthew 26:63-65).

Not only did the high priest officially declare that Jesus had blasphemed, but his tearing of his clothes was a sign of mourning and revulsion over blasphemy.

Other Holy Books Fail the Prophecy Test

Given that prophecy is a true test of something from God it is not surprising that very few holy books attempt any prophecy. After all, since only God can prophesy—and we would expect that most supposed "holy books" are not really from God—it would be difficult to concoct testable prophecy that would be verifiable (like the Bible).

We should not underestimate the significance of vast numbers of Jews switching so quickly to a belief that Jesus was God incarnate—part of a Trinity. *First,* religion was far more indoctrinated in their society than in Western culture today. Hence, making a dramatic change in thinking would be far more difficult. *Second,* the Jews were used to thinking of God in only one person—not three, in the sense of a Trinity. *Third,* there would have been vast political and social pressure to remain steadfast to the Jewish leadership.

Considering other well-known religions, we find the following:

Eastern religions (Hinduism, Buddhism, Confucius, Shinto). These religions are essentially "mystical–philosophical" religions and therefore tend not to use or depend on prophecy.

Islam (and the Qur'an). Although Islam is history-based and agrees with many of the same historical figures mentioned in the Bible (Abraham, Ishmael, Jesus, Mary, and so on), it cannot prove its inspiration from God using prophecy.[1] The Qur'an was written based on dictation by Muhammad (570–632 A.D.). Islamic leaders say there are 22 predictive prophecies in the Qur'an (Sura 2:23-24; 3:10,106,107,144; 5:70; 8:7; 9:14; 15:9,96; 24:55; 28:85; 30:2-4; 41:42; 48:16-21, 27-28; 54:44-48; 56:1-56; 110:1-2).

However, of those listed, Sura 2:23-24,88-89; Sura 3:10, 106,107,144; Sura 8:7; Sura 9:14; Sura 28:85; Sura 48:16-21,27,28; Sura 54:44-48; and Sura 56:1-56 all deal with end-time prophecy and can't be tested (just like the biblical prophecy that was excluded). Sura 5:70; 15:9; 41:42; and 15:96 are not prophecies, but generalities and warnings. Sura 24:55 is a promise of a blessing of land and wealth to believers in Islam. However it does not specify what land, as in the case of Israel. Sura 54:44-48 prophesies military action against enemies of the religion—but this doesn't say much, as it is what people tend to do anyway. And Sura 110:1-2 promises help from Allah (Islam's God) in time of war. Again, this isn't specific—as, for instance, a claim to victory in a specific battle or war.

Sura 30:2-4 is the only potential historical prophecy, although it has problems. It essentially says that, "The Roman Empire has been defeated in a land close by; but they, (even) after (this) defeat of theirs, will soon be victorious within a few years. With Allah is the Decision, in the past and in the Future: on that Day shall the Believers rejoice." In history, the Persians were victorious over the Eastern Roman Empire in A.D. 615, and then the Romans returned to defeat the Persians 13 years later in 628. According to Muhammad, "a few" years in this prophecy was meant to mean 3 to 9 years, with 13 falling outside of this range. Even so, the prophecy would not be particularly surprising since there was an ongoing war in this region, and it was not uncommon for territory to be recaptured.

Mormons (the Book of Mormon, Doctrines and Covenants). The Book of Mormon was actually written in the early 1800s, supposedly translated from golden plates written before the time of Jesus (unfortunately, these valuable plates have never been available for verification). Even so, giving the plates the benefit of the doubt, the Book of Mormon contains two prophecies about Jesus, both of which are false:

> And behold, he shall be born of Mary, at Jerusalem which is the land of our forefathers, she being a virgin, a precious and chosen vessel, who shall be overshadowed and conceive by the power of the Holy Ghost, and bring forth a son, yes even the Son of God (Alma 7:10, Book of Mormon).

Of course Jesus was born in *Bethlehem,* not Jerusalem. Some may claim that Bethlehem is a suburb of Jerusalem; however when transportation was by foot, a town an hour and a half away would not be considered a suburb. Even the Book of Mormon indicates it is a separate city (1 Nephi 1:4).

Here's another example:

> But behold, thus saith the Lord God: "When the day cometh that they (the Jews) shall believe in me, that

I am Christ, then have I covenanted with their fathers that they shall be restored in the flesh, upon the earth unto the lands of their inheritance" (2 Nephi 10:7, Book of Mormon).

Of course the Jews did return to the land in 1948 despite not yet "believing" in Jesus.

The Mormon book of Doctrine and Covenants contains several prophetic errors (with none right, in fact) regarding a Temple that was to be built in western Missouri within a generation of Joseph Smith's prediction in the early 1800s: 1) A temple was to be built at a consecrated site in Jackson County, Missouri ("Zion"), within a generation of 1832 (Doctrines and Covenants 84:5,31). 2) The city ("Zion") was "never to be moved" out of that place (97:19; 101:17-21). Over 150 years have passed with no temple built there.

The Jehovah's Witnesses (The Watchtower, Studies in Scripture). This non-Christian group has repeatedly failed in attempts to prophesy the end of time.

- (2:101)—1914 to be the year of the "battle" of the great day of God Almighty (Revelation 16:14)

- (1914 edition)—"end of the world" date changed to 1915

- (7:62)—date changed to 1918

- (7:542)—date changed to 1920

- (Miscellaneous other publications)—date of the end of the world repeatedly changed to 1925, 1942, 1975, 1980...

With continuing research, one would find that there is no religion, person, or holy book that contains prophecy of any substance whatsoever—and certainly nothing close to the prophecy in the Bible. This would lead one to carefully heed the words of the Bible as truth.

Test Yourself

1. Name at least five messianic prophecies with your estimate of odds that you believe you could defend. How would you explain the certainty of Jesus' deity?

2. How many Gospel references indicate Jesus' prophecy of death and resurrection?

3. What Gospel references indicate Jesus' claim of deity?

4. Why is the resurrection vital to the claim of deity?

5. What other holy books attempt prophecy? What is the result?

Chapter 23 Group Study

Homework Preparation (do prior to group)

Read: Jesus' prophecies of his death and resurrection—see pages 355–357) and pages 26–29 in *Does the Bible Predict the Future?* ✝.

Opening Prayer

Discussion: Discuss the probability estimates on pages 353–355. As a group review each of them, and reduce them to as ridiculously low a level as the group deems "reasonable." Does this new low level still support the claim that prophecy shows Jesus as divine? Now, consider and add in the prophecy of the resurrection. Does that change anything?

Practical-Experience Game

Press conference: The "press corps" is challenging the "Christian spokesperson" on his claim that prophecy sets Christianity apart from all other religions.

Closing Prayer

Part 3

Evidence of God, the Bible, and Jesus in Prophecy: Summary and Conclusion

The Bible tells us that it is important to "test everything" to see if it is from God. Furthermore, it tells us what test to use—100-percent perfect prophecy. Only God can predict the future. The Bible does not exclude itself from this test.

Prophecy takes three basic forms. Short-term prophecy is prophecy that was made and fulfilled within a relatively short period of time. Often prophecies were written in the same books of the Bible in which they were fulfilled. While short-term prophecy might not satisfy a modern-day skeptic about supernatural inspiration, it was vital for the early Jews to determine what people were prophets and what writings were holy Scripture.

Long-term prophecy is prophecy that was given at one point in time and fulfilled in history, often verified in archaeology, many years later. These prophecies provide assurance to later generations that the Bible is inspired and that its words, including those about Jesus, can be trusted.

End-time prophecy is prophecy about the end of time, heaven, and life after death. While there is no way of verifying such prophecy, the vast number of other prophecies fulfilled in the Bible encourages us to trust the prophecies about the future.

Prophecy lends itself to statistical analysis. Although the odds of most prophecies are difficult to ascertain, a reasonable order of magnitude can be estimated. We find that the probability of many biblical prophecies is extremely remote. However, even if the odds are greatly over- or understated, the vast number of correct prophecies in the Bible, with none being wrong, allows us to apply statistical analysis to reach a conclusion even if a single prophecy's odds are greatly changed. One example was given, in which an absurdly conservative probability of only one chance in ten was applied to 118 long-term prophecies, when in fact the odds would be far more remote. The conclusion did not require the more realistic odds—proof of God's inspiration was apparent anyway.

Likewise, we find that the large number of prophecies of Jesus verify his claim to deity. It is not even necessary to have a large number of prophecies regarding his deity since his own prophecies about one event—his death and his resurrection in three days—are alone enough to prove his deity.

Only Christianity has been able to prove itself through divine prophecy. The few other attempts made by other religions have failed. The most important conclusions we can draw from the hundreds of perfectly fulfilled prophecies in the Bible are

1. God is real (only God can perfectly prophesy)

2. the Bible is inspired by God

3. Jesus is the Messiah—God incarnate

Part 4

Evidence of the Resurrection of Jesus

The apostle Paul did not mince words regarding the importance of the resurrection for the Christian faith. As indicated in the above verses, the entire Christian faith hinges on the historical fact of the resurrection. Without the resurrection, there is no basis for faith in Christ, and all people remain unforgiven and are still "dead" in their sins.

Some Christians may ask why the resurrection is necessary. After all, the Bible makes it clear that it was the *crucifixion* that was the ultimate sacrifice for our sin, not the resurrection (Romans 4:25). Why couldn't Jesus be crucified, with believers obtaining redemption on that alone, without the resurrection? Part 3 (Prophecy) provides us the answer. Prophecy indicated that the Messiah would not see death. First, we find it in Old Testament prophecy about the Messiah:

A Verse to Memorize

...nor will you let your Holy One see decay (Psalm 16:10).

The only ways that the "Holy One" (Messiah) could not "see decay" would be for him 1) to not experience death, or 2) to be resurrected. Since we know that a blood sacrifice had to take place in order that humans become redeemed, *the only remaining alternative (to not "see decay") would be the resurrection.*

Likewise, there are 18 references in the Gospels to Jesus' prophecy about his death and resurrection in three days (see pages 355-357).

The resurrection of Jesus is important for many reasons: 1) It demonstrates hope for all mankind and reveals the ultimate triumph of God over evil. 2) It indicates the eternal life that is available to all believers. However, first and foremost, the resurrection is important because it verifies Jesus' claim to be God. As we have seen, only 100-percent perfect prophecy proves that something is from God. In this case, the resurrection was prophesied before Jesus and fulfilled by him. Moreover, it was prophesied by Jesus himself many times. Because of his fulfilling the resurrection, we can be certain that Jesus is God incarnate as he claimed. By fulfilling the resurrection, we can trust the words he spoke regarding his blood sacrifice as the ultimate sin offering:

Just as Moses lifted up the snake in the desert, so the Son of Man must be lifted up, that everyone who believes in him may have eternal life (John 3:14-15).

Also, if the resurrection did not happen, it would indicate that Jesus was, in fact, a false prophet. We could not trust his claim, and his blood sacrifice would have been worthless. As Paul indicated, without it we would be eternally dead in our sin (see 1 Corinthians 15:17-18).

Along with helping us trust Jesus regarding the all-important words of his primary mission on earth—to be a sacrifice to redeem believers to a relationship with God—the resurrection provides us assurance of *all of the words of Jesus' teaching*. Hence we find the resurrection is of priceless importance.

Why Test the Bible's Claims About Jesus?

History readily provides us with reasons to test the basis for our faith. Let's look at two remarkably similar examples of faith, nearly 2000 years apart, with two very different leaders.

Two Examples of Faith

Example 1: On November 18, 1978, a small group of investigators entered the camp of Jonestown, Guyana. It was a scene of horror. Piles upon piles of dead bodies huddled together. Families. Young children. More than 900 people lay dead—276 were children.

Investigation later told the story of how a religious leader, Jim Jones, had wooed his followers along a path of faith and trust in him to the point that they willingly drank cyanide-laced Kool-Aid.

Example 2: In the years of Emperor Trajan (98–117), followers of Jesus Christ were asked to either deny the faith or face a painful martyr's death. To gain freedom, all they needed to do was 1) renounce allegiance to Jesus and 2) worship Emperor Trajan by bowing to his statue. Many Christians

willingly gave their lives for their belief that Jesus was the
Son of God.

—w— —w— —w—

Jim Jones or Jesus Christ? In each case the people felt
strongly about their leader before they met their deaths.
How do we really know who was right? As the Jim Jones
example pointed out, there are many documented cases
where a leader gained the confidence of others and eventually seduced them into an untimely death. Recent examples
include David Koresh in Waco, Texas, and Marshall Applewhite, who deluded Heaven's Gate followers in San Diego,
California. These kinds of leaders, however, are extreme
and rare.

Perhaps even more dangerous, though, are the leaders
who draw people into a religion that is really false by making
such wonderful promises that the people follow them and
reject the one true way. These types of leaders are common-
place. And such leaders seem far more acceptable than the
extreme ones. But isn't the end result—luring people into a
false hope that ends in eternal death—just as deadly? Their
ability to attract much, much larger crowds than the extreme
leaders makes them far more dangerous. Examples of such
dangerous leaders are those in well-known organizations
such as the Mormon Church, The Watchtower (Jehovah's
Witnesses), Christian Science, and Unity School of Christianity. All of these use a "guise" of Christianity while
denying the deity and blood sacrifice of Jesus—thereby
denying eternal life to their members.

Choosing Jesus Christ as a leader is serious. He said we
must follow him and reject the false teaching of others. As
with the early Christians, for some people in certain countries, following Jesus is a potential life-or-death decision. For

most people today, however, it is not a fatal decision for life on Earth. However, according to Jesus, in all situations, following him or not has consequences regarding eternal life. The options are simply stated: Follow him and have eternal life; reject him and miss eternal life.

> *Whoever believes in the Son has eternal life, but whoever rejects the Son will not see life, for God's wrath remains on him* (John 3:36).

So the decision to follow Jesus is of enormous importance. And the decision to reject every other teaching is likewise of extreme importance. Many people rightfully ask, "How can we know that the Bible's teaching about Jesus is right?" "Aren't all religions basically the same?" Some people ask, "Why wouldn't God reveal himself in other holy books?" or, "Why wouldn't he reveal himself through other people as well?" Many also ask, "Why does Christianity have to be so narrow? It doesn't seem to make sense that such a big God would be 'boxed' into such a narrow religion as the Christianity taught by the Bible."

However, it doesn't matter what we "think" should be right. What really matters is what *is* right, whether it fits our personal view or not. *In that regard, we should consider what evidence is available to make an informed decision.*

As already has been pointed out in this book, the Bible does not ask us to accept it on blind faith. In fact, the Bible commands us to "test everything," including the Bible itself:

> *Test everything. Hold on to the good* (1 Thessalonians 5:21).

The above examples indicate why the Bible would prescribe such a test. Blind faith can lead to faith in anything. It can lead to faith in the religious leader of one's parents. It can

The Bible makes it clear that following Jesus leads to eternal life with God, while rejecting Jesus leads to eternal wrath. The above verse is one of the most specific, clear verses in the Bible that define the choice to follow or not follow Jesus.

lead to the most popular faith in the community. It can lead to the faith of friends. And it can even lead to faith in people such as Jim Jones, David Koresh, and Marshall Applewhite. However, *properly tested faith will lead only to the truth*. Therefore, if Jesus Christ is real and if the claims of the Bible regarding him are real, faith in him should be able to withstand being tested. People already having faith in the Bible should have nothing to fear. And if the Bible is wrong, shouldn't it be rejected anyway?

Testing the Truth of the Resurrection

Already we have analyzed several issues regarding the validity of Jesus:

1. We have examined the historical record of Jesus as supported through archaeology (part 2) and have found that there are many archaeological finds that support the biblical account of Jesus, with none that dispute the record.

2. We have examined the prophecies about the coming Messiah and have concluded that a statistical analysis of the probability of all of the Messianic prophecies coming true in one person is beyond reason—without divine intervention. Yet all have come true in Jesus.

3. Likewise, we have reviewed the prophecies of Jesus himself (pages 355-357) and have discovered that his prophecies of the resurrection alone are spectacular enough to warrant his claim to be God incarnate (not to mention his many other prophecies).

4. We have reviewed the manuscript evidence (pages 187-194) and have concluded that the manuscripts of the prophecies were reliably written prior to Jesus' birth and are therefore trustworthy.

5. We have reviewed the manuscript evidence (pages 197-205) and have concluded that the New Testament account of Jesus is reliable, therefore providing, among other things, evidence that the prophecies about Jesus were fulfilled.

So we can see that many vital points already corroborate the resurrection of Jesus. Most important of all is the prophetic verification of the resurrection. However, this prophecy would be worthless if the documents that contain the prophecies or their fulfillment are shown to be untrustworthy. Fortunately, there exists overwhelming evidence that both the prophetic documents (the Old Testament) and those indicating fulfillment (the Gospels) are trustworthy (see again, part 2).

Additionally, archaeology supports many facts that are claimed in the Bible (see chapters 15 and 16). While this in and of itself doesn't prove the resurrection, if there were a number of archaeological inconsistencies, then it would cast doubt on the reliability of the written record. Instead, archaeology adds to its trustworthiness.

Test Yourself

1. Quote two verses from Paul about the importance of the resurrection.

2. What is the difference between the role of the crucifixion and that of the resurrection?

3. Give some examples of how blind faith can be deadly.

4. Cite a very specific verse in the Bible about the consequences of accepting or rejecting Jesus.

5. What are some ways in which the resurrection can be verified?

Chapter 24 Group Study

Homework Preparation (do prior to group)
Read: Psalm 16:10; John 3:36; 1 Thessalonians 5:21; chapter 24 of this text; and pages 34–35 in *What is the Proof for the Resurrection?* ✝.

Opening Prayer
Discussion: Review the two examples of the stories on pages 373–374. Discuss why these stories are not so far fetched. See if the group can imagine being faced with a life-or-death choice for Jesus. What would each individual's choice be based on?

Practical-Experience Game
Role-playing: The "Christian" encounters a "non-Christian" who is excited about a new religious group he or she has been introduced to. Explain the importance of tested faith.

Closing Prayer

The Empty Tomb

We can only imagine what it was like in Jerusalem the day Jesus rose from the dead. Undoubtedly the news of the "missing" body was greeted differently depending on the perspective of each individual.

The tomb was empty.

From the perspective of Herod, Pontius Pilate, and other Roman authorities, this introduced a new dilemma. Due to pressure from the local religious figures, they had acquiesced or agreed to the capital punishment of Jesus, despite unusual circumstances. Now they faced a potentially troublesome situation. How would the Pharisees and Sadducees maintain religious control if there was a groundswell of belief that Jesus rose from the dead? Jesus had prophesied his resurrection several times. His disciples were aware of it. The religious leaders were aware of it. And perhaps worst of all, part of the population of Jerusalem was aware of it. How would this news affect public opinion? Would people believe that Jesus had truly overcome death? Would they believe he was God? Would this cause volatile disputes between groups of Jewish people and disrupt Roman rule?

From the perspective of the Jewish religious leaders, it was a great disaster. They had presumed the execution of Jesus would eliminate this threat to their power once and for all. Now, Jesus' disciples might proclaim that he rose from the dead and was in fact God. If the disciples gained control of public opinion, they would further emphasize the teachings of Jesus, which had always undermined the power of the religious leaders. The very authority of the Jewish Council could be threatened. It might even mean the start of a new religion that could, perhaps, shake the foundations of centuries-old Judaism.

From the perspective of the people, there was confusion. The disciples were telling everyone that Jesus had been seen after he had died. What did this mean? Had Jesus really risen from the dead? Where was he? Exactly what had the disciples seen? If Jesus had really risen from the dead, did it verify his claim to be God? To many this might mean hope...hope in the many things that Jesus had taught during his life on Earth. Hope of eternal life.

Original Concerns About the Corpse of Jesus

The Jewish leaders had concerns about the corpse of Jesus from the outset. They realized that an unaccounted-for body would cause tremendous problems and feared the potential public response if it should be found missing. So great was this concern that they approached Pontius Pilate for a special favor, as indicated in Matthew's Gospel:

The next day, the one after Preparation Day, the chief priests and the Pharisees went to Pilate. "Sir," they said, "we remember that while he was still alive that deceiver said, 'After three days I will rise again.' So give the order for the tomb to be made secure until the third day. Otherwise, his disciples may come and steal the body and tell the people that he has been raised from the dead. This last deception will be worse than the first" (Matthew 27:62-64).

This request brought the issue of Jesus' teachings back into Pilate's domain. Would Pilate's interest go beyond merely appeasing the Jewish leaders? Was he also concerned about the potential public impact if Jesus' corpse were to disappear? Did Pilate's concern reveal a deep-seated fear that Jesus might really be who he claimed to be? After all, on the day of Jesus' death Pilate's wife had warned him not to have anything to do with the man because of a premonition she had had:

While Pilate was sitting on the judge's seat, his wife sent him this message: "Don't have anything to do with that innocent man, for I have suffered a great deal today in a dream because of him" (27:19).

This message suggests that Pilate had been discussing Jesus in his private home with his wife. Jesus' status must have been of some particular interest to him prior to the night of the trial.

Furthermore, Pilate had seemed to do everything he could to set Jesus free, even to the extent of offering the criminal Barabbas as a "replacement." When the crowd insisted upon crucifying Jesus while Pilate was on the judgment seat, the procurator "washed his hands in front of the crowd. 'I am innocent of this man's blood,' he said. 'It is your responsibility'" (27:24).

Whether Pilate's interest in monitoring the existence of Jesus' corpse was because of his fear of political problems or because of his curiosity or fear about Jesus' claims of deity, he quickly acquiesced to the high priest's requests to make the tomb secure:

> "Take a guard," Pilate answered. "Go, make the tomb as secure as you know how." So they went and made the tomb secure by putting a seal on the stone and posting the guard (27:65).

The Response of the Guard

The Roman guard responsible for the tomb of Jesus (which would have consisted of at least 16 soldiers) was in obvious shock with the events of the resurrection. When they observed the angel who rolled away the stone covering the tomb, the Bible says they became "like dead men" (Matthew 28:4). The absence of Jesus' corpse presented them with a difficult problem. Typically, if such guards allowed a prisoner (or in this case a corpse) to escape while they were sleeping or had deserted their posts,

The Romans, at the request of the Jewish leaders, did everything they could to secure the body of Jesus. This was because of the prophecy that Jesus would rise from the dead—which, as has been indicated, would have verified his claim to be God.

they would face the same sentence as the prisoner—in this case, crucifixion. The guards were clearly concerned for their fate, because they first approached the religious leaders to obtain help in approaching the political authority, probably so the military leaders wouldn't punish them. In addition, there was a need to provide a cover-up for the disappearance of the corpse:

> *Some of the guards went into the city and reported to the chief priests everything that had happened. When the chief priests had met with the elders and devised a plan, they gave the soldiers a large sum of money, telling them, "You are to say, 'His disciples came during the night and stole him away while we were asleep.' If this report gets to the governor, we will satisfy him and keep you out of trouble." So the soldiers took the money and did as they were instructed. And this story has been widely circulated among the Jews to this very day* (28:11-15).

So the Roman guard was essentially forced to concoct the story that they were sleeping while Jesus' disciples stole the body. In return for propagating the story, they received a large payment and protection from the highest local authority—the governor. *But if they were sleeping, how would they have known the disciples had stolen the body?* They wouldn't have witnessed it. On the other hand, it would have been difficult for 16 separate guards to keep the story of an angel with an appearance "like lightning" a secret for long (28:3). Someone would have likely told another person eventually. Just like today, when such a story leaks out, it eventually ends up in print—in the Bible, in this case.

Nevertheless, the "official" story of the guards falling asleep and the disciples stealing the body was supported by the religious and political establishment, so it is easy to understand why it became the ongoing popular story amongst the Jews who opposed the Christians.

The Response of the Religious Leaders

The Jewish authorities had a serious problem. Jesus, who had prophesied that he would be raised from the dead in three days, was nowhere to be found three days after his crucifixion. It was their worst nightmare. Now the followers of Jesus could call him God and have evidence to back it up. It didn't take long for the effects of the resurrection to have a major impact. Jesus' disciples immediately started celebrating his deity and began promoting it throughout the region. Within days, thousands were following Jesus as the Savior of the world. The authority of the official Jewish leaders and their teachings started waning among many.

With no corpse to prove Jesus' human mortality, the authorities couldn't prove that Jesus was simply another human being. Since they desperately needed Jesus' corpse, the Jewish leaders would have certainly used every means at their disposal to hunt down and find it. Families, friends, acquaintances, and anyone who had known Jesus would have been questioned. Workers in the synagogues would have been enlisted to search the places where a body might have been placed. In short, if the body of Jesus could be found, Christianity would be stopped dead in its tracks and the threat to historical Judaism would end. The Jewish authorities would maintain their rule.

> The religious leaders would have used every tool at their disposal to locate the corpse of Jesus. This would certainly have meant enlisting help from all of their loyal followers, of which there would have been many. No corpse could be found.

However if the corpse could *not* be produced, the religious leaders had a problem.

The Response of the Roman Leaders

The political establishment of Rome also had a stake in finding the corpse of Jesus. After all, Israel was a volatile religious state that could be upset by any serious challenge to traditional Judaism. The teachings of Jesus were anti-establishment at their best and heretical and revolutionary at their worst. However, they went even further, when we consider that he positioned himself as God incarnate. Many Jews would be forced to begin to deal with the complex and hard-to-understand issue of God being three persons in one Nature (the Trinity—Jesus refers to this in Matthew 28:19).

The Roman leaders would have used every tool at their disposal to locate the corpse of Jesus. This would certainly have involved ordering troops to search the surrounding area. No corpse could be found.

So a conflict between the religious leaders and followers of Jesus seemed inevitable. It would clearly be in the best interest of the Roman establishment to find Jesus' corpse to keep the peace.

The Romans had great resources at their disposal to attempt to find a body. Most importantly, they could invoke capital punishment on anyone found to be hiding the body. In fact, archaeology has located a first-century tomb in Nazareth that has an engraved message specifying the death penalty for anyone found to be grave-robbing. This unusually harsh penalty, interestingly, was found in Jesus' hometown. It was placed on a grave site soon after the resurrection. Perhaps it was in response to it?

The Response of the Disciples

When we consider the disciples during the time of the crucifixion and resurrection, we realize it would be absurd to think they might have stolen the body of Jesus. First, we must consider the disciples' unstable state of mind. Even though they had been warned repeatedly by Jesus that he would be crucified and later raised from the dead, it was obvious they doubted the prophecy. On the critical night of the betrayal, the disciples didn't even stay awake. During the period of Jesus' trial, Peter denied him three times. When he was crucified, the disciples were scattered and there was reluctance to believe in the resurrection. For instance, Thomas stated he would believe only when he placed his hand into Jesus' wounds. None of these events are indicative of a band of well-organized disciples capable of quickly formulating a clever plan to steal a body under professional Roman guard.

Second, even if the disciples had been motivated and ready to steal the body of Jesus, it would have been extremely difficult. The timing of the event would have been during the Sabbath. Movement during the Sabbath was limited and would have been an obvious problem if the disciples were planning the major theft of a body. Then there was the issue of a ragtag band of followers sneaking past the best-trained guards in the world. Finally, there were the problems of moving a two-ton stone and breaking an official Roman seal without detection.

The entire ministry of Jesus was focused on his role as the Son of God. In that role, his triumph over death through the resurrection was paramount. A dead Messiah would serve no purpose for the disciples. They had no motivation to steal the corpse of Jesus; it would be much simpler to just acknowledge they had been mistaken about Jesus. Furthermore, there would be nothing to gain by concocting a story of a resurrection and spreading it. To the contrary, once the persecution started, it would have been obvious that there was everything to lose by perpetuating a story of a phony Messiah.

Key Concept

The disciples would have had no motive to steal the body of Jesus because its presence would have identified Jesus as a false prophet—and the only future then faced by the disciples would have been persecution.

The Response of the Other Eyewitnesses

The 12 disciples were not the only ones to see the risen Christ! For instance, we know that several women saw him on the day of the resurrection. There were Mary Magdalene, Salome, and "the other Mary" (possibly the wife of Clopas or the mother of James and Joses). We also know that Jesus appeared to many other people, including 500 people at one time (1 Corinthians 15:6).

Having so many other witnesses would have made it more difficult for the religious leaders and Romans to sell the story of the disciples stealing the body. After all, why would other people, beyond the disciples themselves, claim to see the risen Christ?

Response of the City of Jerusalem

Jerusalem was faced with two opposing vantage points. On one side, the religious and political authorities indicated there was no corpse of Jesus because "against all odds" the disciples had stolen the body. Certainly these leaders would have commanded enormous respect from the populace. On the other hand, there were the disciples and other people who claimed to have witnessed the risen Jesus; hence, there would be no corpse. Of course, such a supernatural resurrection would also be against all odds. So the city had the dilemma of choosing between their leaders and credible witnesses. At

stake was a foundational change in religious belief. At stake
were the lives of many.

The result of Jerusalem's decision to believe the leaders or
the disciples immediately following the resurrection is
recorded by history. *The disciples and eyewitnesses won
easily. Christianity exploded in the city—and within days,
thousands of people became followers of Christ.* This is particularly significant because strict religious belief was of
paramount importance to the Jews. The idea of a God that
included Jesus (the beginning of the doctrine of the Trinity)
was revolutionary. Yet by A.D. 70, some estimate that an
enormous percentage of Jerusalem had become Christian.
Even today, in a culture far more tolerant of diversity, it
would be unheard of to envision a new religion taking over
such a large part of the populace in such a short period of
time. Yet we know Christianity grew very quickly. Otherwise there would not have been persecution, which history
records as occurring immediately. Christianity continued to
spread in spite of the persecution.

Security Measures at the Tomb

As we have indicated, the Jewish religious leaders had a
great concern about protecting the corpse of Jesus because
they recognized that if the body were to disappear, it would
be proclaimed a resurrection. Both the Pharisees and the
Romans presumed that by taking extraordinary security
measures, they could prevent a theft (they certainly didn't
take the resurrection prophecy by Jesus seriously).

When analyzing the issue of the guard posted at Jesus'
tomb, some people have wondered if the guard posted was
a Temple guard, not a Roman guard, as is usually assumed.
But even the Temple guard members were highly trained.
The Temple guard would have consisted of about ten men—
any one of whom would have been executed if he fell asleep
at an inappropriate time.

However, evidence overwhelmingly suggests that a Roman guard was dispatched to guard the body of Jesus, for the following reasons:

1. In the Bible, the Greek word *koustodia* (guard), when used in the context of Matthew 27:65, implied a Roman guard.

2. Pilate issued the order, implying he was in ultimate command of the guard. (If only a Temple guard had been used, why would the Pharisees have gone to Pilate to request help?)

3. When the guards approached the Jewish religious leaders after the resurrection, they were obviously concerned about the reaction of Pilate—not the religious leaders themselves. This is evident by the Jewish leaders' stating, "If this report [the report of the guards sleeping] gets to the governor, we will satisfy him and keep you out of trouble" (Matthew 28:14). If it were only a Temple guard, which was under the authority of the religious leaders, serious consequences would have resulted immediately. In this case, the religious leaders were sought out to try to avoid a sentence of execution that might be issued by the Roman authorities.

The Roman guard would have consisted of 16 soldiers for an important political prisoner like Jesus. These guards were typically arranged four on each side of whatever they were to protect. At night, four guards would have been placed directly in front of the entrance to the tomb, with the other 12 sleeping "face in" in a semicircle in front of the four that were at watch. Guards slept in shifts so that there would always be a minimum of four on watch at a time. As noted earlier any guard who deserted his post or fell asleep would face crucifixion.[1]

─────────Key Concept─────────

The guard posted in front of the tomb was almost certainly a Roman guard, which would normally have been 16 soldiers with alternating sleeping shifts to ensure constant protection. Penalty for sleeping out of shift or desertion was execution.

The Two-Ton Stone

The biblical historical record indicates that a stone covered the entrance to the tomb of Jesus, and it was a formidable barrier:

> *When the Sabbath was over, Mary Magdalene, Mary the mother of James, and Salome bought spices so that they might go to anoint Jesus' body. Very early on the first day of the week, just after sunrise, they were on their way to the tomb and they asked each other, "Who will roll the stone away from the entrance of the tomb?"* (Mark 16:1-3).

Scholars estimate that the stone enclosing the tomb of Jesus weighed about two tons. It was typical of the stones used in burial tombs at the time.[2]

Some critics suggest a rather outlandish alternative to the story of the disciples stealing the body. They say that Jesus never died, but simply regained his strength and rolled the stone away. But if he had not died, he most certainly would have been very weak. Additionally, it would have been logistically impossible for him to move the stone from inside the tomb. Not only was the weight far too heavy, but since the stone covered the opening, he wouldn't have been able to find a handhold. For others outside the tomb, it could have been moved with enough strength. But it was an obstacle to be reckoned with, as shown by the concern of the women approaching the tomb the day of the resurrection.

The Seal Protecting the Tomb

One of the security measures taken was to attach a seal to the stone covering the entrance to the tomb: "They went and made the tomb secure by putting a seal on the stone and posting the guard" (Matthew 27:66).

The seal was a cord stretched across the entrance to the tomb with a waxlike connection in the middle. It would have prevented the opening of the tomb without breaking the bond. The "seal" of the administrative authority in charge was pressed into the wax, signifying its importance. Only the captain of the guard was permitted to give permission for the breaking of the seal. Anyone breaking it without permission would be executed.

Certainly the seal alone was breakable and could be easily overcome. However, it did provide a psychological barrier to rolling away the stone without permission. It also reinforced the importance of protecting the grave site from opening without agreement by the Romans.

Overall Impact of Security Precautions at the Tomb

No doubt the security precautions at Jesus' tomb were widely known. It would have been impossible for anyone to tamper with the tomb without the knowledge and approval of those charged with protecting it. Overcoming a Roman guard of 16 soldiers, moving a two-ton rock, and breaking a seal—which would have meant certain death—all of these measures helped ensure that the body of Jesus would not be disturbed without the Romans knowing about it.

The high security at the tomb of Jesus provides assurance that the tomb was empty because of the resurrection of Jesus, not a theft or any other form of disturbance.

Can We Be Certain Jesus Was Really Dead?

Some people who attempt to explain away the resurrection claim that Jesus was not really dead—he simply "swooned" and therefore *appeared* to come back from the dead.

This idea makes absolutely no sense when one considers several things:

1. The Romans were professional executioners. The centurions who would have been assigned the job would have doubtless had experience with dozens, perhaps hundreds, of executions. They would be following standardized methods and procedures under the watchful eye of the Jewish leadership, who would have wanted to be certain that the execution was handled properly.

2. Jesus was an important political prisoner. This would have brought extreme importance and attention to the execution, making its desired result more certain than ever.

3. The process of death by crucifixion was extremely slow and certain. The victim had to push up off of his feet to breath (when he was hanging from his hands, the diaphragm was pulled up, making breathing impossible). Hence, it was quite obvious when the victim stopped pushing himself up that he had died of asphyxiation. As with drowning, after someone has been submerged ten minutes or so, it can be certain that death has occurred.

4. The spear thrust further ensured that Jesus had died.

Summary

In the days following the crucifixion, many precautions were taken to protect the corpse of Jesus. Even so, since the day of the resurrection, no body of Jesus has ever been located. There was every reason for the Jewish leaders to do everything they could in order to locate Jesus' body. Failure to do so would, and did, result in the undermining of their religious authority. Likewise, the Roman leaders would have had every incentive to do everything they could have to locate the body of Jesus. Otherwise, a volatile dispute between the traditional Jews and followers of Jesus could ensue—and it did. This meant a threat to the Roman rule of Jerusalem and the surrounding territory.

It would have been virtually impossible for the misfit band of disciples to overcome the Roman guard and steal the body of Jesus. Nor would there have been any reason for them to do so. Despite the explanation presented by the Jewish leaders and the Roman guards that the disciples had stolen the body, the city of Jerusalem was not accepting it. Instead, the people accepted the story presented by the eyewitnesses that Jesus had risen from the dead. Many gave their lives to verify this strong belief.

In a nutshell, all the Jewish leaders and Romans had to do in order to end Christianity forever was produce the corpse of Jesus. They couldn't do it. And Christianity has since become the largest religion in the world. *The tomb was empty.*

Test Yourself

1. Why were the Jewish leaders concerned about the security of the body of Jesus?

2. What would the religious leaders and Romans have done upon hearing that the tomb was empty? Why was the corpse so important?

3. What state of mind were the disciples in following the crucifixion?

4. Describe the Roman guard. What other precautions were taken against theft?

5. What problems did the stone pose?

Chapter 25 Group Study

Homework Preparation (do prior to group)

Read: Matthew 27:24; 28:11-15; chapter 25 of this text; and pages 10, 11, 18-19 in *What Is the Proof for the Resurrection?* ✝.

Opening Prayer

Discussion: As a group, pretend you are the disciples and that you intend to steal the body of Jesus. See if you can plot a strategy to succeed. Be sure to address how you will deal with all of the security problems (including such things as people noticing your movements on the Sabbath).

Practical-Experience Game

Press conference: A "press corps" has assembled in Jerusalem that is predisposed to believe the prevailing notion that the body of Jesus was stolen. The objective of the "Christian" is to defend against such claims.

Closing Prayer

The Martyrdom of
the Apostles

Salome, sobbing uncontrollably, tears in her eyes, clung tightly to her husband, Zebedee. She'd seen it before. She'd seen what someone with absolute power could do. First it was her Lord, Jesus himself. Then it was Stephen, who gave up his spirit as people threw stone after stone (Acts 7:54-60). Now it was her eldest son, James, a disciple of Jesus, who was being dragged through the streets like a piece of garbage to be disposed of. Salome knew she should be forgiving, but this was her own son. She held King Herod Agrippa I in angry contempt.

Finally they reached the site of execution. Then a shocking event happened. To everyone's astonishment, one of the Roman guards suddenly fell to his knees and cried out to James for forgiveness. He had seen such incredible courage from the apostle that he too began to weep uncontrollably and asked James to allow him into the kingdom of God.

"Don't kill him alone," the guard said. "Take me too. James, quickly, tell me what to do!"

"Just believe in the Lord Jesus and you will be saved," James cried as his head was being positioned on the executioner's block. As the seconds dragged by, Zebedee held Salome tightly. She didn't want to look—oh, how she didn't want to look. But this was her last chance to see her son.

James looked over at his mother with an expression of serenity and deep love that only a mother would recognize. He smiled. And then it was over.

In about 190, the early writer Clemens Alexandrinus documented the story of the execution of James, the elder brother of the apostle John and son of Zebedee and Salome. The story, which I have retold in modern language, reveals the enormous courage of the early apostles, who faced cruel death on a daily basis simply for believing in Jesus and spreading his truth.

But this story of James is not an isolated case of martyrdom among the disciples. All of them, except John, would face a similar fate. All died horrible, cruel deaths simply because they believed in and spread the gospel message.[1]

Peter

After Jesus' crucifixion, Peter was despondent. If Jesus really had remained dead and not been resurrected, one would expect Peter to return to the life of a fisherman. After all, he was an expert in fishing, but he was a rather rough, unpolished public speaker. Yet he immediately launched into a highly uncharacteristic career as an apostle and probably never returned to fishing. Obviously the resurrection changed his life forever. And Peter would have certainly been in a position to know whether or not the resurrection was real. He had just spent about three years with Jesus on a daily basis. He was there the night before and the day of the crucifixion. And Peter was among the first to see the resurrected Christ.

Peter started his new career by giving emboldened speeches that persuaded thousands of local Jews to follow the risen Christ. Although Peter started his evangelism in Jerusalem, he soon left to spread the message elsewhere, after having been imprisoned twice. History indicates that he traveled to preach in Corinth for a short time after Paul had established a church there.

The historian Eusebius states that Peter established the Syrian Church in Antioch shortly after the resurrection. Church tradition holds that Peter continued in leadership as its first "bishop" from 33 to 40 A.D. During that time, he ministered to the region of Mesopotamia, a region of strength and importance for the Jews. It is likely that Peter continued his missionary work in Babylon and the eastern region for many of the remaining years leading up to his death in 67, though there is considerable evidence that during that time he also spent time in Great Britain, Gaul, and Rome.

Although Peter undoubtedly faced the ongoing persecution common to Christians during his years of ministry, the brutality he endured at the end of his life is an amazing testimony to the strength of his faith in the resurrection of Jesus. Nero had declared himself the "enemy of God" and was bent on promoting this pride-filled position. He, therefore, had every reason to maximize the story about the treachery of Christians—especially the leaders like Peter and Paul.

Peter was maliciously condemned and thrown into the infamous Mamertine Prison in Rome. The Mamertine was a deep, dark vault carved into solid rock, consisting of two chambers, one atop the other. A narrow slit on the roof provided the only access and light to the upper chamber. The lower chamber, known as the "death cell," was in total darkness—and was never cleaned. A horrid stench filled the prison, so great that it fatally poisoned many inmates.

In the Mamertine "living hell," Peter was chained upright to a post, in a physically exhausting position that didn't allow him to recline. There, alone, wallowing in filth, in total darkness, Peter awaited his death for nine long months—the monotony broken only by periods of intense torture. All Peter had to do to be set free was to renounce Jesus. But the gospel spread as Nero continued to build his personal claim as the enemy of God.

One day in 67, Peter was led into Nero's circus to be executed. There the apostle demanded that he be crucified head down, as he was not fit to be crucified in the same position as his Lord Jesus Christ. The taunting Romans granted his request.

As Peter was led away to be crucified, he looked over at his wife, who likewise was being led away to be executed. In his volume *Church History,* Eusebius quotes Peter's last words of encouragement to his wife: "O thou, remember the Lord."

Rather than submit to Roman authorities, who had tried using every means to break his spirit and to have him renounce the resurrection, Peter remained firm—as did his wife—and faced horrendous hardships to glorify Jesus. Certainly Peter knew the truth of the resurrection. Would he and his wife have gone through this for a known lie?

Andrew

Andrew was the first person to be approached as a follower of Jesus. He was present at the first miracle and many thereafter. Andrew knew Jesus very well and would certainly have known if, in fact, Jesus had actually appeared alive after the crucifixion. Andrew's evangelical actions following the resurrection demonstrate his belief that Jesus was the Son of God.

There are several nonbiblical accounts of the ministry of Andrew following the resurrection. While they differ in some respects, there are many points of agreement. It is not certain when Andrew left Jerusalem to spread the gospel. He is believed to have spent most of his ministry in Scythia, in southern Russia, around the Black Sea (according to Eusebius). Other sources indicate that Andrew also spent time evangelizing in Asia Minor in the city of Ephesus, where some people believe John's Gospel was written, based in part on a revelation given to Andrew. It is possible the time spent in Asia Minor followed Andrew's ministry to Scythia, while Andrew was on his way to Greece, where sources generally agree that he spent his final years and was executed.

In Patras, Greece, tradition (confirmed by several non-biblical sources) indicates that Andrew angered the governor of the region because he converted the governor's wife to Christianity, causing their estrangement. As a consequence, the governor had Andrew crucified on a cross in the form of an "X," not the traditional cross of Jesus. (This form of cross is now referred to as the St. Andrew's cross.)

Like Paul and other apostles, Andrew endured torture prior to his execution. Instead of being nailed to the cross, like others, Andrew was tied in order to prolong the suffering. Hour after hour he bore extreme pain and humiliation while being exposed to the elements with no clothing. Even so, during this time it is recorded that Andrew exhorted Christians and other onlookers, praising God. His torture went on for two days until he finally succumbed to death on the last day of November in approximately 69. Andrew's last words were said to have been, "Accept me, O Christ Jesus, whom I love, whose I am; accept my spirit in peace in your eternal realm."

Thomas

The apostle Thomas is best known for his doubting of the resurrection of Jesus: "Unless I see the nail marks in his hands and put my finger where the nails were, and put my hand into his side, I will not believe it" (John 20: 25). However, this doubting turned into determined commitment once he did encounter the risen Christ. After leaving Jerusalem, Thomas traveled east to Babylon and beyond to India where he became known as the founder of the church of the East. His ministry is said to have started in about 52 in the city of Crangamore. Ancient records indicate he didn't want to serve in India due to the harshness of the environment, yet chose to follow his calling by Jesus anyway.

Details of Thomas' ministry vary, but accounts generally agree regarding his martyrdom. Apparently Thomas had discredited the Brahmins, a Hindu sect, before the king. They became envious of his missionary success and set out to kill him. It is reported that one day Thomas was deep in prayer in a cave on the slopes of Mount Antenodur. The Brahmins attacked him, tortured him, thrust a spear through his side, and then fled. Thomas left the cave in agony and dragged himself up the slope, where he died.

Matthew

Tradition has it that Matthew traveled to Ethiopia and became associated with Candace (see Acts 8:27). Reports of his martyrdom vary. The Jewish Talmud indicates he was condemned by the Sanhedrin. Some writings indicate he was pinned to the ground and beheaded for his faith in about 60.

Philip

Philip traveled into Scythia (southern Russia) soon after the resurrection. There he preached the gospel for 20 years. Some reports indicate that he also spent time in Gaul (modern-day France); however, they are not confirmed.

Records indicate that Philip was martyred at the age of 87 in the city of Hierapolis in Phrygia. It is reported that pagan priests crucified him upside down by piercing him through the thighs. He was then stoned as he hung upon the cross. Before yielding up his spirit Philip is said to have prayed for his enemies like Jesus did.

Bartholomew (Nathaniel)

Bartholomew is always named along with Philip in the Gospels. Following the resurrection, he traveled with Philip to Scythia where they worked together in Hierapolis. Bartholomew escaped crucifixion, however, at the time Philip was crucified.

From Hierapolis, Bartholomew traveled to Armenia, where he is said to have started the Christian church in that region. He was martyred at Albana (now Derbend, Russia). One account indicates that pagan priests and the king's brother, Astyages, became hostile as Bartholomew spoke out against the local idols (and healed the king's daughter). Bartholomew's enemies eventually were able to have him arrested, beaten, and crucified in 68.

Jude Thaddaeus

Sometimes the names of the 12 disciples are confusing. For example, Jude appears in some cases and Thaddaeus in others. However, Thaddaeus was the surname of Jude. (The ancient historian Jerome refers to him as "Trionius," which means the man with three names—Judas Thaddaeus Lebbaeus—see Matthew 10:3 NKJV). He was the son of James (Luke 6:16).

The early church historian Nicephorus Callistus reviews the ministry of Jude in Syria, Arabia, Mesopotamia, and Persia. Other sources document extensive involvement of Jude with the Armenian church from 35 to 43. It is believed that he served with Bartholomew and Thomas in the region for several years. Sources indicate that Jude was martyred by a barrage of arrows on Mount Ararat.

James, Son of Alphaeus

James, son of Alphaeus, often called "James the Less," is sometimes confused with James the brother of Jesus. Much of this confusion stems from early Roman Catholic and Armenian Orthodox attempts to utilize obscure Greek references to demonstrate that both were one and the same person in order to explain the perpetual virginity of Mary. These explanations, however, fall short in that they must consider James the Less either 1) a brother with two sisters named "Mary" in the same family; or 2) a half-brother (not scripturally correct); or 3) a "cousin" (which meant Paul chose the wrong word). None of these seems to be a satisfactory answer.

Separating James, son of Alphaeus, and James, Jesus' brother, makes it much easier to understand the Scripture and much easier to research. Sources indicate that James the Less traveled to Syria soon after the resurrection, where he became the first "bishop" of the Syrian Church. (Jesus' brother James, on the other hand, became the chairman of the church of Jerusalem.) Tradition further indicates that James the Less later returned to Jerusalem, where he was stoned to death by the Jews for preaching the gospel of Christ.

Simon the Zealot

Simon became a disciple at the Sea of Tiberius, along with Andrew, Peter, James (the Great), John, Thaddaeus, and Judas Iscariot. There are many ancient documents that record the ministry of Simon following the resurrection. Though differing in details, they indicate that he first began his missionary work in Egypt and North Africa. From there he traveled to Carthage, Spain, and Britain. After a short stay, he traveled to London and went back to Palestine.

Simon is then believed to have traveled to Persia, where records indicate he evangelized with Jude. Ancient documents describe Simon as having to endure "infinite troubles and difficulties." In Persia, Simon was eventually sawn in two for preaching about the resurrection of Jesus.

John

Of the 12 disciples, only John died a natural death (but he was exiled for his faith in Jesus).

Other Apostles (Not of the Twelve) Who Were Martyred

James, brother of Jesus. James was the early leader of the church in Jerusalem (Acts 12:17; 15:13-29; 21:18-24) and the author of the book of James. The Jewish historian Josephus records the martyrdom of James by stoning. It is believed to have occurred in about 66.

Matthias. Matthias was elected to fill the vacancy created by Judas. It is said he was stoned and then beheaded.

Mark. Tradition indicates that Mark was dragged to pieces in Alexandria after speaking out against the local idol Serapis.

Paul. Paul spent a great deal of time in the prisons of Rome, where he wrote many of his epistles. In 66, Emperor Nero condemned Paul to death and had him beheaded.

Barnabas. Barnabas spread the gospel to many countries, yet on a return to Cyprus he was martyred by the Jews for his evangelism. History records that John Mark secretly buried his body in an empty sepulcher outside the city of Salamis.

Who Would Die for a Lie?

Fact 1. All of these apostles (except Paul and Barnabas) knew Jesus intimately *before* he was crucified. (Paul and Barnabas may have seen Jesus before his crucifixion also.) There would be absolutely no doubt about their ability to recognize Jesus and distinguish between him and any other person who might simply look like him.

Fact 2. All of the Twelve (and others) saw Jesus *after* his resurrection from the dead.

Fact 3. All of the apostles *changed radically* after seeing the risen Christ—from being inept followers to being bold speakers and leaders.

Fact 4. All the apostles *started preaching* the good news about the death and resurrection of Jesus—an action that threatened their lives.

Fact 5. All the apostles *would have had their lives spared* if they had simply renounced Jesus and stopped their evangelism.

Fact 6. All of the apostles willingly, even joyfully, *laid down their lives* in the most horrible, painful ways, to spread the good news about Jesus' death and resurrection.

Why Did They Willingly Die?

The obvious question from an objective outside observer would be, "Why would people willingly endure horrible executions when they could avoid it by a simple renunciation of their faith?" The only answer is that they were *absolutely, totally convinced that Jesus had died and risen from the dead,* verifying his claim to be the Son of God.

When people question the authenticity of the account of the resurrection, they should consider that, in the case of the apostles, we have at least ten people *who certainly knew the truth* and decided to choose death over rejecting Jesus. If Jesus' resurrection was a lie, why would they have died? Some people say these followers of Jesus were insane. But is it likely that *all ten* were insane? Or was Jesus just an illusion? Would all the disciples have seen the same illusion at once? Hardly.

Key Concept

All the disciples, with the exception of John, died horrific martyr's deaths in order to tell the gospel. "All" that was required to escape death was to renounce Jesus. The obvious question is, "Why would anyone, let alone all twelve, die for what they would certainly have known was a lie?"

Furthermore, the apostles were martyred over a long period of time and in various locations. There wasn't a mass execution. This indicates the continuing conviction they held. It wasn't a short-term belief of little consequence; it was a life-changing belief of enormous importance.

The martyrdom of the apostles, who knew Jesus intimately, is a powerful example of eyewitnesses who were absolutely convinced that Jesus Christ had died and risen again from the dead, just as he had prophesied he would. Any of the martyred apostles could have easily chosen to avoid execution by renouncing Jesus. None of them did. The disciples died so that others might believe in Christ and live.

Test Yourself

1. Why is the willing martyrdom of the apostles among the most powerful evidence of all that the death and resurrection of Jesus are historically true?

2. The martyrdom of which apostle was recorded by Clement Alexandrinus?

3. How was Peter martyred? Andrew? Paul?

4. What could the apostles have done to avoid martyrdom?

5. Why is it significant that the apostles were martyred over a period of time, in different locations?

Chapter 26 Group Study

Homework Preparation (do prior to group)

Read: John 21:17-18; chapter 26 of this text; and pages 20-21 in *What Is the Proof for the Resurrection?* ✝.

Opening Prayer

Discussion: Read John 21:17-18. How does this verse relate to the sacrifice the disciples were called to make? Discuss why the martyrdom of the apostles is vitally important to us today.

Practical-Experience Game

Role-playing: The "Christian" should discuss with the "nonbeliever" the fact that the apostles all willingly gave their lives for the historical events of the crucifixion and resurrection. Be sure to indicate the significance of this.

Closing Prayer

Witnesses at the Time of Jesus

We can understand today how memorable an event such as the World Trade Center attack, the explosion of a space shuttle, or the assassination of a president of the United States is. Why would anyone suppose for even a second that the events surrounding Jesus Christ were any less significant to the people at the time? The only difference would be that they did not have mass media to communicate what the eyewitnesses saw. In Jesus' time, the people would talk to the eyewitnesses themselves or to others who were credible sources of eyewitness testimony. The resurrection of Jesus might well have been thought to be as shocking then as the World Trade Center attack or the assassination of JFK is today.

Incredible and disastrous events burn vivid detail into the minds of those witnessing them. Consequently, the facts are not forgotten and versions of the events can easily be compared. Eventually, when they are recorded, as in the New Testament, the accuracy of the writings is easily verified.

While his resurrection was certainly the highlight, there were also many other extraordinary things that happened concerning Jesus. For example:

1. *The miraculous birth of John the Baptist* (Luke 1:13-14,18,21-22)

2. *The supernatural announcement of Jesus' birth* (Luke 2:9-13,17-18)

3. *The recognition of Jesus as Messiah by a respected elder* (Luke 2:27-33)

4. *The recognition of Jesus as Messiah by a respected prophetess* (Luke 2:36-38)

5. *The supernatural warning to flee to Egypt* (Matthew 2:13-15)

6. *Herod's killing of babies* (Matthew 2:16)

7. *The many miracles of Jesus*

8. *The crucifixion of Jesus*

9. *The resurrection of Jesus*

10. *The miracles performed by the disciples* (Acts 3:2,6-10)

11. *The appearance of the resurrected Jesus to 500* (1 Corinthians 15:3-6)

People Talked

People in Jesus' day were like people today. They loved to talk. In fact, we would expect that, with fewer distractions such as TV, computers, and video games, they probably talked even more than today.

Every one of the events just mentioned was far from ordinary. Each one was highly memorable. These events were witnessed by many people and

> Like today, in biblical times people inevitably talked. The amazing events at the time of Jesus would have burned vivid memories into people's minds.

were widely discussed throughout the land. Like the events of September 11, 2001, they would have been remembered vividly by many people for a long period of time. The people would also have been able to easily corroborate written reports in the New Testament, thus verifying its accuracy. People widely discussing memorable events of the day would validate the essentials of the events. The truth would withstand eyewitness scrutiny; the rest would be discarded.

Information Sources for the Gospels

Luke used information from many sources to research the gospel message, making a methodical investigation of the account of the story of Jesus.

> *Many have undertaken to draw up an account of the things that have been fulfilled among us, just as they were handed down to us by those who from the first were eyewitnesses and servants of the word.*
>
> *Therefore, since I myself have carefully investigated everything from the beginning, it seemed good also to me to write an orderly account for you, most excellent Theophilus, so that you may know the certainty of the things you have been taught* (Luke 1:1-4).

Mary

Mary, the mother of Jesus, is without a doubt the most revered mother of all time. When one considers the evidence surrounding the birth, life, death, and resurrection of Jesus, nobody would be in a position to know the full story better than Mary. She was there for almost everything—except for the rigorous journeys during the three-year ministry of Jesus (and even then, there was probably some contact).

People would have talked about the many miraculous events surrounding Jesus' birth, life, and death. Mary was there at the annunciation of the coming of Jesus by angels. She was there at the conception of Jesus. She was there at the miraculous birth, announced by angels appearing to shepherds. She was there when an angel warned Joseph to flee to Egypt. She was nearby when Herod mercilessly slaughtered the infant boys in the region of Bethlehem. She was there when Jesus performed the many miracles, and she is specifically mentioned when Jesus performed his first miracle of turning water into wine (John 2:1-11). She was there at Jesus' crucifixion, standing beneath him at the cross:

> *Near the cross of Jesus stood his mother, his mother's sister, Mary the wife of Clopas, and Mary Magdalene. When Jesus saw his mother there, and the disciple whom he loved standing nearby, he said to his mother, "Dear woman, here is your son," and to the disciple, "Here is your mother." From that time on, this disciple took her into his home* (John 19:25-27).

And she was there at the time of the resurrection of Jesus (Acts 1:14). The evidence of Mary's involvement is apparent in the many churches that were immediately built at venerated sites where she was a participant soon after Constantine allowed Christianity in the Roman Empire. This indicates that the local population was well aware of the events and of Mary's role in them. The belief in Mary and her involvement has not diminished with time.

The Gospel authors almost certainly used Mary as one of their original sources of information.

Conon—A Direct Descendent of Jesus' Family

The Gospel authors would have certainly gathered information from the relatives of Jesus. We know that such relatives existed. It was difficult to maintain the lineage of Jesus, given the persecution that occurred shortly after the resurrection. We would expect that most of the ancestors of Jesus would be martyred. The last recorded descendent of Jesus was a gardener named Conon, who lived in Pamphylia in Asia Minor. Just prior to his death, Conon was asked if he was of the lineage of King David. He replied, "I am of the city of Nazareth in Galilee, I am of the family of Christ, whose worship I have inherited from my ancestors."[1]

Other Relatives of Jesus

The Bible indicates that Jesus had brothers and sisters: "Isn't his mother's name Mary, and aren't his brothers James, Joseph, Simon and Judas? Aren't all his sisters with us?" (Matthew 13:55—see also pages 262–263). These brothers and sisters or relatives would have been used by the Gospel authors to corroborate facts about Jesus' life, death, and resurrection.

Apart from mention of relatives in the Bible, we find mention of other relatives in extrabiblical sources (see page 262). Hegesippus writes of Symeon, son of Clopas (who was thought to be Joseph's brother—see John 19:25), describing his lengthy torture and eventual martyrdom:

> Certain of these heretics brought accusation against Symeon, the son of Clopas, on the ground that he was a descendant of David and a Christian; and thus he suffered martyrdom, at the age of one hundred and twenty years, while Trajan was emperor and Atticus governor.[2]

Hegesippus also briefly refers to the grandsons of Jude, the brother of Jesus.

James, Brother of Jesus

The Bible refers to James (and Jude) as brothers of Jesus:

> I saw none of the other apostles—only James, the Lord's brother (Paul, in Galatians 1:19).

> Jude, a servant of Jesus Christ and a brother of James (Jude 1).

However, we also find evidence of Jesus' brother James outside the Bible, including what may be his actual ossuary (see page 276). But evidence of the existence and role of James, brother of Jesus, goes beyond the ossuary. Josephus (a non-Christian, Jewish historian, about 37 to 96) speaks of the execution of James:

> Albinus…assembled the Sanhedrim of the judges, and brought before them the brother of Jesus, who was called Christ, whose name was James, and some others [or some of his companions;] and when he had formed an accusation against them as breakers of the law, he delivered them to be stoned.[3]

The noncanonical "Gospel of Thomas" (see pages 207-209) speaks of James as "the Lord's brother, who had been elected by the Apostles to the Episcopal throne at Jerusalem."[4] Other writings that speak of James and his election to lead the church of Jerusalem include the Syriac Apostolic Constitutions (second century), Clement of Rome (30–97), Eusebius of Caesarea (260–340), Clement of Alexandria (180–216, surviving in a document by Eusebius), Origen (185–253), and Jerome (342–420).

Mary Magdelene, the "Other Mary," and Salome

Mary, the "other Mary," and Salome were three women who were closely involved in the life of Jesus (see Mark 15:40; 16:1). We know that by the fact that they were going to the tomb to finish preparing Jesus' body the day of the resurrection; hence, they were intimately involved in the many events on that fateful day. Most certainly the Gospel writers would have obtained eyewitness testimony from these three loyal women, along with any others like them.

500 Who Saw the Resurrected Jesus

We know that in at least one instance Jesus appeared to 500 people at once (see 1 Corinthians 15:3-7). What is particularly significant is that Paul is reporting this fact to the Corinthians in a letter sometime prior to A.D. 64—it is stated that many of the eyewitnesses are still alive. Since this letter to the Corinthians was copied and passed around to a wide audience throughout the Roman Empire, it most certainly was "reviewable" by some of the eyewitnesses themselves. This means that if it were incorrect, it would have been challenged. Yet it was not—and it remains in the most widely read book of all time, the Bible.

Throughout the period of Jesus' birth, ministry, death, and resurrection, there were many incredible reasons for people to remember spectacular events and discuss them. As we've seen, Matthew, Mark, Luke, and John would have had no trouble finding eyewitnesses to corroborate the Gospel events. And if there had been any inconsistencies in the widely discussed accounts, there would have been criticism and correction since written copies were circulated during the time of the eyewitnesses.

There were many highly memorable events during Jesus' time, capped by his resurrection. These would certainly have gained attention and would have been widely discussed. The many witnesses of the events and the resurrection—including the apostles, the friends and family of Jesus, and at least 500 others who saw the risen Christ—would have attested to his resurrection.

Hostile Witnesses

The wind moaned through the trees in an eerie song that forebode the bloodshed to come. A damp mist clung to his face as the battle-worn emperor slumped to his knees, deep in thought outside an army camp a few miles north of Rome. It was October 28, 312. Carved in his mind were words he had heard from his Christian mother, Helena, since childhood: "Give to Caesar what is Caesar's, and to God what is God's" (Matthew 22:21).

Slowly Emperor Constantine raised his head and saw, through the mist, an apparition—seemingly coming from an infinite distance...he saw a vision of a cross of light above the sun bearing an inscription: "Conquer by this." Word quickly spread throughout the camp as the many soldiers excitedly related their versions of sighting the same apparition.

Later in the day, after a fitful sleep, Constantine had a second vision. The "Christ of God" appeared to him with the same sign and commanded him to make a likeness of it to use as a safeguard in all battles. It was to have a spear with a transverse bar giving it the shape of a cross; the Greek letters X and P intersecting within a golden wreath on the point of the spear, forming the monogram *chi-rho,* the first two letters of *Christ* in Greek.

Stunned by the vision, Constantine sent for Christian leaders. Surely they expected to be executed by the pagan emperor. However, far from executing them, Constantine asked their advice regarding the "God of the Christians." In his discussions he received information about the incarnation and immortality of Christ.

Constantine obeyed the command. Battle standards were made. Uplifting them with the sudden cry that Constantine could not be defeated, the army brandished their swords as their enemy Maxentius and his soldiers crossed a bridge of boats to meet them. Earlier in the day, Maxentius had consulted an oracle that indicated the Roman army of Constantine would be soundly defeated. It was destined to be a battle of the newly received Christian God against the pagan god of Maxentius.

The intensity of the inspired Romans was overwhelming. Constantine's army charged Maxentius' troops, destroyed the bridge behind them, and forced them into the Tiber River, where they "went to the depths like a stone." The world was changed forever. (Based on Eusebius' account and retold by the author.)

The above account of Emperor Constantine is an example of hostile witness testimony—someone previously committed to eliminating Christianity, who then changed. Hostile witnesses have long been regarded in courts of law as among the most compelling. When they make significant points supporting the claim of a side they are opposed to (or were opposed to), they are very credible. In this chapter, we review hostile witnesses from three most unusual viewpoints: 1) from the viewpoint of a Roman emperor originally bent on defeating Christianity; 2) from the viewpoint of a Pharisee originally determined to annihilate Christians; and 3) from the blood relatives of Jesus who at first did not believe in Jesus' divinity.

Emperor Constantine

Few events have changed world history to a greater extent than Constantine's visions, as retold above. The historian

Eusebius claimed that Constantine recounted his experience and "confirmed it with an oath." There is no doubt that Eusebius had lengthy conversations with Constantine—they are well-documented historically.

At the time Constantine was battling with Maxentius, tax breaks were being offered to cities that uncovered Christians for execution. A fraudulent document was being circulated throughout the Roman Empire to whip up hatred toward Christians, and prostitutes were being rounded up and forced to create false "confessions" of vile Christian perversions. Hatred of Christians was everywhere, and persecution was at its peak.

Overnight, Constantine changed all of that. In 313, Constantine, based on his newfound belief in Jesus, entered into a pact with the Eastern Roman emperor, Licinius. An edict was issued to everyone that they could "follow the form of worship each desired." In a sense this allowed the two emperors to "hedge their bets" on the Almighty, supposing that eventually the true God would prevail. And eventually one did.

Emperor Licinius eventually abandoned his pact of joint tolerance and resumed horrific persecution of Christians. Eusebius wrote about the impact this had on the enraged Constantine, who marched out "kindling a great beacon of light" and went to war against Licinius. Licinius, soundly defeated, was strangled to death.

The changes Constantine implemented radically changed the world. In 324, Constantine's influence was expanded from being emperor of Rome to emperor of the entire Roman Empire. Efforts were made immediately to correct the improprieties of the past. Christians illegally held for their faith were released. All property and goods that had been seized from Christians was to be restored immediately—this included property that was held in the name of the church, and for the first time such property was to be "officially recognized." Clergymen were given freedom from civic duties and also some tax breaks. The first day of the week (Sunday) was to be a day of rest. And key holidays were established (such as December 25—Christmas—and probably also Easter and Lent).

Constantine's mother, Helena, a devout Christian already, was dispatched to the Holy Land to locate key sites to be venerated. This action established many of the important archaeological sites we revere today. However, despite all the efforts of Constantine, old feelings about Christians—caused by extensive misinformation by enemies—were slow to die. It wasn't until 391 that Christianity enjoyed a definitive monopoly as a state religion.

During his lifetime, Constantine was wary of alienating his subjects and was cautious about obliterating pagan sites and temples. However, upon his death in 337, the pace of destroying such sites quickened. Rome, of course, had become the seat of the church that was destined to become the largest religion in the world.

Paul

"Saul of Tarsus" (later Paul), was the leading persecutor of Christians in the years immediately following Jesus' crucifixion (Acts 7:57–8:3). He was the overseer at the stoning of Stephen, the first recorded Christian martyr. Saul was his Hebrew name, although in most of the New Testament he is referred to by his Greek name, Paul.

Paul took his attack against Christians to Damascus, having received "letters of commendation" from the priests in Jerusalem to make his job easier. His goal was to round up Christians and deliver them back to Jerusalem for trial and execution. On the way, he suddenly encountered a blinding light and heard the words of Jesus:

> *"Saul, Saul, why do you persecute me?"*
> *"Who are you, Lord?" Saul asked.*
> *"I am Jesus, whom you are persecuting," he*
> *replied. "Now get up and go into the city, and you*
> *will be told what you must do"* (Acts 9:4-6).

Paul had been blinded, a condition that was to last for three days—until a man named Ananias, called by God, went to him and restored his sight. Ananias took on this task with great fear at first because the reputation of Paul had preceded him, and all the followers of Christ in Damascus knew of his deadly mission.

However, Paul's experience upon encountering the risen Christ had made him a changed man. Immediately his mission changed from rounding up Christians for execution to preaching the gospel of Jesus. He then went out to local synagogues and preached that Jesus was the Son of God, to the startled amazement of the Christians in attendance (Acts 9:21): "Saul [Paul] became more and more powerful and baffled the Jews living in Damascus by proving that Jesus is the Christ" (verse 22).

After many days of testifying about Jesus, angry Jews plotted to kill Paul to end this embarrassing change in attitude about Jesus. With the help of local Christians, Paul escaped. His new mission in life was now established; he would become, perhaps, the most influential advocate of Jesus Christ of all time.

For the remainder of his life, Paul traveled throughout much of the Roman Empire preaching the good news about the resurrection of Jesus. He was especially suited for this task. He was a Pharisee and the son of a Pharisee (Acts 23:6). His family was obviously of some wealth, and he had been tutored by Gamaliel, regarded as one of the leading educators. So Paul came from a position of great status, wealth, and education.

His journeys took him to most of Asia Minor and eventually to Rome. He established churches in all of his travels. During this time he wrote many letters encouraging churches and instructing them in the teachings of Jesus. These letters became, for the most part, books of the New Testament. *Paul is responsible for writing more books of the New Testament than any other author.*

But his conversion came at a great personal, "earthly" cost. He was beaten many times, shipwrecked, stoned, and left for dead. He traded his great reputation among the established nation of the Jews for a leadership role in a ragged band of new believers in Christ. In the end he gave the ultimate sacrifice for Jesus—his life.

Paul's conversion speaks volumes about the historical validity of Jesus and his resurrection. After all, Paul had seen Jesus *after* the resurrection, and as a practicing Pharisee, may very likely have been in Jerusalem at Passover at the time of Jesus' crucifixion. Paul initially was a "hostile witness," influenced, undoubtedly, by the peer pressure of the religious leaders. This is made obvious by his rigorous goal to exterminate the fledgling church of Christ. So when his conversion took place, with his claim to have encountered the risen Christ, it became a powerful message to all who listened. So great was the embarrassment to the Jewish establishment that they did their best to rid the region of Paul's teaching. But in the end, God prevailed through Paul. Consider those onlookers who had witnessed Paul's stern eyes at the stoning of Stephen (Acts 7:57-60). Who would have thought that Paul's words now impact more people for Christ than perhaps any other writer in history!

James and Jude

So much attention is given to Jesus' adult life and ministry that it's easy to forget that he, along with his brothers and sisters, had a childhood too. One can only wonder what the relationships of this family were really like. After all, Mary, Joseph, and other relatives were well aware Jesus was supposed to be the Savior of the world.

We do know that when Jesus began his ministry, he was rejected in the town he had grown up in:

> *Coming to his hometown, he began teaching the people in their synagogue, and they were amazed. "Where did this man get this wisdom and these miraculous powers?" they asked. "Isn't this the carpenter's son? Isn't his mother's name Mary, and aren't his brothers James, Joseph, Simon and Judas? Aren't all his sisters with us? Where then did this man get all these things?" And they took offense at him. But Jesus said to them, "Only in his hometown and in his own house is a prophet without honor." And he did not do many miracles there because of their lack of faith* (Matthew 13:54-58).

To fully comprehend the reaction to Jesus in Nazareth—including that of James and Jude—we must look at Jesus' bold claim to deity when he taught in the synagogue:

> *The scroll of the prophet Isaiah was handed to him. Unrolling it, he found the place where it is written: "The Spirit of the Lord is on me, because he has anointed me to preach good news to the poor. He has sent me to proclaim freedom for the prisoners and recovery of sight for the blind, to release the oppressed, to proclaim the year of the Lord's favor." Then he rolled up the scroll, gave it back to the attendant and sat down. The eyes of everyone in the synagogue were fastened on him,*

and he began by saying to them, "Today this scripture is fulfilled in your hearing" (Luke 4:17-21).

This was a clear claim by Jesus that he was the long-awaited Messiah. The reaction by the religious people and the others in Nazareth emphasizes their outrage:

All the people in the synagogue were furious when they heard this. They got up, drove him out of the town, and took him to the brow of the hill on which the town was built, in order to throw him down the cliff. But he walked right through the crowd and went on his way (verses 28-30).

What makes the eventual reaction of James and Jude so important in regard to evidence of the claim to deity by Jesus is that

1. the two had known Jesus since childhood

2. the two were part of the crowd in Nazareth who rejected him

3. the two later changed and recognized him as the Messiah

We know this because both James and Jude wrote books of the New Testament. Also, James was the leader of the early church in Jerusalem. Paul emphasizes the importance of James by mentioning the appearance of the resurrected Jesus to him: "Then he appeared to James, then to all the apostles, and last of all he appeared to me also, as to one abnormally born" (1 Corinthians 15:7-8).

> Hostile witnesses are among the most valuable in supporting a testimony. In the case of the resurrection, Paul, James, Jude, and Constantine all changed dramatically upon experiencing the risen Christ.

So two half-brothers close to Jesus rejected him early on, then changed their minds after the resurrection.

A wide range of hostile witnesses changed their minds after seeing the risen Christ. First, the brothers of Jesus accepted him as Lord after the resurrection. Second, Paul—who probably had accepted the "official story" of the corpse of Jesus being stolen—had a radical change of mind upon meeting the risen Christ. And finally, after three centuries of Roman persecution of Christians, Emperor Constantine saw a vision of Christ, causing him to end the persecution. Together, the testimony of these hostile witnesses makes an exceptionally strong claim that the risen Christ is real.

Test Yourself

1. List five unusual events involving Jesus that would cause wide-spread discussion.

2. Why do highly memorable events matter in accurate documentation?

3. What relatives of Jesus have been recorded by historians?

4. Why are hostile witnesses particularly valuable?

5. Review how Paul, Constantine, James, and Jude changed after the resurrection.

Chapter 27 Group Study

Homework Preparation (do prior to group)

Read: Matthew 13:55; Galatians 1:19; chapter 27 of this text; and pages 16–19 in *What Is the Proof for the Resurrection?* ✝.

Opening Prayer

Discussion: Read Matthew 13:55 and Galatians 1:19 and discuss Jesus' relatives. What impact would relatives have in passing on information?

Practical-Experience Game

TV interview: The events surrounding Jesus' birth, death, and resurrection are hard to believe. The "TV interviewer" will ask the "Christian" questions regarding the transmission of information to ascertain whether or not the sources are reliable.

Closing Prayer

The Early Christian Martyrs and the Christian Church

Much like the disciples, many early Christians were in a unique position to know for certain whether or not the story of Jesus was true. Many were eyewitnesses of the events; others knew eyewitnesses. Some witnessed the convicting martyrdom of the disciples and the apostles. Many, many Christians were willing to joyfully give their lives for Christ. As Luke said, they considered it an honor to be considered worthy of suffering for Jesus: "The apostles left the Sanhedrin, rejoicing because they had been counted worthy of suffering disgrace for the Name" (Acts 5:41-42).

The Roman emperor Nero was the first to encourage persecution of Christians on a mass scale. Nero, who had been blamed for the great fire of Rome, attempted to shift the blame to the Christians, whom he condemned. Many unimaginably cruel executions were devised. Some Christians were sewn inside skins of wild animals and torn by fierce dogs. Some were dressed in wax-soaked shirts and then impaled on poles and set afire to provide light for orgies held for Nero's pleasure.

As tales of horror spread throughout the Roman Empire, Nero's strategy to break the spirit of the Christians backfired. Rather than melt away in fear, the spirit of early Christians was strengthened—a sign of their enormous conviction and belief in Christ. Many of the 72 men appointed by Jesus (Luke 10:1) were martyred, including such people as Erastus (Romans 16:23), Aristarchus (Acts 19:29), Trophimus (Acts 21:29), Barsabbas (Acts 1:23), and Ananias (Acts 9:10).

Ignatius is one later martyr whose death was recorded by early church historians. He was a courageous church leader who helped many other Christians in hiding during the persecution. However, like so many other Christians at the time, he welcomed the chance to joyously give his life for Christ. When Ignatius realized he would soon be executed for spreading the gospel, he said, "[As for the lions...] I will entice them to devour me quickly....Let come on me fire and cross and conflicts with wild beasts, wrenching of bones, mangling of limbs...only let me reach Jesus Christ."[1]

Later the inevitable happened, and Ignatius was captured and rushed to the Colosseum to be executed. He stood stock-still before a bloodthirsty crowd hungry for his demise. Then he looked to the heavens and said, "I am the wheat of Christ: I am going to be ground with the teeth of wild beasts that I may be found pure bread."[2]

The gates were opened, and the lions bounded toward him as if in slow motion. Ignatius looked up, joyfully singing songs of praise until the claws finally reached him, the end came, and he was silent. It was the year 107.

Nero was the first of a long string of emperors who carried out such persecution. Emperor Domitian was the first to issue the order that Christians be brought before the tribunal to be questioned about their faith. All they had to do to escape horrific execution was to renounce their faith. Again, many stood strong, willingly facing death instead of renouncing Christ. Among those martyred during this time was Paul's dear friend Timothy (1 Corinthians 4:17).

Emperor Trajan continued the practice of forcing Christians to renounce their faith; however, he added the twist that they also had to bow down to a statue of him and worship him to be set free. Christians continued to choose death.

Trajan was succeeded by Hadrian, who was responsible for some 10,000 martyrs. He was especially known for placing crowns of thorns on Christians' heads, crucifying them, and thrusting spears in their sides in a cruel mockery of Jesus' crucifixion. This practice, however, *corroborated the written account of Christ's final days.* In one case a Roman commander was asked by Hadrian to join in idolatrous sacrifice to celebrate his victories. When the commander refused because of his faith in Christ, Hadrian had him and his family put to death.

The list of atrocities goes on and on. Perhaps most important to us today is the vast number of martyrs who died during the early years after Jesus. Some would have been in a position to directly ascertain the truth. *The key point about Christian martyrdom is that it was for a historical event, not merely some philosophical idea, as with martyrs in other religions.*

Key Concept

Emperor Nero was the first Roman Emperor to purposely carry out persecution on a major scale. His policies were followed and even made more stringent by the following emperors, notably Trajan and Hadrian.

Even knowing the truth, how many of us today would willingly face a horrible execution when a "simple renunciation" would forestall it? Certainly the early martyrs had incredible conviction. Fortunately for us, the early martyrs provide compelling evidence that those closest to resurrection—and most likely to be direct witnesses to the truth—died because it was of utmost importance to them.

The Catacombs

Anyone visiting Rome today can see the catacombs, where early Christians buried their dead outside the city of Rome. The catacomb caves are an awe-inspiring testimony to the many early Christian martyrs who gave their lives to spread the gospel of Jesus. Tens of thousands of early Christians were buried in more than 60 underground labyrinths, where individual tombs and family crypts were hewn out of narrow rock passageways. (Five of the catacombs are currently open to the public.) Hundreds of miles of tunnels are connected over vast acres of ground—like the strands of a spider's web. In some cases there are many levels of passages to save space, which was very limited for Christians during the time of persecution.

Contrary to popular belief, the catacombs were not used as secret hiding places during persecution; however, at times they were used as places of refuge for celebration of the Lord's Supper.

Standing in one of the open "worship areas" or even in a large "family crypt," a visitor can't help but sense the spirit and powerful commitment to Jesus at a time so close to his crucifixion, when people would have strong direct evidence of his resurrection. Evidence of early belief in Jesus is everywhere. Symbols prevalent throughout the catacombs are

- *the Good Shepherd*—a shepherd with a lamb around his neck, which symbolized Christ and the souls he was saving; found in frescoes, on sarcophagi, and on facings of tombs

- *the orante*—a praying figure with open arms symbolizing the soul of the deceased living eternally in peace

- *the monogram of Christ*—the Greek letters *chi* and *rho,* which represented the first two letters of "Christ," indicating a Christian was buried there

- *the fish*—the Greek letters "IXTHYS," which, placed vertically, formed an acrostic that stood for "Jesus Christ, Son of God, Savior"

- *the dove holding an olive branch*—symbolizing the soul reaching divine peace

- *the Greek letters alpha and omega*—representing Christ as the beginning and the end

The thousands of martyrs in the catacombs are often identified by the Greek abbreviation "MPT" (which stood for *martyr*).

In February of 313, Constantine ended the persecution of Christians. However, the catacombs continued to be used as a cemetery until the following century. Eventually the church returned to the practice of above-ground burial. With the passage of time, people forgot about the catacombs, and thick vegetation grew over the entrances, hiding them from view. It wasn't until the late 1500s that Antonio Bosio (1575–1629) began the search and scientific exploration of the ancient catacombs. Most important is the irrefutable evidence the catacombs provide us today that early Christians held strongly to the truth of Jesus.

> The catacombs in Rome offer powerful evidence of the conviction of early Christian martyrs who joyfully gave their lives for the historical fact of the gospel.

The people close to the time of the resurrection of Jesus had the greatest ability to judge the veracity of the historical accuracy of the events. Many believed, beyond a shadow of a doubt, that Jesus Christ had risen from the dead. And the early Christians—who existed so close to the time of Jesus and were clearly in a good position to know the eyewitnesses—chose to honor Jesus and die to spread the gospel, rather than bow down to some other "god." Historical and archaeological evidence supports their widespread martyrdom. The fact that so many early Christians died to tell the story lends especially strong credibility to the assertion that the crucifixion and resurrection of Jesus is true.

The Existence of the Christian Church

Nobody doubts the existence of the Christian church. Not only is it the largest religion in the world (some 33 percent of the world's population claims to be Christian), but it has survived persecution ever since its founding shortly after the crucifixion of Jesus in about A.D. 33. Christianity exists in every corner of the world, even where it is strictly prohibited under the threat of death.

The World of Christianity

Today, approximately one-third of the world claims to be Christian. In the year 33, the Jewish population is estimated to have been less than one-half of one percent of the world— a level that it still approximates.

Christianity started from this base of Jews. In fact, early on almost *all* Christians were Jews. However, Christianity quickly spread to the Gentiles as well. As martyrdom took its toll and Christianity became *more removed in both time and geography from the Palestine* of the time of Jesus, the percentage of Jews who were Christians dropped, while the percentage of the world population who became Christian soared. Thus, the world's decision—with "votes being cast" by people's very lives—indicated that more people believed in the resurrection of Jesus than in the widely circulated story that his body had been stolen by the disciples.

The Foundation of Christianity—the Historical Resurrection

> Christianity started from the small base of Jews familiar with Jesus and the historical crucifixion and resurrection. It exploded into the Gentile world because of the conviction of the early missionaries and martyrs and was well entrenched in the Roman Empire before Constantine.

As this part stresses, the foundation of the Christian church is the historical reliability of the resurrection of Jesus Christ. As noted before, the apostle Paul said, "If Christ has not been raised, your faith is futile; you are still in your sins" (1 Corinthians 15:17). This is an extremely powerful fact. The Christian church is *not* a philosophical religion like Hinduism, Buddhism, or various "new spiritualities." Instead, it is tied to one overwhelmingly central issue—*that the resurrection of Jesus Christ is a historical fact!*

This is not to say that the resurrection of Jesus Christ is the *only* important theological issue in Christianity; far from it. The *crucifixion* of Jesus was the event that provided salvation (it was the sacrifice) for those who have a personal relationship with him. However, it was the *resurrection* of Jesus that verified his prophetic claim that he was the Son of God—the Messiah—and *that he would overcome death so that we might have eternal life.* Only God could achieve this resurrection. It was absolutely necessary that it happen in order for Jesus' promise of salvation to have any significance. No other religious leaders have done anything similar. The resurrection caused the early disciples to rejoice in knowing that Jesus was who he said he was and that eternal life was assured. The resurrection gave the disciples the confidence to joyfully face death knowing that a greater reward existed for them in heaven.

Because Christianity is based on a *historical event* that demonstrates the divinity of Jesus, it is very different from any other religion. Christianity can be tested and verified by that single historical event. If it occurred, then Jesus is in fact Lord and Savior. If it did not, he is not.

The means of proving any such historical event is by "legal" proof—that is, proof by eyewitness testimony and by other, often circumstantial, evidence.

As indicated already, there is vast eyewitness testimony that the resurrection occurred. It was provided by many witnesses, including the disciples who had a radical change in attitude as they became bold proponents of Christ immediately following the resurrection.

Overcoming a Theological Dilemma— One God or Three?

As a theocracy, the Jews took their religion very seriously. The laws of Moses (the first five books of the Bible) were well-known. Central to this theological thinking was the importance of a single God, which was at odds with the polytheistic cultures of the time.

The teachings of Jesus pointed to the concept of a three-in-one God. Even with the last words he spoke before ascending into heaven, Jesus exhorted his disciples to baptize others in the name of the three-in-one God: "Go and make disciples of all nations, baptizing them in the name of the *Father* and of the *Son* and of the *Holy Spirit*" (Matthew 28:19).

To the Jews, the idea of Jesus as a man being God—while also praying to God the Father and teaching the existence of the Holy Spirit—was confusing at a minimum, and blasphemy at worst. In some people's eyes it would be like worshiping three separate gods, which is strictly forbidden by the Mosaic Law. Therefore, any change in thinking to accept Jesus as God (along with the Holy Spirit) was a fundamental theological shift that would have been difficult to make in such a serious theocracy. Yet it was a change required by Christianity.

When we consider the existence of the church in light of the conditions at the time, we should not only consider the difficulty of 1) the miracle of the resurrection itself and 2) the horror of the persecution, but we should also consider 3) the theological difficulty of accepting the idea of the Trinity—in which Jesus was God. The existence of the church shows that *the majority of the population overcame all three of these difficulties and believed in the historical resurrection!*

Again, what makes this so very important is that the essence of Christianity rests on the truth of this one historical event—an event that verified the deity of Jesus. No other religion has anything remotely like it.

The Early History and Persecution of the Church

The early history and persecution of the Christian church are well-documented. We know that 3000 people were added to the disciples of Jesus within days after the resurrection (see Acts 2:41). Peter, previously an inarticulate though impulsive fisherman, spoke boldly to a crowd of people immediately after the resurrection. His words had a profound impact on a city aware of the resurrection—in many cases due to eyewitness testimony. After addressing the crowd and describing what the crucifixion and resurrection were all about, he said to them,

> *"Let all Israel be assured of this: God has made this Jesus, whom you crucified, both Lord and Christ."*

> *When the people heard this, they were cut to the heart and said to Peter and the other apostles, "Brothers, what shall we do?"*
>
> *Peter replied, "Repent and be baptized, every one of you, in the name of Jesus Christ for the forgiveness of your sins. And you will receive the gift of the Holy Spirit. The promise is for you and your children and for all who are far off—for all whom the Lord our God will call."*
>
> *With many other words he warned them; and he pleaded with them, "Save yourselves from this corrupt generation." Those who accepted his message were baptized, and about three thousand were added to their number that day* (Acts 2:36-47).

Shortly thereafter, we know that the number of people in the early church jumped to 5000 men (Acts 4:4). Since it was normal at that time to count the men only, as the leaders of the household—and since the women and older children usually held the same belief, we can probably at least double this estimate of the church's size at that time. That would conservatively place the size of the church in Jerusalem between 10,000 and 15,000 people very shortly after the resurrection. The church continued to grow rapidly (Acts 5:14; 6:7). Just how rapid might this growth have been?

I estimate that by the time Jerusalem fell in the year 70, about 70 percent of the city were followers of Jesus. This would place the number at about 70,000 people. When we consider that there were probably about 10,000 to 15,000 Christians in Jerusalem shortly after the resurrection, then that number does not seem odd at all. In fact, growth in Christianity would have *had to have averaged only about 1.8 percent per year* to reach that number. We know that in the first few years, it exploded far beyond that 1.8 percent per year. The growth may have been far greater even than that, when one considers that 1) Jesus' teaching would have made known the value of following him and the cost of rejecting him; 2) Jesus was well-known for his miracles—one of which was raising Lazarus from the dead; 3) the decision to follow Jesus would have been made at a time very close to the resurrection, and there were many confirming eyewitnesses.

Christians in and around Jerusalem were persecuted from the outset. Stephen is the first recorded Christian martyr. His martyrdom is estimated to have occurred in about 35, not long after the resurrection. Stephen was the first of seven to be elected to be a deacon in the church, responsible for the charitable distribution of food and money. He was accused of blasphemy in much the same way as Jesus was—he essentially confirmed Jesus as the Son of God and worshiped him as such. The Bible describes how Stephen inflamed the religious leaders and chronicles the events that followed:

> *"You stiff-necked people, with uncircumcised hearts and ears! You are just like your fathers: You always resist the Holy Spirit! Was there ever a prophet your fathers did not persecute? They even killed those who predicted the coming of the Righteous One. And now you have betrayed and murdered him—you who have received the law that was put into effect through angels but have not obeyed it."*
>
> *When they heard this, they were furious and gnashed their teeth at him. But Stephen, full of the Holy Spirit, looked up to heaven and saw the glory of God, and Jesus standing at the right hand of God. "Look," he said, "I see heaven open and the Son of Man standing at the right hand of God."*

At this they covered their ears and, yelling at the top of their voices, they all rushed at him, dragged him out of the city and began to stone him. Meanwhile, the witnesses laid their clothes at the feet of a young man named Saul.

While they were stoning him, Stephen prayed, "Lord Jesus, receive my spirit." Then he fell on his knees and cried out, "Lord, do not hold this sin against them." When he had said this, he fell asleep (Acts 7:51-60).

This act of stoning Stephen was a violation of Roman law; the Roman authorities alone held the ultimate right to prescribe the death penalty.

As we saw in the previous chapter, the Saul mentioned in this account of the martyrdom of Stephen became known later as Paul, and he was responsible for initiating the expansion of Christianity after he was converted. He started by establishing a base of operation in Antioch (a city that is located today in Syria). From there he embarked on three major missionary journeys throughout Asia Minor (now Turkey) and Macedonia (Greece). During these travels, many new churches were established.

Paul's first trip took him to Cyprus, then Asia Minor. He journeyed with Barnabas and John Mark (who failed to complete the trip) to the cities of Salamis, Paphos, Perga, Antioch in Pisidia, and Attalia.

On his next trip Paul traveled to both Asia Minor and Macedonia. During this journey, he worked with Silas and Timothy and set up churches in Philippi, Thessalonica, and Ephesus.

On Paul's third and final missionary journey, he worked with Apollos and others and established new churches in Philippi and Corinth.

Throughout Paul's missionary days, up until the time of his own martyrdom, he communicated to the churches he had established through letters. These letters have become known as the *Pauline Epistles* and are now books of the New Testament—of which they make up about one-third.

The persecution of Christianity outside of Jerusalem increased considerably under Nero, when in 64 he blamed the great fire of Rome on the Christians and initiated the first of many mass executions. Nero was ruthless. Fear was widespread in the Christian community, although believers accepted their fate as martyrs with joy—as recorded in many historical writings. (Joy in suffering as their Savior had and in the knowledge that they would be with him in heaven.)

Instead of killing off the church as Nero intended, persecution actually caused it to flourish. As the previous chapter pointed out, persecution expanded after Nero: 1) Emperor Domitian ordered Christians to be brought to Roman tribunals to be questioned about their faith; 2) Trajan forced Christians to renounce their faith by bowing down to statues of him; 3) Hadrian killed 10,000 Christians; 4) Hadrian also established pagan landmarks on the Christian holy sites and murdered Christians. The list goes on and on until Emperor Constantine stopped the persecution in 313.

Key Concept

Thousands upon thousands of Christians died because of belief in one historical fact—the resurrection.

So from the time of Jesus until 313, the Christian church flourished in spite of extreme persecution. These years would have probably been the easiest years for Christianity to disappear. The eyewitnesses all eventually died, yet faith in Jesus continued more intensely than ever. In 303, an edict from Rome stated that anyone caught with sacred writings of the Christian church would be executed. Christianity moved totally underground, but still it continued to grow.

Constantine made Christianity an acceptable religion of the Roman Empire. People in the empire were free to reject Christianity (they were just not permitted to persecute Christians any longer). In the years that followed, the church grew by leaps and bounds. (A continuation of the summary of the development of the Christian church is included in part 6.)

Test Yourself

1. Give at least one example of Christians joyfully giving their life for Christ.

2. What Roman emperor started persecution on a mass scale? What emperor ended it? When?

3. What Roman emperors followed with increased persecution? Which Roman emperor actually "marked" Christian holy sites with pagan statues?

4. What are the catacombs?

5. Why is the fact that Christianity is *historical*, so critical?

Chapter 28 Group Study

Homework Preparation (do prior to group)
Read: Acts 5:41,42; chapter 28 of this text; and page 20 in *What Is the Proof for the Resurrection?* ✝.

Opening Prayer
Discussion: Discuss what it must have been like to have been an early martyr for Christianity. What benefit do the martyrs provide us today? Discuss the reasons why the fact that Christianity is *historical* is important.

Practical-Experience Game
Role-playing: The "Christian's" role is to present the case for the early Christian martyrs to the "nonbeliever" in such a way that he or she understands the strength of conviction behind their belief.

Closing Prayer

Part 4

Evidence of the Resurrection of Jesus: Summary and Conclusion

The resurrection of Jesus as a real, historical event has been the cornerstone of Christianity through the centuries. The fact that it has been believed by countless individuals over an unbroken succession of generations has allowed little opportunity for the arising of sudden "Jesus myths" or legends. In addition, we may always compare modern belief to thousands of ancient New Testament and non-Christian writings to verify the consistency of various accounts and ensure historical accuracy in doctrine and beliefs.

Unlike other religions, Christianity is based on *historical fact*. It is not a factless philosophy. If the resurrection of Jesus never happened, there would be absolutely no basis for the Christian church. It would not exist. As we've seen, there is a continuous history of the church without any break. We can go all the way back to the earliest church documents (early manuscripts of the New Testament) and find the essential dogma of the church unchanged.

The many martyrs of the Christian faith all died for essentially one thing—to defend the historical fact that Jesus Christ rose from the dead. Enemies of the church had hoped that the execution of church leaders would stop the expansion of Christianity. Instead, it increased the resolve of Christians and provided poignant evidence of the historicity of the resurrection of Jesus to later generations.

Some people point to martyrs in other religions (for example, Muslims, or in cults) that commit suicide for something not true. However, there is a major diference from the martyrdom of the apostles. They knew for certain about the historical truth of the resurrection (and related claims). In the case of other beliefs, martyrs die for obscure, untestable philosophies.

The existence of the Christian church is undeniable. It exists solely because of the widespread belief in the historical event of the resurrection of Jesus Christ. If the resurrection did not take place historically, the Christian church would not have existed at the outset, nor would it exist today. It stands apart from any other religion in that *it depends upon one single historical, supernatural event for its existence.*

Part 5

Common Biblical Questions

A Verse to Memorize

Whoever believes in the Son has eternal life, but whoever rejects the Son will not see life, for God's wrath remains on him (John 3:36).

Sometimes issues arise from life's enigmas and dilemmas, or from biblical teaching that is difficult for non-Christians—or even Christians themselves—to understand. While no text could possibly address all of the questions one might conceive of, this section will attempt to address some of the most common issues that face people attempting to understand the teaching of the Bible.

Significance of Issues

All people naturally want all of their questions answered to complete satisfaction. Yet as we consider the myriad of potential questions, we should always remain focused on the primary message of the Bible—that which means "life" for believers. No matter what issues we may have with understanding the Bible, we must always remember that accepting Jesus Christ as both Lord and Savior is fundamental; everything else is secondary. (Take another look at the Scripture verse on the previous page.)

To this end, the following pages deal with the issue of building belief in order that solid faith in God and the Bible may be achieved. Using evidence and logic in discussing hard-to-understand sections in the Bible, or biblical doctrine, will be reviewed. The *final step of faith* involves a *trusting* of things that are taught by Jesus and in the Bible that we might not fully understand.

So within the space limitations of this book, commonly asked questions and issues that are difficult for some people will be addressed. Readers are encouraged to seek out other Bible-based sources, including the Examine the Evidence series, books listed in the bibliography, and discussions with leaders in Bible-based churches.

Why Does God Allow Suffering?

The question is asked all the time—why does God allow someone to suffer, or to die? And the most general and important answer is that we are mere human beings with a very limited perspective on God's purpose and on eternity. We are not God, and we must learn to trust that God has a "good purpose" in all that he does. As the Bible says,

A Verse to Memorize

We know that in all things God works for the good of those who love him, who have been called according to his purpose (Romans 8:28-29).

Yet this answer is not "good enough" for many who grieve the loss of a child, or experience a rape, or are struggling with an addiction. Human beings don't tend to think of the paradise that may await them upon death, or the great benefit that can be provided to the world through the experiences of those who suffer.

In an attempt to provide some perspective on why a loving God allows suffering, it is helpful to understand first why God created humans and how God's plan frames the world we live in.

Why Did God Create Humans?

No one can be certain why God created humans, or for that matter, why he created anything in the universe. However, we can get some clues and indications from the Bible, which, as has already been established, is a trustworthy authority that gives us insight into God's will. Below are some conclusions we can draw from Scripture:

1. *Humans are uniquely planned by God.* How do we know this? First, God intended from the beginning that human beings would exist with him in an eternal paradise forever (Revelation 21:3). Second, God created, from a cosmic chaos, an environment that is precisely right for the existence of mankind. Finally, we can see that, out of all the creatures God made to populate the earth, only humans worship him—and they will continue to worship him forever in heaven (Revelation 4:9-11).

2. *God created mankind in his image* (Genesis 1:26). In English, the word "image" often refers to a physical likeness. But the meaning of the original biblical Hebrew word is actually quite broad; it can also mean a spiritual or other type of likeness. Therefore, God may have created humans with a "likeness" to him in his qualities of love, justice, forgiveness, and many other areas—including the attribute of free will.

3. *God provided a means of redemption because he realized that humans would sometimes use free will for*

evil. In his perfect love, God allowed humans freedom of choice—free will—which would allow corruption of his perfect creation by imperfect choices. However, God also provided human beings with a choice of redemption that would permit them to be reconciled with him in all his perfection, even though they had misused their free will to make corrupt choices.

The steps for humans to be reconciled with God are 1) believe that God exists and that he came to earth in the form of Jesus; 2) desire to turn to him and away from evil; 3) acceptance of the sacrifice of Jesus as forgiveness for their evil thoughts and deeds—that is, making Jesus their Savior; thus 4) sincerely giving Jesus (God) control of their lives, putting all of their trust in him, therefore making him their Lord.

4. *God wants perfect humans in heaven with him forever.* Of course nobody is perfect, since all human beings have used their free will to make imperfect decisions. But the Bible tells us that any person can be "made perfect" through the sacrifice of Jesus (Hebrews 10:12-18). Though this is hard to understand, we have already established the Bible as a credible authority, inspired by God. Therefore we can trust anything that it says. So by choosing God's plan to reconcile himself to an imperfect world, any person can be made perfect and be afforded the opportunity to exist with him forever in heaven.

5. *Bottom line: God wants eternal fellowship with humans.* But because he loves all humans perfectly and wants only the best for them, he wants his fellowship with them to be based only on his character of perfect love, perfect holiness, and perfect justice. His perfect love brings him to let humans make free

will choices. His perfect holiness requires humans, if they wish to be forgiven of their evil, to choose to accept the sacrifice of Jesus. And his perfect justice requires humans to accept the awful consequences—hell—if they choose to not accept his love.

Why Did God Create This Kind of Earth?

God's ultimate purposes for human beings are often mentioned in the Bible, our only reliable authority about him. Among his many purposes, God created the earth and its creatures for the dominion of human beings (Genesis 1:26-28). But his ultimate objectives for humans are that they

- freely love him with all their heart, soul, mind, and strength (Mark 12:30)

- worship him forever (Revelation 4:21-22)

- enjoy direct fellowship with him (Revelation 21:3)

- enjoy an eternal life that is beyond earthly imagination (Matthew 13:44-46)

How God's Objectives Fit with the Kind of World We Live In

1. *God had to create something.* Otherwise his objectives could not have been expressed.

2. *God could have created a world without evil.* Humans could have been "programmed" to always choose the right and holy path. This would have resulted in a world of God-directed "robots." Love would not exist, because love requires a free-will choice. You cannot program something to love you. (For example, one could program a computer to say "I love you"—but naturally that would not be real love.)

3. *Since God loves perfectly, and since he desires human beings to love him perfectly in turn, mankind was allowed free will.* This gave human beings the opportunity to choose to love both God and others. However, it also allowed them the choice not to love. God's decision to allow free will resulted in a perfect world—but one that has been and is being used for imperfect choices.

4. *Though God created everything perfect, perfect things can be and are used for evil.*

   • Fire can heat or cook, but it can also injure and kill.

   • Nuclear energy can generate electricity, but it can also be used for bombs.

   • Metal can be used for many wonderful things, but it can also be made into guns.

   • Our minds can be used to help people, but they can also be used to hate people.

5. *Evil is a choice to misuse perfect things, thus bringing corrupt results.* Evil is not a "thing"; it is the *absence* of a thing—the absence of purity and holiness. It is the misuse of things that were created perfect and were meant to be used perfectly. In other words, evil could not be defined, nor could it even exist, if there were no holy, pure things in the first place. To give a couple of rough examples, if no sight existed, how would we know the evil of someone's gouging out another's eyes with his perfect thumbs? If humans had no legs to begin with, how would we know the evil of becoming paralyzed in an accident caused by a drunk driver—the result of misusing God's perfect gift of a mind and a properly functioning car?

6. *A loving God could let everyone—even very evil people—into heaven.* After all, wouldn't that be perfect forgiveness and love? However, it would *contradict the other attributes of God's character*—his perfect holiness and justice—because evil would enter the holy place where God lives, and because it would be unjust—evil would not receive its proper penalty. Consequently, the world God created required 1) *choice,* so that we can show perfect love for him; and 2) *redemption,* so that his perfect justice and holiness can be expressed (Romans 3:21-26).

Through Jesus we can be "made perfect" (Hebrews 10:1-4). But we need to accept Jesus as Lord and Savior, turning from evil, so we can gain his ultimate perfection. Jesus came to earth as a human, suffering all the temptations and trials of a human being so we could relate to him. Then he allowed himself to be executed in one of the most horrible, painful, and humiliating ways ever conceived by humans—to demonstrate God's great love for us and to provide forgiveness *for all who want it.* Rejecting, or not accepting, this free gift of love and forgiveness is the ultimate demonstration of disdain for God.

What Causes Suffering?

We've already established that the existence of free will allows people to choose evil, which results in suffering for the individual who chooses the evil and usually for other people as well. What are the other causes of suffering?

Satan and Demons Can Cause Suffering

It's amazing how many people don't believe in Satan or demons even though the Bible is filled with accounts of their existence. The book of Job gives an excellent picture of how

If God Is All-Powerful and Loving, How Do We Reconcile This with the Existence of Evil?

Questions	Answers
1. Doesn't logic imply that God created evil?	**1. No. Evil is a *lack* of the pure and holy use of things—not a "thing."**
• God created everything.	• God created *everything* pure and holy.
• Evil is something.	• Evil is not a thing—it is the *misuse* of pure and holy things.
• Therefore, God created evil.	• Therefore, God did not create evil. Humans chose to misuse pure and holy things—thus causing evil.
2. Didn't God create imperfect beings?	**2. Perfect love requires freedom of choice, thus allowing the possibility of evil.**
• Every being God made should be perfect.	• God originally made everything perfect, including love.
• But perfect beings would not do imperfect things.	• Perfect love requires a free-will choice—including freedom to not love and freedom to do evil.
• Therefore, God created imperfect beings.	• Therefore, God did not create imperfect beings. His creation uses its free will to choose to do evil.
3. Why can't God stop evil?	**3. Evil can and will be stopped.**
• If God is all-good, he *would* destroy evil.	• Since God is all-good, he *will* destroy evil.
• If God is all-powerful, he *could* destroy evil.	• Since God is all-powerful, he *can* destroy evil.
• But evil has not been destroyed.	• But evil is not yet destroyed.
• Therefore, either God is not all-good, or else he is not all-powerful.	• Therefore, one day God will destroy evil.
4. Why does God wait to stop evil?	**4. God waits to destroy evil to allow more people to be saved.**
• If God can and will stop evil, he would stop it.	• God could stop evil now, yet he allows it to continue.
• If God were all-good, he wouldn't wait to stop evil.	• When God destroys evil, free will will also be stopped.
• Yet evil continues to exist.	• When free will is stopped, the *choice* to love God stops.
• Therefore, either God is not all-good, or else he cannot stop evil.	• Therefore, God will stop evil when his will for people to be saved is completed.

Why Did God Create a World He Knew Would Become Evil?

God's purpose for humans is that they:

- have eternal fellowship with him
- freely choose to love him
- freely choose to worship him
- become holy through forgiveness
- live eternally with him in a perfectly holy paradise

Why this world is the *best solution* to achieve God's purposes:

1. God wants fellowship with human beings who love him, so it was necessary for him to make a world in which people could live, be given the choice to love him, and be given the opportunity to develop holy character.

2. God wants humans to love him perfectly. His desire made it necessary that he create a world of totally free choice.

3. The free choice that God granted to human beings also allows them to use his choice for evil. Humans made the choice of evil in the beginning, though they may still turn from evil and choose the good.

4. God has provided a means for imperfect humans to choose to love him and be forgiven for their past evil. The means he provided for forgiveness were the sacrifice of himself in the person of his Son, Jesus.

5. Those people who do not accept Jesus' perfect sacrifice and his resurrection (which proves his deity) reject God's love, reject God's forgiveness, and reject Jesus—who is God—as Lord. Essentially they show disdain, not love, for God.

6. So this world of good and evil is essentially a sorting ground to determine who will choose to seek holiness and love God by freely accepting his gift of forgiveness—by freely accepting Jesus as Lord and Savior.

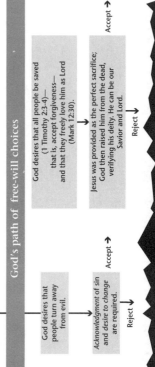

Heaven
Believers can perfectly experience their God-granted holiness and justification (Romans 3:23-24) and are completely free to express perfect love.

God's path of free-will choices

God desires that all people be saved (1 Timothy 2:3-4)—that is, accept forgiveness—and that they freely love him as Lord (Mark 12:30).

Jesus was provided as the perfect sacrifice; God then raised him from the dead, verifying his deity. He can be our Savior and Lord.

Accept → Reject →

Free-Will Choice of — **Eternal Separation from God**

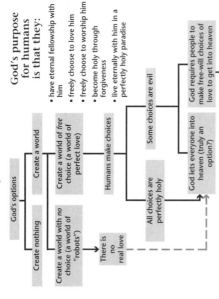

God's options

- Create nothing
- Create a world
  - Create a world with *no* choice (a world of "robots")
    - There is no real love
  - Create a world of *free* choice (a world of perfect love)
    - Humans make choices
      - All choices are perfectly holy
      - Some choices are evil
        - God lets everyone into heaven (truly an option?)
        - God requires people to make free-will choices of love to get into heaven

God desires that people turn away from evil.

Acknowledgment of sin and desire to change are required.

Accept → Reject →

God's path of free-will choices provides for

1. *perfect love*—freely choosing the love of God by accepting Jesus, God's gift of love
2. *perfect holiness*—freely chosen by confession and turning from sin—perfection through Jesus' redemption
3. *perfect justice*—freely chosen through the death and resurrection of Jesus, who as our substitute took the penalty for sin (Romans 3:23-24)

Satan can bring suffering on people. Notice how powerful Satan is:

- He influenced armies to steal Job's herds and kill his servants (1:4-15).

- He brought fire from the sky to wipe out Job's sheep and servants (verse 16).

- He influenced raiding parties to steal Job's camels (verse 17).

- He directed a wind that blew down a house, killing Job's children (verses 18-19).

- He afflicted Job with excruciatingly painful sores all over his body (2:7-8).

Satan clearly has vast power, and he and his demons will create as much suffering as they can. But he still must have God's approval to exercise his power (see Job 1:12; 2:6).

God Can Cause Suffering

The idea that God would cause suffering might at first seem unimaginable. Why would a loving God himself cause suffering? We must remember that God's purpose and understanding is greater than we often conceive of. Consider the following:

- *We have a finite mind limited to four dimensions.* Fully understanding the mind of God is impossible for us.

- *Evil is not the same as suffering.* Evil always has its origin in an intent to do wrong or harm. However, suffering can be caused for good reasons. For example, people often choose the pain of surgery and recovery in order to have a better-functioning body later. And suffering for Christ brings eternal rewards, even though evil may be the cause of the suffering.

- *God's intentions are much greater than ours.* It's difficult for human beings to look beyond their immediate circumstances. But God always considers the eternal perspective (for example, sometimes our suffering can bring other people to eternal life in Christ).

God is perfectly holy, loving, and just. To our limited human minds, these attributes often seem to conflict with one another. In fact, from our viewpoint it seems that God sometimes chooses one over the other:

- God struck down Aaron's sons because they used unauthorized fire in the tabernacle (Leviticus 10:1-3). Note that the fire that killed the sons came "from the presence of the Lord." In this case God displayed his holiness even though it caused suffering in Aaron's family.

- God struck down David's firstborn son and caused calamity within David's household because of his adultery with Bathsheba and his murder of Uriah, her husband (2 Samuel 12:7-14). Notice that the Lord said, "I am going to bring calamity... I will take your wives and give them to one who is close to you." God displayed his justice even though it caused David to suffer.

There are several other cases in the Bible where God caused suffering. But for those people who have accepted Jesus, whatever the source of their difficulty, there is a great message from God as we have seen—that all things work together for good (Romans 8:28).

Are Suffering and Death Always Bad?

People often ask why suffering exists. We've all experienced pain at some point in our life, and it usually seems that our suffering has no good purpose. We just want it to be over. Seldom do we actually consider the benefits of pain, suffering, and even death.

It is the causes and the "justness" of pain, suffering, and death that we often understand the least. Sometimes pain and suffering are clearly the result of an evil action (sin)—either our own or another's. For example, a drunk driver causes an auto accident, paralyzing for life both himself and the occupant of the car he crashed into. There seems to be some justice for the one committing the sin of drunkenness, but it's hard to understand why the innocent victim must also suffer.

The Benefits of Suffering

How can we comprehend the benefits of pain and suffering? Some pain is easy to understand. In fact, it's a protective gift from God. Touch a hot stove, and you learn not to do it again. Feel pain in a part of your body, and you seek a doctor to help you. But long-term suffering is more difficult to understand. Often we don't understand it for many years, and sometimes not at all in this life. Some possible benefits of suffering we might not think about when we are going through it are that God may have planned to

- teach us something
- help us learn to love others
- test our faith in him
- develop our character
- build our trust in him
- inspire us to hope in eternal things

The Benefits of Death

Most people think of death as a horrible event—and it is for those people who refuse to accept Jesus as Lord and Savior. But for those of us who do accept God's love through Jesus, death is a wonderful thing! Imagine being transported from a world of evil and unsolvable problems to a perfect paradise, where we will live in God's presence forever! What many Christians fear is the suffering that going through the process of death may bring. As awful and drawn-out as it may be, this temporary suffering is still small in comparison to eternity.

The Suffering of Jesus

A God who created the universe could certainly have created a world without suffering. But the reasons why he did not—and why the existence of our kind of world makes perfect sense—have already been explored. However, some people may think that God is evil and unfeeling because he "sits up there in a perfect paradise" while we are suffering "down here." This is far from the truth.

God came to Earth in the person of Jesus Christ and went through all the types of suffering that most people go through—until about A.D. 33. At that time, Jesus voluntarily exposed himself to the most painful, horrible, and humiliating death ever devised by man: crucifixion.

Whenever we doubt God's existence—whenever we wonder whether any God worth the name would create a world he knew would be overwhelmed by pain, suffering, and death—we should remember that he chose to enter this world, to suffer more than anyone, and to die in the most painful manner, just to allow us to choose to have eternal life with him in heaven. Jesus didn't have to do this. He chose

Fascinating Facts

How to know that life after death is real: Jesus frequently referred to life after death when he talked about 1) the kingdom of God—heaven; 2) hell; 3) eternal life; and 4) the soul and spirit of human beings. In fact, in the Bible (New International Version) the following number of references are found:

Related Words	Number of References
Heaven / Kingdom of God	420+
Hell / Fire / Abyss	150+
Soul / Spirit	660+
Eternity / Forever	370+

This alone is a strong enough reason to believe in life after death in either heaven or hell. Yet, there is good scientific and logical reason to believe in life after death as well. *Consider that the atoms in your body are in a constant state of replacement. Scientists calculate that once every five years, every atom in your body has been replaced.* Even so, you are still the same person. You remember most of the same things. And your character and personality remain unchanged. Likewise, even if you were to have a traumatic accident that left you physically unrecognizable, your friends would know you by your experiences, personality, and mannerisms.

Essentially, this demonstrates that something exists that identifies you beyond the physical part of your body, which is made up of atoms. What is that "other part" of you? If it doesn't die, when all of the cells of your body die and are replaced, *why would you expect it to die when all of the body dies at once?* Logic would say that it doesn't. And logic might define this "essence," beyond the material being, as one's spirit or soul. (See the Examine the Evidence series book *What Really Happens When You Die?*)

this horrible sacrifice for people who didn't deserve it. He chose it to demonstrate his great love.

> *God so loved the world that he gave his one and only Son, that whoever believes in him shall not perish but have eternal life. For God did not send his Son into the world to condemn the world, but to save the world through him* (John 3:16-18).

When we reject, or simply do not accept, Jesus as our Lord and Savior, we are in effect thumbing our nose at God—saying in essence that the blood of Jesus is not "good enough."

Placing Suffering in Perspective

Would it be worth suffering a 30-second vaccine injection to avoid the long-term effects of smallpox? Would you endure a few months of chemotherapy so you could live a long life free of cancer? Sometimes an enormous long-term benefit requires suffering to attain it. Jesus himself said we would have to suffer to follow him and obtain eternal life in paradise (Matthew 10:21-22,38-39). Isn't a second or two of suffering worth billions of years (really, an infinity) of an inconceivably wonderful eternity?

Its obvious God sometimes allows suffering. As shown, God even uses it to accomplish his greater purposes. Whatever suffering we experience, whether little, much, or every moment of our lives, our human minds are still mostly preoccupied with the present—the here and now. *God is focused on eternity—an eternity of good.*

The point is, what humans regard as unbearable suffering will come to an end—and is really a very small part of eternity. How we deal with that suffering is all-important; it actually tests us in regard to true love and trust, the love and trust that can be anchored only in God. One good example is how God allowed suffering to be a major part of evangelism. Consider what the Bible says:

- *"Suffering produces perseverance"* (Romans 5:3).

- *All this is evidence that God's judgment is right, and as a result you will be counted worthy of the kingdom of God, for which you are suffering* (2 Thessalonians 1:5).

- *This is my gospel, for which I am suffering even to the point of being chained like a criminal. But God's word is not chained* (2 Timothy 2:8-9).

- *In bringing many sons to glory, it was fitting that God, for whom and through whom everything exists, should make the author of their salvation perfect through suffering* (Hebrews 2:10).

- *Remember those earlier days after you had received the light, when you stood your ground in a great contest in the face of suffering* (Hebrews 10:32).

- *Brothers, as an example of patience in the face of suffering, take the prophets who spoke in the name of the Lord. As you know, we consider blessed those who have persevered. You have heard of Job's perseverance and have seen what the Lord finally brought about. The Lord is full of compassion and mercy* (James 5:10-11).

Apart from suffering for the gospel, we should recognize that only through various kinds of suffering can we truly appreciate God's ultimate good—in contrast to evil.

However, nothing presented here is intended to minimize the tremendous pain, hurt, and grief that result from suffering. But our lives continue while we are suffering, even though we might wish they would stop. And through it all we need to keep facing the central issues of human existence. We must ultimately realize that God is in control—and that he is loving, he is just, and he is holy. His acts of love, justice, and holiness have been documented over thousands of years. We are not in a position to judge God. The final answers to suffering lie in a dimension beyond ours—because they lie with God himself.

Remember—our entire lifetime, even if it is 100 years of suffering, is like the smallest fraction of a second when compared to billions of years (actually an infinity) of eternity. Since God knows both the end and the beginning (Isaiah 46:9-10), he is the One who can help us develop an attitude of joy in suffering, as did the early Christians who came to know Jesus (1 Thessalonians 1:5-10).

Test Yourself

1. How is suffering related to love? Give some examples of how you have experienced suffering in the process of being loved.

2. Why did God create human beings? What do you envision heaven and hell to be like? How do we know heaven and hell exist?

3. Explain why God created a world he knew would become evil.

4. What causes suffering? Give some examples.

5. How did God suffer in the same way, or an even greater way, than humans?

Chapter 29 Group Study

Homework Preparation (do prior to group)

Read: chapter 29 of this text; *Why Does God Allow Suffering?;* and *What Really Happens When You Die?* ✝.

Opening Prayer

Discussion: As a group, review the chart on page 452. Be sure everyone understands the process. Discuss death. How is it a benefit? Why is it so important that nonbelievers understand death?

Practical-Experience Game

Debate: The "Christian" debates an "atheist" who uses, as his primary defense, the idea that if God was real, he wouldn't allow suffering. Be sure to bring the issue of death into the debate.

Closing Prayer

The Trinity

Christians speak of the holy Trinity, the three "persons" of God, as a foundational aspect of their faith. The holy Trinity is the Father, the Son (Jesus), and the Holy Spirit—somehow existing as a single "God." At the very least it sounds confusing. Some people think it's irrational.*

Why is the Trinity such an issue? Perhaps because it's basic to knowing God. After all, to know God, we should know who he is and what he is like. The Trinity is a biblical concept, carried throughout the Scripture:

- The Bible defines God as three "Persons" (many references will be reviewed below).

- We can trust the Bible's definition.

The Bible proclaims that the Trinity is real and personal. If we worship, pray to, and think we know a "god" who is not real, we are deceived. It is important to know the nature of the God we presume to know. The Trinity is the biblical

---

* Perhaps much confusion comes from referring to the triune Godhead as three persons in one God. In reality, however the Trinity is three Persons in one Nature—that of God.

and Christian definition. While it may be difficult to understand, if it is indeed a true description of God, we need to know enough to at least accept it. Below, we will attempt to clarify the issue of the Trinity so we can know who God is.

Defining the Holy Trinity

Webster defines the Trinity in the simplest terms:

> The union of three divine figures, the Father, Son, and Holy Ghost, in one Godhead.

Accurate from a biblical standpoint? Yes. Understandable to most people? No. Misleading? Possibly. (More description is necessary, the word *ghost* has changed in meaning over the last few centuries and now gives the wrong impression, and there is no mention of the co-equal, personal nature of the Trinity.)

A much better and more complete definition of the Trinity is given by a well-known theological dictionary. It defines the Trinity as

> the term designating one God in three persons. Although not itself a biblical term,...[it is] a convenient designation for the one God self-revealed in Scripture as the one essence of the Godhead. We have to distinguish three "persons" who are neither three gods on the one side, nor three parts or modes of God on the other, but coequally and coeternally God."[1]

Why Isn't the Word Trinity *in the Bible?*

As the above definition states, although the word *Trinity* never appears in the Bible, the concept is "self-revealed" by God. Biblical scholars merely gave the concept of the three-in-one God a name so it would be easy to refer to and discuss.

There are other concepts in the Bible that have been given a name that doesn't appear in the Bible. For instance, the omnipotence ("all-powerfulness") of God is very clear from the Scriptures (for example, in Job 38 and 39). No Christian would deny this doctrine—yet the word *omnipotence* is never used in the English Bible. For ease of reference, the concept of God's "all-powerfulness" was given the name *omnipotence*.

The Trinity Is Three Persons

A *person* is someone who can know you, can counsel and help you, can care about you, and might even sacrifice himself for you. So the suggestion that God is an "it," or that the Holy Spirit is an "it," is essentially saying that God is a "force" that doesn't 1) know, 2) care about, 3) help, or 4) sacrifice itself for human beings. The Bible repeatedly states that God knows each of us, that he lovingly cares about us, that he counsels and helps us, and that he even sacrificed himself for us. Clearly, God is not an "it."

The Persons of the Trinity (Father, Son, and Holy Spirit), while co-equal and co-eternal, do fulfill different roles.

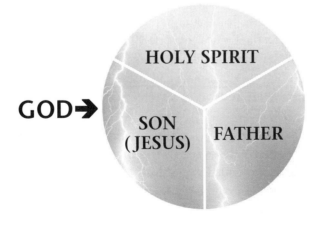

The Persons of the Trinity Are Co-Equal and Co-Eternal

The words *co-equal* and *co-eternal* indicate that the Son and the Holy Spirit are totally equal with God the Father. At first glance, this seems to contradict the Bible. For instance, Jesus prayed to the Father in the garden of Gethsemane, "Not what I will, but what you will" (Mark 14:36). This seems to imply that the Father was above Jesus.

The answer is revealed by defining the *purpose* of Jesus while he was on Earth. Jesus' purpose was to assume the role of humanity to become not only a sacrifice for human sin but also to teach us how to relate to an all-powerful, all-holy God. To accomplish this, Jesus "gave up" the right to exercise his power as God while he was on Earth (this concept is called *kenosis* in theology). He was still 100-percent God, but he simply limited his power while on Earth (though he still had access to it). Jesus thus took on humanity with all its attributes. As a human, he taught us to pray to God. He taught us how to relate to God. And he taught us that the will of God is not always our will.

Did this short-term subjugation to God the Father make Jesus "less equal"? No! It served a teaching purpose. The Bible clearly describes Jesus as equal to God (for example, "I and the Father are one"—see John 10:30). Jesus also received worship and forgave sin, something only God could do. And Jesus proclaimed his ultimate authority as God: "All authority in heaven and on earth has been given to me" (Matthew 28:18).

The eternal existence of Jesus along with the Father is evident in John chapter 1. Jesus is a Person of the Godhead from the beginning to the end (Revelation 22:13). Likewise, the Holy Spirit is a Person of the Godhead who is co-equal and exists from beginning to end. Notice that in the *beginning* (Genesis 1:2) the Spirit of God hovered over the surface of the deep. Also, at the *end of time,* the Spirit of God is again present (Revelation 22:17).

The Trinity in the Old Testament

There is substantial evidence supporting the concept of the Trinity in the Old Testament (the Hebrew Scriptures). Apart from the individual references to each of the three "parts" of the Trinity, we also find other indications that God is made up of multiple "persons."

God the Father

God the Father is presented in the Old Testament in absolute, total glory. So holy and so glorious is his majesty that anyone who saw his face would die (Genesis 32:30; Isaiah 6:1-5).

The presence of God the Father *(theophany)* was perceived in many miraculous ways:

- an angel appeared to Hagar (Genesis 16:9)
- the Lord appeared again to Abraham (Genesis 22:11-12)
- the burning bush to Moses (Exodus 3:2)
- clouds and fire to the Israelites (Exodus 14:19)
- the tabernacle (Exodus 40:34)
- the Lord appeared to Moses (Exodus 33:11)
- the Lord appeared to Isaiah (Isaiah 6:1-5)

God the Son

The Old Testament is also filled with writings that point toward Jesus. There are hundreds of prophecies contained in the Old Testament that are exactly fulfilled by Jesus. (Scholars have actually identified 322 distinct prophecies.)

Fascinating Facts

A *theophany* is a visual or spoken presence of God. There were many theophanies in the Old Testament (such as the burning bush—see Exodus 3:2), possibly because God needed to provide unmistakable evidence of his divine authority over the rebellious nation of Israel.

Some theophanies clearly show the glory of God (for example, the presence of the Lord on Mount Sinai—Exodus 19:18-19; the cloud over the tabernacle—Exodus 40:34). Other theophanies are apparently manifestations of God in human form—often described as the appearance of "an angel of the Lord," a term which implies a special reverence reserved for God. Scholars debate many issues about "angel of the Lord" theophanies. Some believe they are appearances of Christ before he came to earth as a human being.

God has declared that prophecy is the key test to determine whether something is "from him" (Deuteronomy 18:9-22; Isaiah 46:10).

Certainly the Jews themselves were well aware of a coming Messiah ("Anointed One"). Perhaps the single most important indication of the coming Messiah in relation to the Trinity is Isaiah's prophecy of a "son" who was to be called "Immanuel" (Isaiah 7:14). *Immanuel means "God with us."*

Matthew makes this prophetic parallel very clear in his Gospel (1:23). The early apostles, who lived continuously with Jesus for three years, not only understood the important role of the Son, Jesus, as part of the Trinity—they actually used the Old Testament prophecy of a coming "God incarnate" to persuade the monotheistic* Jews that Jesus was

* *Monotheistic* means "believing in a single God." *Monotheism* means "belief in a single God.

God. When we consider the very strong monotheistic attitude of the Jewish nation, and add to this the very large number of Jews who quickly adopted Christianity (largely due to fulfilled Old Testament prophecy), this leads us to the conclusion that those who were in the best position to "know for certain" the facts about Jesus (including his role as a Person of the Trinity) accepted the prophecy about Jesus, including Matthew's key point of Jesus being "God with us."

God the Spirit

The third component of the Trinity, the Spirit of God, is mentioned throughout the Old Testament. Starting at the very beginning of Genesis (1:2), we find this important verse:

> Some scholars believe that Christ appeared in the Old Testament era. Melchizedek—whom Abram (later Abraham) encountered—may be such a case. At least he is a "model" of Jesus (Genesis 14:18).
>
> Melchizedek was honored as a "priest of God Most High" (Hebrews 7:1-2)—just as Jesus is a priest. He offered Abram bread and wine, possibly a foreshadowing of the last supper. And Abram gave him a tenth of everything, an early example of the tithe which was later instituted in the Law of Moses.

The Spirit of God was hovering over the surface of the waters.

The Hebrew word used for spirit is *ruwach*, which in essence means "a resemblance of breath"—but "only by a rational being."[2] So we can recognize immediately that this "Spirit" is differentiated from God the Father and God the Son. And we also see that he is a "rational being," not merely some "force." Furthermore, we see the Holy Spirit involved immediately from the beginning of creation.

The Spirit of God is also seen in the Old Testament as a counselor or helper—indwelling people to allow them to accomplish things that God wills (as in the New Testament). For example, Bezalel was filled with the Spirit of God so that he would have certain abilities in handcrafts in making the tabernacle (Exodus 31:3). Even some people who *rejected* God were inspired by the Holy Spirit, as indicated by the pagan prophet Balaam's blessing of Israel despite the enemy king Balak's attempt to purchase a curse (Numbers 24:2-3).

The Trinity in the New Testament

The concept of the Trinity is clearly expressed throughout the New Testament. If we accept the Bible as truth, we do not need to wonder about the doctrine of the Trinity, because we have distinct evidence from both the start of Jesus' ministry and also the end, with a great deal of supporting evidence in between.

The Beginning of Jesus' Ministry

When Jesus was about 30 years old, he started his ministry by being baptized by John the Baptist. It's significant that Jesus appeared very human and humble.

John claimed to be "unworthy" of baptizing Jesus; then, when the baptism took place at Jesus' insistence, we again find all three Persons of the Trinity:

- *The Son* was humbly submitting himself in human form to the Father, as a model for all of the world (Matthew 3:15).

- *The Father* spoke from heaven, saying, "This is my Son, whom I love; with him I am well pleased" (Matthew 3:17).

- *The Holy Spirit*—the "Spirit of God"—descended "like a dove," lighting on Jesus (Matthew 3:16).

The End of Jesus' Ministry

The last words of a person are often especially significant. After all, we all want to leave the people we love with the most important thing we want them to remember. (Advertising is an ideal example. The last words are almost always the brand name and the primary attribute—often a slogan). Keeping this in mind, what were the last words of Jesus? They were spoken just prior to his ascension into heaven.

> Go and make disciples of all nations, baptizing them in the name of the Father and of the Son and of the Holy Spirit, and teaching them to obey everything I have commanded you. And surely I am with you always, to the very end of the age (Matthew 28:19-20).

No doubt Jesus especially wanted people to recognize the three-in-one nature of God. Otherwise, why would he use his final words to emphasize the three Persons of the Trinity?

Baptism is an important part of one's commitment to the Christian faith and to Jesus Christ. So Jesus' last commandment (often called the "Great Commission") deals with the issue of a public proclamation—baptism—during which all three Persons of the Godhead are recognized—the Father, the Son, and the Holy Spirit. Hence, when people are baptized as Christians, the Trinity is an integral part of their commitment.

More New Testament References

The New Testament differentiates, yet also unites, the Father, the Son, and the Holy Spirit in many ways in addition to those indicated at the beginning and end of Jesus' ministry. For example, Paul speaks of God's three-in-one nature in his letter to Corinth. He describes the differences in roles, but the oneness of "essence":

There are different kinds of gifts, *but the* same Spirit. *There are* different kinds of service, *but the* same Lord. *There are* different kinds of working, *but the* same God *works all of them in all men* (1 Corinthians 12:4-6).

And the clear distinction in the roles of the three Persons of the Trinity was laid out by Jesus, who spoke of his role as intercessor, the Father's as the ultimate authority, and the Holy Spirit's as our helper in day-to-day decisions in the following verse:

Some references to the triune God in the New Testament:

- Matthew 3:16-17
- John 14:16
- 1 Corinthians 12:4-6
- 2 Corinthians 13:14
- Ephesians 3:14-19
- Ephesians 4:4-13
- 1 Peter 1:1-2
- Revelation 1:4-6

I will ask the Father, and he will give you another Counselor to be with you forever—the Spirit of truth. The world cannot accept him, because it neither sees him nor knows him (Jesus, in John 14:16-17).

God's Love in the Trinity

God existed as the Trinity before time began (Genesis 1:1; 1:26; John 1). Yet the reality of God's love has been displayed in his three-in-one nature since before anything else existed. God's total and complete love is shown forth in the three Persons as they exemplify grace, love, and fellowship:

May the grace of the Lord Jesus Christ, and the love of God, and the fellowship of the Holy Spirit be with you all (2 Corinthians 13:14).

One God in Three Persons Meets All Human Needs

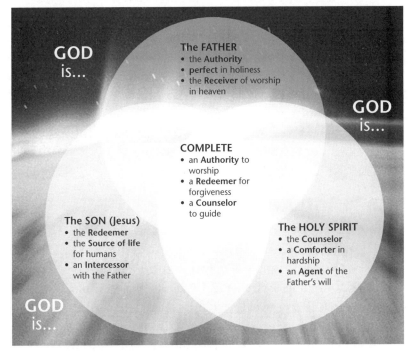

GOD is...

The FATHER
- the **Authority**
- **perfect** in holiness
- the **Receiver** of worship in heaven

GOD is...

COMPLETE
- an **Authority** to worship
- a **Redeemer** for forgiveness
- a **Counselor** to guide

The SON (Jesus)
- the **Redeemer**
- the **Source of life** for humans
- an **Intercessor** with the Father

The HOLY SPIRIT
- the **Counselor**
- a **Comforter** in hardship
- an **Agent** of the Father's will

GOD is...

The Persons of the Trinity Described

The Father—The First Person of the Godhead

A precise description of the Person of the Father is beyond human ability and comprehension. Though anyone who "saw the *face* of God would die" (Genesis 32:30; Isaiah 6:1-5), the *glory* of God was displayed in the Old Testament to the Israelites several times (see page 467). It was also expressed audibly at the baptism of Jesus (Matthew 3:17) and at the transfiguration (Matthew 17:5).

John's revelation from Jesus provides some clues as to the appearance of the Father. He describes him as "someone" sitting on a throne in heaven. He has the "appearance of jasper and carnelian," and from his throne come "flashes of lightning" and "peals of thunder" (Revelation 4:3,5)—similar to the glory of God at Mt. Sinai (Exodus 19:16-18). Finally, God is often referred to as "light" (for example, in 1 John 1:5—whether this is a reference to the Father alone or the entire Godhead is not clear). However, God Himself is called a light so incredible as to eliminate the need for the sun or for lamps (Revelation 22:5).

It is important to point out that the Bible's teaching stresses the essence of God the Father, not as being a physical human father, but as being a heavenly Father—the Creator of all things (Job 38:4-7; Psalm 33:6).

The Son—The Second Person of the Godhead

Jesus, the Son, was fully human and fully God (John 10:30). Therefore, the physical being of Jesus is completely that of a human. Jesus was conceived through the Holy Spirit within a human body—the body of Mary (Luke 1:35; Matthew 1:20). However, to Jesus' complete human nature was joined the complete nature of God, and both natures were in one Person, Jesus. This made it easy for us to relate to God, and for Jesus to experience everything we experience (Hebrews 2:9,12,18). It also provided the necessary utterly perfect sacrifice for sin (Hebrews 10:1-14).

Perhaps the most difficult thing about Jesus to understand from our limited human viewpoint is his pre-existence. We know that Jesus was co-eternal with God, since he was there in the beginning and then came to Earth.

In the beginning was the Word (John 1:1).

The Word became flesh and made his dwelling among us (John 1:14).

As the Son, Jesus never referred to his special relationship with the Father in a way that might imply that the disciples had an equal relationship. Jesus claimed to be the pre-existent eternal Son, fully God and fully equal with the Father, incarnated to fulfill God's purpose of providing salvation. For this reason he was appointed as the sole mediator between humans and God the Father (Matthew 11:27; John 5:22; 8:58; 10:30,38; 14:9; 16:28). As a human who was also fully God, Jesus accepted prayer and worship (Matthew 14:33; 28:9; John 14:14).

The Holy Spirit—The Third Person of the Godhead

The original Hebrew and Greek words referring to the Holy Spirit *(ruwach* and *pneuma)* mean "wind" or "breath." We cannot see wind, but from its effects, we know it exists. The Holy Spirit is the all-powerful Person who was involved in creation (Genesis 1:2), and he will be involved at the end of time summoning people into the new heaven and earth (Revelation 22:17). The Holy Spirit is involved with human beings who are believers on a daily basis as a "comforter," guiding us, communicating the presence of the living Christ to us, and doing everything for us that Christ himself did for the disciples (John 14:15-17; 16:13-15). He is an invisible supporter of good (Zechariah 4:6; 1 Corinthians 12:3) and a restrainer and convicter of evil (Genesis 6:3; John 16:8-11; 1 Corinthians 12:3).

The Three-in-One Nature of the Trinity

Could we ever understand a multidimensional God? Though the concept of the Trinity has been known since the time of Christ, it has often been misunderstood. Why? It's because humans exist in a world that consists of three dimensions of space and one dimension of time. How can we know or even conceive of dimensions beyond our own—such as the spiritual dimension? This has been a large problem for people who can't accept God because he is too far beyond our understanding.

As we have seen, the Bible is very clear in its references to the triune nature of God. We also know there was a widespread, rapid acceptance of Jesus as God (co-equal with the Father) by the Jews around Jerusalem in the months immediately after Jesus' death. At first glance, this would seem to contradict the traditional Jewish monotheism (was Jesus an "additional" god?). Yet the early Jewish Christians accepted Jesus as "one" with the Father: co-existent and co-equal.

Helpful Analogies

The concept of a three-in-one God is difficult to understand because our finite human minds tend to think that $1+1+1=3$, not $1+1+1=1$. Yet neither equation accurately reflects the true three-in-one reality—in which all three Persons are distinct, yet inseparable in nature.

A better mathematical model, which is also quite easy to understand, is $1 \times 1 \times 1 = 1$. Here, all parts are distinct yet interrelated mathematically.

Another useful illustration can be drawn from the realm of moral realities:

> Augustine suggested an illustration of how God is both three and one at the same time. The Bible informs us that "God is love" (1 John 4:16). Love involves a lover, a beloved, and a spirit of love between lover and beloved. The Father night be likened to the Lover; the Son to the One loved, and the Holy Spirit is the Spirit of love. Yet love does not exist unless these three are united as one. This illustration has the advantage of being personal since it involves love, a characteristic that flows from persons.[3]

The Expression of God's Love Required the Full Resources of the Trinity

In order to demonstrate complete love to human beings, who were made in the image of God, all three Persons of God are necessary. First, an authority figure (the Father) was necessary to display perfect love, justice, and holiness. The Father provided us a chance to love him perfectly by giving us free choice—which also allowed sin to enter the world. Second, a human figure (the Son, Jesus) was necessary 1) to give himself as the perfect sacrifice to redeem humans from the sin he knew they would choose, and 2) to be our ongoing source of life and relationship with the Father. Finally, the Holy Spirit was necessary to provide humans daily guidance, assurance, and counsel by being the continual presence of Christ within us.

The Roles of the Persons of the Trinity

In many aspects of God's activities, we see the Persons of the Trinity each taking a role.

- *In creation:*

Father	Revelation 4:11
Son	Hebrews 1:1-2, John 1:1,14
Holy Spirit	Genesis 1:2, Psalm 33:6

- *In God's plan:*

Father	Ephesians 1:11-12
Son	Colossians 1:15-16
Holy Spirit	Isaiah 11:2-3

- *In God's Word:*

Father	Isaiah 55:11
Son	John 1:14, Hebrews 1:3
Holy Spirit	1 Corinthians 2:12-14

- *In God's advent in human form:*

Father	Hebrews 10:5-7
Son	Matthew 16:15-17
Holy Spirit	Matthew 1:20; John 3:34

- *In salvation through Jesus' sacrifice:*

Father	John 3:16; 1 John 4:10-11
Son	John 19:30; Hebrews 9:28
Holy Spirit	John 3:34

- *In reconciliation with God:*

Father	1 John 1:3; 2 Corinthians 5:17-19
Son	Hebrews 2:13-15
Holy Spirit	2 Corinthians 13:14

- *In providing holiness to believers:*

Father	1 Peter 1:15-16
Son	1 Corinthians 1:30-31
Holy Spirit	Galatians 5:16; Romans 8:3-4

- *In providing love, faith, and hope:*

Father	John 3:16
Son	John 14:6; Hebrews 12:2-3
Holy Spirit	Romans 15:13

The Trinity Is Necessary for Eternal Life with God

We have noted the roles of the Persons of the Trinity and the biblical support for them. We can see that

- The concept of the Trinity is clear throughout the Bible

- Each person of the Trinity has had a clear role from the beginning in all human relationships with God

Yet we are still left with the question, "Why was a triune God necessary in the first place?" Just asking that question (though many people have) seems presumptuous. What right do we have to ask God *why* he is who he is? Even so, though it is impossible for human minds to comprehend an infinite God, the Bible does give us some clues why the Trinity is necessary for our eternal relationship with God. Consider the following:

1. God is perfectly holy. He was once in complete fellowship with a sinless Adam and Eve.

2. Once Adam and Eve sinned, humanity became separated from God.

3. A perfect blood sacrifice was required to pay for human sin.

4. Even after the giving of this perfect sacrifice, humans still continue to sin.

5. God's ultimate goal is complete fellowship with humans in a perfectly sinless place—heaven.

In summary, the Trinity, while difficult to understand from a human point of view, is an integral and necessary aspect of God—and it is indispensable to his great love and his many temporal and eternal provisions for humanity.

Test Yourself

1. Define the holy Trinity.

2. Provide at least one example of the Trinity in the Old Testament.

3. Provide at least one example of the Trinity in the New Testament.

4. How is the Trinity involved in the beginning and ending of Jesus' ministry?

5. List at least three of the roles of the Trinity.

Chapter 30 Group Study

Homework Preparation (do prior to group)
Read: chapter 30 of this text and *What Is the Trinity?* ✝.

Opening Prayer
Discussion: Review the many roles of the Trinity on pages 28–41 of *What Is the Trinity?* Select those that are most interesting to the group and discuss them. Some cults claim that the Trinity doesn't exist (for example, the Jehovah's Witnesses). How would you speak to a member of such a group to convince him or her that the Trinity is essential to the Bible's message?

Practical-Experience Game
TV interview: The "TV host" is interviewing the "Christian" regarding the difficulty of understanding the Trinity. Be prepared to explain it and its importance.

Closing Prayer

How to Analyze
Alleged Contradictions
in the Bible

Some people claim that the Bible has a lot of contradictions within it. Yet it continues to be a source of inspiration and the foundation of the Christian faith after more than 2000 years. Are there really contradictions?

If God truly inspired all the words of the Bible, he would certainly not contradict himself. Yet we know that people actually wrote down the words of the Bible. Did the human authors make mistakes? Did they misunderstand God's inspiration in some cases? Or did mistakes creep in later during copying and translating? In the case of apparent contradictions, is it possible we aren't digging deep enough to really understand the message?

Since Christians claim the Bible is inspired by God, it is important to establish that it doesn't contain contradictions at the heart of its message. Why?

- How could the Bible be trusted otherwise?

- How would people know which parts of the Bible to believe or not believe?

- Wouldn't a contradictory Bible allow "picking and choosing" of what to follow regarding its messages and truths?

481

When people research supposed contradictions in the Bible, they find that the Bible is *still in agreement with the earliest manuscripts* on all issues, despite thousands of years of copying and translating. Does that mean today's Bibles are a word-for-word match with the originals? No, of course not. For one thing, the originals were written in different languages. For instance, the original Hebrew Bible contains no vowels. The evidence suggests, however, that the Bible still accurately reflects the original manuscripts, with only minor variations. The question then becomes, are there contradictions within the Bible itself?

Defining Contradictions

What constitutes a biblical "contradiction"? Webster defines *contradiction* and *contradictory* as follows:

- *Contradiction:* "Something containing contradictory elements."

- *Contradictory:* "Either of two propositions related in such a way that it is impossible for both to be true or both to be false."

So when dealing with the Bible, the "something" that would have to contain "contradictory elements" would be the Bible itself.

The Importance of Similarities and Differences

Some sections of the Bible, most notably the Gospel accounts of Jesus, contain similarities and differences in their reports of the same event. Do these constitute contradictions? Not necessarily. In fact, there is a benefit to having both similarities and differences in eyewitness accounts. Consider this example:

Group 1 Eyewitness Accounts

- *Witness 1:* "A lady was hit by a truck. Two men watched on the sidewalk. One was about 5'10" and wore a black shirt; the other was tall and wore a red shirt."

- *Witness 2:* "A lady was hit by a truck. Two men watched on the sidewalk. One was about 5'10" and wore a black shirt; the other was tall and wore a red shirt."

- *Witness 3:* "A lady was hit by a truck. Two men watched on the sidewalk. One was about 5'10" and wore a black shirt; the other was tall and wore a red shirt."

Group 2 Eyewitness Accounts:

- *Witness 1:* "A lady was hit by a truck. A man rushed out to see if she was okay. He was about 5'10" and wore black. It occurred at 12:00."

- *Witness 2:* "A lady was hit by a truck. Two men watched on the sidewalk. One was about 5'10" and wore a black shirt; the other was tall and wore a red shirt. It occurred about noon."

- *Witness 3:* "A lady was hit by a truck. Several witnessed it. The paramedics were the first to arrive. I looked at my watch; it was 12:02."

Which group more fully described the events? The first "cookie cutter" group provided less credible information because the information was identical. Perhaps there was collusion for some purpose. Although each account is different within the second group, they are not inconsistent. The similarities indicate corroboration of—support for—the fundamentals of the event. The differences, however, add depth, meaning, and insight.

The real story: Slightly before 12:00 a lady was hit by a truck. There were several witnesses, including two men. One was about 5'10" and wore a black shirt. The other was a tall man wearing a red shirt. The one wearing black rushed out to see if the lady was okay. The paramedics were the first officials to arrive, at 12:02.

Both similarities and differences are important for a trustworthy and complete account!

Genesis 1 Versus Genesis 2

Some critics claim that Genesis 1 is inconsistent with Genesis 2. Here is a summary of the apparent contradictions:

1. Genesis 2:5-7 seems to indicate that man was created before vegetation.

2. Genesis 1:12 indicates vegetation was created on day 3; Genesis 1:27 indicates man and woman were created on day 6.

3. Genesis 2:7 and 2:19 seem to indicate that animals were created after mankind.

4. Genesis 1:20-25 indicates animals were created on days 5 and 6; in Genesis 1:26-27, the Bible indicates man and woman were created later on day 6.

Response to Contradiction Claims

Genesis 1 is clearly a methodical account of creation. We know this from the opening words "in the beginning" and by the methodical system of steps, or "days," each highlighted with "bookends" that mark the beginning and ending (evening and morning). The chapter 1 account describes exactly what happened on each day.

Genesis 2 has an entirely different purpose. It discusses what happened to heaven and earth *once they were created,* with particular emphasis on the creation of mankind, and God's relationship to mankind, which is the focal point of God's Word.

Many scholars approach Genesis 1 and 2 as a single unit, with Genesis 1 providing the chronology and Genesis 2 adding complementary information. Genesis 2 focuses on the details that relate to humanity's relationship with God and his creation. For instance, the report that "God planted a garden" doesn't rule out the possibility that other vegetation had already been formed. The phrase could be referring to a special place God created for the man and woman to live.

Fascinating Fact

Where did Cain get his wife? Genesis 4:17 states that, "Cain lay with his wife, and she became pregnant and gave birth to Enoch." Yet up to this point, no potential females have been mentioned.

The Bible states that Adam had other sons and daughters besides Cain, Abel, and Seth (who was born when Adam was 130 years old—Genesis 5:4). Seth, in turn, also had sons and daughters (verse 7). Considering the long life spans of that era, Cain had plenty of time to take a wife from among either Adam's or Seth's daughters.

Conclusion

There is no contradiction between Genesis 1 and 2. Genesis 1 is chronological; Genesis 2 complements Genesis 1 by adding more details and focusing on how man and woman relate to God and creation.

The Importance of Biblical Names

Today, names are given for a number of reasons: 1) to honor ancestors, 2) to honor relatives, 3) because of an attraction to a celebrity, 4) because they "sound nice," and so on. Seldom in the Western world is the naming of someone given the importance it had in biblical times. Back then, names were given for a purpose. They were considered equivalent to the person, and they often represented a person's reputation. In fact, even the word *name* is often translated to mean *reputation* (see Mark 6:14; Revelation 3:1). Another example is in 1 Samuel 25:25: "...Nabal. He is just like his name—his name is Fool, and folly goes with him."

So important were names of individuals that even the word *name* appears more than a thousand times in the Bible.

Name Changes

Name changes were often made, usually noting a "promotion." For example, when Jacob was wrestling with God (who was manifest in the form of a person) and requested a blessing, he was rewarded with a name change to *Israel* (Genesis 32:28).

Even today, orthodox Jews (those who strictly adhere to the literal words of the Torah) will often change someone's name when he approaches death in hopes of healing or a new life.[1]

Prayer in Jesus' Name

Believing in Jesus' name is tantamount to believing in Jesus himself. John 3:18 states clearly that those not believing in Jesus' name are condemned because they don't believe in him.

Therefore, prayer in Jesus' name is not a ritualistic or mystical formula. It is a statement of belief in Jesus as the Savior. When said at the end of a prayer, it presumes that all preceding it is based on the desire to serve and please God.

God Gives Names

Several times in the Bible, God named people or changed their names:[2]

- *Abram*—"exalted father"—became *Abraham*—"father of multitudes" (Genesis 17:5)

- *Sarai* became *Sarah*—"princess" (Genesis 17:15)

- *Jacob*—"may God protect"—became *Israel*—"he strives with God" (Genesis 32:28).

- *Isaac* means "he laughs" (Genesis 17:19)

- *John,* prescribed for John the Baptist, means "God shows favor" (Luke 1:13)

- *Simeon* (or *Simon*)—"hearing"—became *Peter*—"rock" (John 1:42)

- *Jesus,* prescribed for Jesus the Christ, means "savior" (Luke 1:31)

The Names of God Are Said to Be an Inconsistency

Some have claimed that the change in the identifying names of God in Genesis 1 *(Elohiym)* and Genesis 2 *(Yahweh),* indicate an inconsistency.

Response

The first key to understanding the names of God is understanding that God's name was (and is) more than a label. It reflects God himself. Exodus 6:3 indicates this: "I appeared to Abraham, to Isaac and to Jacob as God Almighty, but by my name the LORD I did not make myself known to them." What this means is that God appeared to the patriarchs as God Almighty *(El Shaddai),* not the miraculous, covenant-keeping God who was about to deliver his people from bondage (Exodus 5:2).

So important was the name of God at the time the Bible was originally written that it is referred to in the third commandment: "You shall not misuse the name of the LORD your God" (Exodus 20:7). When copies of the Old Testament were made, scribes omitted specific letters to avoid using the Lord's name in vain. They also said a sanctification prayer before writing it down.

The vastness of God requires a large set of names with various meanings to provide the respect and reputation due him:[3]

- *Elohim* (Elohiym): "God of Majesty"—emphasizing him as Creator of all things

- *El:* the root of the word for God

- *El Elyon:* "God most high" (over all things)

- *El Shaddai:* "God Almighty" (all-powerful)

- *El-Eloe-Yisrael:* "God of Jacob" (or "God of Israel")

- *Yahweh* (spelled *YHWH* in early Hebrew): "I AM" (represents God's personal character) Jesus later referred to himself as such (John 8:58).

- *Yahweh Elohe (Jehovah Elohim)* defines the "personal" Yaweh as the same God as that of the patriarchs (Exodus 3:13-16).

- Compounds of *Yahweh:*

    —*Yahweh-yireh (Jehovah-jireh):* "The LORD Will Provide"

    —*Yahweh-shaalom (Jehovah-shalom):* "The LORD Is Peace"

    —*Yahweh-shaamah (Jehovah-shammah):* "The LORD Is There"

—*Yahweh-tsabaaot (Jehovah-sabaoth):* "The LORD of Hosts"

—*Yahweh Yisraael Elohe:* "The LORD God of Israel"

* *Abba:* "Daddy" or "Papa"

* *Adonai:* "LORD and Father," or, more generally, "LORD" in the Old Testament

Inconsistencies in References to People

There are several supposed discrepancies in referring to some people. As noted earlier, some of these are traceable to name changes that were used to "promote" people. Here are some other commonly cited examples and their explanations.

* *Who was the correct father of Jotham?* Matthew 1:9, in the genealogy of Jesus, lists "Uzziah the father of Jotham." However, in the Old Testament, *Azariah* is referred to as Jotham's father (2 Kings 15:1-7; 1 Chronicles 3:12). Later in 2 Kings, he is referred to as Uzziah (15:32,34). Likewise he was referred to elsewhere as Uzziah (2 Chronicles 26; 27:2; Isaiah 1:1; 6:1; 7:1). This is a classic case of an individual bearing two names that are similar in meaning. *Azariah* means "God has helped." *Uzziah* means "God is my strength."[4]

* *Was Zechariah, son of Berekiah, the last martyr?* Jesus said that Zechariah son of Berekiah was the last martyr of the Old Testament (Matthew 23:34-35). Most people assume that the last martyr was Zechariah, son of Jehoiada, who was stoned in the Temple court as ordered by King Joash (2 Chronicles 24:20-22). However, there were many martyrs after Zechariah ben Jehoiada, who died about 800 B.C. In fact, the

last martyr mentioned in Scripture is Zechariah, son of Berekiah, just as Jesus indicated (Zechariah 1:1).

- *Who came to Jesus, a centurion or Jewish elders?* According to Matthew 8:5-13, a centurion approached Jesus directly to request the healing of his sick servant. Luke 7:2 says that some elders of the Jews were sent. It would not be uncommon for a Roman centurion to send Jews, who were familiar with the culture of Jesus, to request the healing first, then make a direct personal request.

- *Who approached Jesus about James and John?* Matthew 20:20-21 indicates that the mother of James and John came to Jesus to request preferential treatment after he came into his kingdom. Mark 10:35 states that it was James and John themselves. Similar to question 3, it would not be unusual during those days for a mother and her children to agree on such a request and then have the mother present it first, followed by the sons.

- *What did the centurion and soldiers say at Jesus' death?* Both Matthew 27:54 and Mark 15:39 indicate that the soldiers exclaimed the same thing: "Surely he was the son of God!" The only difference between the two is that Mark identified a particular centurion (at the foot of the cross) and recorded "this man" in place of "he." Luke 23:47, on the other hand, indicated a single centurion saying "Surely this was a righteous man."

This is certainly easy to reconcile considering the events going on around Jesus—utter darkness, an earthquake, tombs opening with many holy people raised to life. There were numerous soldiers present, and we could easily imagine them all being impressed enough to make remarks that the Gospel writers might have heard.

Is the Old Testament God Different Than the New Testament God?

Many people think the God of the Old Testament is significantly different than the God of the New Testament. To some, this is so troubling that they refuse to trust the Bible at all. To others, it provides an excuse to not consider the importance of the teachings of the Old Testament. Are there two different Gods? Did God's nature change?

The Claimed Contradiction

The Old Testament is filled with examples of God's wrath and judgment, which directly contrasts with the loving, forgiving God of the New Testament. Here are some examples of God's Old Testament wrath:

- expelling Adam and Eve out of Eden and causing great hardship and death simply for eating a piece of fruit (Genesis 3:16-19,22,23)

- killing all the inhabitants of the Earth (including children) with a great flood for widespread evil (Genesis 6–8)

- destroying Sodom and Gomorrah (including children) for the evil of adults (Genesis 19)

- killing the firstborn children of the Egyptians because of an unyielding Pharaoh (Exodus 11:5)

- killing Aaron's sons Nadab and Abihu because they offered "unauthorized fire" before him (Leviticus 10:1-2)

- striking the Israelites with a plague because of their grumbling about food (Numbers 11:4,20,33)

- destroying Korah, Dathan, and Abiram, along with 250 men, for rebelling against Moses and Aaron (Numbers 16)

- ordering the Israelites to "take vengeance" on the Midianites for their worship of Baal, including killing all boys and every woman "who has slept with a man" (Numbers 31:1,11-18)

- destroying every living thing—men, women, children, and animals—in the city of Jericho, except Rahab, who helped the spies (Joshua 6:21)

These are but a few examples of God's wrath poured out in the Hebrew Scriptures.

Then, in supposed contradiction, the New Testament is filled with examples of God's forgiveness and love in the person of Jesus Christ:

- "Do not resist an evil person" (Matthew 5:39).

- "Love one another. As I have loved you, so you must love one another" (John 13:34).

- "If you hold anything against anyone, forgive him" (Mark 11:25).

How These Differences Can Be Reconciled

It is important to understand the status of, and God's objectives for, the spiritual development of the Israelites and Jews in each setting. In the Old Testament, God is *revealing his nature* to the Israelites and *preparing them for a Savior* to come (who will eventually lead them to eternal life). In the New Testament, God *has revealed the Savior* and *is offering eternal life.* God hasn't changed, but the environment has. *The teaching emphasis has moved from the temporal to the eternal.* Nonetheless, God's eternal nature has never changed.

Response to Contradiction Claim

Apart from God's nature remaining the same in both the Old and New Testaments, we find there seem to be a proportionate number of examples of the wrath of God and love of God in both Testaments. (Since the Old Testament is longer, it contains more of each.)

Following are some examples of New Testament wrath:

God's nature is made up of three basics: 1) He is perfectly holy (Leviticus 11:45; Revelation 4:8); 2) he is perfectly just (Deuteronomy 32:4; 2 Thessalonians 1:6); and he is perfectly loving (Deuteronomy 7:9; 1 John 4:16). This fundamental information is included in *both* the New and Old Testaments. Further inspection will reveal hundreds of such examples.

These basics of God's nature cannot always be manifested together on Earth in a way humankind understands. For example, a perfectly holy God might need a pagan land purged of sin, even if it means innocent children might suffer. (This seems to contradict love from a human standpoint.) Yet God is also perfectly just and can deal with such "human-perspective" injustices in an eternal stage (after death).

- "Whoever believes in the Son has eternal life, but whoever rejects the Son will not see life, for God's wrath remains on him" (John 3:36).

- "The wrath of God is being revealed from heaven against all the godlessness and wickedness of men who suppress the truth by their wickedness" (Romans 1:18).

- "Put to death, therefore, whatever belongs to your earthly nature: sexual immorality, impurity, lust, evil desires, and greed, which is idolatry. Because of these, the wrath of God is coming" (Colossians 3:5-6).

- "God remembered Babylon the Great and gave her the cup filled with the wine of the fury of his wrath" (Revelation 16:19).

- "They will weed out of his kingdom everything that causes sin and all who do evil. They will throw them into the fiery furnace, where there will be weeping and gnashing of teeth" (Matthew 13:41-42).

- "The angels will come and separate the wicked from the righteous and throw them into the fiery furnace, where there will be weeping and gnashing of teeth" (Matthew 13:49-50).

> The Old and New Testaments reveal the same God.

Then, compare the following examples of God's love in the Old Testament:

- "...the compassionate and gracious God, slow to anger, abounding in love" (Exodus 34:6).

- "He is the faithful God, keeping his covenant of love" (Deuteronomy 7:9).

- "You, O Lord, are a compassionate and gracious God ...abounding in love and faithfulness" (Psalm 86:15).

Analysis Example: Is There a Contradiction in Jesus' Ancestry?

Why is the ancestry of Jesus, from David on, reported differently in Matthew and Luke? Genealogies were important to

How to Analyze Contradictions

Issue	Genesis 1	Genesis 2
Step 1—Overview State in simple terms the alleged contradiction.	Genesis 1 says both vegetation and animals were created before mankind.	Genesis 2 seems to indicate creation of mankind prior to discussion of vegetation and livestock.
Step 2—Definition List all key elements that seem to indicate a conflict.	Summarize the verses and claims of each issue.	
	Specifics • Verse 12 indicates vegetation was created on day 3. • Verses 20-25 indicate animals were created on days 5 and 6 (early). • Verse 27 indicates man and woman were created on day 6.	*Specifics* • Verses 7-8 indicate the creation of man and woman. • Verses 9-10 indicate trees and a garden planted. • Verse 19 indicates animals and birds created.
Step 3—Hypothesis State all potential means of resolving the apparent conflict.	1. Address the intent of each. 2. Address the language of each.	
	Proposition A Because Genesis 2 reveals creation of vegetation, beasts, and birds *after* man, and Genesis 1 clearly states their creation *before* man, they are in conflict.	*Proposition B* 1. Perhaps Genesis 2 complements Genesis 1 instead of presenting creation again. 2. Perhaps the language provides latitude for the difference. Perhaps perspective can harmonize both accounts.
Step 4—Research Research necessary areas. This may include original languages, culture, and sentence structure.	1. Review each side carefully for context and content. 2. Research words and grammar in each proposition.	
Step 5—Judge Decide if any alternative explanation is plausible. (Remember, you are trying to detect *impossibility* of resolution.)	There were two separate purposes for Genesis 1 and Genesis 2.	
	Purpose Genesis 1 provides the basic structure of the creation of the universe.	*Purpose* Genesis 2 complements Genesis 1 by providing details of God's creation of mankind and how he prepared the earth for the first humans.
Step 6—Conclude Reach a conclusion according to the definition of contradiction.	There is *no contradiction* between Genesis 1 and Genesis 2 in regard to the order of creation.	
	Context Genesis 1 is clearly a chronological overview of creation itself.	*Context* The context of Genesis 2 is clearly mankind's creation and place in relation to God and his creation.

the Jews for many reasons, not the least of which included property rights. So how could two biblical authors be at odds like this? The likely answer is really quite simple: There is one genealogy for each of Jesus' human parents.

The genealogy listed in *Luke* was based on the ancestry of Mary, the human progenitor of Jesus. *Matthew* gave the more common genealogy—through the male line to Joseph, husband of Mary. This is not surprising, since Luke was a physician who dealt with human problems, and Matthew was a tax collector who dealt with legal issues (transferred through the male line). Jesus was the legal heir of Joseph.

Further, Luke was a Gentile and connected Jesus with the entire world through Adam. Matthew was Jewish, and he connected Jesus with the Jewish race (particulary Abraham and David). His concern was Jesus' claim to be the Messiah.[5]

There is evidence of this in the text. Luke 3:23 provides a clue when it includes the words "He was the son, *so it was thought*, of Joseph." This odd choice of words calls attention to the other parent—the only human parent—Mary.

The genealogy of Matthew deals strictly with the *legal* line down through Joseph. The Greek word for "was the father of" (traditionally, "begat")—*egenneesen*—is used in the entire genealogy from Abraham to Joseph. However Joseph is *not* said to have been the father of Jesus (because Jesus was conceived by the Holy Spirit). Instead, Joseph is called the "husband of Mary."[6]

In Luke, Joseph was mentioned as the "son" of Heli, who was his father-in-law. It was normal to mention the father (instead of the mother) because Joseph would have the legal rights. There is no contradiction since both Jesus' human and legal lines, through each parent, are provided.

Test Yourself

1. How can we account for the many different names used for the same person? For God?

2. What are the apparent contradictions between Genesis 1 and Genesis 2? Explain them.

3. How can you explain that the God of the Old Testament is identical to the God of the New Testament?

4. Why are both similarities and differences crucial to an accurate account of an event?

5. Explain the basis for the different genealogies of Jesus.

Chapter 31 Group Study

Homework Preparation (do prior to group)
Read: Genesis 1 and 2; chapter 31 of this text; and *Are There Contradictions in the Bible?* ✝.

Opening Prayer
Discussion: Discuss the perception that the God of the Old Testament differs from the God of the New Testament. How is this not true? How would you defend the consistency of God to a nonbeliever?

Practical-Experience Game

Role-playing: The "nonbeliever" the "Christian" approaches is aware of the many names of God, the differing accounts in Genesis 1 and 2, and the differing genealogies of Jesus. Defend the Bible.

Closing Prayer

Review of Specific Alleged Contradictions

Over many centuries the Bible has stood the test of time. It is deemed a reliable, even miraculous, book—with consistency on a vast number of controversial issues despite being written by more than 40 authors, in different centuries, and in a wide variety of circumstances. Nonetheless, enemies of God (and agnostic or questioning skeptics) continue to attack the Bible in a seemingly never-ending attempt to discredit it. Some of the more common questions concerning apparent contradictions are addressed in this chapter.

In reviewing this and the prior chapter, it is important to keep in mind that we would expect the original Bible to be inspired and accurate. Of course there have been many translations by many groups since then, and the degree of subsequent "inspiration" certainly varies. In some instances the original words were purposely changed (as in Bibles written by "Christian" cults—for example, the *New World Translation*, written by the Jehovah's Witnesses for the purpose of espousing their own unorthodox doctrines).

Answers to Some Commonly Alleged Biblical Contradictions

The Temptations of Jesus—A Sequencing Contradiction?

Matthew 4:5-7 indicates that the second temptation of Jesus is Satan's enticement to jump from the pinnacle of the Temple—relying on God's angels to save him. Luke 4:5-12 makes the temptation of "world empire" number two and the pinnacle temptation number three. How can this be reconciled?

Recognizing that we have different authors, each with a different degree of interest in various temptations and their importance, it would be natural for each author to represent them in a different order. Chronology is not necessarily critical. Just as in a court of law today, witnesses often relate different events in different time frames. As indicated on pages 482-483, the fact that there are similarities and differences in testimony adds strength, not weakness.[1]

The Fig Tree—A Sequencing Contradiction?

Following Palm Sunday, Matthew makes it clear that Jesus went straight to the Temple to expel the "money changers" (Matthew 21:10-12). He does not speak of "cursing the fig tree" until verse 18. Mark, on the other hand, seems to indicate that the "Temple incident" occurred after the cursing of the fig tree (Mark 11:12-16). This appears to be a direct contradiction.

Resolving this apparent problem requires understanding the typical writing style of the authors. *Matthew* tended to place importance on topics at the expense of strict chronology. This is evident in his writing about the Sermon on the Mount, which was undoubtedly given over a period of time in several settings. *Mark*, on the other hand, tended to write a strict chronology of events. Both Matthew and Mark do agree that Jesus went immediately to the Temple upon his arrival on Palm Sunday (Matthew 21:12; Mark 11:11—Mark says that Jesus "looked around in indignation," and then returned to Bethany.) They also agree that the cursing of the fig tree occurred the day after Jesus' entry into Jerusalem, when he was on his way back to the Temple (his second Temple visit).[2]

Entering or Leaving Jericho?

Matthew 20:29 indicates that Jesus and his disciples were leaving Jericho when he healed two blind men. Mark 10:46-47 agrees with the leaving of Jericho but mentions only one blind man. Luke mentions one blind man but indicates Jesus was entering Jericho. (Mentioning only one blind man does not mean there weren't two.)

The issue of whether it was one or two blind men can be easily dealt with in respect to the importance of similarities and differences in the Bible, with different authors emphasizing different things. Mark names the blind man (Bartimaeus), and Luke indicates a "certain blind man," indicating that one of them had some distinction.

Archaeology has answered the entering–leaving issue.[3] During the time of Jesus there was an "old Jericho" and a "new Jericho." Jesus was simply going from one to the other.[4]

Alleged Date and Time Contradictions About Jesus' Final Week

1. *How long was Jesus in the tomb?* Matthew states that Jesus would be dead and buried (like Jonah was metaphorically in the whale) for 3 days and 3 nights (Matthew 12:40). Generally, people acknowledge Jesus was crucified on Friday before the Sabbath,

which started at sunset on Friday. How can we arrive at three full days—let alone three full nights?[5]

2. *Was the crucifixion on a Thursday or a Friday?* The synoptic Gospels (Matthew, Mark, and Luke) seem to indicate a crucifixion the day before a Sabbath (generally starting at sunset on Friday).

3. *At which hour was Jesus crucified?* Mark states Jesus was crucified at the "third hour" (Mark 15:25), while John indicates that his trial was still going on at the sixth hour (John 19:14).

In analyzing this entire scenario, it is valuable to research the role Jesus played.

Jesus as the Passover Lamb

Jesus was clearly identified as the Passover lamb. Revelation 21:22 states,

> *I did not see a temple in the city, because the Lord God Almighty and the Lamb are its temple.*

Some Passover Rules

1. On the tenth of Nisan, a perfect lamb was to be selected for slaughter (Exodus 12:3).

2. On the fourteenth of Nisan—Passover—the lamb was to be slaughtered (2 Chronicles 30:15).

3. The day after Passover was a "holy convocation day" or "special Sabbath" since it was the first day of the feast of unleavened bread (Leviticus 23:7-8). Hence, any day after the Passover would be a "special Sabbath"—it didn't need to be Saturday. John identifies it as such (John 19:31).

4. No bones would be broken in the Passover lamb (Numbers 9:12).

For Jesus to precisely meet those requirements for the "perfect Passover lamb," several things had to happen:

1. He had to be "selected" on the tenth of Nisan (today called "Palm Sunday"—but it wasn't necessarily a Sunday).

2. He had to be crucified on the fourteenth of Nisan (Passover). This would be after sundown on Wednesday, which could be Thursday morning.

3. Because there was always a "holy convocation" day or "special Sabbath" after the Passover, the next day would always be a Sabbath. In Matthew 28:1, the word "Sabbath" in the Greek is plural.

4. No bones would be broken during Jesus' crucifixion (John 19:33).

A Response to the Apparent "Day Contradictions"

While the specific day is somewhat undetermined, the result doesn't change. Most scholars hold to the traditional Friday crucifixion day on the basis of several things:

- First, they say that "Palm Sunday" was really "Palm Monday."

- Second, they consider what John refers to as the "day of Preparation" (for Passover—Greek *paraskeue*) as commonly meaning Friday at that time.[6] This is important because, in some versions of the Bible, the Gospel of John (19:14) indicates the trial of Jesus was on the day of preparation, not on Passover itself. It represents a translational difficulty. Was it Friday? Or was it the day of Preparation?

- Finally, regarding the view on Matthew 12:40 ("as Jonah was three days and three nights in the belly of a huge fish"), scholars point out that Jewish use of idioms included part days as full days. Therefore, Friday, Saturday (Sabbath), and Sunday would constitute three days and three nights idiomatically.[7]

Other scholars have a strong opinion for a Thursday crucifixion with an entry into Jerusalem on a Sunday (Palm Sunday). This would fit John's report that the Last Supper was on a "day of Preparation" (John 19:14). Assuming the tenth of Nisan fell on that Sunday, it would fit all criteria, including three days and three nights (Matthew 12:40).

A Response to the Apparent "Hour Contradiction"

Again, John's statement that it was the "day of Preparation" at "about the sixth hour" when Jesus was still standing "trial" presents a possible contradiction (John 19:14), since the other Gospels have Jesus being crucified at the third hour on Passover. This "day of Preparation" can be reconciled in the original Greek in the context of the day. As previously mentioned, this phrase had come into common parlance to mean Friday. More importantly, since the Feast of Unleavened Bread was immediately on the heels of Passover, the day of Passover was essentially a day of preparation for the seven-day feast to follow.

Then, as now, this period is commonly referred to as "Passover week." Just "Passover" was understood as such, so much so that there was no need to insert the word "week" *(sabua)*. The "preparation of Passover" could be understood as the Friday (or day before) Passover week.[8]

Conclusion

Though there remain some disputes about the precise timing of the final week of Jesus, reconciling these is possible within the realm of good scholarly evidence.

Apparent Contradictions About the Resurrection

There are several supposed contradictions in the all-important account of the resurrection of Jesus.

- *How many women went to the tomb?*

    1. Matthew says Mary Magdalene and the other Mary (Matthew 28:1).
    2. Mark says Mary Magdalene, Mary the mother of James, and Salome (Mark 16:1).
    3. Luke says "the women" (Luke 24:10).
    4. John says Mary Magdalene (John 20:1).

- *Who was at the tomb?*

    1. Matthew says an angel came down, opened the tomb, then sat on the stone. His appearance was like lightning, and he was dressed in white clothes (Matthew 28:2).
    2. Mark says a young man dressed in a white robe was sitting on the right (Mark 16:5).
    3. Luke says two men in clothes that gleamed like lightning stood beside them (the women—Luke 24:4).
    4. John says two angels were seen at the head and foot of where Jesus had been laid. This was *after* the earlier trip and *after* Peter and John had visited (John 20:11-12).

Response to Contradictions

This is how similarities and differences of eyewitnesses can add depth and meaning to historical events (see pages 482-483). Each eyewitness, or those recording what eyewitnesses said, focuses on a different part of the full picture, the part of particular interest to them. Yet when the entire story is read in chronological order, the gaps are filled in, and we find a very complete account of the events of that day.

Chronological Account of the Resurrection

WOMEN COME TO THE TOMB. When the Sabbath was over, Mary Magdalene, Mary the mother of James, and Salome bought spices so that they might go to anoint Jesus' body. Very early on the first day of the week, just after sunrise, they were on their way to the tomb and they asked each other, "Who will roll the stone away from the entrance of the tomb?"

But when they looked up, they saw that the stone, which was very large, had already been rolled away. [See Mark 16:1-4.]

RESURRECTION ANNOUNCED. As they entered the tomb, they saw a young man dressed in a white robe sitting on the right side, and they were alarmed. "Don't be alarmed," he said. "You are looking for Jesus the Nazarene, who was crucified. He has risen! He is not here. See the place where they laid him. But go, tell his disciples and Peter, 'He is going ahead of you into Galilee. There you will see him, just as he told you.'" [See Matthew 28:5-7.]

WOMEN REMINDED OF PROPHECY. While they were wondering about this, suddenly two men in clothes that gleamed like lightning stood beside them. In their fright the women bowed down to them with their faces to the ground, but the men said to them, "Why do you look for the living among the dead? He is not here; he has risen! Remember how he told you, while he was still with you in Galilee: 'The Son of Man must be delivered into the hands of sinful men, be crucified and on the third day be raised again.'" Then they remembered his words. [See Luke 24:4-8.]

WOMEN GO AWAY FEARFUL. Trembling and bewildered, the women went out and fled from the tomb. They said nothing to anyone, because they were afraid. [See Mark 16:8].

PETER AND JOHN TOLD. So [Mary of Magdala] came running to Simon Peter and the other disciple, the one Jesus loved, and said, "They have taken the Lord out of the tomb, and we don't know where they have put him!" [See John 20:2.]

PETER AND JOHN VIEW THE TOMB. So Peter and the other disciple started for the tomb. Both were running, but the other disciple outran Peter and reached the tomb first. He bent over and looked in at the strips of linen lying there but did not go in. Then Simon Peter, who was behind him, arrived and went into the tomb. He saw the strips of linen lying there, as well as the burial cloth that had been around Jesus' head. The cloth was folded up by itself, separate from the linen. Finally the other disciple, who had reached the tomb first, also went inside. He saw and believed. (They still did not understand from Scripture that Jesus had to rise from the dead.)

Then the disciples went back to their homes. [See John 20:3-10.]

JESUS WITH MARY MAGDALENE. [When Jesus rose early on the first day of the week, he appeared first to Mary Magdalene, out of whom he had driven seven demons.] [See Mark 16:9.]...Mary stood outside the tomb crying. As she wept, she bent over to look into the tomb and saw two angels in white, seated where Jesus' body had been, one at the head and the other at the foot.

They asked her, "Woman, why are you crying?"

"They have taken my Lord away," she said, "and I don't know where they have put him." At this, she turned around and saw Jesus standing there, but she did not realize that it was Jesus.

"Woman," he said, "why are you crying? Who is it you are looking for?"

Thinking he was the gardener, she said, "Sir, if you have carried him away, tell me where you have put him, and I will get him."

Jesus said to her, "Mary."

She turned toward him and cried out in Aramaic, "Rabboni!" (which means Teacher).

Jesus said, "Do not hold on to me, for I have not yet returned to the Father. Go instead to my brothers and tell them, 'I am returning to my Father and your Father, to my God and your God.'" [See John 20:11-17.]

JESUS APPEARS TO WOMEN. So the women hurried away from the tomb, afraid yet filled with joy, and ran to tell his disciples. Suddenly Jesus met them. "Greetings," he said. They came to him, clasped his feet and worshiped him. Then Jesus said to them, "Do not be afraid. Go and tell my brothers to go to Galilee; there they will see me." [See Matthew 28:8-10.][9]

Conclusions

The Gospel writers certainly had access to the eyewitnesses. The fundamentals of this account are found in each Gospel record: 1) Women went to the tomb, 2) they encountered angels, 3) the tomb was empty, 4) they were told Jesus had arisen from the dead, and 5) the disciples checked the tomb as well.

In a court of law, these fundamentals, testified to by key eyewitnesses, would be irrefutable, especially when corroborated by the account of the Roman guard. The differences in the stories are easily accounted for simply by reviewing the similarities and differences of eyewitness accounts, which add credibility and clarity to a historical event. The chronology indicates no contradiction.*

Test Yourself

1. Explain the sequencing "problems," in which different Gospel writers appear to indicate a differing sequence of the events of Jesus' life.

2. Explain how Jesus could have been in the tomb for three days and three nights.

3. Explain the differing accounts of which women went to the tomb the morning of the resurrection.

4. Explain the differing accounts of Jesus and the angels on the morning of the resurrection.

5. Name at least two other apparent contradictions and how you would reconcile them.

---

* For discussion of other supposed contradictions in the Bible, refer to *Are There Contradictions in the Bible?*

Chapter 32 Group Study

Homework Preparation (do prior to group)
Read: Matthew 28; Mark 16; Luke 24; John 20; chapter 32 of this text; and *Are There Contradictions in the Bible?* ✝.

Opening Prayer
Discussion: Review the apparent conflicts of the day of the resurrection of Jesus. Discuss as a group how you would defend the Bible to a skeptic by reconciling each one.

Practical-Experience Game
Debate: The "nonbeliever" is confronting the "Christian" by arguing that there are many unresolved contradictions in the Bible, and therefore it can't be trusted. Be prepared to address specific alleged contradictions.

Closing Prayer

How Is Jesus Different from Other Religious Leaders?

Religious leaders assume many roles. It's important to understand the role that a leader plays within a religion so that we can evaluate him or her from the right perspective. Does a leader maintain he possesses unique insight into ancient holy books? Does he say he is a prophet? Does he say he is a god? These three roles are very different.

Leaders should be evaluated by their claims. Assuming that the leaders we are considering are human, we can evaluate their roles within a religion by using the following criteria:

1. Do they claim to authoritatively interpret something old?

2. Do they proclaim something new?

3. Do they claim divine insight?

4. Do they claim to be God (or a god)?

It's important to consider the priority of these roles. For instance, merely *interpreting* something is obviously less important than actually *being* God. However, even more important is the central issue—*can the person prove his or her claims?* Hence, in our analysis of roles and claims, it will

511

be important to look both at what is claimed and at the strength of the evidence that supports those claims. Someone who maintains that he is God *and can prove it* should carry far more weight with us—and be far more worthy of our attention—than someone who simply claims to interpret ancient holy writings.

Some practical questions to ask about religious leaders and their teachings might be as follows:

1. Is the religion based on *untestable philosophy* or on *historical events?*

2. Is there some undeniable fact about the religion that reveals *divine confirmation,* such as perfect prediction of the future?

3. Are the daily words and actions of a religious leader *consistent* with the proclamations he or she makes and the beliefs he or she espouses?

Note: Pages 513–528 utilize the following sources:

- Ankerberg, John, and John Weldon. *Encyclopedia of Cults and New Religions.* Eugene, OR: Harvest House, 1999.

- Draper, Edythe, ed. *Almanac of the Christian World.* Wheaton, IL: Tyndale House Publishers, Inc., 1992.

- Geisler, Norman. *Baker Encyclopedia of Christian Apologetics.* Grand Rapids, MI: Baker Books, 1999.

- Halverson, Dean. *The Compact Guide to World Religions.* Minneapolis, MN: Bethany House, 1996.

- Martin, Walter. *The Kingdom of the Cults.* Minneapolis, MN: Bethany House, 1996.

- McDowell, Josh. *Handbook of Today's Religions.* San Bernardino, CA: Campus Crusade for Christ, 1983.

Leaders of World Religions in History

The chart below shows some of the world religious leaders who have had the greatest impact in history. All of them have led millions of people to a belief in a "god" (or "gods")—whether right or wrong. For each of them, we must assess

1. whether the "god" (or "gods") each leader promotes is real and true

2. whether the leader is a legitimate spokesman for God

The Heritage of World Religions

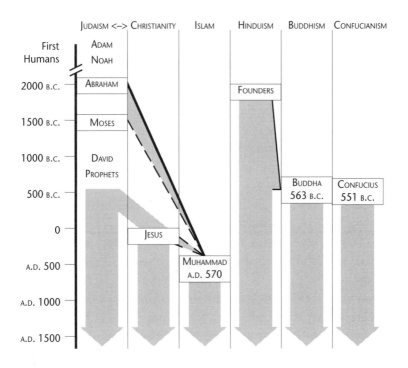

The Founders and Leaders of Judaism

Judaism is the foundation of the history-based religions of Christianity and (to some extent) Islam, which together claim more than 50 percent of the world's population. Hence, even though the followers of Judaism are relatively few (less than 1 percent of the world's population), it is an extremely important religion, as are its founders and leaders who are described in the Bible.

Abraham

Abraham was unique because he was called by the God of the universe to go to the land of Canaan (Palestine—now mostly modern Israel) to be the "father" of a nation. The people of this nation would become God's messengers to carry his Word to all mankind. God promised Abraham that he and his wife, Sarah, would have a child despite their age (each of them was very old—beyond childbearing age). After a number of years passed without fulfillment of this promise, the couple decided to fulfill it themselves without God's involvement. Sarah gave her servant, Hagar, to Abraham as a "concubine" (a wife of secondary status). This union produced the child Ishmael, whom the Arab nations claim as their father. And it is among the Arabs that Islam was founded and has its greatest strength.

Later Abraham and Sarah were blessed with the miracle child God had promised—Isaac—who became the father of the nation of Israel. The line of Isaac's descendants led to Jesus, who claimed to be the long-promised Messiah whose coming was predicted by the prophets of Israel. (These prophecies are recorded in the books of the prophets in the Hebrew Scriptures—the Old Testament.)

Jesus is the foundation of Christianity. He is also claimed by Islam—as one of their greatest prophets. Thus the two major history-based religions of the world, Christianity and Islam, rest upon this single historical person.

Moses

Moses is considered by some people to be the founder of Judaism. Under the inspiration of God, he wrote the Torah—the first five books of the Hebrew Scriptures—which is the foundation for Judaism.

Moses did not claim to be a god, but merely a messenger who transmitted words from God. The key evidence in support of his claim to divine appointment is his prophecy—perfectly fulfilled in history, no prophecies ever wrong, even though some of his predictions were made hundreds of years in advance of the actual events.

The Basic Doctrine and Key Leaders of Judaism*

God: There is one God, who created the universe and everything in it.

Mankind: People are separated from God by sin.

Sin: People are sinful, but can be reconciled to God by making sacrifices for their sin.

Eternity: People can gain an eternal dwelling with God by following the laws of Moses.

Key leaders: Abraham, Moses, David, the prophets

Period of foundation: 2000 B.C. to 400 B.C.

Holy writings: The Hebrew Scriptures (The Old Testament of the Bible)

Key claims:* One God; mankind is sinful; Jews elected by God

Key evidence: Archaeology and history

Divine evidence: Fulfilled prophecy in the "Books of the Prophets" and the "Books of Moses"

---

*The three major branches of Judaism differ on specific doctrines.

_____Key Concept_____

> *Judaism—defined as practicing Jews who have not received Jesus Christ as their Savior—is essentially a religion of "works," not grace. Their belief is that one must "earn" the way to heaven by following the Laws of Moses, which include sacrifice for sin.*

Jesus (Christianity)

Jesus is the foundation of the Christian faith. Apart from his teaching, he made a claim that was far more special— something that no other major religious leader asserted: *He claimed to be God in human form.*

Jesus fits precisely with the Jewish beliefs about a coming *Messiah** (literally, the "anointed one [anointed by God]"). These beliefs are not new—they are built firmly upon the words of the Old Testament of the Bible. In turn, Jesus' teaching supports Abraham, Moses, and the entire Hebrew Scriptures. He personally fulfills the prophecies given in these Scriptures. And Christianity is founded upon his life, death, and resurrection, all of which are historically documented events.

Jesus' life and words often gave clues that would help people recognize that he was God in human form. For instance, the manner, circumstances, and location of his birth all fulfilled ancient prophecies—and they were just the beginning of the record of divine evidence in support of his claims. Jesus' earthly father, Joseph, had been given a dream to confirm that Jesus would be called *Immanuel* (Matthew 1:23),

---

* The word *Christ* comes from the Greek word that means the same thing as the Hebrew word *messiah.*

which means "God with us"—just as had been predicted by the prophet Isaiah (Isaiah 7:14). Furthermore, throughout his public life, Jesus himself showed that his claim to be God was true by 1) performing miracles that "only God could perform" and 2) perfectly fulfilling his own prophecy of his death and resurrection (see pages 355–357).

These miracles, these prophecies, and their fulfillment are recorded in thousands of surviving copies of documents that were written by eyewitnesses to the events surrounding Jesus' life: the Gospels of the New Testament. The Gospels are written accounts of the same evidence that Jesus presented personally to the people of his time. All of these documents withstood the test of scrutiny by eyewitnesses of Jesus' life.

Key Concept

Leader: Jesus

Active period: A.D. 30 to 33

Holy writings: The Bible—the Old and New Testament

Key claims: Jesus claimed to be God; everyone is sinful and needs redemption, Jesus is the Redeemer; salvation is by grace—God's gift

Key evidence: Prophecy, history, archaeology

Divine evidence: Extraordinary prophecy, resurrection from death

The Basic Doctrine of Jesus (Christianity)

God: There is one God. Jesus is the Son—one of the three "Persons" of the three-in-one Godhead (Father, Son, and Holy Spirit).

Mankind: People are sinful by nature.

Sin: People are separated from God by sin and must accept God's gift of Jesus' sacrifice on their behalf in order to be reconciled with God.

Eternity: Eternity is a gift from God, given freely to people as a result of their committing themselves to Jesus.

Jesus' Teaching

The greatest commandment—"Love the Lord your God with all your heart and with all your soul and with all your mind and with all your strength" (Mark 12:30).

The second-greatest commandment—"Love your neighbor as [in the same way you love] yourself" (Mark 12:31).

The new commandment—"Love one another. *As I have loved you,* so you must love one another. By this all men will know that you are my disciples, if you love one another" (John 13:34).

Jesus' great commission—"Make disciples of all nations, baptizing them in the name of the Father, the Son, and the Holy Spirit [the triune God]; and teaching them to obey everything I have commanded you. And surely I am with you always, to the very end of the age" (Matthew 28:19-20).

The Fate of Jesus

Jesus was crucified in A.D. 32 or 33. He *rose from the dead,* an event attested to by hundreds of people.

Muhammad (Islam)

Muhammad is the founder of Islam, whose followers (called Muslims) make up about 20 percent of the world's population. (The Arabic word *islam* means "submission [to the will of God].") Some Islamic beliefs were influenced by the Jewish Scriptures (the Old Testament) or the Christian New Testament—both Judaism and Christianity were highly influential in the region where Muhammad started his work. Muhammad is considered by Muslims to be the ultimate prophet—above Jesus, Moses, and others.

History

Islam is the third of the major history-based religions, after Judaism and Christianity. None of these three denies the historical existence of Abraham, Moses, David, Jesus, or Muhammad. Only the teachings and actions of each are in dispute.

Muhammad was born in A.D. 570, into an Arabian tribe that controlled the important trade city of Mecca. Local custom called for every spiritual person to go to a "place of solitude" once a year to pay homage to various gods. Muhammad alleged that, in one such experience he had at age 40, the angel Gabriel had given him his first revelation about the one single God—Allah. This revelation gave him insights that later became the basis of the writings of the Qur'an.

Muhammad doubted this first revelation because monotheism (belief in one single God) was not common or popular in the region. As time went on, other people convinced him to become bolder; and his preaching about monotheism eventually resulted in his expulsion from Mecca. He embraced both Christianity and Judaism to a degree, and though he was later rejected, the Qur'an actually contains much material from extrabiblical Jewish sources and from heretical "Christian" writings such as the Gospel of Thomas[1] (see pages 207–209). In the year 630 he returned triumphantly to Mecca, taking control without a struggle, and began to institute his new religion of Islam.

The Teachings of Islam

Major groups: *Sunni* Muslims (about 80 percent of Muslims) recognize only written traditions as authoritative. *Shi'ite* Muslims also recognize the authority of certain living people. The groups disagree over who the rightful successors to Muhammad were.

God: God is a single unit. Considering Jesus and the Holy Spirit to be God is blasphemous.

Mankind: People are, by nature, good.

Sin: People can be forgiven of sin through repentance. Jesus' involvement is not necessary.

Jesus: Jesus "was" a great prophet, but to identify him as God is blasphemous.

Salvation: People are saved by virtue of their deeds. Their good deeds must outweigh their bad deeds at the day of judgment.

Leadership issues: Muhammad seemed to be receptive to Christians and Jews until they rejected him. Among other things, this caused him to turn from Jerusalem to Mecca as the most holy city. This raises the question as to how much of Muhammad's theology was a reaction to Judaism and Christianity, as opposed to revelation from God.

The fate of Muhammad: Muhammad died on June 8, 632 and remained dead.

_____Key Concept_____

Leader: Muhammad

Dates: A.D. 570 to 632

Holy writings: The Qur'an; the Bible—the Torah and Psalms (revised); the Bible—the Gospels (revised)

Key claims: One God—Allah

The prophets of God include Adam, Noah, Abraham, Moses, David, Solomon, Jonah, John the Baptist, Jesus, Muhammad

Key prophet: Muhammad

Key evidence: History

Divine evidence: The "beauty" of the Qur'an

Confucius (Confucianism)

China, with its large population, is the home of several of the largest Eastern world religions: Confucianism, Taoism, and their variations, all of which are philosophy-based. Confucianism remains strong today, but Taoism has greatly waned during the Communist era in China. Of the philosophy-based religions in the Far East, Confucianism claims the most followers.

History

Confucius* lived during the sixth and fifth centuries B.C., about the time of Buddha. His teachings gained popularity during the decline of Taoism, a ritual-based religion that had previously been widespread in China. Confucius taught moral laws, not just rituals. As Confucianism spread and became dominant, it was often combined with the practice of Buddhism, as it still is today.

---

* The name *Confucius* is a Latin form of the Chinese name *K'ung-Fu-tzu*.

The Teaching of Confucius

Summary: Confucianism is essentially a set of moral–philosophical beliefs. For this reason, many people do not consider it a religion.

God: He (it) is not really personal, but is the ultimate reality. Confucius himself did not profess to be divine, though some sects later deified him.

Mankind: People are good by nature and are potentially perfect.

Sin: Sin only occurs when people are forced to act in evil ways, or when they allow their minds to wander to evil thoughts.

Jesus: Jesus has no bearing on Confucian thought.

Salvation: There is no precise definition. It is sometimes viewed as a creative moral power or an impersonal principle.

Leadership issues: Confucius was more of a politician than a religious leader. He held many official positions and was able to convince many of his contemporaries that his moral–political system was the best way to restructure Chinese society. His wisdom was revered and his sayings were well-known, but they remained mostly in the philosophical arena (much like the teachings of Socrates and Plato, who were active not long after Confucius' time). After Confucius' death, some of his followers began to venerate him as divine.

The fate of Confucius: Confucius died in 479 B.C. and remained dead.

_____Key Concept_____

> **Leader:** Confucius
> **Dates:** 551 to 479 B.C.
> **Holy writings:** The Five Classics
> **Key claims:** Ancestor worship; obedience to elders; doctrinal principles of worship; ethical doctrines
> **Key prophet:** Confucius
> **Key evidence:** Philosophy
> **Divine evidence:** None

Hindu Leaders

Hinduism centers in India, the world's second most populous nation, whose population is about 82 percent Hindu. Strictly defined, the followers of Hinduism make up about 13 percent of the world's population. However, it has a much more far-reaching impact because it forms the basis for the "Christian" mind-science cults (for example, Christian Science); New Age religions and practices (transcendental meditation, for instance); and other philosophies and religions as well. Furthermore, Buddhism resulted from Gautama Buddha's reforms of Hinduism.

History

There is no single leader who has been identified as the founder of Hinduism. In fact, the religion has many variants, any of which may have had its own founder. Hinduism is one of the world's oldest religions, dating back to about 1500 B.C. Its doctrines and variations developed over a period of centuries, as did its holy books and writings.

Hindu Beliefs and Doctrines

Major beliefs: Several doctrines are consistent through all Hindu sects.

Brahma—The impersonal life-force within all things; "god."

Karma—The concept of moral cause and effect, or "you reap what you sow." Considered to be an actual "force."

Caste system—People are born to different statuses in life, depending upon their karma from past lives.

Reincarnation—A cycle of successive rebirths enabling people to work off their karma and eventually to reach the ultimate dissolution that brings them freedom from the cycle.

Dharma—The moral order that people must follow to eliminate karma.

God: "God" is an impersonal force; an undefinable, all-pervading deity. Hinduism recognizes hundreds, even thousands, of lesser gods.

Mankind: People are morally neutral, but their status reflects their karma from past lives, which they must work off in order to reach nirvana.

Sin: Actions and thoughts inconsistent with dharma, the moral order. "Sin" does not affect a person's relationship to Brahma.

Jesus: He is not an issue.

Salvation: Nirvana can be achieved by working off karma through actions, knowledge, or devotion on the part of an individual. Working off karma to achieve nirvana—the state of dissolution—may require millions of reincarnations.

Leadership issues: Since we do not know who the founders of Hinduism are, we cannot examine their lives and actions. However, many modern leaders of variants of Hinduism, New-Age religions, and mind-science cults have had enormous problems with personal credibility and honesty.

Fate of Hindu leaders: All known leaders in Hinduism and of Hinduism-based religions who have died, have remained dead.

Key Concept

Leader: No identified founder

Dates: About 1500 B.C.

Holy writings: The Vedas; Mahabharata; Ramayana; Bhagavad-Gita

Key claims: Great variation: Work your way to nirvana through successive reincarnations; religions are all related; many paths to god

Key evidence: Philosophy

Divine evidence: None

Buddha (Buddhism)

Buddhism currently claims about 6 percent of the world's population and is sometimes combined with other major religions (mainly Confucianism or Shintoism). Two of the major sects of Buddhism are *Theravada*, which is based on the original form of Buddha's teachings and is prevalent in southern Asia; and *Mahayana*, which centers in China and Japan. Theravada Buddhism emphasizes the individuality of humans and the necessity of self-effort to achieve salvation, which is limited to the worthy. Mahayana stresses social concern and people's interdependence, accepts many writings as Scripture, and teaches that everyone will receive the "grace" necessary for salvation.

History

Buddha, originally named Siddhartha Gautama, was born in 563 B.C. in a part of northern India that is now part of Nepal. Tradition says that Buddha was sheltered by his family in a palace so that he would never see the enormous suffering in the world from old age, sickness, poverty, and death. One day, Buddha ventured out and encountered all these forms of suffering, which inspired him to devote his life to discovering the source of suffering and finding a way to eliminate it. After six years of extreme self-denial, he realized that self-induced suffering would not bring him enlightenment. He then ate some food and sat under a fig tree to meditate, vowing not to rise until he was enlightened. After a time, he asserted that he had received the enlightenment he was seeking, and he became the "Buddha," which means "the enlightened one."

Key Concept

Key leader: Buddha

Dates: 563 to 483 B.C.

Holy writings: The "Three Baskets" (The Pali Scriptures); (The Mahayana canon is open and contains many holy writings)

Key claims: Moral conduct for enlightenment: Take no life; do not steal; remain sexually moral; do not tell falsehoods; do not take intoxicants

Key evidence: Philosophy

Divine evidence: None

The Teachings of Buddhism

Main groups: *Theravada* puts emphasis on the necessity of the individual to achieve enlightenment through worthy acts. Enlightenment is not granted to all. *Mahayana* teaches universal salvation and the mutual interdependence of people. *Vajrayana* (a third Buddhist sect) is closest to Hinduism and centers on occult practices.

God: God is an abstract. In essence, Buddhism is an atheistic philosophy.

Man: We suffer because of our desires for temporary things.

Sin: Suffering is the focus, not sin as such.

Jesus: He is not a factor.

Salvation: Total enlightenment brings us to nirvana, a state of blessedness in which all desire and individual consciousness is extinguished.

Leadership issues: Though Buddha was later deified by some of his followers, he never professed to be a god. He didn't pretend to be something he was not, but attempted to improve upon Hindu philosophy, based upon his discoveries from his personal "enlightenment."

The fate of Buddha: He died about the year 483 B.C. and remained dead.

Cults of Christianity

For our purposes here, a *cult* is defined as a religion claiming to be based on Christian doctrine, yet differing substantially from established orthodox theology. The most common cults of Christianity are

- the Mormons (Latter-day Saints)
- the Jehovah's Witnesses (Watchtower)

- Christian Science

- the Unity School of Christianity

- various New Age groups

Information regarding these cults and their leaders can be found in the Examine the Evidence booklet *How Is Jesus Different from Other Religious Leaders?* or from the resources cited on page 512.

Jesus Is Different—Jesus Claimed to Be God

Many times Jesus either unequivocally asserted that he was God or made statements and performed actions that implied the same thing. His words and actions so infuriated the religious leaders of the day that they tried several times to kill him for "blasphemy" (claiming that he was God). Eventually they succeeded in putting him into the hands of the Roman government, which technically crucified him (though Pilate "washed his hands" of the act, which he opposed—see Matthew 27:24).

If we look at Jesus' actions and words, we can see four specific ways in which he indicated he was divine:

1. *Jesus indicated he could forgive sins.* The Jews believed that only the single God of the universe could forgive sins. When Jesus made this claim, the religious leaders said he was blaspheming (Matthew 9:1-8— see below for more about this incident).

2. *Jesus accepted worship.* In the Law of Moses, God specifically commanded the Israelites to worship only him. Jesus demonstrated that he was in fact God by accepting the worship of, among others, his disciples (Luke 5:8; John 20:28).

3. *Jesus specifically said he was God.* Besides the examples given on the next page, Jesus said "I and the Father are one" (John 10:30). He also told the religious leaders, "Before Abraham was born, I am!" (John 8:58—"I am" was one of the names that God used of himself). The leaders clearly recognized what Jesus was saying and started to pick up stones to stone him for blasphemy.

4. *Jesus performed miracles only God could do.* Jesus did the same miracles Isaiah had prophesied would be signs of God's presence (Isaiah 35:4-6).

Here are more examples of Jesus' actions and claims:

• He forgave the sins of a man who had been paralyzed since birth. The religious leaders recognized his action as either evidence that he was God ("only God can forgive sins")—or blasphemy. Jesus silenced them by healing the paralyzed man in front of them and other witnesses—a miracle that only God could perform (Matthew 9:1-8).

• The Jewish religious laws forbade the gathering of food or the performing of any work at all on the Sabbath (Saturday), which was a ceremonial day of rest God had commanded. On one Sabbath, Jesus allowed his disciples to pick some wheat to satisfy their hunger. He also healed a man with a deformed hand. When the religious leaders tried to condemn him, he proclaimed that he was "Lord of the Sabbath"—indicating that he was equal to the One who had created the Sabbath. The religious leaders began plotting to kill him after this (Matthew 12:1-14).

- Jesus called himself the "capstone" (the highest and most critical part of a building) that was rejected by the "builders"—in this case the religious leaders. Again they tried to find a way to arrest him (Matthew 21:42-46).

- At his final trial, when Jesus was asked whether he was the "Christ, the Son of God," he replied that he was. At this point the high priest tore his own clothes—a sign of great distress over, among other things, blasphemy—and the religious leaders emphatically demanded that Jesus die for his "blasphemy" (Matthew 26:63-66).

Jesus' Miracles Were a Sign

The Jewish religious tradition regarded certain miracles as indication of God's presence. They included making the blind see, the lame walk, the deaf hear; the curing of leprosy; and the raising of the dead. Isaiah listed several of these miracles as those that would occur when "your God will come" (Isaiah 35:4-6). Jesus did all these things, many times in the presence of numerous witnesses, and later spoke of these same miracles when confirming his deity to John the Baptist (Matthew 11:2-5).

Jesus Proved He Was God

How can anyone prove he is God? Based on God's words in the Bible, there is literally only one way that Jesus or anyone else can prove he is God:

1. *Demonstrate first that he is a prophet of God by proclaiming perfectly fulfilled prophecy.* Only God can predict the future (Isaiah 46:10). The Bible tell us to "test everything" (1 Thessalonians 5:21) and specifically tells us to use prophecy as the test to

confirm that something is from God (Deuteronomy 18:14-22).

2. *Then prophesy that he is God—and that he will prove it by performing miracles only God can perform.* In addition to maintaining that he was God, Jesus told both his disciples and the Jewish religious leaders that he would be *resurrected from the dead,* which would be a confirmation of all his words and prophecies.

3. *Finally, fulfill the prophecy and perform the miracle that he predicted.* Jesus fulfilled his prophecy of the miracle of the resurrection. *Its fulfillment verified his claim to be God* and confirmed his triumph over death.

In addition to fulfilling his own prophecies, Jesus fulfilled more than 100 Old Testament Mesianic prophecies (see part 3), giving further evidence that he is God.

The Miracle of the Resurrection

Jesus precisely prophesied his own miraculous resurrection from the dead. Despite making this remarkable prophecy many times—along with others—he did not make any errors in any predictions. Furthermore, he professed to be God. And God tells us to use prophecy as a test to know whether something is from him. Therefore, *the prophecies Jesus made, along with their fulfillment by the events of his death and resurrection, verify his claim to be God.*

Conclusions

Jesus Is Vastly Different from Other Religious Leaders

1. Jesus' claim was very special. He maintained he was God in human flesh.

2. Jesus' claim was verified by Old Testament prophecy and by the historical events of his death and resurrection.

3. Jesus' own prophecy, along with the divine miracle of the resurrection, provided evidence of God's involvement.

4. Jesus' pure, sinless life—in perfect accord with his teaching and his claims—supports his claim to be God.

How Can We Know Whether a Leader Is Really Leading Us Toward Jesus?

Many religious leaders profess to teach the truth about Jesus, or even to be "extensions" of him, yet in reality they are far from him. And some religious groups that call themselves "Christian" are not. It's important to be wise and careful in choosing who you will meet with.* Here are a few guidelines:

- Observe how often, how clearly, and how accurately the Bible is used in teaching.

- Is Jesus referred to as God and as part of the Trinity (Father, Son, and Holy Spirit)?

- Who is being glorified—Jesus? Or some other individual or thing?

- Does the group believe that Jesus was crucified to provide forgiveness and redemption from sin?

- Does the group believe that Jesus was physically raised from the dead, and that he was miraculously born from a virgin?

---

* Some of the references listed in the notes and bibliography can help guide you in your choice. You may also contact the Christian Research Institute at 949-858-6100, ext. 301, or at www.equip.org, for information about a specific religious group or leader.

Test Yourself

1. Review the basic doctrines of Christianity and the other major religions.

2. Where in the Bible did Jesus claim to be God?

3. Besides his words, what actions did Jesus take that indicated he claimed to be God?

4. What major miracle separates Jesus from others?

5. How does prophecy differentiate Jesus from other leaders?

Chapter 33 Group Study

Homework Preparation (do prior to group)
Read: Luke 5:8; John 20:28; chapter 33 of this text; and *How Is Jesus Different from Other Religious Leaders?* ✝.

Opening Prayer
Discussion: Read Luke 5:8 and John 20:28. Discuss Jesus' acceptance of worship, forgiveness of sin, and other things that indicate he claimed to be God. Discuss these claims with actual verification. Compare this issue with other religious leaders.

Practical-Experience Game

Role-playing: A "nonbeliever" thinks all religions are the same. The "Christian" should review other religious leaders and point out their differences from Jesus.

Closing Prayer

Part 6

Seven Independent Studies of World and Bible History

As noted throughout this volume, Christianity is the only religion in which the fundamental doctrine is based on one set of historical events—the crucifixion and resurrection of Jesus Christ. Without these events there is no basis whatsoever for Christianity. Hence, historical context is of indispensable importance.

Part 2 reviewed the historical reliability of the Bible, including archaeology. This part provides a framework for the history of the Bible and Christian church within the history of the world. It is intended to provide a simple outline for reference and for additional outside study.

Seven independent study sessions in this part will help people explore history of the world, the Bible, and the church on their own using the guidelines provided. Readers are encouraged to make extensive use of references listed in the notes and bibliography of this book. *In particular, the author has established a special section on his Web site to assist the reader in dealing with this historical framework in this part.* Please visit www.evidenceofgod.com.

Of special importance in this part are the charts that list world and Bible–church events side by side. Pay particular attention to any dates or people in **bold**. They should be memorized for any in-depth study.

Creation Through Noah's Flood

The events of the creation of the universe and life on Earth took place in a systematic fashion, as outlined in Genesis. Whatever the timing of these events (see pages 62–64), the essential truth is that God, in all of his glory and omnipotence, created everything specifically for humans. Of particular interest is the fact that modern science and the Bible are in complete agreement regarding the order of events of creation.

Key Concept

Do not let issues like the age of the universe and Earth, dinosaurs, or the type of flood that occurred during Noah's time create a problem with acceptance of the Bible as factual. To understand how these issues can be reconciled, see chapters 3 and 4.

World History | Creation Steps | Bible History

World History	Old Earth	Young Earth	Bible History
There was a **beginning** when the heavens, Earth, and time came to be (general relativity).		[1]	In the **beginning** God created the heavens and the earth (and time).
The Earth was formless and void.	4.6 bil B.C.	6-10 thou B.C.	The earth was formless and void.
Opaque, dark clouds covered the Earth.			The spirit of God was at the surface of the water.
The atmosphere became translucent, allowing **light** to reach the surface of the Earth.		[2]	Let there be **light**. (From God's vantage point at the surface of the deep, there was light.)
Oceans and clouds separated.		[3]	Water above is separated from water below.
Volcanos and earthquakes created continents.		[4]	Continents and seas are formed.
Eukaryotic cells (with a nucleus) appear.	1.5 bil B.C.		
Angiosperm (flowering) **plants** appear.	Pre-cambrian**	6-10 thou B.C.*	First seed-bearing **plants** created.
Cambrian explosion of many plants and **sea animals.**	545 mil B.C.*	6-10 thou B.C.*	Fish were created.
Amphibians and insects appear.	350 mil B.C.		
Reptiles appear.	250 mil B.C.		
First dinosaurs appear.	230 mil B.C.		
First **birds** appear.	150 mil B.C.	6-10 thou B.C.	**Birds** were created.
Rats, mice, and squirrels appear.	60 mil B.C.	6-10 thou B.C.	**Livestock and wild animals** created.
Larger mammals and apes appear.	20 mil B.C.		
Man appears (Chaurat cave paintings).	15,000 B.C.	6-10 thou B.C.	**Man** was created.
Early man (Altamira cave paintings).	9000 B.C.		
First Law of thermodynamics. Matter and energy are constant. **Universe complete.**		[10]	Creation is complete.
Evidence of a great **flood.*****	7000 B.C.		Noah's **flood.***
			Tower of Babel.*

Creation Step numbers shown in middle column: 5 (between Precambrian / 6-10 thou B.C.), 6 (between 545 mil B.C. / 6-10 thou B.C.), 7, 8, 9.

* Note: There is substantial uncertainty about early biblical dates.
** www.grisda.org/origins/08007.htm.
*** www.cnn.com/2000/NATURE/09/13/great.flood.finds.ap/.

Test Yourself

1. The Bible takes care to state the initial conditions and frame of reference for creation. What were they? How is this important from a scientific perspective?

2. How does the command "Let there be light" take on a new meaning when we consider it from the frame of reference stated in the Bible?

3. What are the ten steps of creation?

4. How does creation coincide with the Bible?

5. What explanation(s) is (are) there for the dinosaurs?

Chapter 34 Group Study

Homework Preparation (do prior to group)

Read: Genesis chapter 1; chapter 34 of this text; *Creation vs. Evolution*✝; *Dinosaurs and the Bible* ✝. Familiarize yourself with appendix B. Also go to www.evidenceofgod.com and familiarize yourself with tools regarding creation vs. evolution.

Opening Prayer

Discussion: Discuss general and special revelation (see pages 61–65). In particular, discuss how the events of creation and science are in agreement. Discuss any potential areas of discord (such as the issue of dinosaurs) and how they might successfully be addressed.

Practical-Experience Game

Role-playing: The "Christian" should attempt to demonstrate to a "nonbeliever" how the creation account in the Bible is identical to scientific knowledge.

Closing Prayer

Noah Through the Period of the Judges

Fundamental events and people during this period are the patriarchs, starting with Abraham in the city of Ur (Genesis 11–50); the Exodus from Egypt; the conquest of Palestine; and the relatively dark period of the judges.

Key Concepts

The line of key patriarchs was Abraham, Isaac, Jacob, Joseph. This was the foundation leading up to 400 years of slavery in Egypt, which Moses later led the Hebrews out of in the Exodus.

—※— —※— —※—

The first five books of the Bible—Genesis, Exodus, Leviticus, Numbers, and Deuteronomy—are called the Torah. They were written by Moses about 1450 B.C. and were considered inspired by God (canonical) immediately.

World History		Bible History
■ Copper first used to make tools.	6200 B.C.	
■ Cuneiform writing in Mesopotamia (Abrahams' hometown of Ur).	3500 B.C.	
■ First pyramid built. ■ First treatise on surgery written (by Imhotep, in Egypt).	2670 B.C.	
■ Sargon creates first Mesopotamian empire.	2340 B.C.	
■ Stonehenge is built.	**2166 B.C.**	■ **Abraham** born in Mesopotamia.
■ Ziggurat (tower) of Ur (Abraham's town) built.	2100 B.C.	
	2066 B.C.	■ **Isaac** is born.
	2006 B.C.	■ **Jacob** is born. ❑ Book of Job is written.
	1915 B.C.	■ **Joseph** is born to Jacob and Rachel.
	1805 B.C.	■ Joseph dies. His body is mummified.
■ First law code established (by Hammurabi).	1728 B.C.	
■ Crete: the palace of Knossos is rebuilt after an earthquake.	1700 B.C.	
■ Hyksos overrun most of Egypt (and are expelled in 1567). ■ Horse and chariot introduced.	1675 B.C.	■ Hebrews suffer as slaves in Egypt.
■ Egypt reaches its height of power under Thutmose III.	1504 B.C.	
■ **Hinduism** begins.	**1500 B.C.**	
■ Amenhotep II rules Egypt. ■ Mycenaeans rule Mediterranean.	**1446 B.C.***	■ **Moses leads Exodus** from Egypt. ❑ Torah (First five books of Old Testament) are written.
■ Hittites forge iron (1400).	1406 B.C.	■ **Joshua** leads Hebrews into Canann.
■ Akhenaton introduces monotheistic worship of sun in Egypt.	1379 B.C.	❑ Book of Joshua is written. ■ Othniel becomes judge of Israel (1367*).
■ Tut rules Egypt as boy king.	1361 B.C.	
■ Canaanites develp extensive sea trade.	1300 B.C.	■ Deborah becomes judge of Israel (1209*).
	1162 B.C.	■ Gideon becomes judge of Israel.
	1110 B.C.	❑ Book of Ruth is written.
	1105 B.C.	■ **Samuel** is born.
■ Egypt: The New Kingdom period ends.	1085 B.C.	
* Note: There is substantial uncertainty about biblical dates.	1075 B.C.	■ Samuel becomes judge of Israel (1075*).

Test Yourself

1. Name the first five books of the Bible. What is the group of books called?

2. List the patriarchs. What events were going on in the nonbiblical world at the time?

3. How is Abraham's near-sacrifice of Isaac relevant to Jesus?

4. How was Jacob renamed? Why? What did it mean? Why was Jacob key to the long-term development of Israel?

Chapter 35 Group Study

Homework Preparation (do prior to group)
Scan: Genesis chapters 11–50; read chapter 35 of this text; go to www.evidenceofgod.com.

Opening Prayer
Discussion: Review each of the patriarchs. Discuss the personalities and the strengths and weaknesses of each. How did God use them in spite of their shortcomings? What other events were going on in the world at the time?

Practical-Experience Game
TV interview: The "Christian" is being interviewed to provide the basic historical facts about the Old Testament patriarchs.

Closing Prayer

The United Kingdom of Israel to Alexander the Great

One of the pivotal points in the history of the Jews was the United Kingdom under Saul, David, and Solomon (starting 1050 B.C.). For the first time, this consolidated and established the Israelites as a nation. It also set the stage for their later division—and after a dramatic exile, an eventual time when the Jews would be brought together in unity.

Key Concepts

The three united kingdom reigns were each about 40 years, starting in 1050 B.C.—Saul, 1050–1010; David, 1010–970; Solomon, 970–930.

The Torah (the first five books of the Bible) was officially canonized sometime soon after the first exile.

World History		Bible History
	1050 B.C.	■ **Saul** becomes first king of Israel. ❏ Book of Joshua is written (1045*).
■ China: refrigeration developed using block ice.	**1010 B.C.**	■ **David** becomes second king of Israel.
		❏ Many psalms written by David. ❏ 1 Samuel written. ❏ Many proverbs written by Solomon.
	970 B.C.	■ **Solomon** becomes third king of Israel. ❏ 1 Chronicles written. ❏ 2 Samuel written.
	959 B.C.	■ The Temple is completed.
	930 B.C.	■ The kingdom is divided: Israel—north, Judah—south. ❏ Song of Solomon is written.
	875 B.C.	■ Elijah the prophet begins ministry in Judah.
	851 B.C.	❏ 1 Kings is written.
	848 B.C.	■ Elisha the prophet serves in Judah.
■ Homer writes *The Iliad* and *The Odyssey*.	**800 B.C.**	
■ The first Olympics are held. Temple of Artemis begun.	**776 B.C.**	
■ Rome is founded.	**753 B.C.**	■ Micah prophesies to Israel (742).
		■ Isaiah prophesies to Judah (740).
■ Greeks actively start colonies in Asia Minor, Sicily, southern Italy, and elsewhere.	**772 B.C.**	■ **Samaria falls:** Israel exiled to **Assyria**.
	639 TO 622 B.C.	■ Zephaniah, Jeremiah, Nahum, Habakkuk prophesy to Judah (639, 627, 625, 622).
	606 B.C.	■ Daniel prophesies in exile. Ezekiel (593), Zechariah, Haggai, and Malachi in Judah (521, 521, 500).
■ Nebuchadnezzar becomes king of Babylon.	**586 B.C.**	■ **Jesusalem falls to Babylon:** Judah to exile.
■ **Buddha** (563). ■ **Confucius** (551).	**563 B.C.**	❏ Obadiah. ❏ Lamentations is written (580).
	537 B.C.	■ Cyrus' decree allowing Jews to return from exile.
■ Persians under Darius capture Macedonia and northern Greece (512).	**516 B.C.**	■ The rebuilding of the Temple is complete.
■ Rome establishes itself as a republic. ■ The Temple of Jupiter is built.	**509 B.C.**	
■ Socrates executed for undermining values (399).		❏ Esther is written (474). ❏ Ezra (450). ❏ Nehemiah is written (433).
■ Plato active (397–347).	**399 B.C.**	❏ Ecclesiastes is written (400). ❏ Joel is written (380).
■ Aristotle founds a school of philosophy near Athens.	**335 B.C.**	

* Note: There is substantial uncertainty about biblical dates.

————————Key Concepts————————

The exile of the Northern Kingdom to Assyria took place in 722 B.C., when Samaria (the capital) fell. The exile of the Southern Kingdom to Babylon was complete in 586 B.C., when the capital city of Jerusalem was taken.

—ɯ— —ɯ— —ɯ—

The Persians ruled Palestine after the Babylonians. Starting in 538 B.C. Cyrus was the ruler of Persia, who after defeating the Medes, controlled Babylon and allowed the Jews to return to rebuild Jerusalem and the Temple. This fulfilled a prophecy by Isaiah made over 100 years in advance of the destruction of Jerusalem and the Temple, and about 160 years before Cyrus was even born (Isaiah 44:28). Archaeology has uncovered the Cyrus cylinder, which confirms Cyrus's decree.[2]

Test Yourself

1. List the three kings of Israel's united kingdom and the dates of their reigns.

2. Who is the one king who remained loyal to God?

3. What faults did each king have? Why would the Bible list faults as well as successes?

4. When and where was the exile of Israel? Of Judah? What did the prophets identify as the reason for exile, and why was Judah spared for a few years?

5. Review the empires that controlled Palestine from the time of the united kingdom to that of Alexander the Great.

Chapter 36 Group Study

Homework Preparation (do prior to group)
Read: chapter 36 of this text; go to www.evidenceof god.com.

Opening Prayer
Discussion: Review the strengths and weaknesses of Saul, David, and Solomon. Discuss how some leaders were used for good despite their later falling away—in particular Solomon. How could the wisest man on earth make such a change? Why is the Bible so forthright about mistakes? Discuss, in general, the later kings of Israel and Judah.

Practical-Experience Game
Debate: The "nonbeliever" is critical of the leaders described in the Bible, claiming that God wouldn't place such misfits in such important positions. Defend God's choices.

Closing Prayer

37

Alexander
the Great
to Nero

After exile into Babylon and rule by the tyrant Nebuchadnezzar, the Jews continued to face a myriad of harsh
conquerors. Alexander the Great, while conquering with an
iron hand, ended up contributing valuable Greek (Hel-
lenistic) culture and education. The Seleucid ruler Antiochus
Epiphanes IV sacrificed a pig on the Temple altar and abol-
ished worship—inflaming the Jews and leading to the Maccabean revolt. A series of Roman leaders followed,
eventually leading to the hated emperor Nero, who blamed
the great fire of Rome on the Christians in order to justify
mass persecution.

World History		Bible History
■ **Alexander the Great** begins conquests for Greece.	**333** B.C.	■ Alexander quickly overruns Palestine.
	323 B.C.	■ After Alexander's untimely death, control of Palestine is divided. The **Ptolemies** (Egypt) take over.
	280 B.C.	■ The **Septuagint** translation of the Hebrew Scriptures is written.
■ Parchment is developed.	**250** B.C.	■ Early manuscripts of the **Dead Sea scolls** are written.
■ Hannibal crosses Alps—captures much of Italy.	**218** B.C.	
■ Antiochus IV (Seleucid) invades Egypt. A Roman ultimatum forces him to withdraw.	**198** B.C.	■ **Seleucids** capture Jerusalem.
■ Roman streets paved (170).	**167** B.C.	■ **Old Testament canon unofficially established.** ■ Antiochus IV Epiphanes desecrates the Temple by sacrificing a pig on the altar.
	164 B.C.	■ **Maccabean Revolt** overthrows Antiochus IV (Hanukkah).
■ Pompey conquers Syria and Palestine.	**63** B.C.	■ Roman general Pompey captures Jerusalem.
■ Julius Caesar assassinated.	**44** B.C.	■ Herod flees to Rome when Parthians invade Syria and Palestine (40).
	4 B.C.	■ Herod dies. Palestine divided among his children. ■ **Jesus Christ born.**
■ World population at 250 million (A.D. 1). ■ Tiberius becomes emperor (14).	**A.D. 33**	■ **Crucifixion and resurrection** of Jesus Christ.
■ Emperor Caligula of Rome becomes convinced of his own divinity (37).	**A.D. 35**	■ Paul changes from Pharisee to Christian. ■ Paul visits Peter and Jesus' brother James (38).
■ Caligula assassinated. Claudius becomes emperor.	**A.D. 41** **A.D. 43**	■ Herod Agrippa I given control of all Palestine: ■ Opposes Christians, beheads James, son of Zebedee.
	A.D. 46	■ Paul's first missionary trip, to Cyprus, Asia Minor. ❏ Galatians written (49). ❏ James written (49).
	A.D. 50	■ Jerusalem Council. ■ Ignatius born. ■ Paul's second missionary trip, to Macedonia, Asia Minor. ❏ 1 and 2 Thessalonians (51–52).
	A.D. 52	■ Paul's third missionary trip, to Macedonia, Asia Minor.
■ Claudius is poisoned so Nero can become emperor.	**A.D. 54**	❏ 1 and 2 Corinthians (55–57). ❏ Romans (57). ❏ Ephesians (60). ❏ Colossians (60). ❏ Philippians (61). ❏ 1 and 2 Timothy (64–67). ❏ Philemon (64). ❏ Titus (64). ❏ 1 Peter (62–64).
■ **Great fire of Rome.** Nero blames Christians and inaugurates mass persecution.	**A.D. 64**	❏ Matthew, Mark, Luke, and Acts probably written prior to the persecution of 64—no later than 80.

Key Concept

Following the divided kingdom, the Jews were ruled by
1. *the Assyrians (starting in 722 B.C.)*
2. *the Babylonians (starting in 586)*
3. *the Medo-Persians (starting in 538)*
4. *the Greeks (starting in 333)*
5. *the Ptolemies and Seleucids (starting in 323)*
6. *the Hasmoneans (starting in 164)*
7. *the Romans (starting in 63 B.C.)*

The Romans destroyed Jerusalem and the Temple in A.D. 70.

Test Yourself

1. Review the governments in control of Palestine from Alexander the Great to the Roman Empire.

2. What is Antiochus IV famous for? When? What happened three years later?

3. When did Rome conquer Jerusalem? When did Julius Caesar die? How was Israel divided after Herod the Great's death?

4. Why is the martyrdom of the apostles and early Christians so important?

5. When did Nero inaugurate mass persecution of Christians? When did the Romans destroy the Temple?

Chapter 37 Group Study

Homework Preparation (do prior to group)

Read: chapter 37 of this text; go to www.evidenceof
god.com.

Opening Prayer

Discussion: Discuss the situation of the world at the time
of the birth of Jesus. Why was it ideal for the introduction of
a Savior and the spreading of the gospel? What is so important about Paul's change to Christianity and his missionary
journeys?

Practical-Experience Game

Role-playing: The "Christian" should use the martyrdom
of the apostles and early Christians as evidence to convince
the "nonbeliever" that the crucifixion and resurrection were
historical.

Closing Prayer

Nero to Emperor Constantine

Probably the most critical period in the survival of Christianity was the period from the beginning of mass persecution by Nero until Emperor Constantine. First, there were still several apostles alive early in that period, along with many other eyewitnesses of the crucifixion and resurrection. Together they could verify any writings and oral accounts. Secondly, it was a period of enormous persecution when extensive attempts were made to end Christianity once and for all, through repeated mass persecution and executions. And third, it was a critical period to ensure a continuum of communication of the gospel message from the apostles through later leaders (until Christianity was made acceptable in the Roman Empire and Bibles were safe from mass destruction).

The early church fathers start an unbroken line of communication from the eyewitnesses—the apostles themselves—to the present day. The message is consistent throughout regarding the essentials of the events of the crucifixion and resurrection. This provides assurance regarding the accuracy of the original message.

World History		Bible History
▦ Emperor Vespasian	A.D. 69	▦ **Polycarp born.** ❑ Book of Jude is written (65). ❑ 2 Peter is written (67).
	A.D. 70	▦ Rome overcomes Jewish revolt. Temple destroyed. ❑ Book of Hebrews is written.
▦ Pompeii, Herculaneum destroyed by volcano (79). ▦ Josephus writes *The Jewish War* (79). ▦ Colosseum is dedicated by Titus (80). ▦ Emperor Domitian (81).	A.D. 79	▦ All apostles except John are martyred between 60 and about 75.
	A.D. 88	▦ **Clement** ("of Rome") becomes fourth "bishop" of Rome. ❑ Book of 1 John is written. (85–90). ❑ Books of 2 and 3 John are written (90). ❑ Book of Revelation is written (95).
▦ Emperor Trajan	A.D. 95	▦ The *Didache* is written (a guide of church teaching from the apostles).
▦ Britain: Romans build first "London bridge" ▦ China: Paper is invented.	A.D. 100	▦ **John,** the last remaining apostle, dies. ▦ **Justin Martyr** born. ▦ 1 Clement, a key early church document, is written. ▦ Heretical "Gospel" of Thomas is written. ▦ **Irenaeus** born (c. 97).
▦ Tacitus, historian, writes *Annals* of Roman history. ▦ Hadrian becomes emperor (117). ▦ Emperor Antoninus Pius (138–161). ▦ Emperor Marcus Aurelius (161–180).	A.D. 115	▦ **Ignatius** is martyred (107).
	A.D. 150	▦ Tatian writes *Diatessaron* (a harmony of the Gospels). ▦ **Tertullian** born (c. 155).
	A.D. 185	▦ Irenaeus writes *Against Heresies*.
	A.D. 197	▦ Tertullian writes *Apologeticus*.
	A.D. 200	▦ **Hippolytus** writes *Apostolic Tradition*. ▦ Irenaeus martyred.
▦ Goths invade Asia Minor (200–249).	A.D. 202–232	▦ **Origen** leads school in Alexandria.
▦ Emperor Decius establishes systematic persecution of Christians—sacrificial commissions in all cities, demanding recognition of Roman deity.	A.D. 249	
▦ Emperor Valerian orders sacrifices to Roman gods.	A.D. 253	
▦ **Emperor Diocletian decrees** anyone with a Bible would be executed.	**A.D. 303**	▦ Worst period of persecution (303–312).
▦ Eusebius writes history. Friend of Constantine.	A.D. 260–340	
▦ **Constantine ends persecution.**	**A.D. 313**	▦ Edict of Milan ends persecution and makes Christianity official religion of the Empire.

Jerome (347 to 419 or 420) authored the Vulgate—a translation of the Bible from the original languages of Greek and Hebrew into Latin. This was the Bible on which the first English Bibles were based—and thus was the root of the King James translation of the Bible.

Timeline of Overlapping Communication: From Jesus and the Apostles to Constantine

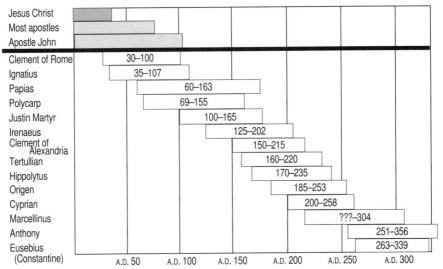

Note: Most dates are approximate.

Key Concept

Those books in the biblical canon are accepted as "God-breathed," or inspired by God.

Test Yourself

1. What early church fathers probably communicated with the apostle John?

2. Why is the unbroken chain of communication from the apostles to the mass copying of Bibles after persecution important?

3. Name at least three important church fathers and what they produced.

4. When did persecution end? What effect did this have?

5. Who wrote the Vulgate? What is it?

Chapter 38 Group Study

Homework Preparation (do prior to group)
Read: chapter 38 of this text; go to www.evidence ofgod.com.

Opening Prayer
Discussion: Review the chart on page 555 of the overlapping timeline of early church fathers. First, consider that several of the early church fathers had actual contact with the apostles. Second, consider that there is an unbroken chain of church fathers that communicated with each other both verbally and in writing. Now, considering that Christianity is based on history, how does this help us trust the reliability of the biblical account?

Practical-Experience Game
Press conference: The "Christian" will field questions regarding the trustworthiness of the transmission of the Bible.

Closing Prayer

Emperor Constantine to the Protestant Reformation

When he suddenly and dramatically reversed years of persecution in the Roman Empire, Constantine finally opened the door to mass duplication of the Bible, along with official councils regarding church doctrine. Fortunately, as pointed out earlier, there was an unbroken chain of communication from Jesus, through the apostles, through early church fathers. There also exist early biblical manuscripts that predate even Constantine. Hence, we have good reason to believe that the many ancient biblical manuscripts we can review today are accurate.

> The Apostles' Creed, the Nicene Creed, and the Athanasian Creed are the three major creeds of early Christendom. They have defined the Christian faith for centuries. Originally they were written to rebuke common heresies.

Even so, during the period of time from Constantine to the Reformation, the church encountered problems of a different kind. It evolved into an instrument of power and prestige that was misused by many. Eventually reformations were necessary to resolve the problems.

World History		Bible History
## World History		## Bible History
■ Constantine convenes Council of Nicaea.	325	■ Council of Nicaea condemns Arianism (a heresy denying the Trinity and deity of Jesus).
	330	■ Constantinople is dedicated as the capital of the Christian empire.
■ Huns invade Europe (350–399). ■ Valens rules Rome (364–378). ■ Valens defeated at Adrianople (378). ■ Emperor Theodosius proclaims Christianity the official religion of the Roman Empire (394).	354–430	■ **Augustine**
	397	■ Third Council of Carthage. ■ **Bible officially canonized.**
	345–420	■ **Jerome translates the Vulgate** (complete in **405**).
	440–461	■ Pope Leo I prevents Attila the Hun from ransacking Rome.
	592	■ Pope Gregory the Great reaches peaceful agreement with the Lombards.
■ **Muhammad** flees from Mecca to Medina. ■ Arabs attack north Africa (670).	**622**	
	715	■ Pope Gregory II brings stabilizing force to church.
	731	■ Pope Gregory III increases cooperation between church and state.
■ Alfred the Great becomes king of Britain (871), defeats Danish invaders (878). ■ Vikings discover Greenland (c. 900). ■ Leif Eriksson discovers America (c. 1000).	**800**	■ Charlemagne crowned emperor of the new Holy Roman Empire.
	1054	■ Traditional date for split of Church into Catholic and Orthodox branches.
	1095	■ Beginning of Crusades.
■ Universities of Paris and Oxford are founded.	1150–1167	
■ Richard I (the "Lionhearted") succeeds Henry II as king in Britain (1189). ■ Genghis Khan invades China (1211).	1227	■ Inquisition comes into final form under Pope Gregory IX.
■ Marco Polo of Venice travels to China. ■ Thomas Aquinas stops working on *Summa Theologica* (the basis for all Catholic theological teaching) and never completes it (1273).	1271	
■ Beginning of the Italian **renaissance**.	1325	■ **John Wycliffe, John Hus** initiate reform beliefs (1320–1384).
■ Hundred Years' War between England and France (1337–1453).	1378–1417	■ Papacy schism.
■ Black Plague hits Europe (1346).	1417	■ **John Hus** martyred by church for reform beliefs (1415).
		■ Papacy hits low. Three Popes at once, all are deposed.

Test Yourself

1. What is Gnosticism? What creed was written to counter it?

2. What is Arianism? What council was convened to address it?

3. Who is Pope Gregory the Great? What were his major accomplishments?

4. What caused the decline of the papacy?

Chapter 39 Group Study

Homework Preparation (do prior to group)
Read: chapter 39 of this text; go to www.evidenceof god.com.

Opening Prayer
Discussion: Discuss the problems that caused the decline of the papacy. Discuss how these problems could have arisen. What may have been done to prevent the problems? Is there any chance such problems could come up today? Compare problems in the papacy with problems in the church today.

Practical-Experience Game
TV interview: The "interviewer" is interested in obtaining basic information from the "Christian" to inform viewers about the development of the Christian church.

Closing Prayer

The Reformation to the Modern Church

While Wycliffe and Hus were early reformers, the Protestant Reformation gained its greatest burst of momentum under Martin Luther. Condemning many obvious heretical practices of the church, Luther used his following to launch a new theology based only upon the carefully considered words of holy Scripture.

In the years following Luther, Protestantism began to take on many forms based on various readings of Scripture alone. Leaders like Calvin, then Wesley, Spurgeon, and Moody, all played key roles in shaping the many Bible-based denominations of the modern church.

The Catholic Counter-Reformation of the mid and late 1500s also attempted to address many problems in the Roman Catholic Church. However, religious conflict between Catholics and Protestants ignited a series of disputes that often ended in bloodshed.

World History		Bible History
▨ Invention of **printing**.	**1455**	▨ First Bible Printed (1456).
▨ **Columbus** discovers New World. ▨ Moors stopped in attack against Spain.	**1492**	
▨ Leonardo da Vinci paints Mona Lisa (1503). ▨ Michelangelo sculpts David (1504). ▨ St. Peter's Church started in Rome (1506). ▨ Henry VIII takes throne in England (1509), breaks ties with Pope.	1517	▨ **Martin Luther** posts famous Ninety-five Theses, founding Protestantism.
▨ Copernicus' theory that the Earth revolves around the sun is published after his death, since he feared being executed as a heretic (1543).	1509–1564	▨ **John Calvin** initiates extensive reforms with broad influence. ❑ Tyndale Bible (1526). ▨ War breaks out between Protestants and Catholics (1546).
	1545	▨ Council of Trent—Catholic Counter-Reformation addresses church problems. Defines doctrine.
	1558	▨ Queen Elizabeth I ascends to throne in England, establishes Anglican state church.
▨ Defeat of Spanish Armada by English. Henry IV of France converts to Catholicism in an attempt to end religious wars (1588).	1572	▨ St. Bartholomew's Day massacre in France, when thousands of Protestant Huguenots were murdered by Catholics.
▨ **Kepler** discovers elliptical orbit of planets (1609).	1608	▨ John Smith baptizes first "Baptists."
▨ **Galileo** denounced as a heretic for supporting Copernicus and Kepler that the Earth revolved around the sun and rotated on its axis (1616).	1611	▨ **King James Version**—translated by a team of 54 scholars—is completed. Although immediate basis is "Bishop's Bible," root of prior English Bibles is Vulgate.
▨ **Galileo** forced by Church to recant belief (1633).	1738	▨ **John Wesley's** conversion eventually leads to founding of the Methodists.
▨ United States of America is formed (1776).	1854	▨ **Charles H. Spurgeon** becomes influential pastor.
	1855	▨ **Dwight L. Moody** converted, later becomes leading evangelist.
▨ United States Civil War ends.	1865	▨ William Booth founds the Salvation Army.
▨ **Charles Darwin** writes *On the Origin of Species,* launches evolution theory (1859).	1870	▨ Pope Pius IX proclaims doctrine of papal infallibility.
▨ Scopes Monkey Trial ushers evolution into schools, pushes biblical creation out (1925).	1906	▨ Azusa Street Revival launches Pentecostalism.
	1949	▨ **Billy Graham** launched into evangelism career at Los Angeles crusade.
	1962	▨ Vatican II—A Council that modified Catholic Church doctrine to promote broader, more contemporary acceptance.
	1992	▨ Roman Catholic church finally overturns 1616 condemnation of Galileo as a heretic.

Test Yourself

1. Who was John Wycliffe? Why was his contribution so important?

2. Name at least two church problems that inspired the Reformation.

3. Who is regarded as the father of Protestantism? What are the key doctrines he introduced? When did he start the movement?

4. What and when was the Council of Trent? What were its purpose and conclusions?

5. Who is Calvin? Wesley? Spurgeon? Moody?

Chapter 40 Group Study

Homework Preparation (do prior to group)

Read: chapter 40 of this text; go to www.evidenceof god.com.

Opening Prayer

Discussion: Discuss Church practices rejected by the Protestants. Which does the group think are unbiblical, and which are acceptable? Discuss the Roman Catholic Church's reluctance to have the Bible translated into English. Does there seem to be any relationship of the Church's intention then to the continuation of Catholic masses in Latin (until recently)? Or was the Latin mass an honest attempt to not alter anything from Jerome's Vulgate?

Practical-Experience Game

Debate: Two people take the sides of the Protestants and the Counter-Reformation Catholics and discuss the pros and cons of each issue.

Closing Prayer

How to Know God

If you would like to have a relationship with the God of the universe, a relationship ensuring eternal life, all you need to do is the following:

1. Believe that God exists and that he came to earth in the human form of Jesus Christ (John 3:16; Romans 10:9).

2. Accept God's free forgiveness of sins and gift of new life through the death and resurrection of Jesus Christ (Ephesians 2:8-10; 1:7-8).

3. Switch to God's plan for your life (1 Peter 1:21-23; Ephesians 2:1-7).

4. Expressly make Jesus Christ the director of your life (Matthew 7:21-27; 1 John 4:15).

Prayer for Eternal Life with God

"Dear God, I believe you sent your Son, Jesus, to die for my sins so I can be forgiven. I'm sorry for my sins, and I want to live the rest of my life the way you want me to. Please put your spirit in my life to direct me. Amen."

Then What?

- Find a Bible-based church you like and attend regularly.

- Set aside some time each day to pray and read the Bible.

- Locate other Christians to spend time with on a regular basis.

Special Group-Study Tools

The 40-chapter group-study recommendations offer a systematic program of group study, designed for Bible study groups, small groups, workshops, and special gatherings. Any topic or series of topics in the chapters can be selected from the 40 depending on a group's interest.

The group study recommendations are designed to use the smaller, "topical" Examine the Evidence series booklets in combination with the use of *Examine the Evidence*. Each session's topic will always consist of

1. homework—generally consisting of reading

2. opening and closing prayers

3. topic(s) for discussion

4. a practical-experience game

The Opening Prayer

The opening prayer is up to the direction and inspiration of the group leader. Using the model for prayer provided by Jesus (Matthew 6:9-13), the prayer should 1) glorify and worship God, 2) thank God (be specific) for the things he has done, 3) ask for forgiveness for sins committed, 4) request

God's blessings (be specific according to group's individual needs), and 5) request guidance and insights for the meeting.

Topics for Discussion

Every chapter will contain a few topics for discussion. They will be relevant to the chapter and often will draw from information included in the companion Examine the Evidence series booklets—information not contained in the larger *Examine the Evidence* text.

A leader (moderator) should be selected to guide the discussion. A time-limit guideline should be established. Twenty minutes normally is sufficient for a good discussion. Free-thinking participation from the entire group is encouraged.

A Practical-Experience Game

Each session should include a practical-experience game that allows group members to practice skills and knowledge about the topic. Listed below are the forms of games used in the chapter group-study recommendations. Keeping the game light, humorous, and fun is essential to success. In that vein, one way to keep it humorous is to appoint a panel of "experts" that evaluates the "performance" for the game. Be sure to appoint one person to break any tension by always making some outlandishly derogatory remark. For fun, give that character a name, like "Simon." If done in the right spirit, this approach will minimize the danger of anyone taking themselves too seriously. Yet it also will provide insight.

Game 1: Role-Playing

Assign one person to be the Christian and another to be the nonbeliever. On folded pieces of paper, write down various locations where someone might have a chance meeting with a nonbeliever. Examples might be a Little League game, an airport coffee shop, a charity gathering, or an outing such as a friendly golf game. The Christian selects a location and announces it to the group.

Also use folded pieces of paper to define the attitude of the nonbeliever. Use the following designations: 1) *seeker*—someone who happens to be searching for God and is currently attending church on a periodic basis; 2) *apathetic*—someone who really hasn't thought at all about God and doesn't attend church, except maybe Easter and Christmas; 3) *hostile*—one who is antagonistic about religion, and though he or she loves to argue, never attends church. The nonbeliever blindly selects his or her "attitude" and does not tell anyone. It is up to the Christian to determine how to deal with the person.

The game consists of the Christian entering into a conversation with the nonbeliever about the assigned topic and attempting to use gentleness and respect (1 Peter 3:15) to open discussion about God, Jesus, and the Bible.

Allow ten minutes for the role-playing and ten minutes for discussion.

Important note: Refer to *How to Talk About Jesus with the Skeptics in Your Life*—an Examine the Evidence booklet—to learn a detailed step-by-step approach to dealing with all types of skeptics.

Game 2: The Press Conference

Everyone is familiar with the basic press conference given by a U.S. president or some other notable figure—it has hordes of anxious reporters screaming to get their questions answered.

In this game, a person is selected to be the "apologist" (defender of the faith) to answer questions about the topic. Several others are selected to be the reporters. The game has the most appeal if reporters are selected the week before and have a chance to prepare a list of questions, thereby allowing for "reporter bedlam" in the game.

Schedule the press conference to be ten minutes followed by ten minutes of discussion.

Game 3: The Debate

Two people are selected—a Christian and a nonbeliever. They will be on a "college campus" debating the topic assigned. Having the "panel" review the debaters' skill can be especially fun and useful here.

Schedule the debate to be twenty minutes, followed by ten minutes of discussion.

Game 4: The TV Interview

Try to imagine a situation where you, being an expert in the topic at hand, are suddenly whisked onto a TV set where a skilled reporter is ready to interview you in front of millions of viewers. This happens frequently in real life, and the interviewers are not always friendly—confrontation often can increase ratings.

One person is assigned to be the expert and another to be the interviewer on the topic assigned. Schedule the interview to be ten minutes, followed by ten minutes of discussion.

As experience and comfort is gained by using the above games, variations and other ideas may surface. Don't hesitate to experiment with new techniques, keeping in mind that any means of having fun while trying to learn to be more open and encouraging about your faith is worthwhile.

Closing Prayer

The leader may select a person to lead a closing prayer. Thank God for what he has revealed and request guidance in the future.

S.H.A.R.E. Program

The Examine the Evidence tools coordinate together to provide 1) education to build belief and faith (*Examine the Evidence: Exploring the Case for Christianity*); 2) ready answers to common questions *(One-Minute Answers—The Evidence for Christianity);* and 3) topic-oriented booklets (the Examine the Evidence series) ideal for evangelism.

Steps to **S.H.A.R.E.**:

- *Study the Word and the evidence* in support of the gospel. Read the Word daily. *Examine the Evidence: Exploring the Case for Christianity* is a thorough self-teaching course designed to prepare people to answer questions.

- *Hear others.* Develop the habit of listening to others. A relationship can be developed in a short period of time. By hearing what others have to say, you can learn what keeps them from learning more about God, or from embracing him. Look for opportunities to encourage questions.

- *Answer questions.* Use *One-Minute Answers—The Evidence for Christianity* to deal with issues immediately. With this tool, there is no need to be intimidated—you can be ready with quick answers.

- *Respond and research.* Immediate answers often lead to deeper questions. Respond with a follow-up meeting. Research any incomplete answers or remaining roadblocks using the references provided. Look for chances to share the gospel.

- *Evangelize.* When the time is right, let others know about the gift of salvation through Jesus Christ. Sometimes in-depth study of a particular issue is helpful. The 48-page Examine the Evidence booklets are designed to break down specific barriers to Christ. Each one tells the reader how to establish a personal relationship with God at its end.

A Checklist of Questions for Evolutionists

Regarding evolutionary teaching:

1. *Presuppositions.* Why do evolutionists presuppose evolution is true? Why not start in a more objective manner and consider that the origin of life could have come about either by random process or by intelligent design, and let the evidence lead people to the more logical conclusion?

2. *Macroevolution versus microevolution.* After acknowledging the existence of microevolution, ask, What evidence is there of macroevolution?

3. *Homology.* What does the observation of common body parts really prove? Isn't it likely that a good designer would use a "well-designed" body part within different creatures for a specific application?

4. *Embryology.* Embryology in regard to evolution is mere speculation. What evidence is there that embryology means anything?

5. *Common ancestry?* If someone can draw pictures of a frog turning into a prince, why would we expect that someone would not likewise draw pictures of an ape becoming a man?

6. *Miller–Urey experiments #1.* The experiments are criticized for not properly representing early-Earth conditions. Yet even if they did, how can life-specific amino acids survive when, according to the experiments, the by-product of destructive tar is far more abundant?

7. *Miller–Urey experiments #2.* Even if we were to accept the highly unlikely position that all life-specific amino acids were randomly generated by the experiments, how far does this *really* take us towards random development of life itself? In other words, this would be a far cry from creating *all* of the materials and overcoming all the assembly problems. Isn't it like claiming random development of black ink proves that an encyclopedia came about randomly?

Regarding the fossil record:

1. *Soft-science conclusions.* Isn't the entire premise of using the fossil record to support evolution based on soft-science conjectures? In other words, doesn't it simply use "order of appearance" of creatures, combined with homology, to create a "story" of how things evolved?

2. *Hard-science evidence.* What hard evidence is there that evolution is real? Since there are no "missing links" to test, is it not impossible to demonstrate hard evidence of DNA mutational change? On the other hand, previous conjectures such as the "Neanderthal man" have been shown to be nonhuman using DNA testing.

3. *Missing links.* Why are there no true missing links (transitional creatures showing, for instance, partially formed feathers, not fully functional ones)?

4. *The Cambrian explosion.* Given that neo-Darwinism requires gradual change over long periods of time, how do we explain the sudden appearance of many new life forms on Earth?

Regarding the statistical analysis of life:

1. *Chirality.* Can anyone provide one piece of hard evidence that the issue of chirality can be resolved using random processes?

2. *Statistical origin.* How can someone believe that components of life randomly came together when the odds of this random event are far less than picking one marked subatomic particle out of the entire universe (in fact, many universes!)?

3. *Addition of "life."* Even if the right atoms came together in precisely the right way at precisely the right time (statistically impossible, as shown above) how do we account for life being added to make such an assembly "work"?

4. *Statistical development.* Even if life could randomly start, how can we account for the random development of more than 1.7 million very different, highly complex species, along with the many necessary transitional forms, in only a few hundred million years? Keep in mind that this "evolution" would require change from a simple cell of only about 100,000 to 500,000 base pairs of DNA to a human with 3.2 billion base pairs of DNA—all precisely arranged.

5. *Mutations #1.* Since mutations do not add information, how would DNA gain the vast amount of additional information needed for change?

6. *Mutations #2.* Even if mutations could add information, how does one overcome the statistical problem that shows that there is not enough time for required positive mutations to take place to provide for evolution (pages 132–135)?

7. *Irreducible complexity.* How can we account for the problem of irreducible complexity?

Appendix C

Analyzed Prophecies of the Old Testament

In addition to the prophecies analyzed in part 3, the following prophecies were used in the statistical analysis of fulfillment of non-Messianic prophecy in the Old Testament.

1. Abraham's son Ishmael would be father of a great nation (Genesis 17:20).

   Fulfillment: Ishmael is considered the father of the Arab nations.

2. The Amalekites would be destroyed (Moses, c. 1450 B.C., Exodus 17:14).

   Fulfillment: About 1000 B.C., 1 Chronicles 4:43).

3. Assyria would fall and be destroyed (Isaiah, c. 735 B.C., Isaiah 14:24-27).

   Fulfillment: Completed with the destruction of Nineveh in 612 B.C.

4. Destruction of Damascus predicted (Isaiah, c. 735 B.C., Isaiah 17:1-4).

   Fulfillment: Destruction by Assyria (history).

5. Prophecy against Egypt (Isaiah, c. 740 B.C., Isaiah 19:1-17).

   Fulfillment: Invasion by Assyria and Babylon along with internal fighting (history).

6. Prophecy against Babylon (Isaiah, c. 740 B.C., Isaiah 21:1-10).

   Fulfillment: Conquest by Medes and Persians in 539 B.C.

7. Prophecies against Edom and Petra (Isaiah, c. 745 B.C., Isaiah 34:5-15; Jeremiah, c. 600 B.C., Jeremiah 49:17-18; Ezekiel 25; 35).

   Fulfillment: History. "Unpopulated," conquered by heathen (500s B.C.), conquered by Israel (Ezekiel 25:14); desolate to Teman (Ezekiel 25:13); void of trade (Isaiah 34:10; Jeremiah 49:17); inhabited by wild animals (Isaiah 34:11-15; Ezekiel 35:7). All of these prophetic elements have transpired.

8. Prophecy of Jerusalem being destroyed, yet with blessings to follow (Isaiah 29:1-24).

   Fulfillment: 2 Chronicles 36:15-21.

9. Israel would not be helped by Egypt after their alliance with them (Isaiah 30:1–31:9).

   Fulfillment: History.

10. Jerusalem would be destroyed along with other towns of Judah (Jeremiah, c. 620 B.C., Jeremiah 9:11).

    Fulfillment: History.

11. Children and young would be killed, as well as those in Egypt, Edom, Ammon, and Moab (Jeremiah, c. 620 B.C., Jeremiah 9:17-26).

    Fulfillment: 2 Chronicles 36:15-21.

12. Those living in the land God promised to Abraham would experience God's wrath, and by breaking the covenants of Moses, Israel would experience curses (Jeremiah, c. 600 B.C., Jeremiah 10:17-25; 11:1-8).

    Fulfillment: 2 Chronicles 36:15-21.

13. Israel would have drought, famine, and wars. Their prophets would die (Jeremiah, c. 620 B.C., Jeremiah 14:1-16).

    Fulfillment: 2 Chronicles 36:15-21.

14. Jeremiah would be saved, but Jerusalem would fall and be plundered (Jeremiah, c. 600 B.C., Jeremiah 15:5-21).

    Fulfillment: History—exile to Babylon.

15. Israel would be hunted—to exile its people into captivity (Jeremiah, c. 620 B.C., Jeremiah 16:16-18).

    Fulfillment: 2 Chronicles 36:15-21.

16. Judah's wealth would be taken, its people would be enslaved, and they would lose their inheritance (Jeremiah, c. 620 B.C., Jeremiah 17:1-14).

    Fulfillment: History.

17. Israel would be destroyed and its treasure would be taken to Babylon (Jeremiah, c. 620 B.C., Jeremiah 20:1-6).

    Fulfillment: 2 Chronicles 36:15-21.

18. Jerusalem would be destroyed unless it surrendered (Jeremiah, c. 620 B.C., Jeremiah 21:8-14).

    Fulfillment: 2 Chronicles 36:15-21.

19. Judah's kings and holy places would be destroyed (Jeremiah, c. 620 B.C., Jeremiah 22:1-23).

    Fulfillment: 2 Chronicles 36:15-21.

20. God would judge lying prophets (Jeremiah, c. 620 B.C., Jeremiah 23:9-40).

    Fulfillment: 2 Chronicles 36:15-21.

21. Babylon would conquer Israel; Israel would surrender (Jeremiah, c. 620 B.C., Jeremiah 27:1-22).

    Fulfillment: 2 Chronicles 36:11-21.

22. Jerusalem would be rebuilt "from the Tower of Hananel to the Corner Gate" (Jeremiah, c. 620 B.C., Jeremiah 31:38-40).

    Fulfillment: History.

23. Jerusalem would be conquered; its houses would be filled with dead (Jeremiah, c. 620 B.C., Jeremiah 33:1-5).

    Fulfillment: 2 Chronicles 36:11-15.

24. Babylon would conquer and burn Jerusalem; King Zedekiah would face punishment (Jeremiah, c. 620 B.C., Jeremiah 34:1-22).

    Fulfillment: 2 Kings 24:18–25:10.

25. The Babylonians would come back after fighting Egypt and attack Jerusalem and destroy it (Jeremiah, c. 620 B.C., Jeremiah 37:1-17).

    Fulfillment: 2 Chronicles 36:11-15.

26. Fall of Jerusalem predicted several times (Jeremiah, c. 620 B.C., Jeremiah 38).

    Fulfillment: 2 Chronicles 36:11-15.

27. Egypt would be defeated by Babylon (Jeremiah, c. 620 B.C., Jeremiah 46:1-26).

    Fulfillment: History, in approximately 605 B.C.

28. The land of the Philistines would be destroyed (Jeremiah, c. 620 B.C., Jeremiah 47:1-7).

    Fulfillment: History, in 609 B.C.

29. Moab would be destroyed as described (Jeremiah, c. 620 B.C., Jeremiah 48:1-47).

    Fulfillment: History, in 585 B.C., by the Babylonians.

30. Ammon would be destroyed (Jeremiah, c. 620 B.C., Jeremiah 49:1-6).

    Fulfillment: History.

31. Edom would be destroyed (Jeremiah, c. 620 B.C., Jeremiah 49:7-22).

    Fulfillment: History, about 550 B.C.

32. Damascus would be destroyed by fire (Jeremiah, c. 620 B.C., Jeremiah 49:23-27).

    Fulfillment: Many times in history.

33. Kedar and Hazor would be destroyed (Jeremiah, c. 620 B.C., Jeremiah 49:28-33).

    Fulfillment: History—the Babylonian invasion.

34. Jerusalem falls and captivity begins (Jeremiah, c. 620 B.C., Jeremiah 52:1-31).

    Fulfillment: History, 586 B.C.

35. Israel would be destroyed and their property taken from them (c. 590 B.C., Ezekiel 7:1-27).

    Fulfillment: 2 Chronicles 36:11-15.

36. Israel would be restored to its land (c. 590 B.C., Ezekiel 11: 16-25.

    Fulfillment: History, in 537 B.C.

37. Jerusalem portrayed as an "unfaithful wife" who would be subject to judgment (c. 590 B.C., Ezekiel 16:1-63).

    Fulfillment: 2 Chronicles 36:11-15.

38. Jerusalem would be enticed by Egypt, conquered by Babylonians, and ultimately destroyed (c. 590 B.C., Ezekiel 17:1-24).

    Fulfillment: 2 Kings 24:17–25:10; 2 Chronicles 36:11-15.

39. Israel would be judged through a defeat at the hands of Babylon (c. 590 B.C., Ezekiel 21:1-27).

    Fulfillment: 2 Chronicles 36:11-15.

40. Ammon would fall by sin (c. 590 B.C., Ezekiel 21:28-32).

    Fulfillment: History.

41. Samaria and Jerusalem depicted as two "sinful sisters" being judged for sin (c. 590 B.C., Ezekiel 23:1-48).

    Fulfillment: History—conquest by the Assyrians and Babylonians.

42. There would be no time for mourning when many in Israel were killed (c. 590 B.C., Ezekiel 24:15-27).

    Fulfillment: 2 Chronicles 36:11-20.

43. Ammon would be destroyed (c. 590 B.C., Ezekiel 25:1-7).

    Fulfillment: The race disappeared from history.

44. Moab would be destroyed (c. 590 B.C., Ezekiel 25:8-11).

    Fulfillment: The race disappeared from history.

45. Edom would be destroyed (c. 590 B.C., Ezekiel 25:12-14).

    Fulfillment: The race disappeared from history.

46. The Philistines would be judged by God (c. 590 B.C., Ezekiel 25:15-17).

    Fulfillment: The race disappeared from history.

47. Destruction of Egypt (Ezekiel 31:1-18).

    Fulfillment: History—in 663 B.C. and 571 B.C., when Egypt was invaded by the Babylonians.

48. Another prophecy against Edom (c. 590 B.C., Ezekiel 35:1-15).

    Fulfillment: The race disappeared from history.

49. The impending doom of Israel (c. 830 B.C., Joel 2:1-11).

    Fulfillment: Assyria started devastation of the land beginning about 722 B.C.

50. Tyre and Sidon would be judged for selling the children of Israel as slaves to the Greeks; their children in turn would be sold to the people of Judah (c. 830 B.C., Joel 3:4-8).

    Fulfillment: History—Alexander the Great's conquest, 326–323 B.C.

51. Israel would again enjoy abundant food and water (c. 830 B.C., Joel 3:16-21).

    Fulfillment: History, following the first exile; and again, following the second exile—today.

52. Destruction of Damascus, Gaza, Tyre, Edom, Ammon, and Moab (c. 760 B.C., Amos 1:1–2:5).

    Fulfillment: History—under the Assyrians, Babylonians, Medo-Persians, and Greeks.

53. Judgment of Israel for specific sins (c. 760 B.C., Amos 5:1-27).

    Fulfillment: 722 B.C.—Assyrian captivity; and 587–586 B.C.—Babylonian captivity.

54. Judgment of Israel for complacent and luxurious living (c. 760 B.C., Amos 6:1-14).

Fulfillment: 722 B.C.—Assyrian captivity; and 587–586 B.C.—Babylonian captivity.

55. Judgment of Israel—enemies would "strip the land clean" and Israel's sons and daughters would die by the sword (c. 760 B.C., Amos 7:1-17).

    Fulfillment: 722 B.C.—Assyrian captivity; and 587–586 B.C.—Babylonian captivity.

56. Israel ripe for judgment—like a basket of ripe figs (c. 760 B.C., Amos 8:1-14).

    Fulfillment: 722 B.C.—Assyrian captivity; and 587–586 B.C.—Babylonian captivity.

57. Prophecy that Israel would never be uprooted from its land after returning from exile (Amos 9:14-15).

    Fulfillment: History, since 1948—against all odds, the nation of Israel has survived repeated attacks.

58. Edom would be destroyed (c. 650 B.C., Obadiah 1:1-21).

    Fulfillment: History—by invading Arabs.

59. The city of Nineveh would be destroyed (c. 785 B.C., Jonah 1:1).

    Fulfillment: In 612 B.C., when conquered by the Medes and Scythians.

60. The destruction of Israel (c. 740 B.C., Micah 1:2–3:12).

    Fulfillment: 722 B.C.—Assyrian captivity; and 587–586 B.C.—Babylonian captivity.

61. Israel would be regathered (c. 740 B.C., Micah 2:12).

    Fulfillment: Both in 538–537 B.C. after the first exile and in 1948 after the second exile.

62. Babylonian captivity for Israel (c. 740 B.C., Micah 4:9-13).

    Fulfillment: In 587–586 B.C. under Nebuchadnezzar.

63. Judgment of Nineveh (c. 660 B.C., Nahum 1:1-14).

    Fulfillment: The conquest of Nineveh by the Medes and Scythians in 612 B.C.

64. Nineveh's destruction would be complete (c. 660 B.C., Nahum 3:1-19).

    Fulfillment: The conquest of Nineveh by the Medes and Scythians in 612 B.C. was destructive to the point that the city remained hidden under the sand for centuries until discovered by archaeologists in 1845.

65. Babylon would conquer the land of Israel (c. 610 B.C., Habakkuk 1:1-11).

    Fulfillment: The conquest by Babylon in 605–586 B.C.

66. Judgment of Babylon after the conquest (c. 610 B.C., Habakkuk 2:4-17).

    Fulfillment: Babylon's conquest by the Medo-Persian Empire.

67. The coming judgment upon Judah (c. 625 B.C., Zephaniah 1:2-18).

    Fulfillment: The conquest of Judah by Babylon in 587–586 B.C.

68. The invading nations would later be judged (c. 625 B.C., Zephaniah 2:1-15).

    Fulfillment: The conquest of Babylon by the Medo-Persians.

69. Joshua was promised a chance to enter the Promised Land, with God's blessing (Moses, c. 1450 B.C., Deuteronomy 31:23).

    Fulfillment: c. 1406-1375 B.C., Joshua 21:43-45.

70. A curse would come upon the one who would rebuild Jericho (c. 620 B.C., Joshua 6:26).

    Fulfillment: c. 874 B.C., 1 Kings 16:34.

71. Bodies of the pagan priests of "high places" would be burned on an altar (c. 970 B.C., 1 Kings 13:1-3).

    Fulfillment: c. 640 B.C., 2 Kings 23:15-16.

72. Jezebel would be eaten by dogs (c. 870 B.C., 1 Kings 21:23).

    Fulfillment: c. 840 B.C., 2 Kings 9:30-37.

73. Hezekiah would be delivered from a siege by Sennacherib (c. 735 B.C., Isaiah 37:21-35).

    Fulfillment: c. 700 B.C., 2 Kings 19:35-37.

74. Those who plotted to kill Jeremiah would die (c. 620 B.C., Jeremiah 11:18-23).

    Fulfillment: 2 Chronicles 36:15-21.

75. King Zedekiah would die and others would not receive pity (c. 620 B.C., Jeremiah 21:1-7).

    Fulfillment: 2 Chronicles 36:15-21.

76. King Jehoiachin (also called "Coniah") cursed as "childless" regarding an heir to the throne (c. 620 B.C., Jeremiah 22:24-30).

    Fulfillment: None of Jehoiachin's descendants became king of Israel. (Jehoiachin's legal heir, Jesus, was not his physical descendant, since Jesus had been conceived in Mary by the Holy Spirit.)

77. Shemaiah (a false prophet) would be punished (c. 620 B.C., Jeremiah 29:24-32).

    Fulfillment: 2 Chronicles 36:11-15.

78. Jehoiakim's descendants would not have the throne of David (c. 620 B.C., Jeremiah 36:27-31).

    Fulfillment: 2 Chronicles 36:11-21.

79. False prophets would be destroyed (c. 590 B.C., Ezekiel 13:1-23).

    Fulfillment: 2 Chronicles 36:11-15.

80. Idolaters to be judged (c. 590 B.C., Ezekiel 14:1-23).

    Fulfillment: 2 Chronicles 36:11-15.

Notes

Chapter 1—Observational Evidence of Creation

1. David Rosevear, "The Myth of Chemical Evolution," *Impact*, July 1999, p. iv; as cited in Richard A. Swenson, *More Than Meets the Eye* (Colorado Springs, CO: NavPress, 2000), p. 188.
2. Gerald L. Schroeder, *The Hidden Face of God* (New York: The Free Press, 2001), p. 189.
3. *Earth Science*, California ed. (Woodland Hills, CA: Glencoe/McGraw-Hill, 2001), pp. 383, 391, 395.
4. Robert Wright, "Science and the Original Sin," *Time* magazine, October 26, 1996, p. 76.
5. As cited in Jonathan Wells, *Icons of Evolution: Science or Myth?* (Washington, DC: Regnery Publishing, Inc., 2000), pp. 81-109.

Chapter 2—Analyzing the Fossil Record

1. William A. Shear, "Millipedes," *American Scientist*, vol. 87 (May/June 1999), p. 234.
2. National Park Service, Geologic Resources Division, "Geology Fieldnotes, Florissant Fossil Beds National Monument, Colorado," www.aqd.nps.gov/grd/parks/fifo/ accessed on 11/21/01.
3. Andrew Bridges, "Rare Fossilized Jellyfish Found," January 25, 2002, http://dailynews.yahoo.com/h/ap/20020125/sc/fossiljellyfish1.html, accessed on 1/28/02.
4. Charles Darwin, *On the Origin of Species* (Cambridge, MA: Harvard University Press, 2000), p. 95.
5. Darwin, p. 171.
6. Darwin, p. 172.
7. The Brown University News Bureau, February 25, 1999, http://brown.edu/Administration/NewsBureau/1998-99/98-077.html, accessed on 12/17/01.
8. Mark Ridley, *New Scientist* 90:830 (1981); as cited in Duane T. Gish, PhD, *Creation Scientists Answer Their Critics* (El Cajon, CA: Institute for Creation Research, 1993), p. 113.
9. T.N. George, *Science Progress* 48:1 (1960); as cited in Gish, *Creation Scientists*, p. 113.
10. Michael Denton, *Evolution: A Theory in Crisis* (Chevy Chase, MD: Adler & Adler, 1997).
11. G.G. Simpson, *Tempo and Mode in Evolution* (New York: Columbia University Press, 1944), p. 105; as cited in Duane T. Gish, *Evolution: The Fossils Still Say No!* (El Cajon, CA: Institute for Creation Research, 1995), p. 334.
12. Simpson, p. 107; as cited in Gish, *Evolution*, p. 334.

13. Jeffrey H. Schwartz, *Sudden Origins* (Hoboken, NJ: John Wiley & Sons, 1999), p. 89; as cited in Genesis Park: "Dinosaurs: Living Evidence of a Powerful Creator (www.genesispark.org), Genesis Park Exhibit Hall, "Room 3—The Story of the Fossils," www.genesispark.org/genpark/gaps/gaps.htm. Used by permission.

14. David B. Kitts, "Paleontology and Evolutionary Theory," *Evolution*, vol. 28, 1974, p. 467; as cited in Genesis Park. Used by permission.

15. Cited in David Raup, "Geology," *New Scientist*, vol. 90 (1981), p. 832; as cited in Genesis Park. Used by permission.

16. Niles Eldredge, *The Myths of Human Evolution* (New York: Columbia University Press, 1982), p. 59; as cited in Genesis Park. Used by permission.

17. Stephen J. Gould, "Is a New and General Theory of Evolution Emerging?" *Paleobiology*, vol. 6 (1980), p. 40; as cited in Genesis Park. Used by permission.

18. Donald Lindsay, "Speciation by Punctuated Equilibrium," University of Colorado Computer Science Department Web site, www.cs.colorado.edu/~lindsay/creation/punk_eek.html.

19. Steven M. Stanley, *The New Evolutionary Timetable: Fossils, Genes, and the Origin of Species* (New York: Basic Books, 1981), p. 99; as cited in Genesis Park.

20. Donald R. Prothero, PhD, "Punctuated Equilibrium at Twenty: A Paleontological Perspective," *Skeptic*, vol. 1, no. 3 (Fall 1992), pp. 38-47.

21. Gareth Cook, the *Boston Globe;* as reported in the *Orange County* (California) *Register,* July 11, 2002, p. 1.

22. Cook.

Chapter 3—Using Science as Powerful Evidence of God

1. Dr. Hugh Ross, "Responses to Young Earth Universe 'Answers,'" as cited on www.reasons.org/resources/apologetics/younguniverse.shtml?main.

2. J. P. Moreland, *The Age of the Earth,* a lecture given to Northshore Church in Everett, WA, on February 2, 2002; as cited by www.reasons.org/resources/apologetics/moreland_jp_age_of_earth.shtml?main.

3. Hugh Ross, *A Matter of Days* (Colorado Springs, CO: NavPress, 2004), pp. 30-32.

4. J. H. Taylor in *Ancient Christian Writers,* (Newman Press, 1982), vol. 41, as cited at http://www.pibburns.com/augustin.htm.

5. www.thinkexist.com/english/Author/x/Author_4145_1.htm.

Chapter 4—Creation, Science, and the Bible

1. *The Columbia Electronic Encyclopedia.* Copyright © 1994, 2000, Columbia University Press.

2. *The Columbia Electronic Encyclopedia.*

3. As cited in Hugh Ross, *The Creator and the Cosmos* (Colorado Springs, CO: NavPress, 2001) p. 31.

4. "U.S. Scientists Find a 'Holy Grail': Ripples at Edge of the Universe," London *International Herald Tribune,* April 24, 1992, p. 1; as cited in Ross, *The Creator and the Cosmos,* p. 31.

5. As cited in Ross, *The Creator and the Cosmos,* p. 31.

6. Ross, *The Creator and the Cosmos,* p. 57.

7. P. Jokeosen, et al., "Detection of Intergalactic Ionized Helium Absorption in a High-Redshift Quasar," *Nature*, vol. 370 (1994), pp. 35-39; and Yuri I. Izotov et al., "Helium Abundance in the Most Metal-Deficient Blue Compact Galaxies: I Zw 18 and SBS 0335-052," *Astrophysical Journal*, vol. 527 (1999), pp. 757-77; both as cited in Ross, *The Creator and the Cosmos*, p. 57.

8. Hugh Ross, PhD, interview, September 7, 2001, at Reasons to Believe, Pasadena, CA.

9. Hugh Ross, *The Fingerprint of God*, 2nd ed. (Orange, CA: Promise Publishing, 1991), pp. 45-47; as cited in Hugh Ross, "Another Success for General Relativity," Reasons to Believe Web site, www.reasons.org/resources/apologetics/success.html.

10. Roger Penrose, *Shadows of the Mind* (New York: Oxford University Press, 1994), p. 230; as cited in Hugh Ross, *Beyond the Cosmos* (Colorado Springs, CO: NavPress, 1996), pp. 22-23; as cited in Ross, "Another Success for General Relativity."

11. Lawrence M. Krauss, "The End of the Age Problem and the Case for a Cosmological Constant Revisited," *Astrophysical Journal*, vol. 501 (1998), p. 461; as cited in Ross, *The Creator and the Cosmos*, p. 45.

Chapter 5—The Complexity of Living Things

1. *World Book Encyclopedia*, vol. 3 (Chicago: World Book, Inc., 1988), p. 328.

2. Dr. Lee Spetner, *Not by Chance* (Brooklyn, NY: The Judaica Press, Inc., 1998), p. 30.

3. Mahlon Hoagland and Bert Dodson, *The Way Life Works* (New York: Three Rivers Press, 1998), p. 15.

4. Gerald L. Schroeder, *The Hidden Face of God* (New York: The Free Press, 2001), p. 189.

5. Richard A. Swenson, *More Than Meets the Eye: Fascinating Glimpses of God's Power and Design* (Colorado Springs, CO: NavPress, 2000), p. 20. © 2000. Used by permission of NavPress—www.navpress.com. All rights reserved.

6. Swenson, pp. 17-18. Used by permission—see note 5.

7. John R. Cameron, James G. Skofronick, and Roderick M. Grant, *Physics of the Body* (Madison, WI: Medical Physics Publishing, 199), p. 38; as cited in Swenson, p. 188. Used by permission—see note 5.

8. David Rosevear, "The Myth of Chemical Evolution," *Impact*, July 1999, p. iv; as cited in Swenson, p. 188. Used by permission—see note 5.

9. Rosevear, p. iv; as cited in Swenson, p. 188. Used by permission—see note 5.

10. Mark Caldwell, "The Clock in the Cell," *Discover*, October 1998, p. 36; as cited in Swenson, p. 188. Used by permission—see note 5.

11. Swenson, p. 21. Used by permission—see note 5.

12. Spetner, p. 30.

13. Swenson, p. 65.

14. Swenson, p. 63.

15. Schroeder, p. 189.

16. John K. Stevens, "Reverse Engineering the Brain," *Byte*, April 1985, pp. 287-99; as cited in Swenson, p. 34. Used by permission—see note 5.

17. This and previous bullet points from Swenson, pp. 23,24,26,28,29,30,32,33. Used by permission—see note 5.

18. This and other bullet points after note 17 from Swenson, pp. 34,36,37,38, 39,40. Used by permission—see note 5.

Chapter 6—Calculating the Impossibility of the Random Origin of Life

1. Mahlon Hoagland and Bert Dodson, *The Way Life Works* (New York: Three Rivers Press, 1998), p. 88.

2. While there are a few ways in which a small increase in proportion of chiral molecules has been observed, none have been shown to adequately come close to solving the chirality problem—and all are fraught with other problems. See Fazale Rana and Hugh Ross, *Origins of Life* (Colorado Springs, CO: NavPress, 2004), chapter 9.

3. Christian de Duve, "Clues from Present-Day Biology in the Thioester World," *The Molecular Origins of Life*, André Brack, ed. (Cambridge, UK: The Cambridge University Press, 1998), p. 222.

4. Alan W. Schwartz, "Origins of the RNA World," Brack, ed., p. 247.

5. J. Cohen, "Getting All Turned Around over the Origins of Life on Earth," *Science*, vol. 267 (1995), pp. 1265-66; as cited in Jonathan Sarfati, "Origin of Life: the Chirality Problem," Answers in Genesis Web site (www.answersingenesis.org).

6. University of California at Davis Web site (www.ucdavis.edu).

7. "Lugodoc's Theory of the Origin of Life on Earth—or the Artificial Origin of DNA," www.lugodoc.demon.co.uk/lugodoc/rant02.htm.

8. "Lugodoc's Theory."

9. R.F. Service, "Chemistry: Does Life's Handedness Come from Within?" *Science*, vol. 286 (1999), pp. 1282-1283.

10. Marcel P. Schutzenberger, "Algorithms and the New Darwinian Theory of Evolution," as cited in John Ankerberg and John Weldon, "Rational Inquiry and the Force of Scientific Data: Are New Horizons Emerging?" *The Creation Hypothesis: Scientific Evidence for an Intelligent Designer,* J.P. Moreland, ed. (Downers Grove, IL: InterVarsity, 1994), p. 274; as cited in Richard A. Swenson, M.D., *More Than Meets the Eye—Fascinating Glimpses of God's Power and Design* (Colorado Springs, CO: NavPress, 2000), p. 69.

11. Harold Morowitz, as cited in Hugh Ross, *The Creator and the Cosmos: How the Greatest Scientific Discoveries of the Century Reveal God* (Colorado Springs, CO: NavPress, 1995), p. 149.

12. Edward Argyle, "Chance and Origin of Life," *Extraterrestrials—Where are They?* Ben Zuckerman and Michael H. Hart, eds. (Cambridge, England: Cambridge University Press, 1995), p. 131; as cited in Fred Heeren, *Show Me God: What the Message from Space Is Telling Us About God* (Wheeling, IL: Day Star Publications, 1998), p. 61.

13. John Horgan, as quoted in Gerald L. Schroeder, *The Science of God: The Convergence of Scientific and Biblical Wisdom* (New York: Broadway Books, 1997), p. 142; as cited in Swenson, p. 70.

14. Fred Hoyle and Chandra Wickramasinghe, *Evolution from Space* (London: J.M. Dent and Sons, 1981), p. 24; as cited in Heeren.

15. David Foster, as quoted in Heeren, p. 68; as cited in Swenson, pp. 70-71.

16. Hoyle and Wickramasinghe, p. 148; as cited in Heeren.

17. Schroeder, p. 93; as cited in Swenson, p. 71, emphasis added.

18. Carl Sagan and Francis Crick, as quoted in Ankerberg and Weldon, in J.P. Moreland, ed., p. 272; as cited in Swenson, pp. 70-71.

19. Stephen C. Meyer, "The Message in the Microcosm: DNA and the Death of Materialism," *Cosmic Pursuit*, Fall 1997, pp. 41-42; as cited in Swenson, p. 72, emphasis added.

20. Ralph O. Muncaster, *Dismantling Evolution* (Eugene, OR: Harvest House Publishers, 2003), pp. 139-142.

Chapter 7—Mutations: A Faulty Mechanism for Evolution

1. Stephen C. Meyer, "The Message from the Microcosm: DNA and the Death of Materialism," *Cosmic Pursuit*, Fall 1977, pp. 41-42; as cited in Richard A. Swenson, *More than Meets the Eye* (Colorado Springs, CO: NavPress, 2000), p. 72.

2. *Science Daily*, Web posting of the University of Texas at Austin, 1/10/2002.

3. John Maynard Smith and Eors Szathmary, *The Origins of Life* (New York: The Oxford University Press, Inc., 2000), p. 1.

4. Mahlon Hoagland and Bert Dodson, *The Way Life Works* (New York: Three Rivers Press, 1998), p. 79.

5. Francisco J. Ayala, "The Mechanisms of Evolution," in *But Is It Science?* Michael Ruse, ed. (Amherst, NY: Prometheus Books, 1996), p. 135.

6. *World Book Encyclopedia*, vol. 13 (Chicago: World Book, Inc., 1987), p. 973.

7. Maynard Smith and Szathmary, p. 1.

8. Hoagland and Dodson, p. 79.

9. Ayala, in Ruse, ed., p. 129.

10. *World Book,* p. 973.

11. Fred Hoyle, *The Mathematics of Evolution* (Memphis, TN: Acorn Press, 1999), p. 98.

12. Hoyle, pp. 135-136.

13. Hoyle, p. 105.

14. As cited in Dr. Lee Spetner, *Not By Chance: Shattering the Modern Theory of Evolution* (Brooklyn, NY: The Judaica Press, Inc., 1998), p. 54. Used by permission of Judaica Press, Inc., www.judaicapress.com.

15. T.K. Gartner and E. Orias, University of Santa Barbara, 1966; in Spetner, p. 131. Used by permission.

16. Spetner, pp. 139-41. Used by permission.

17. Spetner, p. 143. Used by permission.

18. Spetner, p. 146. Used by permission.

19. Spetner, p. 148. Used by permission.

20. Spetner, p. 150. The references are to Lerner et al., 1964; Wu et al., 1968; Rigby et al., 1974; Burleigh et al., 1974; Inderlied and Morlock, 1977; Thompson and Krawiec, 1983. Used by permission.

21. Spetner, pp. 94-103. Used by permission.

22. Fersht, 1981; Drake, 1969, 1991; as cited in Spetner, pp. 39,92. Used by permission.

23. Stebbins, 1966; as cited in Spetner, p. 97. Used by permission.

24. As cited in Spetner, p. 102. Used by permission.

25. Spetner, p. 103. Used by permission.

Chapter 8—Irreducible Complexity: A Major Transitional Problem

1. Michael Behe, *Darwin's Black Box* (New York: The Free Press, 1996), p. 39. © 1996 by Michael J. Behe. By permission of The Free Press, a Division of Simon & Schuster Adult Publishing Group.

2. Frances Hitching, *The Neck of the Giraffe* (London: Pan, 1982), p. 68; as cited in Behe, p. 37. © 1996 by Michael J. Behe. By permission of The Free Press, a Division of Simon & Schuster Adult Publishing Group.

3. Richard Dawkins, *The Blind Watchmaker* (London: W.W. Norton, 1985), p. 81.

4. Behe, pp. 18-20. © 1996 by Michael J. Behe. By permission of The Free Press, a Division of Simon & Schuster Adult Publishing Group.

Part 2—Evidence of the Reliability of the Bible

1. Samuel Davidson, *The Hebrew Text of the Old Testament* (London: 1856), p. 89; as quoted in Norman L. Geisler and William E. Nix, *General Introduction to the Bible* (Chicago: Moody Press, 1986).

Chapter 9—The Bible Is Scientifically Accurate

1. Josh McDowell and Bill Wilson, *A Ready Defense* (San Bernardino, CA: Here's Life Publishers, Inc., 1990).

Chapter 10—The Structure of the Bible

1. Merrill F. Unger, *The New Unger Bible Handbook* (Chicago: Moody Press, 1984), p. 362.

Chapter 11—The Dead Sea Scrolls, the Septuagint, and Their Validation by Jesus

1. Josh McDowell, *The New Evidence That Demands a Verdict* (Nashville: Thomas Nelson Publisher, 1999), p. 80.

2. McDowell, p. 78.

Chapter 12—The New Testament Manuscript Explosion

1. Norman L. Geisler and William E. Nix, *A General Introduction to the Bible* (Chicago: Moody Press, 1980), p. 361.

2. Lee Strobel, *The Case for Christ* (Grand Rapids, MI: Zondervan Publishing House, 1998), pp. 62-63.

3. Josh McDowell, *The New Evidence That Demands a Verdict* (Nashville: Thomas Nelson Publishers, 1999), p. 38.

4. Strobel, *Case for Christ*, p. 64.

5. Geisler and Nix, p. 361.

6. Josh McDowell and Bill Wilson, *A Ready Defense* (San Bernardino, CA: Here's Life Publishers, Inc., 1990).

7. See http://www.geocities.com/worldview_3/reliabletext.html.

8. F.F. Bruce, *The Canon of Scripture* (Downers Grove, IL: InterVarsity Press, 1988).

9. Based on Bruce M. Metzger, *The Text of the New Testament* (New York and Oxford: Oxford University Press, 1968), pp. 43,44; as cited by Josh McDowell, *Evidence that Demands a Verdict*, vol. I (Nashville, TN: Thomas Nelson, 1976), pp. 47-48.

Chapter 13—Non-Christian Documents About Jesus

1. www.sacred-texts.com/chr/thomas.htm.

2. See www.facingthechallenge.org/talmud.htm, July 2003.

3. See http://members.aol.com/FLJOSEPHUS/life.htm, maintained by independent scholar G.J. Goldberg, July 2003.

4. See www.uncc.edu/jdtabor/josephus-jesus.html, July 2003.

5. See http://www.tektonics.org/tekton_01_01_01_TC.html, July 2003.

6. See http://library.thinkquest.org/11402/bio_pliny_young.html.

7. See www.pbs.org/wgbh/pages/frontline/shows/religion/maps/primary/pliny.html, July 2003. Brackets in original.

8. Suetonius, *Life of the Emperor Claudius,* chapter 25 (excerpt), from www.biblehistory.com/nero/NEROSuetonius_on_the_Christians.htm, July 2003.

9. Suetonius.

10. See www.christianstudycenter.com/refs/bios/phlegorphil.htm, July 2003.

11. See www.neverthirsty.org/pp/hist/phlegon.html, July 2003.

12. www.neverthirsty.org.

13. www.tektonics.org/tekton_01_01_01_LUC.html.

14. www.tektonics.org/tekton_01_01_01_LUC.html.

15. www.tektonics.org/tekton_01_01_01_LUC.html.

16. Lucian, "The Death of Peregrine," 11-13, in *The Works of Lucian of Samosata,* tr. H.W. Dowler and F.G. Fowler (Oxford: Clarendon, 1949), vol. 4; cited in Habermas, *The Historical Jesus,* p. 206.

17. John McRay, *Archaeology of the New Testament* (Grand Rapids, MI: Baker Book House, 1991), p. 214.

18. www.westarkchurchofchrist.org/library/extrabiblical.htm.

Chapter 14—The Early Church Fathers Confirm the Bible

1. Bruce M. Metzger, *The Text of the New Testament: Its Transmission, Corruption and Restoration* (New York: Oxford University Press, 1968), p. 86.

2. www.creeds.net/ancient/apostles.htm.

3. See www.bible-researcher.com/canon3.html, July 2003.

Chapter 15—Archaeological Evidence of the Old Testament

1. Joseph P. Free and Howard F. Vos, *Archaeology and Bible History* (Grand Rapids, MI: Zondervan Publishing House, 1992) pp. 108-109.

2. Free and Vos, p. 37.

3. Free and Vos, p. 51.

4. Free and Vos, pp. 56-57.

5. Free and Vos, p. 55.

6. Free and Vos, pp. 59-60.

7. Free and Vos, pp. 126-127.

8. John McRay, *Archaeology and the New Testament* (Grand Rapids, MI: Baker Book House, 1991).

9. Free and Vos, p. 100.

10. James B. Pritchard, ed., *The Harper Atlas of the Bible* (Toronto, Canada: Harper and Row, 1987), p. 27; Free and Vos, p. 47.

11. Free and Vos, p. 104.

12. Free and Vos, p. 116; Pritchard, ed. pp. 46, 47.

13. *Orange County* (California) *Register,* August 6, 1993.

14. Free and Vos, p. 189.

15. https://listhost.uchicago.edu/pipermail/ane/2003-March/007302.html.

Chapter 16—Archaeological Evidence of the New Testament

1. Jack Finegan, *The Archeology of the New Testament* (Princeton, NJ: Princeton University Press), 1992.
2. Finegan.

Chapter 18—Why Prophecy Is a Reliable Test

1. Jeane Dixon, *Parade* magazine, May 13, 1956; as cited by Josh McDowell, *A Ready Defense* (San Bernardino, CA: Here's Life Publishers, 1990), p. 387.
2. www.fingerprintamerica.com/fingerprintHistory.asp.

Chapter 22—Old Testament Prophecy Completely Describes the Messiah

1. Flavius Josephus, "Antiquities of the Jews," VIII, sections 1-5, tr. William Whiston, *The Complete Works of Josephus* (Grand Rapids, MI: Kregel Publications, 1981), p. 375.
2. Anderson calculated the Messiah's year of arrival as A.D. 32, Hoehner as the year 33. Either may be right, since the ancient dates are based on the reigns of kings, which carries a degree of uncertainty in virtually all cases. However, both scholars agree on the exact length of the time period between Artaxerxes' decree and the Messiah's arrival.
3. Harold W. Hoehner, *Chronological Aspects of the Life of Christ* (Grand Rapids, MI: The Zondervan Corporation, 1977), p. 138.

Chapter 23—Statistical Prophecy Proof of Jesus Compared to Others

1. www.geocities.com/worldview_3/quranvbible.html.

Chapter 25—The Empty Tomb

1. Josh McDowell, *The Resurrection Factor* (San Bernardino, CA: Here's Life Publishers, Inc., 1989), pp. 56-57.
2. Josh McDowell and Bill Wilson, *A Ready Defense* (San Bernardino, CA: Here's Life Publishers, 1990), p. 226.

Chapter 26—The Martyrdom of the Apostles

1. Some material in this chapter is drawn from John Foxe, *The New Foxe's Book of Martyrs* (North Brunswick, NJ: Bridge-Logos Publishers, 1997), pp. 5-10.

Chapter 27—Witnesses at the Time of Jesus

1. Quoting from Richard J. Bauckham, "All in the Family: Identifying Jesus' Relatives," *Bible Review*, April 2000, www.rockinauburn.com/columns/jesus_siblings.htm.
2. See http://cbn.org/bibleresources/theology/eusebius/churchhistory/eusebius-b3-33.asp.
3. Flavius Josephus, *The Complete Works of Josephus* (Grand Rapids, MI: Kregel Publications, 1981), p. 423.
4. See Eusebius, "Ecclesiastical History," 2.23; and www.thenazareneway.com/ossuary_of_james.htm, July 2003.

Chapter 28—The Early Christian Martyrs and the Christian Church

1. Flavius Josephus, *The Complete Works of Josephus* (Grand Rapids, MI: Kregel Publications, 1981), p. 423.
2. Josephus, p. 14.

Chapter 30—The Trinity

1. J.B. Heard, "The Tripartite Nature of Man", R.E. Brennan, "History of Psychology from the Standpoint of a Thomist; D.E. Roberts, "Psychotherapy and a Christian View of Man"; W.M. Horton, "A Psychological Approach to Theology"; as cited in Walter A. Elwell, ed., *Evangelical Dictionary of Theology* (Grand Rapids, MI: Baker Book House Co., 1984.), p. 1112.
2. Spiros Zodhiates, *The Complete Word Study of the Old Testament* (Chattanooga, TN: AMG Publishers, 1994).
3. Norman L. Geisler, *Baker Encyclopedia of Christian Apologetics* (Grand Rapids, MI: Baker Book House, 1999), p. 733.

Chapter 31—How to Analyze Alleged Contradictions in the Bible

1. Walter A. Elwell, ed., *Evangelical Dictionary of Theology* (Grand Rapids, MI: Baker Book House Co., 1984).
2. Joseph L. Gardner, ed., *Reader's Digest Who's Who in the Bible* (Pleasantville, NY: Reader's Digest Association, Inc. 1994).
3. Elwell, p. 464; Ronald F. Youngblood, *New Illustrated Bible Dictionary* (Nashville, TN: Nelson, 1995), p. 879.
4. Norman L. Geisler and Thomas Howe, *When Critics Ask* (Grand Rapids, MI: Baker Book House, 1992), p. 325.
5. Geisler and Howe, p. 385.
6. Gleason L. Archer, *Encyclopedia of Bible Difficulties* (Grand Rapids, MI: Zondervan Publishing House, 1982), p. 316.

Chapter 32—Review of Specific Alleged Contradictions

1. Norman L. Geisler and Thomas Howe, *When Critics Ask* (Grand Rapids, MI: Baker Book House, 1992), pp. 328-329.
2. Geisler and Howe, p. 354.
3. John McRay, *Archaeology and the New Testament* (Grand Rapids, MI: Baker Book House, 1991), p. 17.
4. Geisler and Howe, pp. 352-353.
5. Geisler and Howe, pp. 343-344.
6. Gleason L. Archer, *Encyclopedia of Bible Difficulties* (Grand Rapids, MI: Zondervan Publishing House, 1982).
7. Harold W. Hoehner, *Chronological Aspects of the Life of Christ* (Grand Rapids, MI: Zondervan Publishing House, 1977).
8. Hoehner.
9. F. LaGard Smith, *The Daily Bible in Chronological Order* (Eugene, OR: Harvest House), 1984, pp. 1478-1479.

Chapter 33—How Is Jesus Different from Other Religious Leaders?

1. Jay Smith, "Who Is the True Jesus?" debate presented by the Master of Arts Program in Christian Apologetics at Biola University in La Mirada, CA, on October 23, 2000.

Bibliography

General Reference

Archer, Gleason L. *Encyclopedia of Bible Difficulties.* Grand Rapids, MI: Zondervan Publishing House, 1982.

———. *A Survey of Old Testament Introduction,* rev. ed. Chicago: Moody Press, 1994.

Elwell, Walter A., ed. *Evangelical Dictionary of Theology.* Grand Rapids, MI: Baker Book House, 1984.

Geisler, Norman L. *Baker Encyclopedia of Christian Apologetics.* Grand Rapids, MI: Baker Books, 1999.

———. *A Popular Survey of the Old Testament.* Grand Rapids, MI: Baker Book House, 1977.

———. *Systematic Theology,* 2 vols. Minneapolis, MN: Bethany House, 2002 and 2003.

Geisler, Norman L., and Ron Brooks. *When Skeptics Ask: A Handbook on Christian Evidences.* Grand Rapids, MI: Baker Books, 1990.

Geisler, Norman L., and Thomas Howe. *When Critics Ask.* Grand Rapids, MI: Baker Books, 1992.

Geisler, Norman L., and William Nix. *A General Introduction to the Bible.* rev. ed. Chicago: Moody Press, 1986.

Glynn, Patrick. *God: the Evidence—The Reconciliation of Faith and Reason in the Postmodern World.* Rocklin, CA: Prima Publishing, 1999.

Hoehner, Harold W. *Chronological Aspects of the Life of Christ.* Grand Rapids, MI: The Zondervan Corporation, 1977.

Keller, Werner. *The Bible as History,* 2nd ed. New York: Barnes and Noble Books, 1995.

Moreland, J.P., and Kai Nielsen. *Does God Exist?: The Debate Between Theists and Atheists.* Amherst, NY: Prometheus Books, 1993.

Payne, Barton. *Encyclopedia of Biblical Prophecy.* London: Hodder & Stoughton, 1973.

Smith, F. LaGard, commentator. *The Daily Bible.* Eugene, OR: Harvest House Publishers, 1984.

Stoner, Peter. *Science Speaks.* Wheaton, IL: Van Kampen, 1952.

Strobel, Lee, *The Case for Christ.* Grand Rapids, MI: Zondervan Publishing House, 1998.

Youngblood, Ronald F., Herbert Lockyer Sr., F.F. Bruce, and R.K. Harrison, eds. *Nelson's New Illustrated Bible Dictionary.* Nashville, TN: Thomas Nelson Publishers, 1995.

Zodhiates, Spiros, ed. *The Complete Word Study New Testament, King James Version.* Chattanooga, TN: AMG International, Inc., 1991.

Zodhiates, Spiros, and Warren Baker, eds. *The Complete Word Study Old Testament, King James Version.* Chattanooga, TN: AMG International, Inc., 1994.

Creation Versus Evolution and Analytical Evaluation

Alcamo, I. Edward. *Schaum's Outline of Microbiology.* Blacklick, OH: McGraw-Hill, 1998.

Behe, Michael J. *Darwin's Black Box: The Biochemical Challenge to Evolution.* New York, NY: The Free Press, 1996.

Brouwer, Sigmund. *The Unrandom Universe.* Eugene, OR: Harvest House Publishers, 2002.

Darwin, Charles. *On the Origin of Species.* Cambridge, MA: Harvard University Press, 1964. This is the classic book introducing evolution. Obviously the author does not support its points of view.

Dawkins, Richard. *The Blind Watchmaker: Why the Evidence of Evolution Reveals a Universe Without Design.* New York: W.W. Norton, 1996. This book is written by one of the most outspoken modern-day evolutionists. Many conclusions are drawn with no support to back them. The author discourages reading it except as an example of presupposition and typical theoretical claims without hard evidence.

Dembski, William A., ed. *Mere Creation.* Downers Grove, IL: InterVarsity Press, 1998.

Denton, Michael. *Evolution: A Theory in Crisis.* Bethesda, MD: Alder & Alder Publishers, Inc., 1985.

Eastman, Mark, and Chuck Missler. *The Creator Beyond Time and Space.* Costa Mesa, CA: Word For Today, 1996.

Goodsell, David S. *The Machinery of Life.* New York: Springer-Verlag New York, Inc., 1982.

Grange, Robert. *A Scientist Looks at Creation* (videotape). Reel to Real & American Portrait Films. For information call 1-800-736-4567 or go to www.amport.com. The author highly recommends this videotape.

Gross, Michael. *Travels to the Nanoworld: Miniature Machinery in Nature and Technology.* Cambridge, MA: Perseus Publishing, 1999. This book is written by an evolutionist from an evolutionary standpoint, yet demonstrates elements of spectacular design in life.

Hanegraaff, Hank. *The Face That Demonstrates the Farce of Evolution.* Nashville, TN: Word Publishing, 1998.

Hawking, Stephen W. *A Brief History of Time: From the Big Bang to Black Holes.* New York: Bantam Books, 1988.

Heeren, Fred. *Show Me God: What the Message from Space Is Telling Us About God.* Wheeling, IL: Searchlight Publications, 1995.

Herbert, David. *Charles Darwin's Religious Views: From Creationist to Evolutionist.* London, Ontario: Hersil Publishing, 1990.

Hoagland, Mahlon, and Bert Dodson. *The Way Life Works.* New York: Random House, Inc., 1998.

Hoyle, Fred. *Mathematics of Evolution.* Memphis, TN: Acorn Enterprises LLC, 1999.

Maynard Smith, John, and Szathmary, Eors. *The Origins of Life: From the Birth of Life to the Origins of Language.* New York, Oxford University Press, Inc., 1999. This book contains the latest evolutionary theory from highly respected evolutionists, which the author obviously disagrees with.

Milton, Richard. *Shattering the Myths of Darwinism.* Rochester, VT: Park Street Press, 1997.

Moreland, J.P., ed. *The Creation Hypothesis: Scientific Evidence for an Intelligent Designer.* Downers Grove, IL: InterVarsity Press, 1994.

Moreland, J.P., and John Mark Reynolds, eds. *Three Views on Creation and Evolution.* Grand Rapids, MI: Zondervan Publishing House, 1999.

Morris, Henry M., and Gary E. Parker. *What Is Creation Science?* El Cajon, CA: Master Books, 1987.

Muncaster, Ralph O. *Creation vs. Evolution* (videotape). Eugene, OR: Harvest House Publishers, 1999.

Ridley, Matt. *Genome: The Autobiography of a Species in 23 Chapters.* New York: HarperCollins Publishers Inc., 1999.

Ross, Hugh. *The Creator and the Cosmos: How the Greatest Scientific Discoveries of the Century Reveal God.* Colorado Springs, CO: NavPress Publishing Group, 1993.

———. *The Fingerprint of God.* Orange, CA: Promise Publishing Co., 1991.

———. *A Matter of Days.* Colorado Springs, CO: NavPress, 2004.

Ruse, Michael, ed. *But Is It Science? The Philosophical Question in the Creation/Evolution Controversy.* Amherst, NY: Prometheus Books, 1996. The author disagrees with many points of view in this book.

Schroeder, Gerald L. *The Hidden Face of God: How Science Reveals the Ultimate Truth.* New York: The Free Press, 2001.

———. *The Science of God: The Convergence of Scientific and Biblical Wisdom.* New York: Broadway Books, 1997.

Spetner, Lee. *Not By Chance! Shattering the Modern Theory of Evolution.* Brooklyn, NY: Judaica Press, Inc., 1998.

Stewart, Don. *The Bible and Science: Are They In Conflict?* Spokane, WA: AusAmerica Publishers, 1993.

Swenson, Richard A. *More Than Meets the Eye: Fascinating Glimpses of God's Power and Design.* Colorado Springs, CO: NavPress, 2000.

Wells, Jonathan. *Icons of Evolution: Science Or Myth? Why Much of What We Teach About Evolution is Wrong.* Washington, DC: Regnery Publishing, Inc., 2000.

Statistical Evidence

McDowell, Josh. *The New Evidence That Demands a Verdict*. Nashville, TN: Thomas Nelson Publishers, 1999.

———. *A Ready Defense*. San Bernardino, CA: Here's Life Publishers, Inc., 1990.

Walvoord, John F. *The Prophecy Knowledge Handbook*. Wheaton, IL: Victor Books, 1990.

Major Religions

Ali, Maulana Muhammad. *The Religion of Islam*. Columbus, OH: Ahmadiyya Anjuman Isha'at Islam, 1990.

Campbell, William. *The Qur'an and the Bible in the Light of History and Science*. Lake Forest, CA: L.M. Carter, n.d.

Cowell, E.B., ed. *Buddhist Mahayana Texts*. Mineola, NY: Dover Publications, Inc., 1989.

Dawood, N.J. *The Koran*. London, England: Penguin Group, 1993.

Gethin, Rupert. *The Foundations of Buddhism*. Oxford, England: Oxford University Press, 1998.

Goodall, Dominic, ed. *Hindu Scriptures*. Berkeley and Los Angeles, CA: J.M. Dent, Orion Publishing, 1996.

Halverson, Dean C., ed. *The Compact Guide to World Religions*. Minneapolis, MN: Bethany House Publishers, 1996.

McDowell, Josh, and Don Stewart. *Handbook of Today's Religions*. San Bernardino, CA: Here's Life Publishers, Inc., 1983.

Prabhupada A.C. Bhaktivedanta Swami. *Bhagavad-Gita As It Is*. Los Angeles: Bhaktivedanta Book Trust International, Inc., 1997.

References for the Old Testament

Free, Joseph P., and Howard F. Vos. *Archaeology and Bible History*. Grand Rapids, MI: Zondervan Publishing House, 1992.

Josephus, Flavius. *The Complete Works of Josephus*. Grand Rapids, MI: Kregel Publications, 1981.

Kertzer, Morris N. *What Is a Jew?* rev. by Lawrence A. Hoffman. New York: Touchstone, 1996.

Shanks, Hershel, and Dan P. Cole, eds. *Archaeology and the Bible: The Best of BAR*. Vol. 1, *Early Israel*. Washington, DC: Biblical Archaeology Society, 1990.

References for the New Testament

Black, David Alan. *New Testament Textual Criticism: A Concise Guide*. Grand Rapids, MI: Baker Books, 1994.

Finegan, Jack. *The Archeology of the New Testament: The Life of Jesus and the Beginning of the Early Church*, rev. ed. Princeton, NJ: Princeton University Press, 1992.

Green, Michael. *Who Is This Jesus?* Nashville, TN: Thomas Nelson, Inc., 1992.

Habermas, Gary R., and Antony G.N. Flew. *Did Jesus Rise From the Dead? The Resurrection Debate.* San Francisco, CA: Harper & Row, 1987.

Habermas, Gary R., and Michael R. Licona. *The Case for the Resurrection of Jesus.* Grand Rapids, MI: Kregel Publications, 2004.

McBirnie, William Steuart. *The Search for the Twelve Apostles.* Wheaton, IL: Tyndale House Publishers, Inc., 1973.

McDowell, Josh, and Bill Wilson. *He Walked Among Us.* Nashville, TN: Thomas Nelson Publishers, 1993.

McRay, John. *Archaeology and the New Testament.* Grand Rapids, MI: Baker Book House, 1991.

Shanks, Hershel, and Dan P. Cole, eds. *Archaeology and the Bible: The Best of BAR.* Vol. 2, *Archaeology in the World of Herod, Jesus, and Paul.* Washington, DC: Biblical Archaeology Society, 1992.

White, James R. *The Forgotten Trinity.* Minneapolis, MN: Bethany House Publishers, 1998.

Evidence of the Bible's Accuracy

Blomberg, Craig. *The Historical Reliability of the Gospels.* Leicester, England: InterVarsity Press, 1987.

Bruce, F.F. *The Canon of Scripture.* Downers Grove, IL: InterVarsity Press, 1988.

Comfort, Philip Wesley, ed. *The Origin of the Bible.* Wheaton, IL: Tyndale House Publishers, Inc., 1992.

How We Got the Bible. Torrance, CA: Rose Publishing, 1998.

Price, Randall. *Secrets of the Dead Sea Scrolls.* Eugene, OR: Harvest House Publishers, 1996.

Vos, Howard F. *Nelson's Quick Reference: Introduction to Church History.* Nashville, TN: Thomas Nelson Publishers, Inc., 1994.

References for "Alternative Christian" Religions

Bodine, Jerry and Marian. *Witnessing to the Mormons.* Rancho Santa Margarita, CA: The Christian Research Institute, 1978.

The Book of Mormon. Salt Lake City, UT: The Church of Jesus Christ of Latter-day Saints, 1981.

Martin, Walter. *Cults Reference Bible.* Santa Ana, CA: Vision House Publishers, 1981.

———. *The Kingdom of the Cults.* Minneapolis, MN: Bethany House Publishers, 1996.

———. *The Maze of Mormonism.* Ventura, CA: Regal Books, 1978.

McDowell, Josh, and Don Stewart. *The Deceivers.* San Bernardino, CA: Here's Life Publishers, Inc., 1992.

Watson, William. *A Concise Dictionary of Cults & Religions.* Chicago: Moody Press, 1991.

Index

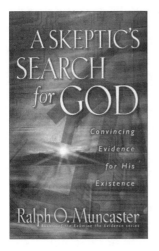

1,456 hours of Sunday school and church turned Ralph Muncaster into a hard-core atheist.

Then he was challenged to honestly investigate the Bible and the facts of modern science. He was stunned. Fact after fact—from biology, history, archaeology, physics—lined up with the Bible's account!

Join Ralph on the intensive personal search that took him—a cynical skeptic with an education in engineering—from disbelief to belief in God and the Jesus of the Bible. Along the way,

- ❖ you'll encounter the same astounding evidence that the author found during his three-year search

- ❖ you'll find solid information that challenges comfortable assumptions and outdated ideas

- ❖ your mind will be opened and your faith will be strengthened

Fascinating, unconventional, and provocative, *A Skeptic's Search for God* will point you to the facts—and to the God of the universe who is behind them.

"The dismantling of Darwinian evolution is long overdue...This book will be particularly helpful to the general reader looking for an easily accessible introduction to intelligent design."

—Dr. William Dembski, author of *Intelligent Design: The Bridge Between Science and Theology*

Enough Time + Enough Stuff = Life ...Right?

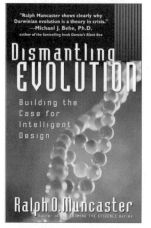

In the few seconds it's taken you to read these words, trillions of molecular interactions have taken place in your eyes and brain. And this is just one of the amazing things that today's molecular biology has revealed about the complex inner workings of our cells.

The conclusion? We now know that even a 15-billion-year-old universe allows *far too little* time for life to arise through evolutionary random chance. As author Ralph Muncaster surveys some of the latest findings from biochemistry, astrophysics, and other fields, you'll discover further that

❖ the mechanisms of evolution—mutations and gradual change—fall apart in the face of the hard facts

❖ the random development of life is statistically impossible

❖ from the nucleus to the cosmos, everything we examine displays evidence of purposeful design

Exploring and revealing the magnificent complexity of the universe, *Dismantling Evolution* takes you beyond the data and gives you a glimpse of the Designer who's behind everything that exists.